Argumentation, Discussion, and Debate

Argumentation, Discussion, and Debate

by A. CRAIG BAIRD

Professor of Speech
State University of Iowa

New York   Toronto   London
McGRAW-HILL BOOK COMPANY, INC.
1950

ARGUMENTATION, DISCUSSION, AND DEBATE

IX

03265

Preface

This text attempts to interpret for the college student of the mid-twentieth century well-established argumentative principles as affected by the current contributions of logic, philosophy, psychology, speech, political science, and related subjects.

Teachers of argument, this author among them, continue to ground their concepts in the rhetorical traditions of Aristotle, Cicero, Quintilian, and their successors. Particularly, too, have we found stimulation and illumination in the twentieth-century contributions to persuasion by such writers and teachers as George Pierce Baker, James Milton O'Neill, James A. Winans, and Charles Woolbert. Alert to the new era and critical of mere scholastic inheritance, they nevertheless identified their thinking and writing with the broad stream of rhetorical development.

What, then, are the increments and modifications attempted in this text?

1. It hopes to reflect the American political thinking and educational philosophy of the post Second World War era of 1949 and later. Argumentation, I assume, is an important art for the discipline of those who are to be properly equipped for political responsibilities. *It is thus central in the college program of general education with its aims of intellectual and political competence.*

2. This volume, moreover, attempts to appropriate the recent contributions of logic, semantics, philosophy, and psychology to argumentation, discussion, and debate. The elementary principles of *applied* logic I have tried to utilize at every stage. The influence of John Dewey and the pragmatic, nonsymbolic, and nonformal school of logicians is apparent in this treatment. Moreover, healthy suggestions have been found in the writings of current semanticists.

This book, furthermore, strengthens the presentation of argumentation, as I have treated it in earlier texts, by reference to contemporary psychological interpretations of personality, motiva-

v

2568

tion, emotional response, social incentives, measurement of social attitudes, suggestion, propaganda, and similar concepts. My attempt has been to relate closely the speaker-speech-audience-occasion configuration to the argumentative processes.

3. I have aimed at developing as comprehensively as is practicable in a limited volume the entire subject of argumentation, discussion, and debate. Part I introduces the student to this field of rhetorical speaking and writing; Part II establishes the fundamentals of argumentation; Part III applies these principles to discussion; and Part IV, to debate. My teaching has convinced me that special instruction in discussion and debate can be given most efficiently by preliminary or coordinate study of argumentative principles and techniques.

4. Discussion is given prominence here in accordance with its high educational and practical values. The applications of discussion, especially during and after the Second World War, have been more and more extensive—in communities, in labor and other economic areas, and in schools and colleges. The chapters included are written out of my own experience with community and campus discussion since the 1920's; out of discussion methods as tried in the armed services; and out of the experimentation (admittedly scant) related to this practice.

5. Debating as a school and college activity has certainly not been neglected in this book. I assume the correlative character of discussion and debate; that democracy necessitates both techniques; and that debate, properly understood, taught, and applied is free from the reprehensible educational indictments offered by thoughtful opponents. We have not been insensitive to those critics who thirty years ago were denouncing debating as sophism institutionalized.

Not only has the practice survived our severe testing of it as education, but it has since taken on most interesting modifications. Within the memory of present teachers of speech have come the debating tournaments; the intercollegiate congresses; the rise of national forensic society programs; the experimentation with cross-examination and other extempore speaking modifications; the extensive multiplication of graduate studies in the field of debate; the inception and, after the Second World War, the revival of international debating; the expansion of radio controversial speaking; and the interest in debating as reflected in the sessions of the Speech Association of America and in the expanding departments of speech. This text, then, attempts to describe, interpret these trends and types, and to furnish for the student a competent guide for his own effective participation in the debates of his generation.

This book is written for college students. Teachers of oral and written communication will find it usable, it is hoped, for units of instruction in argumentation. Teachers of speech who wish to concentrate on discussion may assign Parts I, II, and III. Those who are concerned chiefly with debate may specialize on Parts I, II, and IV. The material may thus be adapted to a three-semester-hour course, to a two- or three-semester-hour course in argumentation, in discussion, or in debate, or a year course totaling six semester hours in all three divisions.

This text from the outset should be accompanied by definite projects. A subject (or subjects) for discussion, debate, or individual speaking or writing should straightway be assigned for presentation before the class, over the radio, in college newspapers or magazines, before campus, community, or intercollegiate audiences.

I have arranged the chapters functionally according to my own preferences. The teacher can easily make shifts to suit his teaching methods. The chapter on briefing, for example, may be delayed; that on delivery may be assigned earlier than the text does—or may be disregarded if the students have had equivalent training in other courses.

The projects at the end of each chapter are suggestive only. Supplementary readings have been listed in the Appendix. A specimen brief, outline of parliamentary law, and further suggestions for library investigation have been included.

My debt in this volume to my speech colleagues at the State University of Iowa, teachers of discussion and debate in many other colleges and universities, the members of my graduate seminar in problems of debate and discussion, and the undergraduates in my discussion and debate courses is a large one. Space does not permit my listing specific names of many to whom I owe a great deal.

The references cited are my partial effort to indicate the influence of my contemporaries and predecessors in the field of rhetoric and argumentation on my thinking.

My thanks are also due to publishers and authors for their kind permission to quote copyright materials. Specific acknowledgment has been made in the footnotes.

A. Craig Baird

Iowa City, Iowa
   December, 1949

Contents

Part I

Approach to Argumentation, Discussion, and Debate

CHAPTER 1

Aims, Relationships, Applications

I. WHY ARGUE?

In the past twenty-four hours you have probably engaged in considerable talking. In the classroom, on the campus, and elsewhere your oral exchange has continued. Much of your conversation has, no doubt, been pointless; some of it has been organized speaking before your fraternity or other group.

No small part of your vocal output has been argumentative or persuasive.

In addition to this routine campus experience, you may be trying out for a debate team, or joining a student discussion squad, or having an eye on radio discussion. Moreover you have enrolled in a course in argumentation, or discussion, or debate.

Just why? Perhaps some student advised you to sign up. Whatever your motive, you will later (if you do not at the outset) come to understand the broad values of training and development as an arguer, debater, and discussant.

College presidents, lawyers, teachers, engineers, journalists, radio commentators, preachers, community leaders, salesmen, professional men and women of all sorts have repeatedly told how much their experience in discussion and debate has helped.

A Middle Western college president and former Rhodes scholar states, "I am an enthusiastic believer in the value of forensics. Such experience affords an opportunity for creative work and analytical thinking which is beneficial in many areas of life. My experiences in forensics are far more valuable than I can convey in words."[1]

II. What Are the Goals of Argumentation, Discussion, and Debate?

According to the testimony of those who have had this training, argumentative speaking and writing aims chiefly to (1) educate you for active and responsible participation in democratic government, (2) assure you more efficiency in your occupation or profession, (3) strengthen your self-confidence and enable you to make more satisfactory social adjustments, (4) provide you with defenses against "bad" propaganda, and (5) widen your general influence in social movements.

Let me comment briefly on these general goals.

A. *Discussion and Debate in the Service of Democracy.* You are now, or soon will be, inextricably involved in the concerns of your community, state, and national life. You will pay taxes, perhaps submit to a military draft, vote for a President of the United States. You may not always have sustained interest in the United Nations, prices, strikes, or highway safety. But these things relate to your permanent welfare.

How do you and the other citizens deal with these public problems? You live under a government of public opinion. You have frequent public meetings, freedom to speak and publish, secret ballot. You select your public representatives, check their votes, and sometimes write postcards of advice to them. This is the American system.

At the bottom yours is a government by talk. Literally, it is government by argumentation, discussion, and debate. As one educator puts it, "We can no more dispense with legislative and forensic debating in a democratic society than we can take a walk to the moon. . . . The surest way to throw ourselves into the hands of a dictator is to outlaw debate."[2]

---

[1] Emory Lindquist, *The Forensic*, Series 29, No. 2, p. 51, January, 1944.
[2] James H. McBurney, "The Role of Discussion and Debate," *The Debater's Magazine*, pp. 60, 70, Summer, 1948.

When World War II engulfed this country, President Roosevelt stated:

I have long been keenly interested in public forums and round-table discussion groups as democratic means of developing popular understanding of pressing issues. Now, under the impact of defense emergency, I am convinced that it is more important than ever that the people, and particularly the students in our colleges and universities, be encouraged freely to assemble and discuss our common problems. Indeed, it is one of the freedoms that we are determined to defend.[3]

B. *Discussion and Debate and Professional Success.* Whether you are to practice law, medicine, teaching, or other occupation, your practical problem is to influence human behavior. Your efficiency will be measured not simply by your knowledge of logic and your array of evidence but by your skill in presenting your case. The application of argumentative principles will certainly strengthen your chances of getting good results.

Donald O. Olson secured from more than 150 former University of Nebraska debaters, representing law, sales and advertising, teaching, and some twenty-five other occupations, attitudes toward debating. "More than 95% believed that debating had given them help in their present occupation; 93% stated that 'probably' and 'yes' they would advise those entering their profession to study debate; 96% said 'probably' and 'yes' they would advise any interested person to take debate."[4]

C. *Discussion, Debate, and Personal and Social Adjustments.* Implied in your occupational achievement and closely related to it is your growth in self-confidence and in social adjustment. Possibly you may enter a discussion class with a feeling of hesitancy and self-consciousness. Your experience there and in related extracurricular speaking situations will give you more and more skill in organizing and presenting your ideas, defending them, and contributing to the clarification of issues. Your confusion will lessen, your confidence and assurance will increase.

Complementary to this satisfactory growth in self-realization will be your adjustment to your associates and your surroundings.

[3] *National Extempore-discussion Contest on Inter-American Affairs,* Bulletin, Washington, D.C., 1942.

[4] Donald O. Olson, "An Evaluation of Debate," *The Gavel,* Vol. 30, pp. 31–34, January, 1948.

Your civilization commits you to group associations. Your role, after all a happy one, is to make these adjustments to the community, to learn the ways of cooperation, perhaps compromise. Your individuality, however, you are determined to save. You propose to be one of the crowd but not to fall into lock step. You would alter but not weaken your own personality, your outlook, and ideals.

Discussion and debate, functioning in a medium of cooperative thinking and analysis, should help you to become a more agreeable member of the group. Your alleged assertiveness will diminish. Your intellectual and personal integrity and initiative will be happily combined with open-mindedness, broad sympathy, and social adaptiveness.

D. *Argumentation, Discussion, and Debate as Defense against Bad Propaganda.* Implied in your activity as a citizen and in your constant occupational and social experience is your constant exposure to propaganda. Radio, television, mail, the public platform, the editorial and columnist pages, and the personal calls on you by skillful persuaders—all give you pause in the face of the appeals. Your job is to apply critical standards to each propagandistic drive directed to you. Training in argumentative principles and their application in discussional and debating situations should increase your ability to discriminate between straight and crooked thinking, between "good" and "bad" propaganda.

E. *Argumentation and Social Change.* College students are also social philosophers. We are interested in "truths" or facts and in the application of these "truths." What is truth? What are facts? Without an excursion into epistemological inquiries, let me merely observe that argument begins with facts. Argumentation does help to get at basic information. Its purpose is to collect and evaluate evidence.

In addition, however, you, the arguer, are interested in making this information and the principles based upon it prevail. Gladiatorial combats, polygamy, social slavery, torture, the chain gang, and similar practices were outlawed through prolonged argumentation, discussion, and debate. Without the steady and insistent argument on these issues the changes would doubtless have come even more slowly.

It is sometimes charged that argumentation merely creates an atmosphere of fighting feudalism and so of confusion. It has been further argued that the cause of right will prevail whether or not we agitate. Debate and argument, on the contrary, clear the atmosphere and hasten progress. As E. A. Ross states it, "Discussion hurries conflicts to a conclusion."[5]

III. What Is Argumentation?

Argumentation is not just excited "name calling." It is not wrangling, a pouring forth of ridicule, of epithets, of slogans, and of appeals to passion. Argumentation, whether written or spoken, is made up primarily of reasoning together with facts for your belief. It is designed to convince and to persuade others to subscribe to your facts and principles and to the conclusions warranted by these premises and evidence. Note the distinctive elements of argumentation.

A. *A Form of Communication.* Argumentation, like other divisions of English composition, is the art of communication. Communication, especially under the impetus of World War II and the rise of the radio, has been more and more recognized as basic in our individual and community association. Training in communication was prominent in the wartime program. The development of the new means of communication, the enormous expansion of undersea, surface, aircraft, and other units, the great dependence on radio and other methods of contact combined to dramatize the place of communication in our new civilization. World War II also reinforced our growing dependence on communication as the key to our civilian cohesion and mobility. Hence the attention of colleges and universities to communication in the postwar era. Because of the radio and airplane development, television, the population expansion, and the ever-multiplying complexity of our national life, the art of exchange by speech and writing has become especially important.

Aside from these practical considerations, educators are viewing the communicative act as the means of giving vitality to the entire college training. Knowledge and wisdom must be appropriated through interpretation and transference to others. Communication, then, is the art by which these ideas and facts are transmuted into new concepts and into programs. College and university training are deemed successful only when the student

[5] E. A. Ross, *Social Psychology*, Chap. XVIII, p. 307, The Macmillan Company, 1908.

has grasped and applied these principles of oral and written discourse.

B. Communication and the Audience. Argument, as communication, requires an audience. The situation is a social one. Readers or hearers are necessarily involved. You may reason with yourself as did Hamlet, but even he envisaged a great audience applauding or condemning his conclusions. Without this audience you have, of course, no communication. However breathtaking may be your ideas, however weighty may be your facts, your speaking or writing gets nowhere as long as your speech falls on deaf ears or resides between uncut pages.

Psychologically, the process is one of providing stimuli and securing response. You, the speaker or writer, provide the stimuli (in this case, words or substitute stimuli for the original sensation); the audience becomes a reactor and furnishes the response. That response is circular. The listeners become active. They talk also. You become the audience. The stimulation is reciprocal.

C. Communication and the Occasion. A third factor in the communicative process is the immediate occasion. The speaker and audience are gathered for a specific purpose. It is a legislature to pass a given law, a court to declare innocence or guilt, a popular assembly to honor Washington or Franklin D. Roosevelt, or it is one hundred thousand readers of an argumentative article in a magazine.

D. Communication and the Speaker or Writer of Argument. On one side is the audience. Either it is totally oblivious to your ideas; or it is indifferent, having once reflected on the problem and dismissed it for one reason or another; or it is openly hostile. On the other side are you, conscious that something is wrong, determined to have some understanding, reconciliation, compromise, or other form of adjustment. Ideas and attitudes crystallize in your thinking. Your initial problem is to select words that duplicate your ideas. The semanticists remind us how difficult it is. Effective communication requires that we make this language comprehensible to others. Straightway you discover that the mind of the audience, its education, its character, cultural experiences, and attitudes are so diverse from each other and from you yourself that the results of your communicative act are sometimes startling and disheartening. Nevertheless, that is your job.

These factors, then, are involved in communication—the audience, the occasion, the speaker, and his argument.

E. Aim of Argumentation to Change Belief and Conduct. The goal of your argumentative process is conversion or complete response. The reactor audience faces a day of judgment. If you succeed, a new man emerges. Belief and conduct change.

Contrast this rhetorical motive with that of the expositor or narrator. If you explain the importance of dust, characterize a college man or woman, or state a problem in nuclear physics, your mood is that of an instructor. Your real undertaking, whatever your selection of materials, is largely to make clear your ideas. On other occasions you may be chiefly concerned with interesting those who listen.

In contrast to such purposes is your aim of affecting belief or conduct. You are still eager to make clear and to entertain, but mainly you wish to move your audience to belief and action.

Specifically, you wish to retain the beliefs of those who at the outset agree with you and to shift the attitude of those who are opposed or uncertain.

What distinction are we to draw between your effort to establish belief and your aim to secure action? Little. Belief and conduct are practically identical. Belief is really identical with conduct. Even if you argue for the proposition, *We should pity our grandchildren,* you hope to influence behavior as well as mental assent. This behavior pattern may be merely verbal response, emotional expression; or if conditions warrant, the convictions should translate themselves into overt action.

F. Argumentation and Reflective Thinking. Argumentation secures its end by appealing to both intellectual and emotional thinking and reaction. Argumentation is chiefly concerned with intellectual elements—with fact, logic, reasoning, as contrasted with loose assertion and unrestrained persuasion. Advocates of argument from the days of Aristotle have insisted on the supremacy of reasoning in argumentative speaking and writing.

G. Argumentation and Motives for Action. Argument, in addition to satisfying the understanding as to the truth of a proposition, must, as I indicated above, reckon with prejudices, impulses, motives, and emotion. We are agreed that, although neither you nor your audience should succumb to mere emotionalism, if you are to secure action or complete response, you must have emotional reinforcement of your reasoning. If, for example, you tried to establish the proposition, *That a federal world government should be established,* your logic would include a chain of reasoning to prove that wars are threatening along various frontiers; that the basis for future conflict is being securely laid; that economic, social, and political realignments threaten the peace; that the machinery of world government can be worked out; and that the proposal is more than a dreamer's dream. Authorities and other types of concrete evidence would supplement your series of deductions. Your arguments, however, to be effective, would become a series of emotional concepts—emotion of national pride, self-interest, duty to other peoples, fear of war, etc. Woodrow Wilson once said, "Life is essentially illogical. The world is governed now by a tumultuous sea of commonalities made up of passions, and we should pray God that the good passions should outvote the bad passions."[6]

IV. What Are the Representative Types of Argumentation?

Argumentation usually occurs not as a strict logical forensic, presented with few or no elements of interest, but more often as persuasive speaking or writing, as discussion, or as debate. Each of these types again may be more concretely described according to occasion and the special procedures accompanying the performance.

A. Persuasion. Persuasive speaking and writing are almost identical with argumentation except for the more obvious motivating elements. Persuasion, as we broadly use the term, attempts to influence an auditor or reader not so much by sheer logic, facts, and opinion as by suggestion, emotional and imaginative coloring, verbal pictures, connotative language, suggestive phrasing, and sentence structure. When you persuade, you may present a direct appeal to be uncritically accepted. As you hurry down the street, you may be interrupted with a "Buy a badge." You automatically respond. That incident furnishes an example of abbreviated persuasion. The one-minute advertising "plugs" over the radio are striking examples of mass appeal through persuasion. Argument, by contrast, stresses proposition and inference. It is probably

[6] Woodrow Wilson, "Training of the Intellect" from *Modern Short Speeches* (J. M. O'Neill, ed.), p. 261, The Century Company, 1923.

in its purest state in the carefully reasoned arguments sometimes presented before the Supreme Court of the United States. Persuasion, when it also obviously proceeds from proposition to conclusion, becomes, of course, argumentation. This book is mainly concerned with methods of influencing human behavior through the more explicit methods of reasoning.

B. *Discussion.* How does discussion differ from argumentation? Discussion is often regarded as conversation or as haphazard, almost aimless, ramification in and out of a subject. Properly understood, discussion is the art of reflective thinking and communication. It is usually oral and involves a group whose aim is to solve a problem cooperatively. The discussant, like the arguer, adheres closely to the logical pattern of thinking. He recognizes the awareness of a problem, focuses upon the definitions of terms involved in the controversy, analyzes the factors which cause the disturbance, states clearly the various hypotheses or representative solutions, weighs in turn both the advantages and disadvantages of each solution, selects that outcome which seems feasible and practicable to the group, and finally concentrates upon the program for setting up the solution as determined.

These characteristic elements of discussion are those of argument. Each type pays strong allegiance to logic, fact, and testimony, the analysis and rejection of bad argument, the thorough organization of main and submaterials, and the accurate use of language.

How do they differ? At every point the discussionist almost entirely ignores the techniques of persuasion. Discussion, strictly speaking, aims chiefly to establish "truth" or facts and to secure a consensus of judgment on the basis of reason alone. When you join a discussion group, you disavow any propagandistic tendencies. This approach sets you off, sometimes sharply, from the debater, the salesman, or the typical arguer in the classroom or elsewhere.[7]

C. *Debating.* Debating and argument are often used interchangeably. Argument, as we have indicated, is the broader term. It applies to all methods, oral or written, that influence conduct and belief by rational or emotional means. Debate is characteristically controversy under definite rules. These include time limits, use of opposing speakers, the activities of judges, main

[7] For further examinations of these types see Chap. 20.

speakers and rebuttals, and methods of audience voting. The
writer of a first-rate forensic or complete argument may have his
article printed in a reputable journal. He may, however, be a
third-rate debater because of lack of ability to think quickly on
his feet, to talk readily on the platform, or to use a hundred other
arts of an experienced debater. Whereas argument was perfected
and applied in early Greece, debate as it is practiced today in
American colleges is a comparatively modern invention. In this
book the terms *argumentation* and *debate* may occasionally be
used as synonyms.

In this text I propose to discuss the general principles of argumentation. My assumption is that these concepts may be applied
effectively both in the general field of argument, spoken or written,
and in debate. The underlying principles apply to editorials, controversial articles, sermons, lectures, and similar forms of discourse
that persuade or convince. Formal discussion, in symposiums and
lecture-forums, likewise reflects definition, analysis, organization,
logical handling of evidence and argumentative types, audience
adaptation, and language skills.

V. What Skills and Techniques Will You Develop?

You who plan to develop in this field will put aside the popular notion that argumentation, discussion, and debate may be
mastered by seizing upon a principle here and there and supple-
menting it with voluble talk. The conquest of the art requires
systematic application and training. These include a frank self-
analysis of your needs, ability to criticize your own work, and a
will to persist and so realize the successive goals to be achieved
in learning these techniques.

More specifically, these goals include ability (1) to select,
frame properly, and analyze a subject; (2) to gather and organize
materials; (3) to develop and test arguments and evidence; (4)
in debate to refute effectively; (5) to express arguments in effective language; (6) to deliver a speech or more informal talk effectively; (7) to adapt the discourse to the audience; and (8) in
argumentative speaking and writing, especially in debate, to use
persuasive devices. Later chapters will discuss the techniques
for developing each of these abilities and skills.

VI. What Attitudes, Habits of Mind, and Action Accompany Such Training?

Your hurdling of the successive goals calls for definite attitudes and habits of mind and action. You will, I hope, be motivated by most of the professional, political, social, and intellectual interests discussed at the outset of this chapter. You will also plan to achieve the specific aims of argumentative technique and skill listed above.

Accompanying these general and specific objectives will be your development in habits of reflective, as contrasted with emotional, thinking; your open-mindedness in your approach to problem solving; your orderly methods of research; your respect for facts; your restraint in drawing conclusions; your systematic and creative reading; your systematic recording, outlining, and briefing; your growing accuracy, simplicity, and clarity in oral and written composition; your patient and persistent industry in all these efforts; your unabated intellectual curiosity and honesty; and your increasing self-confidence combined with the humility of every genuine student.

With such attitudes and habits, including constant practice, you will find increasing pleasure and satisfaction in argumentative speaking and writing.

EXERCISES AND PROBLEMS

1. Report (about 150 words) concerning the argumentative elements in a recent speech, a printed copy of which you have examined.

2. Take notes on a public lecture, sermon, or campaign speech. Report the nature and effectiveness of the appeal.

3. Name and explain four or five ways in which skill in argumentation and debate should increase one's ability in any one of the following situations (let the class judge the validity of your suggestions): (a) selling an insurance policy; (b) organizing and directing a community-chest campaign; (c) acting as counsel for the defendant in a ten-thousand-dollar automobile personal-liability suit; (d) writing an automobile advertisement for a national weekly; (e) writing an editorial for your college newspaper; (f) writing a term paper in zoology (or some other subject); (g) delivering a college classroom lecture; (h) teaching a college class; (i) presiding over a community forum on a problem of public ownership of utilities; (j) delivering a sermon.

4. Review for brief written or oral reports each of the following topics related to the discussion in this chapter: (*a*) Persuasive speaking as a factor in social adjustment. (*b*) Debating as training for citizenship. (*c*) What is persuasion? (*d*) Your aim as an arguer. (*e*) When and why do we believe? (*f*) Are people primarily reasonable? (*g*) The place of emotion in convincing people. (*h*) What is debating? (*i*) What is discussion? (*j*) What does logic contribute to argumentation? (*k*) Does debating produce open-mindedness? (*l*) What results do you hope to have from a course in argumentation, discussion, and debate?

REFERENCES

(For suggested readings see Appendix C.)

Part II

Principles and Techniques

CHAPTER 2

Subjects, Propositions, and Questions

I. The Subject in General

What kind of subject is best suited for discussion or debate? The answer depends upon the exact purpose of the occasion, the circumstances that lead to the framing of the proposition, and the response desired. Is the debate to take place in a courtroom, at a legislative assembly, on a college platform, in a dormitory, on a soapbox in a city park, in a Pullman smoker, at a New England town meeting, or over the radio? In general the subjects may be as broad as human thought and curiosity. Whatever challenges differences of opinion becomes a theme for controversy, whether it be a question of the best brand of cigar or the dimensions of the universe.

What types of subjects, then, shall you discuss or debate? Each representative field of thinking yields a large number of controversial topics, some, to be sure, highly speculative, others perhaps trivial, still others significant and practical.

Effective argumentation depends to a large degree on problems growing out of the immediate circumstances, as when Japan suddenly attacked Pearl Harbor. Other topics are the product of prolonged and careful deliberation by a committee assigned to the preparation of a series of debates or discussions. America's

Town Hall Meeting of the Air, the Chicago Round Table, the American Forum of the Air, the *New York Herald Tribune's* annual forums represent good judgment in the selection of issues. Many conferences and public forums, on the other hand, fall flat because of inappropriate and poorly worded questions.

II. SUGGESTIONS FOR THE SELECTION OF THE SUBJECT

Although you were encouraged at the beginning of this chapter to discuss almost every subject, the application of certain principles, or criteria, in the choosing of your topic will help you to make a discriminating selection. Some subjects are more fully adapted to your own interests and experiences than others; some will appeal much more than others to your audience; some will be more timely than others; some will be preferable because they are sufficiently limited in scope. Let us examine each of these tests of your topic.

A. *Select a Subject Adapted to Your Experience and Interests.* Prefer that subject which relates itself to your experience and your vital thinking. What holds true of subject matter in general, whether it be that of a story you intend to write or a speech you intend to deliver, is to be applied to the field of discussion. Select the material about which you have reflected, about which you have notions, and about which you think you have a real message. Perhaps the single tax means little to you and always will; then you had better discuss some educational or political subject which touches your imagination. The greatest thrill in discussion or debate comes when you work in the field with which you are familiar and in which you are interested. Since interest and attention result from focusing on a problem, in many cases you can develop enthusiasm for a topic apparently dull in itself. In general, however, follow the principle of choosing themes and ideas close to your experience.

B. *Select a Subject Adapted to Your Audience.* What is true of writing and speaking in general is true of the argumentative subject. It should be adapted to the learning level, knowledge, purposes, needs, and interests of the audience. The question should fix and hold attention and should create desire. Curiosity, self-interest, the love of the familiar or the novel should all be appealed to. Sometimes the subject is as old as human experience. *Shall we live again?* was contemporary for Job's audience and is also for ours. Again, heavy though it is, *Shall taxes be reduced?* has been debated again and again in and out of Congress, and the reports of such debates continue to furnish front-page headlines. People are interested in their pocketbooks.

Some audiences or groups are primarily interested in action. *Shall we strike?* may be the immediate question before the higher up board of strategy of a union. Many other audiences are learning groups, such as those at college and high-school assemblies, radio performances, public forums, community service or speakers' clubs. These learning groups are distinct in purpose and interest from the action committees.

Radio debates and discussions are often designed to supply information or to provoke thought or to stimulate public morale and support of worthy causes. Recognition of these purposes will heavily influence the selection of the topic.

Consider, too, the factors of learning levels of listeners and participants. Radio-program directors use all audience-analysis aids to determine types of "shows," including subjects for lectures, commentaries, and debates.

Secondary-school pupils would be interested in such propositions as the following:

The high school should publish a monthly magazine rather than a school annual.

The faculty of my school should have the power to suspend any student for attending a midweek public dance.

National high-school basketball tournaments should be established.

C. Select a Timely Subject. This principle is really a special form of the preceding one, but because of the importance of observing timeliness the suggestion is given prominence. It is hard in these days, at least in undergraduate circles, to create great interest in such subjects as *Resolved, That Senators should be elected by popular vote.* Yet not many years ago college debaters, attired in evening dress, argued this point on the basis of months of preparation. A great many questions, like this one, are rejected because they are obsolete, such as questions having to do with slavery, bigamy, the press gang, and dueling. Yet colonial undergraduates fought fiercely over some of these issues.

At Dartmouth College, according to the diary of one Ephram Smedley, the following questions were among those debated by

Daniel Webster in the United Fraternity Literary Society[1] between Nov. 28, 1797, and June 26, 1798:

Should foreigners be excluded from office?
Is it better to marry a widow or an old maid?
Is celibacy justifiable?
European despotism is beneficial.

Mr. Lyle observes on the debates and decisions: "They reflect
the spirit of the times in opposition to France, slavery, military
laws, and in support of foreign immigration, capital punishment,
and in general a strict rather than a liberal view of moral questions."[2]   Even recent problems quickly lose significance.

It is highly desirable to deal with those issues that are emphasized at the hour—those, for example, that occupy the front pages
of the paper.   The debater's thinking will be vitalized by the
thinking of the immediate audience and by that of the larger
audience which somehow also participates in the controversy.

The development of atomic energy has aroused a whole new
series of issues.   The military, economic, political, and social
transformation in prospect in the atomic age will provide problems for discussion indeed strange even to the collegian of the
late 1940's.

D. Select a Subject about Which Discussion Is Profitable.   The
subject, while appealing to the speaker and the audience, should
also be one which is profitable to discuss.   Sometimes, when the
occasion is one for entertainment, the speakers are justified in
considering the problem presented in Frank R. Stockton's story
"The Lady or the Tiger," the question concerning whether the
beautiful maiden or the beast came out of the door into the arena.
British university students have occasionally engaged in "rag" debates on such topics as *That the Old Should Be Seen and Not
Heard* and *That Humor Is No Longer Funny.*[3]   But if the talk in
the world is increased, there should be also utilitarian justification.

---

[1] The citation was from a photostatic copy, the original copy being in
the possession of Mrs. W. B. Sprague (Olena, Ohio).   Here quoted from
Harry M. Lyle, "Factors in the Early Training and Speech Education of
Daniel Webster," pp. 68–69, unpublished master's thesis, State University of
Iowa, 1941.

[2] Lyle, *op. cit.,* p. 72.

[3] See Norman J. Temple and Edward P. Dunn, "British Debating Is Parliamentary," *Quarterly Journal of Speech,* Vol. XXXIV, pp. 50–53, February, 1948.

Furthermore, if we are to change the opinions of men, we must use subjects with which there is some chance of making headway.

E. *Select a Subject That Can Be Settled on Rational Grounds.* When it is evident that prejudice will dominate the discussion or debate, another subject should be chosen. No moral or legal restraint should be imposed upon those who debate. But it is a fair question whether much of the religious discussion that goes on is worth while. Those who try to convert others to any faith are so deeply moved by sentiment and emotion that the controversy shifts to grounds other than purely rational ones. Some debates on communism in the United States, or on Southern white supremacy have resolved themselves into emotional tirades. Religious topics and others that involve deep feelings should not always be barred, but the limitations of such discussions should be clearly understood in advance.

F. *Usually Select a Subject Capable of Specific Proof.* In childhood we used to speculate on what was on the other side of the moon. Although such mental exercises doubtless developed our spirit of inquiry, their debating value was doubtful. Medieval schoolmen probably found similar mental stimulation and similar barrenness of concrete results when they disputed the ability of angels to stand on the point of a needle. Harvard, Yale, and Dartmouth during the period from 1750 to 1800 staged many syllogistic disputations in Latin and forensic disputations in English —often on abstract subjects. Jesse Edson at Dartmouth, in 1794, engaged in a syllogistic disputation on *An vitae brevitas hominibus sit mala?* (whether brevity of life is an evil for mankind).[4]

American college students, especially after the rise of intercollegiate debating in the 1890's, have selected more tangible propositions. Government ownership of railroads is a hackneyed topic, but at least it provides a wealth of concrete material from which reasonably substantial inferences may be drawn. One desideratum of a good proposition for school or college debate, then, is that abundant evidence may be obtained. A wealth of fact usually makes for a more satisfactory debate.

G. *Select a Controversial Subject.* A controversial subject is one that provides two or more sides. A distinct difference of

[4] Ota Thomas, "The Theory and Practice of Disputation at Yale, Harvard, and Dartmouth from 1750 to 1800," p. 8, unpublished doctoral dissertation, State University of Iowa, 1941.

opinion should be apparent among both the speakers and the audience. There should be a real problem; it should still be unsettled when the debate or discussion begins; and representatives of the differing points of view should express themselves. Recently I read an announcement that a church organization would discuss, "Is there a God?" I assume (and hope) that the adherents of that church were all on the same side. Such propositions as *The United States has become a world power* are manifestly one-sided and therefore undebatable.

H. Select an Important Subject. For learning groups, including school and college students, the preferable topics are those significant economic, political, and other problems of the contemporary world. Such themes are a natural complement to the classroom studies and to the problems analyzed in opinion journals of the day.

Occasionally students may be justified in taking time out for debate on a passing local problem, such as *What can the 500 students of Social Science 113 do to minimize cheating in the three-hour semester examination?* Usually, however, you will count your time for debating and discussion better spent if you undertake a more representative problem that will be of interest to your radio listeners and to the rival debaters representing other colleges. Also your concentration on an important topic in college debate will no doubt pay you dividends ten years later.

I. Limit the Subject. The purpose of the occasion, the nature of the argumentative procedure, and the time limits impose restrictions on the extent of the problem to be treated. If your debate is limited to fifteen minutes over the radio, with four speakers involved, you will cut down the problem to dimensions that may be handled with some completeness. For a ten-minute single argumentative speech or written argument, you are advised to delimit the proposition: *The record of the Democratic party from 1933 to 1949 justifies our approval* should be limited to *The Democratic policy during the 81st Congress concerning individual income taxes deserves our approval.*

The bane of most thirty-minute discussions over the radio and of most one-hour discussions and debates in face-to-face situations is that the problem is too wide in scope to be effectively presented.

J. Select Either a Question of Fact or One of Policy. A problem of fact is typically one that deals with (1) the existence of an entity; (2) the naming of a concept; (3) the occurrence of an action; (4) the establishment of similarity, or resemblance, between objects or relationships; (5) the causes or results of events.

Propositions or subjects of this type are often debated. Questions involving the existence of things include such propositions as *Democracy is a failure;* those naming a concept are illustrated by *Democracy means social-political equality;* those discussing an alleged action are illustrated by *John Doe murdered Richard Roe;* those discussing a possible relationship include such assertions as *A federal world government is preferable to the United Nations;* those suggesting a connection of events are exemplified by *The administration of F. D. Roosevelt resulted in strong gains for American labor,* and *The teaching of phonetics in every American college would produce better speech by undergraduates.*

A proposition of policy raises the question, Should this course of action be followed? This type of proposition aims at action, and he who assumes the burden of proof must establish the workable character of his plan. In each case the term *should be* is equivalent to *is both desirable and practicable.*

III. Suggestions for Wording of the Subject

The exact framing of a question or proposition requires considerable skill. Often what appears to be a single or satisfactory statement turns out to have vague or ambiguous implications that invite quibbling rather than clear-cut exposition of rival ideas.

Propositions for interscholastic or intercollegiate debate are more and more coined by official committees. Each year since 1930 the wording committee of the National University Extension Association has spent weeks in getting the precise statement of the national high-school question for the ensuing year.

The Committee on Intercollegiate Debate and Discussion Activities of the Speech Association of America is at great pains each year to select and frame a proposition to be used by all American colleges.

The prospective debater himself, however, in the classroom and elsewhere, is continually called upon to phrase a subject or to criticize intelligently the phrasing submitted to him. Such intelligent criticism is, of course, the basis of his discerning analysis of the proposition.

A. State the Subject in the Form of a Complete Sentence. It is to be noticed that in each example the statement is in the form of a complete sentence, interrogative or declarative, with subject and predicate. You may present an exposition, a description, or a narration concerning a term. Argument should rest upon a complete statement. A term is the subject or predicate of a single assertion. It is impossible to argue a term. A belief or opinion which deals with the relation of things cannot be expressed in a word or phrase. To have a complete statement or interrogation, two terms connected by a linking verb are necessary. All matters which men discuss can be reduced to this form. Although much debate is carried on without formal words in mind, where accuracy is demanded or where a decision is attempted, such complete statement is needed.

B. *For Formal Debate Use a Resolution, Motion, or Proposition.* In the motions, indictments, and pleas of courts of law, in the bills and resolutions of legislative assemblies, a complete statement is required. The ease with which the matter can be reduced to a proposition is in proportion to the definiteness of the discussion. The proposition is present whether it is definitely stated or not. The chairman announces that "John Smith will discuss the 7-cent gas tax." What Mr. Smith actually discusses is an unannounced proposition: *The State of Iowa should place a tax of 7 cents on every gallon of gasoline.*

The motion form would be: *I move that this council approve a parking-meter system.*

The resolution form is: *Resolved, That this council approves a parking-meter system.*

The proposition form, implying a motion or resolution, would be: *This House favors the adoption by Congress of a Federal sales tax.*

C. *For Discussion Usually State the Subject as an Impartial Question.* Sometimes the subject is stated as a question rather than as a declaration, particularly in public discussions in which only one speaker presents a set speech prior to the open forum. Thus America's Town Meeting of the Air discussed these subjects:

Would you like to turn the clock back?
Would you rather live in a small town or a big city?
Is radio operating in the public interest?
Should there be further limits on the right to strike?
Is science the salvation, or the destroyer of mankind?

D. Frame the Proposition in a Simple Sentence. The chief problem of the debater after he has limited his subject is to reduce it to a simple, specific sentence.

The compound structure, for example, is objectionable because it may include two distinct propositions only vaguely related. One of several reasons for refusing to argue the following proposition is its double-headedness: *Resolved, That the powers of the President should be substantially increased as a settled policy and that he should be ineligible for reelection.*

The dependent clause, moreover, has little place in the propositional sentence. *If the several states should endorse the policy of the retail sale of liquor by a system of state monopoly and sale in state stores, political corruption and graft would increase* may be more conveniently phrased, *For the several states to endorse the policy of the retail sale of liquor by a system of state monopoly and sale in state stores would mean an increase in political corruption and graft.* Further improvement in the wording would be, *Resolved, That each state should adopt a state monopoly and sale of liquor in state stores.* The student of debating and of English will find interest and profit in working over at length the statement of this proposition, or some similar one, in order to make it meet the tests of concise as well as accurate statement.

E. Omit from the Wording Any Ambiguous, Question-begging, or Vague Terms. An apparently innocent and straightforward statement may precipitate endless wrangling. If the occasion is to be a decision debate or one that invites limited and specific treatment, be sure that your proposition is free from such terms as *socialistic system, will of the people, conservatism, best interest, control, progress.* Debates on *Resolved, That the general welfare of the people of the United States would be best promoted by democratic collectivism* led to all sorts of descriptions of *democratic.*

F. Word the Proposition to Make a Standard of Comparison Possible. A satisfactory debate results if we can compare the proposal advanced by the affirmative with an alternate one by the negative. Note how the following statements invite the affirmative and negative each to take a definite position.

The President of the United States should be elected by a direct popular vote instead of by the electoral college.

For a democratic nation the congressional form of government is preferable to the parliamentary form.

G. *Give to the Affirmative the Burden of Proof.* The proposition should be so phrased that those who introduce the resolution or question should assume the burden of proof. Burden of proof is the obligation on one side or the other of influencing the audience to accept a proposition. Logically, the affirmative must assume this obligation, for whoever asserts should also attempt to establish his contention. *The several states should continue the system of private rather than socialized medicine* obviously puts chief burden on the negative. To give to the affirmative the responsibility of proving a case, the statement should be framed so that (1) the affirmative advocates a policy or contention strongly opposed to public opinion, or so that (2) a change from existing affairs is advocated, as in the usual question of policy. *Resolved, That the issuance of tax-exempt securities should be permitted by law* clearly lays the burden on the negative, as does the following proposition, *Each state should refuse to adopt the policy of compulsory voting.*

First of all, decide what mature public opinion over a wide area is in regard to the question; then phrase the proposition so that the affirmative must go against this tide of public sentiment. If you are in doubt about the trend of such social sentiment or if sentiment is not crystallized or is evenly divided, then follow the conventional suggestion of wording the proposition so that a change from existing affairs is proposed. Usually the advocacy of a change will mean also the advocacy of a course of action contrary to popular approval.

EXERCISES AND PROBLEMS

1. Frame satisfactory propositions on three timely topics of national concern; three dealing with present state issues; three on local (county or city) issues; and three on problems related to your campus.

2. Comment on one of the propositions you have worded for exercise 1. Apply each (or most) of the tests listed in this chapter, and show in detail why your proposition and its wording conform to these criteria.

3. Apply the tests of subject matter and phrasing to each of the

following propositions. After the comment, in each case reword to correct the phrasing. (Take wide liberties in such rewording.)

a. The novels of Anthony Trollope deserve wider reading in schools and colleges.

b. The dreadnought is obsolete.

c. The Federal government should reject the principle and practice of providing support for agricultural prices.

d. The control of atomic energy in the United States should be under the exclusive control of the United States military forces.

e. Education at Harvard about 1800 was largely an echo of out-of-date concepts of higher education.

f. The present President of the United States is a superior public speaker.

g. Television will contribute heavily to the obsolescence of the motion picture industry.

h. Congress should provide four-year college scholarships ($1,200 per year) for all American youths who qualify by passing satisfactory entrance examinations and who demonstrate the need for financial aid.

4. On one page give a satisfactory criticism of the current high-school or college question chosen for debate for this year.

5. Draw up five subjects for debate or discussion by your group over the radio. Defend before your group such selections.

6. Examine and comment on the subjects and their wordings for the debates in the current *University Debater's Annual.*

7. Evaluate the subjects and wording of topics used recently in America's Town Meeting of the Air, or similar radio series.

CHAPTER 3

Research Techniques

I. System in Preparation

What are the problems dealing with the collection and selection of materials for argumentation, discussion, and debate? Subjects and subject matter are really a single problem. Certainly if you find a profusion of materials and assemble an array of ideas, you are provided with motivation hardly to be expected from exploration of a topic devoid of supporting details.

What are these materials you are to collect and from which you will shape persuasive discourse? They consist of the framework of general ideas that compose your reflective thinking. These background data include also the evidence, the authorities, the specific examples, facts, figures, raw or systematized, the circumstantial details, the analogies, general illustrations, the events or situations that fall into cause-effect relationships. These materials, in short, are the complex phenomena of this political, social, economic, physical, military, moral, and religious world to which we react in diverse ways.[1]

How shall we go about selecting from this vast range of data and ideas?

Four or five principal techniques or skills are indicated: thinking, listening, talking, systematic and creative reading, and note taking.

[1] For illustration of the types of materials and ideas involved in research, examine the Specimen Brief, Appendix A.

28

II. Thinking as a Source of Materials

The first step, before you rush to the library, is to examine your individual ideas in regard to the proposition. The subject given to you may be so esoteric or complicated that your information and ideas concerning it seem blank. More often, however, you will find that your previous reading, observations, and experience have contributed a respectable body of facts and judgments concerning the issue. College athletes have been known to complain because they could "find no information in regard to the abandonment of intercollegiate athletics." Other students, when confronted with such subjects as *Resolved, That coeducation is a failure,* neglect to consider their fund of personal information.

Make, then, a mental inventory of your ideas on the problem. The steps of thinking in working out a controversial problem will give us a clue for procedure. We ask, "What does this proposition mean?" We may not have the technical answer, but we can use common sense. Further, we inquire, "What is the difficulty or perplexity?" We line up the immediate disturbing factors. Moreover, we ask, "What are the causes of the trouble, and what may be the outcomes?" Pursuing our reflection further, we inquire, "What course or courses are best to consider as possible remedies?" "What suggestions occur to me in favor of 'my side,' and what objections arise?" Other reflective questions that emerge at this and succeeding stages are "What facts do I already have?" "Or are they merely loose opinions?" "What experiences and observations have occurred to me that relate to this problem?" "Do I have the opinion of others?" "Are these sources genuine 'authorities'?" "Are the instances or examples that occur to me of any validity?" Thus you will at the outset exercise some judgment and some ability in analysis and classification of materials. Later chapters will lead you more concretely into these processes of straight and productive thinking.

III. Listening as a Source of Materials

If you are developing a problem over a period of three or four weeks, you will have opportunity to profit in fact and idea gathering through your attendance at classroom recitations, public lectures, and your listening to discussions.

Are you an efficient listener? (1) If so, you will adopt a re-

ceptive attitude toward the speaker. His ideas will be worth your
while if you give him your attention. (2) Concentrate on his remarks. Make mental or other notes. (3) Have an open or inquiring mind. Get the speaker's point of view. Question the
ideas, but don't be antagonistic. If you are in the classroom, help
the lecturer achieve a "lively sense of communication" by your
response to his effort. (4) As he proceeds, raise such reflective
questions as I suggested above.

Especially will you profit from listening to radio discussions.
Hundreds of radio stations, including those owned by educational
institutions, have regular discussion programs. The networks,
National, American, Columbia, Mutual, and others, feature such
debating-discussions as America's Town Meeting of the Air, University of Chicago Round Table, American Forum of the Air,
Wake Up, America, and Northwestern Reviewing Stand.

IV. CONVERSATION, DISCUSSION, AND PERSONAL INTERVIEWS
AS SOURCES OF MATERIALS

If your attentive listening gives knowledge and starts critical
thinking, so do your conversations, informal discussions, and interviews. Edmund Burke, Charles James Fox, Richard Brinsley
Sheridan, Henry Clay, Abraham Lincoln, Albert J. Beveridge,
William Jennings Bryan, Franklin D. Roosevelt, Wendell Willkie,
and other historic debaters or representative speakers derived no
small part of their fund of information for their speeches from
conferences and prolonged talks with their friends. You will no
doubt agree that often your clarification of thinking and added
knowledge have resulted from "bull sessions" and "gab fests." If
you direct the conversation into a channel related to some problem that concerns you, you will sometimes be surprised at the
wealth of ideas uncovered in this group situation.

When the topic does have such a pattern of directed thinking,
the occasion may evolve into an informal discussion. When several participate, you will find the give and take most stimulating
in crystallizing your point of view.

Like discussions, personal interviews with members of the
faculty who are specialists on the particular economic or political
problem under investigation, with businessmen, or with public
officers who may have special knowledge of the subject will be
well worth while. Your mood in the inquiry, however, should be

that of a reporter rather than that of a cross-examiner. Sometimes it is better to postpone this particular plan of gathering points of view until you have enough information to construct in advance of the interview a series of rather definite and pertinent questions.

In any case make the interview brief (great men are busy), frame your questions beforehand, but follow any important clue given by the interviewee. Have the manners of a good conversationalist and a good listener. Make only mental notes and jot down later what you have been told.

V. READING AS A SOURCE OF MATERIALS

In spite of the ocean of printed material, our speaking or writing is too often the product of limited and superficial reading. The truth is that the libraries and their world of books we only vaguely tap. Even though our time is occupied with immediate course requirements and the library resources are only perfunctory experiences to us, we will profit fully only by extensive resort to the printed page as a complement to our thinking, listening, observation, and conversation.

Those who expect to argue, discuss, and debate will find their way easily and often about the library; will know something of the typical books of reference; will be able to select quietly and judiciously books and magazines and newspapers and will know the secret of getting at the riches of government documents and at the pamphlets of nongovernment agencies; will be able to build bibliographies, to read creatively, and to take notes efficiently.[2]

VI. READING TECHNIQUES

In the presence of the plethora of reading material suggested above, what efficient methods of reading will you adopt? Your problem is partly that of selecting wisely what to read from the relevant articles and books; how to use your time to the best advantage in covering the sources you have selected; and how to assimilate these facts and ideas you have comprehended.

A. *The Tendency to Eclecticism.* One of the besetting dangers of wide and specific reading in connection with the preparation of a debate lies in the wholesale appropriation and reproduction of the material. In these days when endless pamphlets,

[2] See Appendix B, "Library Sources for Readings on Current Problems."

articles, reports, and interviews are swamping the reading public, it is not only possible but exceedingly easy to secure excellent ready-made arguments on most debatable subjects. The novice in debating, unable to withstand the temptation offered him by a rich array of arguments, in many cases succumbs. His argument as delivered becomes a series of echoes of some authoritative writer, or writers, on the subject. Usually the speaker gives credit to his sources so that the debate becomes a piecing together of ideas, each prefaced by "Mr. So and So says," or "According to Mr. So and So," or "To quote Mr. So and So in the last number of *Harper's Magazine,* p. 14," etc. The process is eclectic, a dove-tailing of authorities without the hazarding of a single personal opinion. In a few cases the student, regarding as his own whatever he finds, delivers as his own paragraph after paragraph from the *Congressional Record* or other sources without so much as giving credit. It should be added here that the disposition of some "coaches" to phrase the ideas for the debaters has contributed to the student's confusion concerning originality and plagiarism.

B. Proper Indication of Quotations. Although exact rules which guarantee the prevention of plagiarism are impossible, teachers of debate and composition in general agree that any quotation of three or more words should be included within quotation marks and that he who speaks the words of another must make clear to the audience that the statements are not his own.

C. Assimilative Reading. How, then, shall you preserve your own soul in a library rich in evidence and in arguments for your case? The answer lies in the practice of *assimilation* of what you read. Your reading is not principally to the end that the fifty or more quotations on your cards may be strung out one after the other in the form of a so-called speech but rather that you may read reflectively and creatively.

1. Approach your sources with an open mind. Try to be objective. Don't pass by an article that criticizes unfavorably what you wish to defend.

2. Read with a purpose. Keep in mind a framework of what you are after.

3. Sometimes read for details. Close examination is necessary when you are hunting for facts. Even so you can speed up the

process in proportion to your clear understanding of the types of evidence you are looking for.

4. Sometimes read for general ideas. In such cases you may read rapidly. To size up efficiently many pages, you will note the introductory and summarizing passages, the topic sentences, the organization and purpose of each paragraph.

5. If you think you are pretty slow as a reader, consult your faculty. They will give you special guidance that will no doubt increase your skill in silent reading.

6. Read reflectively. Question each statement. If the book belongs to you, write on the margin your reaction to the text.

Thus by avoiding blind acceptance of what is in print, you will not parrot. You will assimilate rather than echo ideas and information. You will be a creative reader.

VII. METHODS OF CONSTRUCTING THE BIBLIOGRAPHY OR LIST OF REFERENCES

A. *Character of a Bibliography.* The discussion above of source material assumes that you have a working bibliography on your topic. A bibliography is a list of sources on a given subject. You should distinguish three kinds of bibliographies: (1) a basic bibliography, a comprehensive listing of all the literature of a subject up to a given date; (2) a current bibliography, a record of the sources of a given period (*e.g.,* one year); (3) a selective bibliography, including a limited list of books and articles best adapted to your purpose. This latter type you should label "List of References." It, rather than a complete bibliography, is really what you want for practical purposes.

B. *Printed Bibliographies.* One of your first tasks as an investigator is to secure any printed, authoritative bibliographies on your proposition.

C. *Preparing Your Own List of References.* Because your subject is almost invariably a live one, you will find it necessary to draw up a selective bibliography.

1. For books, go first to the *Cumulative Book Index,* formerly the *United States Catalog,* with the recent *Monthly Cumulative Supplements.* If you are doubtful about whether a recent book should be included, perhaps the *Book Review Digest* will give you a clue.

2. Next consult your college library card system although the

data given may need to be supplemented by those from the *Cumulative Book Index.* Star those books which are in your local library.

3. Refer next to the recent numbers of the *Readers' Guide to Periodical Literature.*

4. Go next to any other special indexes, for example, the *Public Affairs Information Service.*

5. Then consult government documents by means of the recent indexes to the *Congressional Record* and perhaps of the *Catalogue of Public Documents* with the supplementary *Monthly Catalogue.*

6. Then list a number of selected references to the *New York Times* or equivalent newspapers by means of the *New York Times Index.*

D. Methods of Recording Your Items. 1. Use cards or slips of paper so that you can sort your items systematically and add constantly (a debater's bibliography is complete only after he steps onto the platform for his final debate on the subject).

2. Place only one item on a card.

3. Classify your assembled list into divisions of (*a*) bibliographies; (*b*) books; (*c*) pamphlets and reports; (*d*) periodicals (including newspapers or making a special division for the latter).

4. For books (including pamphlets) include the author's name and initials, the exact title of the book, the name of the publisher, date of publication, and the number of the edition (if revision has been made), thus:

PERKINS, FRANCES: *The Roosevelt I Knew,* The Viking Press, 1946. Note that the entries for books will thus be arranged alphabetically by authors.

5. For periodicals (including newspapers) list the title of the magazine, volume and page, and, if possible, the date, title of article, and the author's name and initials. For example:

Vital Speeches of the Day, 13:272–277, Feb. 15, 1947, "The British Empire in the Modern World," Churchill, Randolph.

6. Use a filing box and alphabetical guide cards. Above all, not only in debate but in every college subject, copy your items accurately and clearly so that typists can read them. If you can thus prepare a worth-while selective bibliography, you have laid the basis for research. Your term papers and other college and professional investigations will thus more easily bear the stamp of genuine scholarship.

VIII. NOTE TAKING

Once the selective bibliography, or list of references, is tentatively arranged or under way, you are confronted with the problem of systematically taking notes on your reading. Here again a proper method is necessary. At no point in debate preparation do students show greater neglect. At no point should you exercise more patience than in putting on paper the results of your study of sources. If you follow a plan, you will save hours. Don't rely on your memory. Don't hastily jot down the ideas or facts on odd scraps of paper and wonder the next day just where or how you found some idea. Don't subject yourself to the embarrassment of having some other debater or some critic judge quietly ask you, "Just where did you learn that alleged fact?" Proceed somewhat as follows:

1. Use cards or sheets of paper of uniform size. Three-by-five-inch cards are standard. They can be quickly classified.

2. Place only one fact or point on a card. Otherwise the material cannot be readily classified. These cards are not to be confused with the bibliography cards. The latter you have carefully pigeonholed in the "bibliography box." Loose-leaf notebooks are sometimes used; but they are usually not so satisfactory as the smaller recording mediums.

3. Place at the top of the card or small sheet of paper the main issue or topic to which the specific fact or evidence refers. See below for suggestions concerning the topics.

4. Indicate, preferably at the bottom of the card, the exact source of your information. Here exercise your will power to make the record accurate. It is unnecessary to copy everything you read; read selectively and take things down discriminately.

5. Quote accurately from each source and indicate omissions by means of dots. Avoid long quotations. Be sure that your citation represents the spirit as well as the letter of your source. Your citation should represent also the context of the article.

6. Let your notes be mainly facts rather than opinions. Statistics, illustrations, and specific cases rather than mere authorities should form the bulk of your data.

7. Assemble your items under general headings. When you begin reading, form a rough program of things to look for; presently a more detailed classification will suggest itself to you. In

some cases you can relabel some of your evidence cards.   Such possible topics would be *history of the case or problem, explanation of terms, main issues, need for the proposal* (subtopics might be *economic evils, social evils, political evils*), *causes of the alleged evils or weaknesses in the present system or situation, alternate proposals for dealing with the problem* (here a number of classifications will develop as your investigation unfolds), *advantages and disadvantages of the proposal* (here break your cards into *economic, social, political, moral, physiological, legal, financial,* and other sections), *practicability of the proposal.* This last-mentioned topic would include groupings such as (*a*) *cost,* (*b*) *precedent for the proposal, i.e.,* its successful or unsuccessful working in various cities, states, or countries, (*c*) *authorities in favor of, or opposed to, the proposal,* (*d*) *machinery for its administration,* (*e*) *justification or justice or injustice of the plan,* and (*f*) the *social and economic results,* or (*g*) the *results to different groups,* such as to the individual, local community, state, and nation. These titles are tentative; of course, they somewhat overlap. If, however, you follow them, you will read more methodically from the beginning.

EXERCISES AND PROBLEMS

1. Present to the instructor your tentative selective bibliography, or list of references, on a question for debate assigned to you. If a full bibliography already exists, supplement it by obtaining more recent references (*e.g.,* those of the most recent twelve months.) Your bibliography should be neatly prepared (but should consist of the original cards ready for any reshuffling) with the proper classifications of books, periodicals, and other divisions suggested in this chapter. Each item should be accurately, completely, and legibly copied. If practicable, let your references indicate that you have consulted the *United States Catalog,* the *Readers' Guide,* and the other special indexes, the *Congressional Record* and other government publications, the *New York Times Index* or other newspapers. (At the option of the instructor this list of references may be secured as a group project, with each member assigned to some special index or division of material for his contribution.) The number of items offered for this assignment will vary with the subject. It may be said, roughly, that each member of the group, if he alone is to give an entire list of references, should probably offer at least thirty or forty cards.

2. Present to the instructor at least twenty evidence cards, that is, cards representing your note taking on the subject investigated for the exercise above. Be sure that each card conforms in every detail to the instructions in this chapter. Be sure that you differentiate your evidence cards from those used for making your selective bibliography. (The latter will comprise an entirely different bundle of material.)

3. Test your knowledge of this chapter and of Appendix B "Library Sources for Readings on Current Problems" by reviewing the following topics (be prepared for oral or written reporting on any one or all):

a. The importance of system in preparation.

b. The importance of personal information in working out the debate topic assigned to you.

c. What you have learned from discussion with your roommate (or an acquaintance) on the topic assigned to you.

d. Letters you should write to secure information on this topic.

e. Recommendation of a general encyclopedia and an explanation for your preference.

f. A special encyclopedia that has material on the subject of your debate or discussion.

g. Three or four authoritative books in the field of your subject for debate or discussion.

h. The value to discussants of the *Cumulative Book Index* and its attendant *Monthly Cumulative Supplements.*

i. Explanation of where to go for a list, with addresses, of propagandistic or learned societies.

j. Five organizations that have material for your specific purpose.

k. Six special periodical indexes in addition to the *Readers' Guide.*

l. Explanation of the *Book Review Digest;* the *Public Affairs Information Service.*

4. Give reasons why your colleagues should subscribe to a certain monthly magazine of opinion.

5. Expound the uses of the *New York Times Index.*

6. Explain the *University Debaters' Annual; The Reference Shelf Series; Speech Activities.*

7. Explain at least six principles or steps which you followed in recording your bibliography.

CHAPTER 4

Reflective Thinking and Argumentative Types: Preliminary Survey

I. Function of Reflective Thinking in Argumentation, Discussion, and Debate

Argumentative writing and speaking, whether general argument or specialized discussion or debate, is primarily logical rather than emotional communication.[1] Although representative techniques of communication by language are involved in argumentation, reason predominates. The old admonition to judge a debater by his skill in evidence and argument more than by delivery or language still holds. The audience, speaker, occasion, and subject in which argumentative discourse functions assume that rational treatment, intellectual exchange, and logical conclusions should prevail. Aristotle wrote his *Rhetoric* partly to restore to a central place logical materials in communication. His contemporaries tended to exalt style and presentation. Aristotle gave full weight and place to audience appeals but insisted, and rightly, on the primacy of rational judgments.

Modern students of argumentation have adhered to this ancient emphasis. They have done so not because of the high respect for

[1] See Chap. 1, pp. 10–11.

tradition but because the proper deliberation of controversial matters demands reason. We who attempt to practice effective argumentation in writing and speaking assume (1) that argumentation is essentially problem solving; (2) that problem-and-solution of this nature, usually in groups and involving usually social or economic problems, can best be done by minimizing the emotional trial and error and by favoring a methodical examination of the controversial factors; (3) that those who attempt to exercise this cognitive technique have sufficient learning, experience, and discriminative skill to arrive at dependable judgments; (4) that a given society (the contemporary United States and the larger civilization which pronounces what are the "right" decisions) "progresses" most satisfactorily when these decisions and courses of action stem from deliberative (rather than demonstrative) occasions.

If your aim, then, is to clarify complicated issues and to move toward stable beliefs and conduct, you will exalt the techniques of logic. It is important for you to understand how people think and to apply techniques that aid in clear thinking. This chapter aims to introduce to you some principles of sound thinking with which every debater should become familiar.

II. Emotionalized Thinking

What distinguishes systematic from emotional thinking? The individual, it is apparent, is a "bundle of emotions." The traditional conceit of "man as a thinker" needs strong qualification. Man in his mighty role as thinker has been deflated by the experimental psychologists. Woodrow Wilson's observation, frequently quoted, that we move on a sea of passion is in point.[2]

What is "emotion"? Psychologists agree that it is a consciousness or awareness of bodily changes. These physiological reactions result from a stimulus, communicated to the higher centers of the nervous system. "This fused complex of sensory experience is what we call an emotion."[3]

Since emotion is a word or a name, there is always a tendency to think that emotion is some *thing*, some discrete, distinct definable unity. Experiments have uniformly shown that emotion, like percep-

[2] See Chap. 1, p. 10.
[3] F. H. Allport, *Social Psychology*, p. 84, Houghton Mifflin Company, 1924.

tion, cognition, and attention, *does not exist as a unique entity*, but that there is a variety of perceptive experiences, attendant reactions and cognitive experiences. It is also true that such emotions as anger, fear, pity, disgust do not exist in unique independence, but in relation to concrete situations—in such phenomena as fighting reactions or fearfulness, in the experience of pity or of withdrawal from obnoxious objects.[4]

These "emotions" or "emotion" whether primary (*e.g.*, hunger) or secondary become motives for action or satisfaction of the needs or wants. The stronger the emotion, the more clearly is it associated with behavior and with motivation. If you are to make progress as an arguer, you should understand something of these emotional states and motivative drives. Hunger drives us to food; fear, to flight or resistance; anger, to personal or international wars. Thus do we catalogue a considerable group of motives or drives, ranging from the elemental reactions to the "higher" impulses to duty and unselfish sacrifice.[5]

Emotional reactions cannot be sharply set off from rational activity. The old "faculty psychology" with its departmentalized intellect, feelings, and will has been long abandoned. Reaction is the product of complicated nervous, muscular, and glandular activity. We are content to describe tendencies as predominantly "intellectual" and "logical" and others as largely "emotional."

Emotional activity is relatively excessive, disorganized, "subcortical," sometimes described as chiefly centering in the thalamus.[6]

Emotional thinking, then, is mainly the expression of these relatively disorganized responses. Emotionalized thinking is largely explained as the demonstration of stereotyped responses,

. . . perceptions or meaningful arrangements of ideas having their origin primarily in feelings and emotions rather than in some characteristics of the stimulating circumstances. In reacting to personal

[4] Edwin Garrigues Boring, Herbert Sidney Langfeld, and Harry Porter Weld, *Introduction to Psychology* (5th printing), p. 183, John Wiley & Sons, Inc., 1944.

[5] For detailed treatment of motives in argument, see Chap. 18. *Cf.* Boring, Langfeld, and Weld, *op. cit.*, Chaps. 5 and 6.

[6] "The unique psychological experience in feeling and emotion has been attributed by various investigators to patterns of response depending upon nervous activity mediated through the *thalamus*." Boring, Langfeld, and Weld, *op. cit.*, p. 217.

and social problems the individual builds up these modes of conduct, and later they may be released by stimuli having elements in common with the original situations.[7]

The emotional speaker or writer, as thinker, in his language and mental processes, is typically a "crooked" thinker. In language usage, for example, he is abstract, verbose, inaccurate, often colorful and bombastic. His sentence structure is complicated and dramatic. His "definitions" are loose, equivocal, framed to echo his biases. He usually substitutes assertion for fact; embellishes or distorts facts to support his drives and motives. He ignores authorities or selects those that coincide with his prejudices. His "evidence" is inconsistent and partial. He generalizes from few instances and ignores negative cases. His analogies are graphic but misleading. He thinks in "absolutes" and moves easily from one ill-supported premise to another equally untenable. All is couched in "allness" terminology and pseudo logic. He is given to name calling, appeals to tradition, humor, and fear. He eulogizes and denounces. He rationalizes, *i.e.*, talks to a conclusion arbitrarily held previously and determined by his wants and hopes alone. At his worst he is a Hitler. He is a "bad" propagandist. Or he is merely ignorant, creating infantile argument and succumbing to the propaganda or specious argument that appeals to his wishes.[8]

III. CHARACTERISTICS OF REFLECTIVE THINKING

Reflective thinking, as suggested above, is the kind of mental activity in which "ideas" and reactions are examined critically. The critical thinker's mental activity is relatively under control.

The systematic "cortical" thinker identifies reactions with causes and results of the stimuli. Although his thought will no doubt be accompanied by much random motivation, his effort—and the outward expression of it in language, voice, and bodily attitudes—will indicate balanced treatment of the stimuli to which he is responding. In essence his technique is that of examining a disturbing problem and solving it. To do so he views critically the facts, language, hypotheses, beliefs, and assumptions attending his diagnosis and prescription.

---

[7] Charles Bird, *Social Psychology*, p. 289, Appleton-Century-Crofts, Inc., 1940.

[8] For further treatment of unsound thinking see Chaps. 14 and 15.

IV. Reflective Thinking and the Logical Pattern

What is this pattern of thinking? The complete act of reflective thought, as John Dewey put it, involves the following steps: (1) recognition of a felt difficulty; (2) the description or diagnosis of the problem; (3) the description of representative hypotheses or solutions of the problem; (4) the rational elaboration of these suggestions and the testing of each; (5) experiment and verification leading to acception or rejection of the preferred solution.[9]

Reflective thinking, then, is first of all a deliberate and conscious awareness of a disturbing situation. Is it that the railroads are strikebound and you wish to get somewhere? Has a member of the faculty flunked you unfairly? Have you run out of cash and wonder how to get more for your immediate needs? Do the headlines of the papers disturb you by suggesting approaching war clouds?

Your second step is an orderly diagnosis of the problem. What are the phenomena or facts which give rise to the difficulty? What are the causes of the irritating situation? What are the probable results?

The third phase of the reflective process consists of an examination of representative solutions of the problem. What are the possibilities for solving the bad situation? Each hypothesis in turn is weighed and compared with the other solutions. You survey advantages and disadvantages, the practicability and impracticability of each.

The final step is a concentration on the preferred "way out" of the difficulty. You firmly establish its comparative superiority and muster evidence and argument to this end. Such in essence is the reflective process underlying all forms of argument, discussion, and debate.

What of this reflective procedure as it relates to the discourse? Essentially, intellectual thinking and expression are based on examinations of facts and on the principles or conclusions to which these facts or phenomena point. You bridge the gap from the well authenticated to the relatively unknown. The exploration ends in some sort of conclusion (a picture or perception of what should be done). Conclusions that grow out of this deliberative

[9] John Dewey, *How We Think* (new edition), pp. 71–78, 91–101, D. C. Heath and Company, 1933.

and evaluative process we call *judgment* or *inference*. The reasoning process, then, is made up of a series of inferences. Your method in arguing is to provide judgments or inferences or reasons that an audience may follow and accept.

V. Details of the Reflective Process

A. Weighing of Facts. The arguer or discussant first confronts the alleged facts that underlie the "felt difficulty." These materials he evaluates with respect to their accuracy, their completeness, their consistency, and their harmony with all other relevant data. He frames his queries as impartial questions and secures whatever disinterested replies are available to him. He thus focuses on "fact" and does so as a critical observer. He has somewhat the spirit of any scientific investigator.[10]

B. Weighing of Language. Your reflective approach will necessitate your sharp scrutiny of language in its relation to thought itself. Does language adequately convey what is intended in the symbolic interpretation of facts, principles, propositions, and conclusions? Are the formal definitions intelligently and functionally conceived? Are the words and phrases throughout the discourse, as used by you or by others, referential, concrete, and contributory to clear thinking? Again, by the aid of impartial and intelligent inquiry, you will check these language usages and thus demonstrate critical thinking of no mean order.[11]

C. Weighing the Analysis of the Subject. Still another aspect of your controlled evaluation of argumentative speaking and writing will be your review of the issues and partition (chief propositions to be developed). What, exactly, is the problem? What main and subissues are at stake? What concrete propositions are developed? What important ones omitted? Have these propositions plumbed the depths of the controversy? These and similar lines of investigation will occupy your thinking. Power of successful analysis characterizes the fruitful thinker. At no point in mental orderliness is constructive reasoning more apparent than in this formulation of main and subdivisions and in the criticism of them.[12]

[10] See Chap. 9 for tests of evidence.

[11] For details of testing definitions and of language usage in general, see Chaps. 5 and 17.

[12] For details of stating and criticizing issues and divisions of a subject see Chap. 6.

D. Weighing of Organization or Structure. Organization is the complement of analysis. The order of the materials, the selection of ideas and their relatively full treatment, the devices by which relevancy, emphasis, and coherence are achieved—all require critical review. Structure is no mere accessory to discourse. Organization is a mirror of the thought pattern. The speech organizer and the critic of such arrangement will test the structural texture of the thought and so will detect the presence or absence of logical validity in his own and others' speeches and writings.[13]

E. Weighing of Inference. What is inference? Roughly it is synonymous with reason and reflective thinking. From facts or general statements based on facts we draw conclusions. This movement from fact or premise to conclusions is reasoning or inference.

1. Inference and orderly thinking. Reason and reflection occur when we mentally explore and take up a position in a heretofore undiscovered region. This thought movement is controlled not by chance or whim, however, but by careful inspection of the facts and principles at hand and by a cautious examination of whatever alleged facts and principles are only dimly seen. Inference is the ability to see and describe connections between terms and statements whose close association may not be immediately apparent. It is guessing, but judicial guessing, based not on "hunches" but on methodical survey of the probabilities and hazards accompanying the new stand (conclusion).

You view, for example, the connection between dictators and international wars. You note that these two phenomena occur together or that wars follow the rise of dictators. There seems to be an obvious connection. You reason, then, "Dictators breed international wars" (one proposition). Later you refer to the history of 1925 to 1945 and examine the rise and fall of Hitler and of Mussolini. "These were simon-pure dictators," you say (a second proposition). Then the association of your first and your second propositions becomes clearer to you. Thus you conclude, "Hitler and Mussolini were among the potent causes of World War II." This experience of identification and association of terms and of statements drawn from such terms constitutes the method of inference or argument.

Note that your inferences in almost every case have an element of speculation. Often they concern the future as when you con-

---

[13] For full treatment of structure see Chaps. 7 and 16.

clude as you survey the heavens, "We shall have good corn-growing weather tomorrow — a hot and dry July day is in prospect." Absolute certainty is seldom possible in your systematic conjectures. But with all your bearings properly surveyed you have enough confidence to hazard the inference. Your mental movement is orderly and precise. Independent thinkers in another room or another country, without consulting you but with your selfsame data and selfsame methods of scientific reflection, arrive at conclusions similar to your own. This is the objective method of science. Research scholars are constantly demonstrating the soundness of this reflective technique.

What is the explanation of this procedure by which you may confidently proceed from simple facts to more remote or speculative situations? How was it that Galileo in 1581 while watching a lamp swing in the cathedral at Pisa was able to visualize and enunciate the principle of the uniform vibration of all pendulums?

2. *Inference and an order system.* The answer to the question of how scientists like Galileo, Darwin, Newton, Pasteur, and political interpreters like Burke, Fox, Webster, and Lincoln reasoned lies in this: *inference is a description of the relationships of various facts, groups of facts, laws, and principles.* The good reasoner quickly sees and understands these relationships. He views the underlying connections. He notes that events or movements are casually connected; that certain phenomena always occur in exact harmony or association with other phenomena.

The logical reasoner is like the astute detectives in the pages of Agatha Christie, Dorothy Sayers, and Conan Doyle. These Sherlock Holmeses piece together threads into a consistent and revealing pattern.

Inference is possible because the world is orderly. Each relationship of nature and of man is a tidy little universe. We operate in a cosmos. The down-East Yankee becomes a duplicate of his kin, once you know him (you are familiar with a certain Maine village). But Yankees are united in the larger aggregation of Easterners; they in turn merge with other orders of Americans; and they in turn fall within the larger order system which circumscribes the whites, browns, and blacks of all nations. What is this "order system"? It is that property of the universe that reveals its "methodical composition." The universe may be physical, spatial, chronological; or it may be a conceptual ideal world. In any case "order is the first law of heaven."

We human beings, and especially we who decry whim and exalt reason, view, describe, and infer in the light of this order system (frequently designated as an "implicative" system or "inferential whole"). Through experience and observation we have come to understand this principle of uniformity, invariability, and consistency. These methods of describing relations—cause and effect, correlation of various properties—as we constantly apply them give us more and more assurance. Nature, if we understand her, does not betray our judgments. If we can only see clearly enough, we can fill out the picture. Sequences are invariable. Constancy is never violated. Every piece fits into the puzzle. Every detail of the circumstantial evidence tallies with every other detail. Reflection, or the drawing of inferences, is the residue of our racial experience in dealing with the universe.

Why do we thus put our faith in reasoning and in reasoning as an interpretation of cause-and-effect resemblance, uniformity, and law? Not simply because philosophy views the world in its spiritual character as directed toward a spiritual end, but because our daily experience strengthens our confidence in such judgments. Every minute produces its little cycles of reflection that are later verified in our personal history. "The uniformity of nature, the conviction that things will continue to occur in the same manner as they have hitherto, is undoubtedly the best founded generalization in the whole range of human experience."[14]

VI. Typical Methods of Inference

When you infer or reason you do so in one or more of several well-defined ways.

1. You may view details that have similarities and so generalize concerning the whole array of such cases or samples. This is reasoning or argument by induction — the thought passage from the particular to the general. Induction may be simple or more complex as used in statistics.

2. You may limit your description and inference to a comparison between specific objects or relationships. One item has certain traits, fully revealed to you; the other case or relationship is comparatively unknown, as when you attempt to compare the earth and Neptune. You attempt, however, to discover sufficient

[14] Columbia Associates in Philosophy, *An Introduction to Reflective Thinking*, p. 93, Houghton Mifflin Company, 1923.

resemblances to warrant your placing these objects or relationships in the same category; you may thus predict the characteristics of the comparatively unknown case. This is reasoning or inference from analogy or example. Analogy may be a comparison of objects or of relationships; of those in the same order and those in a different field—literal and figurative analogy.

3. You may focus on two or more events or particulars that seem to have an invisible but definite connection. You apply various tests to these factors and presently may conclude that one affects the other. This inference is the familiar mode of argument or inference by causal connection. Such reasoning may be from cause to effect, effect to cause, or from effect to effect.

4. You may view the statements of others who speak with surety and experience concerning an event or theory and so infer conclusions from such testimony. This inference is from authority.

5. Finally, you may draw specific conclusions from general statements, such as those erected through induction. This mode is the familiar inference or argument by deduction. Logicians have subdivided deductive reasoning as (a) categorical and (b) conditioned (disjunctive and hypothetical), depending on the way the propositions are worded and matched with each other to lead to the deductive conclusion.

Several observations are in order concerning these types of argument.

They are not *all* the ways of orderly thinking. Logicians reduce deduction to various kinds of syllogisms and refer to enthymemes, prosyllogisms, and sorities; some logicians refer to induction by agreement, by difference, concomitant variations, or residues; some treat statistics as a distinct category; some refer to "argument from circumstantial detail" as a separate concept. The classification I have made above is a somewhat standard one. It is comparatively simple. It will be adequate for your needs as a debater or discussant.

These logical modes you are to view as the practical substance of your discourse. They are not academic forms to be applied as accessories to your speech or written argument. Rather they must compose the very texture of your unfolding argument. They are forms not to be rigidly followed one after the other but are to be flexibly introduced in ways and at points that naturally invite their application.

Later I shall treat at length these typical modes. The following diagrams suggest their relationship:

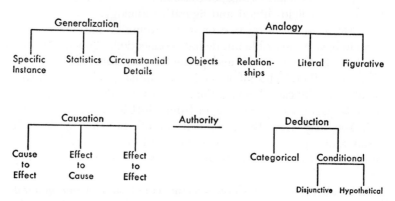

CLASSIFICATION OF ARGUMENTS
(modes of inference)

This further remark should be added: These logical forms are not separate entities except for our convenience in examining each as a phase of the thinking process. Logical argument is a unit. Your systematic illumination of any problem represents a single mental effort. An unfolding of your mental panorama would reveal induction and deduction closely interwoven, with specific instances, authorities, comparisons, causal arguments, and other types of reasoning knit together to produce a single stream of thinking and of effect. The charting of your mental activity would probably reveal a "line of reasoning" without inductive and deductive peaks and valleys. The picture of thinking as inductive or deductive is not dissimilar to the outmoded disunity of the mind as analyzed into compartments of intellect, feeling, and will. The distinctions we retain only as means to describe the different approaches to one process. Debaters have sometimes come into confusion because of their ability to classify a single argument in several ways—as analogy or generalization or causation. Your experience in this direction will merely bring home to you the fact of the totality and unity of the intellectual enterprise.

Whatever the mode of reasoning, we are attempting to penetrate the heart of the order system. Generalization starts with tangible facts. Nevertheless, the reasoner always assumes certain underlying principles (hypotheses, assumptions) into which he hopes his items will fit. Deduction, likewise, operates from initial principles, theories, and hypotheses and progresses toward more specific conclusions. But the deductionist finds that his generalities have been, or should be, traced back to inductive ways of verification. Induction and deduction are thus complementary and, as will be shown below, are phases of a common process. Analogy or causation, too, often listed as separate from deduction or induction, cannot have logical meaning apart from the framework of deduction and induction in which they function.

I shall attempt in later chapters to illustrate in more detail these observations concerning the operation of each of these divisions of inference.

VII. Summary

Reflective or critical thinking is central in controversial speaking and writing. Critical thinking, in contrast to emotional thinking, is controlled, directive, and deliberative. Its pattern is that of problem solving. It analyzes a problem or "felt difficulty"; traces causes and results of the situation in its personal and group impact; sets up hypotheses for solving the problem; tests each solution by applying evidence and inference; weighs the preferred solution in its relations to the other tentative proposals; and if a problem of policy is treated, determines on a practicable course of action.

This logical process, through its word symbols and the typical modes of argument and inference, calls for the evaluation of formal definitions and word meanings; of facts or evidence; of critical examination of divisions and hypotheses; of the various forms of argument. These bases of reasoning comprise the technique of the arguer as a critical thinker. Such creative mental activity comprises one of the fundamentals of higher education. The assumption of this writer and of this book is that the technique of critical thinking, basic both in education and in American life, can be "learned."

The following chapters attempt to indicate in detail these elements of directed thinking in argumentation, discussion, and debate.

EXERCISES AND PROBLEMS

1. Explain what "reflective thinking" is. Comment on the assumptions of argumentation as listed in Section I of this chapter.

2. Distinguish emotionalized thinking from reflective thinking.

3. Outline the "pattern of thinking" as suggested by John Dewey (Section III of this chapter).

4. List the details of the "reflective process" (Section IV of this chapter).

5. What is inference (Section V of this chapter)?

6. Discuss the relation of inference to an "order system."

7. Classify arguments (Section VI of this chapter).

8. Classroom discussion: What does reflective thinking involve? How can we improve in such process?

9. Criticize a speaker's reflective thinking as shown in his treatment of facts, inferences, language, or organization in a recent speech. (Consult any standard collection of recent speeches.)

CHAPTER 5

Definition

I. Definition and Analysis in Argumentation, Discussion, and Debate

Suppose you were asked to participate in a discussion on the question, *Shall the nations immediately enter a federal world government?* Your first impulse, after you had done a bit of desultory reading and consultation of facts, would be to marshal your ideas and perhaps think that you were more or less ready for the panel.

By and by, however, if you were methodical, you would ask yourself, "What, after all, should be talked about? What is this world government about which we are to confer? What is its relation to the United Nations? What would be some of the objections to continuing the present international policies? Can I classify the present difficulties of the nations and the possible bad outcomes?"

This process of making clear the meaning of terms and of listing the various arguments and conflicting points of view and of raising the questions to be answered is that of definition and analysis. Whether you are preparing for discussion, an individual persuasive speech, or a debate, the experience of such preliminary exploration is equally necessary.

Wise discussants clear the air at the outset by arriving at an understanding concerning troublesome terms. They ask sensibly, "What are we talking about?" Debaters try to do so but often march through an entire debate spurning their rival speakers' definitions and insisting on some quite different definitions. Many speakers and writers develop great heat over what they think are fundamental arguments; in reality the confusion and disagreements are often based merely on misunderstanding concerning what each group means by the terms used.

Let us here summarize and apply principles for satisfactory definition and review special methods for clarifying terms.

II. PRINCIPLES OF DEFINITION

Definitions in argument, as in other types of writing and speaking, are governed by logical principles.

A. *State the Class or Group to Which the Object of Definition Belongs.* Economics is "a science that investigates" certain "conditions and laws." Humanism is "a philosophy of general development." Education is "an act or process of developing and cultivating mentally and morally." Once you have pigeonholed your general concept in its field, the rest is comparatively easy. This classification is sometimes hard. Is a democrat one who delegates representation in government? Is a secondary school one that terminates with the twelfth grade? First then, place your subject or term in its proper class.

B. *Regard the Process of Definition as One of Placing the Concept into a Continuous Rather than a Sharply Departmentalized Pattern.* The principle stated above of locating a term with a general field and then of relating the word or words to a particularized section of the area should not commit the definition maker to the Aristotelian technique of putting the thing defined into sharply separated categories.

Thus to define *white, democracy, Republican, insanity, intelligence, capitalism,* we construct a scale representing the general character or property of the thing defined with the opposites of this concept at the extremes of the scale. Thus intelligence might be illustrated: *idiocy, imbecility, mental backwardness, normal intelligence, above-normal intelligence, intellectual brightness, genius.* Somewhere in the scale we attempt to fix the type we are trying to differentiate. The unbroken line from idiocy to genius represents successive but minute changes. The step from normal to above-normal intelligence is imperceptible and is arbitrarily marked out. This principle of describing a term by relating it to a scale as illustrated above and of placing the term at some point on the line is the principle of *continuous variation*.

This method of definition making stresses relative rather than absolute distinctions. Sane moves gradually into the unstable category and so on to a condition more obviously approaching insane. Good finally becomes bad.[1]

Your success in localizing your term in the continuum will depend on the clearness with which you set forth the "property" or character of the broad line, upon the clearness with which you place your concept in the scale, and upon the definiteness with which you describe the term in its relative position.

Your descriptive precision, however, need not compel you to fall into the error of assuming that the word labels you attach to specific divisions within the continuum really imply sharply separated compartments. The low IQ individual is not sharply differentiated from the imbecile. The country residents are not distinct from the small-town population except as census makers arbitrarily mark off "urban" from "rural" groups.

Your demarking of the units, moreover, need not require you to deny the reality of differences between terms even though the continuous variation seems to assume that no differences exist. Certainly a moron is mentally different from a normal person. The man who placed one straw at a time on the camel's back assumed that by such process he could place an indefinite number of straws on the animal. When finally the beast collapsed, he wrongly assumed that the one final straw was the sole cause of "breaking the camel's back." In argument or discussion your definitions are to stem from assumptions that the area of common properties is continuous and yet is an area in which details differ recognizably from each other. For you, however, to press to the limit either the principle of continuous extension or that of differentiation is to miss the point in practical definition.

 C. *Translate the Word or Words under Examination into More Familiar and Concrete Language.* One debater explained "alliance with Russia" in the proposition, *Resolved, That it would be for the best interests of the United States to form a permanent military and economic alliance with Russia in the postwar era:* "By an alliance we mean a definite written agreement between

---

[1] See Robert H. Thouless, *How to Think Straight,* pp. 119*ff.*, Simon and Schuster, Inc., 1941.

these two countries, similar in nature to the twenty-year alliance now in operation between Great Britain and Russia. This alliance in effect proposes that these two countries cooperate and consult in all major economic and military projects for their mutual defense and for the furtherance of world peace."[2] Such concreteness removed a number of doubts as to what proposal was advocated in the debate.

D. *Define Your Terms in Relation to the Context.* In the example just given the debater did not define "alliance" and "Russia" in isolated concepts. "Monroe" and "doctrine" are explained properly as a single term. Occasionally, you may define *alliance* in its political, scientific, and legal details. Also you may interpret Russia as that geographical-political unity more accurately labeled as those "territories of Europe and Asia comprised within the Union of Soviet Socialist Republics." You may even break down this statement into a detailed classification of the "provinces, the autonomous areas, and the autonomous republics." Ultimately, if your proposition is as stated above, you will link the words together for efficient interpretation of "alliance with Russia."

E. *Regard All Definitions as Selective.* No one explanation, let us say, is the "correct one." All depends upon the purpose of the speaker or writer and upon the demands made by the audience. Certainly, the word or words should always be retained in their real character or genus. But the differentiating details will vary according to the point of view of the definer. Communism, for example, may be defined from the point of view of the immediate purpose of the political theorist, the sociologist, the historian, the economist, the Republican, or the Democrat. To affirm that only one of these purposes in framing the definition is permissible is illogical. The only limitation on purpose is that it does not ignore the essential genus of the thing defined and that it satisfies those who are to accept it.

F. *Make Your Definition Sufficiently Complete to Satisfy Those for Whom the Explanation Is Intended.* The aim of the process is to clarify and inform. If the recipients of the process are still incredulous or mystified by your exegesis of the term, then you are to proceed further in your elucidation of the meaning.

[2] *University Debaters' Annual* (1942–43), p. 332, The H. W. Wilson Company.

Such demands for clarity of definition are especially illustrated in discussion. Prolonged discussion may revolve completely around the meaning of a question as tentatively framed. The time spent in such common inquiry on "What is meant by government by the people?" is not a mere dialectic exercise. Rather it is an honest effort to find a common interpretation.

G. Define to Clarify Rather than to Confuse. A University of Chicago Round Table discussed for thirty minutes, "What is equality?" The result was highly satisfactory clarification to listeners. Sometimes in the hands of sharp debaters, definitions are used for confusion or technical advantage. The opponents may be baffled and perhaps "defeated." Such tactics are those of a shyster lawyer. Discussants and debaters have a special obligation to interpret fairly and obviously the propositions.

H. Avoid Bias in Definition Making. Explanation obviously loses its character when it becomes propaganda. Note in the following definition of communism the slanting of words and the emotionalism:

Mr. McDonough: Mr. Speaker, I have introduced House Resolution 99 for the purpose of defining communism. In my opinion it is time that communism is defined so that there will be no question about its insidious influences and the effect it is having on the people of the United States.

I have introduced this resolution for the purpose of establishing a clear definition of communism that can be easily understood. . . .

It should be defined so that all will be aware of its dangers to our way of life in the United States.

I trust that the Members of the House will read this resolution, and urge its passage in the near future.

The resolution reads as follows:

Whereas communism as a political policy, or as a way of life, is inimical to the people of the United States; and

Whereas communism advocates deceit, conspiracy, confusion, subversion, revolution, and the subordination of man to the state; and, because of its practice of deceit and confusion, its real purpose and intentions are clouded and misunderstood to the extent that many persons in the United States have been influenced to believe in and sympathize with communism; and

Whereas there is a pressing need for a clear and easily understandable definition of communism in order to protect the people of the United States from its insidious influence: Now, therefore, be it

Resolved, That communism be defined and declared to be not a political policy, but an international conspiracy and an anti-Christian ideology which advocates and practices deceit, confusion, subversion, revolution, and the subordination of man to the state, and which has for its purpose and intention the overthrow of any democratic form of government by force and violence, if necessary; and be it further

Resolved, That any person, either citizen or alien, adhering to or expounding the purposes and intentions of communism, should be exposed and revealed as an enemy of the United States and dealt with accordingly.[3]

III. Specific Means of Definition

Clear and effective definitions that will withstand careful examination often result from more than reference to the dictionary. Rather they represent wide reading on the subject, technical weighing of the terms, and a good deal of counseling with others.

Specific methods that may well be used to support explanations include (1) authority, (2) history, (3) function or purpose, (4) operation, (5) comparison and contrast, (6) enumeration of details or characteristics, (7) common usage and practice, (8) any combination of these methods.

A. Define by Authority. One excellent method of definition is by authority. Debaters and discussants rely much more on this method than upon the dictionary. The citation of a recognized authority in the use of the term will both make clear the real meaning and will add impressiveness to that meaning for the reader or hearer.

The following section of the introduction to a discussion of the proposition *Resolved, That a permanent policy of price control by the Federal government should be adopted* illustrates the method:

Before outlining our case to you, my colleague and I feel that there is one term in the proposition which requires clarification. That term is "price control." We are adopting the definition of Jules Backman, Instructor of Economics at New York University. Dr. Backman defines price control as "actions which are *deliberately* undertaken for the purpose of affecting, limiting the movements of, or setting . . . prices." In other words we are discussing the advisability of em-

[3] *Congressional Record* (daily edition), Vol. 93, pp. 1051–1052, Feb. 13, 1947.

powering the Federal Government permanently to control the general price level for the purpose of stabilizing our national economy.[4]

B. Define by History. A history of the term is also a common device for definition. The discussion of *Shall we abandon the policy of Pan Americanism?* would inevitably call for a description of Pan Americanism as that policy has evolved. Every controversial subject has its history; that history will in any event be reviewable for evidence throughout the debate or discussion. Highly appropriate and effective is it to use significant features of that history to throw light on the meaning of the institutions under discussion. This history, it should be added, extends to the recent hour. What is America's policy in the Orient? Partly, perhaps, what this nation seems to be doing according to the latest radio information from the East. What is the Monroe Doctrine? That policy which the present administration, according to the latest information, applies in handling Latin-American foreign relations.

C. Define by Function or Purpose. Often you may expound a concept by outlining its purpose or function.

In a Town Meeting debate on "Is World Disarmament Possible Now?" Norman Thomas defined disarmament by outlining five functions:

What do we mean when we say disarmament? Five things:

1. The establishment of an international atomic development authority and other provisions of the Baruch Plan for turning atomic energy only into uses of peace.

2. The universal abolition of peacetime military training.

3. The demilitarization of military and naval bases and the narrow waterways which are the channels of world commerce.

4. Armaments and armed forces, on land, sea, and air must be reduced to a level necessary to preserve internal order.

5. Adequate instrumentalities, freed from the power of any one nation to veto effective action, must be set up to supervise disarmament and positively to guarantee security.[5]

D. Define by Operational Description. Often the most sensible way to expound your term is to say, "This is how it works."

[4] *University Debaters' Annual* (1943–44), p. 235, The H. W. Wilson Company.

[5] *Bulletin of America's Town Meeting of the Air,* Dec. 19, 1946, p. 5, Town Hall, Inc.

The technique is that usually employed in the description of machines or processes. What is atomic energy? A terse but technical explanation would be sufficient for a physicist. The layman would be immensely helped, however, if you were to expound by diagram and otherwise the actual stages in the transformation of uranium into atomic material. In experimental studies the researchers often content themselves by resorting to such method. What are *Federal compulsory economic planning, rent control, cabinet government, censorship of the radio, government ownership of coal mines?* To tell what takes place when the organization or institution is at work is a concrete way of accomplishing definitional results.

In a Town Hall debate on "Should we have Labor-Management Courts to settle labor disputes?" Senator Homer Ferguson, of Michigan, defined Labor-Management Courts by the operational method: "Here, briefly, is how Labor-Management Courts would work. There would be district courts, circuit courts of appeal, and finally, yes, a supreme court of labor." The Senator then explained the method of appointment of the judges, their salaries, the number of judges for each district, the function of lay judges, the relation of the program to collective bargaining, the method initiating the court trials, and the function of mediation and arbitration.[6]

E. Define by Comparison and Contrast. Again the matching of the term under discussion with its contrasted or related institutions will frequently illuminate the concept by such comparison. Capitalism may be compared and contrasted with socialism. Fascism and communism may be compared to establish clearly the unique elements of either one. Cabinet government may be contrasted with Congressional government with respect to the relationship of each to the executive, legislative, and judicial branches. The Republican party may be defined by contrasting it with the Democratic party.

F. Define by Details. The method of classification or enumeration or recital of details is often substituted for more academic explication. The enumerative method has the advantage of concreteness. It is likely to bore readers or listeners unless interestingly handled.

G. Define by Common Usage. In dealing with this entire prob-

[6] *Ibid.,* Jan. 9, 1947, pp. 6–7.

lem of definition in argumentation, the arguer or discussant will not lose sight of his obligation to simplify and even to popularize. Often he should abandon the technical atmosphere surrounding his effort to define and should substitute his own personal interpretation of the language. Town Hall radio programs are so prepared and presented that practically all occasion for wrangling over disputed terms is negligible. The school and college debaters and discussants will do well to adopt more frequently this same unacademic usage.

H. Define by a Combination of Methods. Many a definition, especially if the process is a long one constituting an entire discussion, will be developed by a combination of methods. *Authority* will be supplemented by *function*, and perhaps by a detailed exposition of the *operation*. *Contrast* and *comparison* will frequently complement these other devices. In some examples cited above a combination of these specific techniques was utilized.

IV. CONCLUSION

Explanation of terms, to conclude this chapter, is basic to all good argument as well as to all expert analysis of a problem. The semantic pitfalls are at best numerous. Perhaps half of the disputations in debate and misunderstandings in discussion would be avoided if the speakers or writers cleared up at the outset the language difficulties and continued to seek such clarification throughout the program. You are urged to make clear your meanings at every turn.

EXERCISES AND PROBLEMS

1. Discuss each of the following principles of definition: (*a*) State the class, or group, to which the object of definition belongs. (*b*) Place the concept to be defined in a continuous pattern; observe the principle of continuous variation. (*c*) Translate the word or words into more familiar and concrete language. (*d*) Define your term in relation to the context. (*e*) Regard all definitions as selective; observe the principle of abstracting the significant elements. (*f*) Make the definition sufficiently complete to be acceptable to those for whom the definition is intended. (*g*) Make the explanation or definition in terms of the contemporary meaning; date your terms. (*h*) Free your explanation or definition from bias.

2. Define a term by the method of authority.

3. Define by the method of citing the history of the terms.

4. Define a term in the light of its purpose.

5. Illustrate the method of operational definition.

6. Illustrate definition by the method of contrast or comparison.

7. Illustrate definition by a combination of two or three of the methods suggested in this chapter.

8. Define the terms in the proposition, *Resolved, That the United Nations charter should be amended to convert that organization into a federal world government.*

9. Define the terms in the current national college or high-school question.

10. Define the terms in one of the propositions you framed for the exercise assigned for Chap. 4.

11. (*For the instructor.*) Arrange a speaking exercise in definitions as follows: the first speaker states a proposition and defines terms (two minutes); the second speaker criticizes the definitions of the first speaker (two minutes); the first speaker gives a rejoinder (one minute) in which he defends his interpretation.

12. Be prepared (*a*) to state a proposition, (*b*) to define a term or terms in the proposition as you heard it, (*c*) to discuss and improve the definition or definitions offered by another. Each speech will be limited to two minutes.

13. Explain the terms in the following proposition, proposed by the Oxford University debaters in their American tour of 1949: *Public ownership of basic industries and services is for the best interests of a democracy.*

CHAPTER 6

Analysis and Issues

I. The Aim of Analysis of the Subject

Argumentative speaking and writing are at bottom the discovery and selection of the essential materials to be applied in the conviction-persuasion process, and in the process of problem-and-solution in discussion. Such discovery and selection is primarily a process of analysis or division of the subject.

Your starting point in such analysis is to reduce your nebulous thinking and information on the problem to a clear-cut proposition or question. At first hazy, these controversial facts and opinions later fall into recognizable relationship and order.

Your second step in this inventive approach is to light upon the essential questions and subquestions about which the general problem revolves. Your success will depend on the extent to which you frame searching inquiries that go to the bottom of the problem.

Your third step is one of selection for actual speechmaking, debating, or discussion. Assuming that your questions are comprehensive and detailed, you have probably constructed many more queries than can be answered in your limited time before an audience (or limited space for an article), at a conference, or in a discussion group. Moreover, some of these questions are comparatively trivial; others, though important, are not of primary consequence to your immediate audience. You select, then, those of major concern to these auditors.

61

Your fourth step is to frame these questions in proper language and to arrange them in proper sequence for a round-table or other discussion. Or if you have in mind a written or spoken argument or out-and-out debate, you will form tentative answers to these inquiries. These several declarative sentences or propositions are the *partition propositions,* or *points* or *contentions* to be established.

II. ANALYSIS AND ISSUES

A. What Are Issues? Every controversial subject expresses a division of opinion. If opinion is unanimous concerning any proposition, then controversy ends and exposition succeeds. In any deliberative gathering—legislature, standing committee, informal discussion group, or student club—the procedure is to ask, (1) What is the problem, if any, before this group? And then, (2) What are the differing opinions regarding it?

By a show of hands, attitude, or other ballots, by discussion and debate, those differing points of view are revealed. These differences may have wide range—almost as numerous as the number present. Not two sides, affirmative and negative, but seven, eight, or more may emerge.

The chairman of a university student council, for example, may call a special meeting to deal with the problem of whether a permanent senior-class president should be designated. Informal exchange of opinion by the twelve members may quickly reveal these and similar differences: (1) some want the president appointed by the council; (2) some want him elected; (3) one does not see the need for any permanent senior president; (4) if he is elected, some want the method supervised by close police methods; (5) others regard such policing as impracticable; (6) some want one central voting booth; (7) some want several; (8) some want only those to vote who at the beginning of the semester have to their credit eighty semester hours toward graduation; (9) some think seventy hours would be sufficient.

The formulation of these and kindred attitudes leads to the issues (*i.e.,* questions that bring out these varying points of view). Some issues suggested in this case might be: (1) Shall a permanent senior class president be elected or appointed? (2) If appointed, shall he be so by this council? (3) If he is elected, shall a special election be held within the next month? (4) If such election is held, shall all vote who have not received their degree but who have at the beginning of the semester accumulated at least eighty semester-hour credits?

Issues are the questions that describe the differing opinions concerning any controversial subject. They are the fundamental questions, the answers to which determine the truth or falsity, the acceptability or unacceptability, of a given proposition, assertion, or tentative conclusion.

B. *What Are Main and Minor Issues?* Some of these questions are relatively crucial. These are the main or chief issues. Others, logically falling under these general captions, may be minor or trivial. The student of discussion and argument aims to find these main questions and to discriminate between them and the lesser ones.

C. *Importance of Discovering and Stating the Issues.* Only by bringing to light these all-important questions, or issues, can you have a satisfactory discussion. To talk or write at length without reference to them is to confuse the hearer or the reader, to present an argument lacking in unity, coherence, or force, and to fail in securing the proper response from the audience. The very clearness resulting from keeping the great questions in the foreground is a long step toward the successful end.

III. How Are Issues Discovered?

A. *Read, Think, Discuss as Means of Discovering Issues.* I have already indicated that issues (questions) are discovered by formal or informal conference by a group, and by their oral or written description of their individual opinions regarding any proposition (resolution, proposal, or assertion) to be passed upon.

If you draw up a tentative discussion outline for a round table and if you do so before you can confer with your group, you will have to make the best guess you can as to what are the issues as the group may see them. If you are preparing for a debate against speakers from another college, you and your colleagues will need to do the same thing—make the best guess you can concerning what will be the chief controversial points actually debated. If you are to write a controversial article for your college magazine or for some journal of opinion, the same obligation of determining the chief questions will fall to you.

This "guessing," however, is hardly mere chance selection. You and your associates will think, read extensively, interview informed specialists on the subject, and otherwise try to collect and list the opinions and arguments most relevant to the problem.

B. *Set Up the General Problem as an Over-all Impartial Question.* Often the problem comes to you as a clear-cut proposition for debate. Then convert it into a question. Often it faces you as a question for discussion already formulated. In either case you have before you as the starting point the general interrogation. Your task is to discover the main and subordinate questions to be answered. Your method of such discovery is to ask all sorts of questions that might be raised by a hypothetical audience, nevertheless one composed of highly interested and especially well-informed participants.

C. *Ask Questions Related to the Explanation of Terms Involved in the Question as Framed.* Suppose the query is, "Shall the United States adopt a program of planned economy?" Before you get far in such controversy, you discover that a wide difference arises concerning *planned economy.* Is it the same as *economic planning?* Does it involve government control of the chief means of production, distribution, and consumption? In basic industries only? Under a supreme economic council at Washington, D.C., with mandatory powers? Does it involve government ownership and operation of basic industries and services (socialism)?

Legitimate discussion and debate arise out of these differences.

When a British Universities team debated this problem in the United States in 1948, such issues of definition loomed up.

Successful discussants usually begin by asking, "Are we agreed on the meaning of the representative terms in the problem?"

D. *Ask Questions Related to the Goals Assumed or Set Forth by the Debaters or Discussants.* Since those engaged in any controversy have in mind certain desirable goals, outcomes, or interests that are to be kept clearly before the group, it is important to ask what these objectives are.

In the example above of economic planning, the inquiries centered about such questions as, Do the people of the United States aim at a program calling for maximum production? Full employment? The protection of political liberties? The retention of private enterprise? The retention of our present Federal system of government?

Often these questions are awkward to answer. Often, too, they are awkward to reduce to question form. But the intelligent analyst of a discussion or debate problem will attempt to face and frame them. For many speakers and writers on the subject, whether they realize it or not, are either assuming or challenging these basic propositions that may not at first thought relate to the immediate arguments at stake.

E. *Ask Questions Related to a Problem of Policy.* Here you should revert to the discussion in Chap. 2 in which questions of policy are marked off from questions of fact. For policy-determining issues you are to consider both the *problem* and its *solution,* the latter phase to be regarded as a *program of action.*

Subjects are usually divided or analyzed from the angle of (1) chronology, as in scientific exposition and in narration; (2) classification, as in scientific exposition; (3) topography, as in scientific and artistic description, in which the general scene is set forth with the details then added, or in which the scene is unfolded from the near to the remote; (4) definition, in which the general qualities or characteristics of the object are stated with the differentia in turn expounded, as in the typical speech or essay of definition; and (5) logical partition, as in the typical argument and sometimes in fiction in which a solution is given with the preceding facts then unfolded.

The *logical* method of division is that of stating the *cause* and the *results* of a proposal. The method is illustrated by the (1) problem and (2) solution patterns of the typical discussion and by the (1) need, (2) practicability, and (3) desirability divisions of the conventional debate.

If your question is one of policy, you will inquire, What is the cause of the proposal? and What is the effect of the proposal? You raise these queries because you think more or less as do the rest of the population. The reaction of the audience to a proposition is somewhat of this sort; vaguely or definitely they ask, Why? Your systematic formula of issues as applied to a proposition of policy is somewhat as follows:

I. What are the causes of the proposal?
   A. What principles or goals constitute desirable objectives?
   B. What defects, if any, in the present plan or institution are discoverable? Has the present policy or institution outlived its usefulness?[1]

---

[1] Note that all arguments involve a comparison. Two or more institutions or situations that now exist are under comparison; or you may compare and contrast an existing institution with some ideal one. When you contend that

1. Are there objectionable social characteristics or features? What of population, poverty, crime, race conflict, immigration, home, church, children, women, civilization, and other typical social situations or problems?
2. Are there objectionable economic characteristics or features? What of production, marketing, distribution in detail, supply, price, competition, monopoly, money, rent, interest, wages, profit, taxation, labor, insurance, or similar problems?
3. Are there objectionable financial features? What of investments, cycles, foreign exchange, deposits, loans, credit?
4. What objectionable political or governmental characteristics or features are noted? What of Congressional, governmental, and parliamentary defects? Are there executive, legislative, municipal, state, and national weaknesses?[2]
5. What objectionable weaknesses from an international angle are noted?
6. What of the significant educational features? Are they objectionable? Are the methods of school finance defective? Are the elementary, secondary, and higher schools open to criticism in specific matters? Is the college open to criticism? Are its curriculum, intellectual fields, athletics and recreation, organization, government, and community life faulty?
7. Are any aspects detrimental to health?
8. Are there literary features to be criticized? What are the weaknesses of drama, fiction, poetry? What of plot, dialogue, themes, character? What of emotion, intellectual pattern, form, imagination?
9. Are the legal features open to criticism? What of the judge, jury, criminal?
10. Are there religious and moral criticisms? What of God, man, sin, religious books, immortality, the Church?

---

the American system of government is "bad," you mean that it is "worse" than the British, or French, or some utopian system. The point is that "bad" must have some concrete significance with reference to a specific standard.

[2] These topics are merely illustrative of the range of questions. Other subjects, such as international relations, education, health, literature, law, ethics, religion, psychology, science, each call for specific inquiry. *Cf.* the *Position* (*Constitutio*), *Status,* and *Topoi,* of Aristotle's *Rhetoric and Topics;* and of Cicero's *De inventione,* 1.8.10–16; 2.4–39.

11. What are the psychological weaknesses of the institution under criticism?

12. What scientific features are to be criticized, such as those that relate, for example, to geology?

13. What administrative features are to be included? What of cost, operation, personnel?[3]

C. Are the results of the present condition or situation, if unchecked, likely to be permanently objectionable?

D. Are these alleged defects inherent in the present system?

E. Are proposals other than the solution by the proposition inadequate for dealing with the situation or insufficient to correct the alleged evils?

    1. Is the *status quo* unsatisfactory? (The affirmative has already answered yes. The negative may take any position on this issue.)

    2. Is the alternative proposal, or program A, unsatisfactory? (The affirmative will answer yes with adequate reasons.)

    3. Is proposal B unsatisfactory?

    4. Is proposal C unsatisfactory?

    5. Are proposals A, B, C, or any combination of these unsatisfactory? (Note that by the method of exhausting possibilities the affirmative leads to its own proposal; note further that the questions under I are all designed to bring out the need or lack of need for this proposal.)

II. Are the effects, or results, of the proposal adequate to meet the alleged needs? Will the financial, social, religious, governmental, or other results on the whole be satisfactory? (Note that one or two divisions listed above will demonstrate the chief features of your solution. Note that the affirmative analysis at this point will follow closely the elements of analysis stressed under I.)

III. Will the proposal be practicable?

A. Will the administrative machinery function efficiently?

B. Will the details of the program for operating the proposal be workable?

C. Will the cost be prohibitive?

D. Will the program have popular approval or cooperation?

---

[3] Note that the list above by no means exhausts the general fields of knowledge, and that within each field the classifications are merely suggestive, that items overlap, and that numerous classifications and methods of analysis are to be used. The items above are merely suggestive of the detailed types of inquiry that may be applied to bring out possible issues peculiar to a specific problem.

E. Does precedent indicate the success of the proposed program?[4]

Sometimes other main issues are added:

IV. Is the proposal morally or legally justified?
V. Is the proposal the best solution?   (The issue of legality or moral justification is treated under II, and the problem of "best solution" is analyzed under I.)

Let us apply these stock issues to the proposition *Resolved, That the several states should enact legislation providing a system of complete medical service available to all citizens at public expense.*

I. Are there causes sufficient to justify the proposal as stated above? (Is there need for this proposal?)
   A. Do goals suggest themselves in view of the problem of free medical service?
      1. Is health one of the first concerns of the nation?
      2. Are *all* the people entitled to a high quality of medical service?
      3. Are the people entitled to this service at minimum cost?
      4. Should they be provided with an adequate program of preventive medicine?
      5. Are they entitled to a system in which practitioners are competent and are satisfactorily rewarded?
   B. Do alleged defects exist in the system of private medical care? Are there significant features of the present system which are on the whole detrimental?
      1. Are health conditions in the United States below a reasonable minimum standard?
      2. Can the people in general afford to buy adequate medical and dental care?   Is too much spent for practitioners, patent medicines, and hospitals?
      3. Do the people need a much larger volume of scientific medical service than they now have?
      4. Do the modern public-health services need to be extended to a far greater percentage of the people, including those in rural regions and small towns?

[4] You will note that the queries of II and III attempt to treat the matter of results from both the theoretical and the practical angle.   Unless the issue of practicability is emphasized under a separate category, arguers and discussants sometimes limit their inquiry to the speculative features of their proposition.

5. Is there need for a geographical distribution of doctors and agencies which will more adequately meet the medical requirements of the people than the present distribution?

6. In the rural and semirural areas, are current expenditures for medical care sufficient to ensure adequate medical service and to provide satisfactory remuneration to the practitioners?

7. Do the practitioners as a whole deserve larger incomes than they now have?

8. Should the quality of medical service be improved?

9. Should effective control be exercised over the number and type of trained practitioners?

10. Can the waste of money for unnecessary medication be reduced?

C. Are the alleged weaknesses inherent in the system of private medicine?

D. Are proposals, other than state medicine, for dealing with the situation sufficient to correct the alleged evils?

   1. Would improvement in environment and in health education correct the alleged evils?

      a. Are private medical programs responsible for the alleged bad health conditions?

      b. Are health defects equally common among those with high incomes and those with low incomes?

      c. Is free medical attention available to those unable to pay for it?

   2. Should medical service be provided through organized groups?

      a. Would the group plan be better than the *status quo* or state medicine in providing improved medical care, diagnosis, and treatment, individual responsibility, high standards?

      b. Would the methods of financing the plan be more detrimental than those of the *status quo* or of state medicine?

         (1) Would the financing through insurance (by insurance companies or industrial medical services) be detrimental?

         (2) Would the alternative method of financing through general taxation be more detrimental than that of financing through the *status quo* or through state medicine?

            (*a*) Should taxes, if offered for the financing, be

Federal, state, or local, or some combination of these?

(b) Would the plan of such financing resolve itself into a complete system of state medicine?

3. Should the service be provided under professional sponsorship so that the indigent are taken care of by the country medical society, with a provision through joint use of professional personnel and private group clinics for insurance for high-cost illness?

4. Should the medical service be provided under consumer sponsorship: (a) workmen's compensation, (b) an employer medical service, (c) a plan of employee groups, or (d) a plan of joint employer and employee action?

5. Should the service be provided under community sponsorship with professional participation? Would a program be on the whole successful which provided nominal rates for hospital services, pay clinics, private practice in hospitals, public-health nursing, expansion of government health services, government provision for hospitalization, tax-supported physicians in rural areas, state aid for local medical services, hospitalized illnesses, university medical services, and health, hospital, and nursing councils?

6. Should the service be provided for by joint sponsorship of professional and consumer groups with periodic-payment plans for group clinics?

7. Should the service be provided for under commercial sponsorship, with installment payments through loan companies, health insurance by insurance companies, and medical-benefit corporations operating for profit?

8. Should the service be provided for through a program which would include organization of medical services, strengthening of public-health services, group payment for medical services, coordination of medical services (including control of drugs and medicine) and state agencies, and through basic educational improvements, such as postgraduate education and dental, nursing, and pharmaceutical education?

II. Would a program providing free medical services to all the citizens without cost be beneficial or harmful?

A. Would the quality of medical service be better than under the *status quo* (or under any alternative program other than state medicine)?

B. Would all the people participate in the medical benefits more

fully than under the *status quo* or under any alternative program?
C. Would general health conditions be improved?
D. Would a more equitable distribution of doctors and agencies result?
E. Would the practitioners in general receive a higher wage than they now have?
F. Would the free medical service improve the program of preventive medicine?
G. Would the free medical service strengthen or weaken the Federal form of American government?
III. Would the proposal be practicable?
A. Would the cost of the program be prohibitive?
B. Would the administration be less efficient than that of private medicine?
C. Would the program have popular cooperation?
D. Does precedent indicate the success of the proposal?
E. Can the program be carried out better by the states than by the Federal government?
F. Would the program require or assume assistance by the Federal government?

F. Ask Questions Related to a Problem of Fact. Although a formula for questions of policy seems workable—for the problems are in the main those of cause-and-effect relationship—a suggested series of queries for problems of fact is much harder to construct.

Such questions usually suggest a division by the classification of materials. For example, the proposition, *Resolved, That a policy of high protective tariff is detrimental to the best interests of the United States* would lead to such inquiries as: (1) Is the high protective tariff injurious to the economic welfare of the American people? (2) Would the policy lead to international economic rivalries and breed war? Each of these questions would break down into definite subqueries.

The issues, as the illustration suggests, are usually the classification of material according to economic, social, political, and similar considerations.

Where the question is primarily not one of social or political judgment but rather one where the facts can be rather accurately discovered (as in the investigations of pure science), the method of analysis and statement of issues is usually one of classifying the types of argument and evidence. The formula of applying types of argument and evidence to such problems may be illustrated by a consideration of the resolution *Resolved, That sending a rocket to the moon is feasible.* (*Is the sending of a rocket to the moon feasible?*) Do argument and evidence from analogy support the theory? Do argument and evidence from causal reasoning support the theory? Do argument and evidence from specific instances (factual details) support the theory? Do argument and evidence from authority support the theory?

IV. How Are Issues to Be Organized and Worded?

Your business, as I have suggested, is to find issues by asking major and minor questions bearing on (*a*) definitions of terms used in the problem, (*b*) goals sought by all involved in the discussion or debate, (*c*) the problem-and-solution phases of a question of policy, (*d*) the problem-and-solution phases of a question of fact. I have indicated that you will use as tentative lines of inquiry these questions growing out of cause-and-effect modes of division, and questions based upon a classificational division (such as economic, social, or political categories).

Applying such a formula will yield you a long list. Your next correlated job is to organize and word these questions. You will reject those that are trivial or irrelevant, perhaps insert others that you previously overlooked, and revise the language of each so that it more definitely reflects the actual situation under examination.

1. In your preliminary analysis, aim to cover the field. Your total list should be comprehensive—even though in actual discussion or debate you do not treat all angles.

2. Avoid overlapping of issues. See that questions are arranged under proper headings. Avoid duplication of questions couched in slightly different language.

3. See that the issues represent a genuine division. How many main divisions will you use? Certainly more than one. Otherwise your "division" means nothing. On the other hand, more than four or five will be unnecessary. A grouping under few rather than many headings can usually be effected.

4. In actual discussion or debate select and order the questions according to the interests of the audience. Audiences make the issues. By *audience* in this case I refer either to one you address face to face (or by radio) or to your readers.

5. *Select the questions according to time or space limitations imposed for actual presentation.* Your problem is—what is most important to discuss during my fifteen-minute radio presentation; or my twenty-minute address to the Kiwanis Club; or my ten-minute main speech and five-minute rebuttal in a debate; or my fifty minutes with my colleagues in a discussion; or my maximum of five hundred words in the college paper? Your inquiry is, What are the most important issues? (This suggestion, I hope, is not inconsistent with the advice above to "cover the field.")

6. *In selecting issues for presentation, get to the bottom of the problem.* In your array of major and minor questions, be sure you have hit upon the one (or ones) that are basic. The superior analyst is he who can bring to light such fundamental inquiries.

7. *For the debate or discussion, arrange issues in the order that meets the tests of logical sequence and of audience needs.* Logic, for example, suggests that you treat in order (a) definitions, (b) the goals, (c) the problem, and (d) the solution or solutions. Sometimes, however, the audience and discussion participants are uninterested in steps (a), (b), and (c). They feel that they are agreed at such points. They wish to proceed at once to (d). Debaters, especially the negative, often face the matter of, What issue shall I develop first?

8. *Frame each issue concretely, clearly, and objectively.* State each without biased or prejudicial or slanted language. Let the question be simple, clear cut, free from vagueness or ambiguity.

V. RELATION OF ISSUES TO PARTITION IN ARGUMENT AND DEBATE

In debate, contentions or the main divisions are the answers to the issues. If you have analyzed carefully, you are bound to bring to light the great questions. You do not indicate your attitude in the argument until you answer these questions by an enumeration of the chief ideas which you intend to present or defend.

If the issues are relevant to the subject, mutually exclusive, and comprehensive, the contentions should also be properly set up. Main issues will suggest main contentions; subordinate issues will suggest subordinate contentions. In actual argument or debate you may select only those which best suit your need. Any complete presentation of the affirmative will include each of these contentions and thus will bring to light all the significant arguments. In preparation, which comes first, the issues or the contentions? In truth, asking questions and framing contentions go on simultaneously. In general, however, issues will evolve before an arguer finally concentrates on the proposition he decides to defend.

VI. Application of Definition and Analysis to Types of Discussion and Debate

The work of definition and analysis, you will need to keep in mind, is largely expository. It appears more directly in the introduction of an argument than elsewhere although definitions and explanatory detail appear throughout the discourse. The principles reviewed in this chapter are largely for the benefit of the speaker or writer himself; many of the features of analysis which he works out for a given question will not appear in the completed argument as finally presented or in the discussion as it actually evolves. Below are illustrated some applications to representative types of discussion and debate.

A. *Definition, Analysis, and Oral Debate.* In formal debate the first speaker for the affirmative should explain the subject and otherwise present an analysis which the negative speakers may endorse or qualify. This first speech usually contains the following items in the introduction:

1. *A brief statement of the immediate cause for discussion.* Most formal discussions originate because public policy of the moment leads to agitation of the proposition and because an event of the day brings the problem sharply before the people.

The introductory statement, "Immediate cause for discussion," should occupy only a brief paragraph and should be largely an attention-getting, interest-arousing device.

2. *A definition of terms.*

3. *A brief history of the case.* Sometimes this step is omitted; sometimes it precedes the definitions; sometimes it is interwoven with the definitions or with the cause for discussion. It goes without saying that the entire discussion will be permeated with whatever historical facts are pertinent. This step, as a phase of the introduction, should mention only important items but should refer

to early facts of the institution under discussion and, above all, should mention the latest turns of the problem. *The history, therefore, should be relevant, selective, comprehensive, and up to date.* To stop short of the most recent event is fatal. Every debater of a live problem should glean the daily papers, especially the editions issued just before the debate.

4. *A statement of admitted or waived matter.* Often a debater may need to explain that the teams have agreed to waive certain items that come within the province of the debate; or, for strategic reasons, he may wish to admit certain points or agree with certain arguments to be advanced, or already developed, by the opposing speakers.

5. *A statement of issues and/or a statement of what a speaker will attempt to prove.* A statement of issues gives the audience a clear impression of the field of controversy and is an indispensable feature of every well-organized and effective introduction. This statement of issues (always in the form of impartial questions) should usually be followed by a statement of what the speaker himself will develop.

In oral debate the conventional introduction usually includes (*a*) a brief statement of the cause for discussion and a history of question; (*b*) an explanation of terms; (*c*) a statement of admitted and waived material; (*d*) a statement of issues or of what the speaker intends to prove. The effort of debaters to get away from the highly mechanical methods of analysis has led to an abandonment of almost every feature of the stereotyped introduction. Instead, emphasis is put upon the approach to the audience and upon the persuasive elements of the introduction rather than upon the logical features. Any formal step, such as history or definition, is to be used only if it has value in holding attention, and that value must be made apparent.

B. Definition, Analysis, and a Student Forensic, or Written Argument. In a student forensic, a written or spoken debate in which the writer or speaker develops the entire argument for one side, including the introduction or analysis, every possible step of analysis is included. The typical forensic, a formal composition, develops in succession the following features: (1) the occasion for discussion; (2) the history of the case; (3) definition of the terms; (4) contrasted arguments; (5) narrowing of the question through a statement of the excluded, admitted, and waived material; (6) the main issues; (7) a partition of the subject or enumeration of the points to be proved.

C. *The Speech or Article of Definition and Analysis of a Proposition for Debate.* Frequently, questions for debate are analyzed at length to suggest to those who propose to debate or discuss them the possible and legitimate lines of inquiry. This speech of interpretation is, of course, in no sense an argument; but it does serve well for the opening remarks by the leader of a discussion group or for the explanation to guide school or college debaters in their preparation for contests.

D. *Definition and Analysis and the Editorial or Persuasive Article.* The introduction is informal, and the definitional and analytical elements are used at appropriate points. The main issues and partition are seldom mentioned directly but are implied and, if the article is worth while, are clearly adhered to.

E. *Definition and Analysis and the Persuasive Speech.* The general argumentative or persuasive speech, usually colored by elements of vividness, may range all the way from a conventionally organized debate to a loose oration. In any case you will resort to the definitions and imply, if you do not state literally, the issues and partition.

F. *Definition and Analysis in Round-table Discussion.* Particularly is it important for the members of a discussion group to prepare an analysis of the subject, this draft forming the basis of complete agenda. This draft, under the leader, may take the form of a group outline or series of questions.[5] The transcript of any well-conducted discussion will usually reveal an orderly exposition of terms and a statement of issues.

G. *Definition and Analysis in Radio Debate and Discussion.* Either the moderator or the first speaker—if set speeches are used —will open the program with preliminary definition and analysis sufficient to launch the problem.

EXERCISES AND PROBLEMS

1. What is an issue? Illustrate by naming the issues in a proposition concerning a campus problem.

2. Criticize, by applying the principles of division, each of the fol-

[5] For further discussion of such an outline see Chap. 21.

lowing statements of issues. Present your criticism in written form to the instructor.

a. Resolved, That the Federal government should own and operate the coal mines of the United States.

(1) Is there need for some change of policy toward the coal mines?

(2) Is government ownership and operation of these mines in the interest of good government?

(3) Can we find the money necessary for such purchase?

b. Resolved, That the dissolution of the British Empire would be for the best interests of the world.

(1) Does the British Empire represent imperialism?

(2) Does the British Empire represent colonial exploitation?

(3) Does the British Empire represent discrimination against American foreign trade?

c. Resolved, That a Department of Consumers should be established at Washington.

(1) Do present circumstances necessitate the creation of a Department of Consumers?

(2) Would the creation of this department be satisfactory?

(3) Would this department protect the interests of the consumers as such?

3. Give the main and subissues of one of the following questions: (*a*) The gasoline tax in my state should be increased by 2 cents per gallon. (*b*) The United States should establish a National Theater. (*c*) The principle of democracy has on the whole failed in the United States.

4. Give the main and subissues of the following proposition: *Resolved, That the United States should establish a permanent alliance with the nations of western Europe and of Great Britain.* Include in detail impartial questions relating to the alleged need for such alliance, the economic, social, political, military, and other advantages and disadvantages, the justice or injustice to all nations of such a plan, and the many factors of practicability or impracticability of the proposal.

5. Write a complete introduction (500 words) for a debate to be delivered before a school or college audience.

6. Criticize your introduction (and those of the others as these written speeches are read) by considering such questions as (*a*) whether the approach to the audience is interesting and clear, (*b*) whether the terms are clearly explained, (*c*) whether the issues are properly and clearly set forth, and (*d*) whether the introduction is analytical rather than argumentative.

CHAPTER 7

Organization: The Outline
and the Brief

I. ORGANIZATION AND ARGUMENTATION

Structure or plan is implicit in argumentation just as it is in all other written and oral discourse. The creation and assembling of argumentative material leads in practice to shaping these ideas in such form that both the writer or speaker and his audience can well follow them through. Especially important is it for effective audience adaptation that the structure be properly built with relevancy of each item, with sequence arranged to hold the reader's or listener's attention and interest, and with treatment to each section proportional to its significance in the argument as a whole.

In discussion, too, whether round table or more formal panel, the effectiveness of the total program rests heavily on the completeness with which the discussional pattern and outline (granted that such patterns and outlines are to be most flexible) are clearly delineated.

II. ORGANIZATION AND THE OUTLINE

If you have clearly grasped and applied the principles for the proper definition and analysis of your subject and have set up the main issues and partitions, you have mapped out definite lines

78

for the orderly development of your argument. You have set up a working plan. Your next and necessary step is to construct an outline that will be your blueprint for speaking or writing.

Students of public discussion and debate sometimes frown upon an outline. "Why," they sometimes ask, "should I struggle with a complicated mechanism? I have my ideas and on paper have assembled the notes from which I am to talk." It must be admitted that good speeches have sometimes come seemingly from scattered notes. It is questionable, however, whether any worthwhile speaker has proceeded methodically through an argumentative speech without some deliberate apprenticeship in the ordering of material. Those who boast of not having made an outline usually give evidence of that lamentable fact. You will search long to find a first-class school or college debater who has not disciplined himself at length in the process of outlining.

What will detailed planning do? It will enable you to survey your case conveniently, to test the logic of your assertions, to question the order of your issues, to review the character and amount of evidence, and to construct a unified, forcible, and coherent forensic.

III. THE DISCUSSION OUTLINE

In discussion the outline is especially serviceable, both as a guide to the group and as an aid for your individual preparation. The group outline, with its series of questions, takes on the character of an enlarged series of questions or issues arising out of the analysis. The individual discussion outline incorporates a number of the features, with respect to the mechanics of construction, of the argumentative brief. Full treatment of the discussion outline has been reserved for Chap. 21.

IV. THE BRIEF AND THE SPEAKER'S NOTES

If you are to prepare an argument fully, you will draft two outlines; the first, a complete digest of your entire case; the second, a more highly personal and informal arrangement of ideas with the requirements of the special audience in mind. The first type is a brief; the second, a speaker's outline.

The brief is a storehouse of information, including a complete analysis of a given proposition and all the representative argument and evidence on a given side of the resolution. Professor Baker, of Harvard, who developed and taught the brief in his instruction in argument, apparently borrowed the brief from legal practice.

The student's brief, often called a forensic brief, provides the reader with a bird's-eye view of the complete argument and gives to the debater-author a complete chart to guide him in the development of his spoken argument. Contrary to its name, it is usually long and complicated.

Suppose you were to prepare a brief on the question of limiting annual incomes in the United States to fifty thousand dollars. You would work out a complete argument and evidence on the chief issues suggested in the previous chapter. You would doubtless include all the main headings and subheadings, the sources of your material, and even the rebuttal material so as further to strengthen your points. If you set out to argue the case, however, you would select certain sections for your contest debate (with your colleague). You would frame one case for your contest debate (your colleague would present about half of the case), another for a short talk before the Kiwanis Club, another for a radio debate. You would need to consider the time limits and possible prejudices on the part of the audience. From the same brief you can draft several speeches and different outlines.

V. Rules for Constructing the Brief

For convenience in constructing the brief, rules which students of argumentation and debate have found through experience to be most convenient are followed. It is recognized that no one set of rules is absolutely necessary. The experience of students of debate indicates that the rules given below are highly satisfactory. They are classified as (A) general rules for brief making; (B) rules for the introduction; (C) rules for the discussion; and (D) rule for the conclusion.[1]

A. General Rules for Brief Making. 1. Arrange the brief in three parts, marked "Introduction," "Argument," and "Conclusion." The purpose of the introduction is to present a complete analysis of the question (including a statement of the issues) and a partition of the case. The purpose of the conclusion is to summarize the points as proved.

2. Phrase the ideas as complete statements. The purpose of

[1] See Appendix A for Specimen Brief.

this rule is to guarantee clearness and completeness for every idea contained in the brief. The argumentative outline is intended for the reader as well as for the composer of the brief. A complete statement obviously is less likely to cause confusion than a mere term. A term, although it may be clear to the writer, may be meaningless to the reader.

3. *Indicate the relation of ideas by proper symbols and proper indentions.* The following system of symbols is generally used:

I. . . . . , for
  A. . . . . , for
    1. . . . . , for
      a. . . . . , for
        (1) . . . . , for
          (*a*). . . . .

(The logical completion of such a skeleton outline is assumed.)

The symbols and indentions serve to indicate clearly the relative logical rank of ideas.

4. *Under each heading express a single point.* Since the brief aims to give a logical statement of each line of argument that contributes to the proof, it is necessary that double arguments be carefully separated; therefore, headings or subheadings that express more than one point should be avoided.

5. *Make the brief impersonal.* Frequently the brief is confused with the speaker's notes or with a fully developed argument. In such case the outline contains such expressions as "I believe that," "We argue that," and frequent use of the personal vocabulary. The argumentative outline is intended as an impersonal statement of the facts involved and is in no sense framed to include persuasive elements.

6. *Note on the margin or at appropriate points in the body the exact sources of evidence.* Although these exact sources need not always be recounted when the debater is on the platform, they should be at hand for citation.

B. *Rules for the Introduction.* 7. *Let the introduction contain a full analysis of the proposition,* including a statement of the main issues and main arguments to be established. The analysis should include some or all of the following items: (*a*) a statement of the occasion, or cause, for discussion, (*b*) a history of the case, (*c*) an explanation of terms, (*d*) a statement of admitted or waived matter, (e) the contrasted arguments of each side, (f) a statement of the isssues, and (g) the partition. Each step of the analysis should be sufficiently complete to provide an adequate understanding of the discussion.

8. *Exclude all argument from the introduction.* Since the analysis is intended for the purpose of discovering and stating the issue and the partition, it is clear that argumentative material is irrelevant. This rule, however, need not apply to the introduction as presented in actual debate, where the interests of persuasion may lead to the inclusion of highly debatable statements. Nor is this rule violated by that step of analysis which calls for a contrasting of the affirmative and negative arguments. The listing of arguments is, of course, not an attempt to develop, or even to endorse, those controversial points. Note in the following section of the brief of an introduction that prejudiced language (in italics) shows bias:

II. The history of this movement toward a federal world government is as follows:
  A. The United Nations was established at San Francisco in 1945.
  B. This organization has continued but *has almost completely failed in its purposes and methods.*
  C. The agitation for a federal world government began in earnest soon after the *unnecessary* dropping of bombs on Hiroshima and Nagasaki, in August, 1945.
  D. The proposal for federal world government *has been endorsed by practically all* progressive American leaders.

9. *In the introduction use expository briefing.* Expository briefing requires that each heading shall explain or be a division of the heading to which it is subordinate. Argumentative briefing requires that substatements prove the main statement. Contrast the two types.

A. Expository Briefing

III. The plan provides for a system of world government.
  A. It provides for an Executive branch.
  B. It provides for a two-chambered Legislative branch.
  C. It provides for a Court of Justice to interpret the laws of the Congress and to settle all questions of a justiciable character.
  D. It provides for an international police force to enforce the laws of this world government.

B. ARGUMENTATIVE BRIEFING

III. The plan for a federal world government would be practicable, for
   A. The plan provides for an Executive division.
   B. The plan provides for a practicable organization to deal with international problems, for
      1. It provides for an Executive division.
      2. It provides for a two-chambered Legislative branch.
      3. It provides for a Court of Justice to interpret the laws of the Congress and to settle all questions of a justiciable character.
      4. It provides for an international police force to enforce the laws of this world government.

In the first example above, the subtopics attempt to prove nothing; they merely give information. The mood of the author is that of explaining to his audience certain facts later to be discussed. In the second case, the object of each statement is to convince the reader or hearer, *i.e.*, to induce him to accept the proposal. The subtopics aim to provide a series of reasons.

C. Rules for the Discussion. 10. Let the main headings of the discussion correspond to main arguments listed at the end of the introduction. Compare the following, consisting of (*a*) issues; (*b*) points to be proved, or partition; (*c*) main steps in the discussion:

Should the nations of the world adopt the Baruch proposal for the control of atomic energy?

A. ISSUES

IV. The main issues are thus suggested:
   A. Does the development of atomic energy demand international control of such development?
   B. Is the Baruch proposal practicable?
   C. Are alternative proposals more promising in preventing an atomic war and in controlling atomic energy for peacetime uses?

B. PARTITION

V. The affirmative will establish the following arguments:
   A. The development of atomic energy demands international control of such production and usage.
   B. The Baruch plan is practicable.
   C. The Baruch plan will prevent war and will facilitate peacetime applications of atomic energy.

D. This plan is superior in theory and practice to the alternative Russian proposal for control.

C. ARGUMENT PROPER

The nations of the world should adopt the Baruch plan for control of atomic energy, for

I. The development of atomic energy demands international control of such production and usage, for

(Argument and evidence)

II. The Baruch plan is practicable, for

(Argument and evidence)

III. The Baruch plan will prevent war and will facilitate peace-time applications of atomic energy, for

(Argument and evidence)

11. In the discussion use argumentative briefing, in which each subordinate statement proves the more general statement. A frequent fault in the proof is the presence of expository briefing, with the result that subtopics stand in no logical subordination to the topics under which they are placed. Notice in the following example of classroom briefs that a number of the subtopics fail to follow as logical reasons for the topics which precede:

I. There is need for some action concerning medical conditions in the United States, for

A. Investigation of medical conditions in the United States reveals maldistribution and lack of planning, for

1. There are 100,000 people who need medical attention.

2. Fifty million people have decayed teeth; yet

a. There are 8,000 clinics and out-patient departments of hospitals.

II. Maldistribution is further apparent, for

A. There are many state, county, and municipal health departments.

B. The results of maldistribution are bad, for

1. We have too many cases of tuberculosis.

Note that under IA, above, "50 million people have decayed teeth" does not prove "maldistribution." Note that IIA, should go to establish IA. "Maldistribution is further apparent" is unnecessary, for the statement is merely a repetition of IA.

12. Show the relation between the various statements by the word "for."

13. State clearly the argument to be refuted. This rule assumes that argument is both constructive and destructive; that the purpose of the brief is to establish proof partly by removing inhibitions.

The beginner in briefing often states his refutation in an obscure or negative form that leaves the reader in doubt as to whether that part of the brief is intended as refutation. The supreme advantage of the rule is that it requires a clear and accurate statement of the opposing argument. Note the weakness of the following brief in the handling of refutatory material:

II. The implementation of the Baruch plan for the control of atomic energy would work satisfactorily, for
    A. It is not true that Russia or other powers would continue to make bombs, for
        1. The military and inspection forces would be sufficiently strong and alert to prevent such illegal production.

Note the rewording to indicate the argument to be refuted:

II. The implementation of the Baruch plan for the control of atomic energy would work satisfactorily, for
    A. The argument that Russia or other powers would continue to make bombs is fallacious, for
        1. The military and inspection forces would be sufficiently strong and alert to prevent such illegal production.

14. Admitted matter in the discussion should be placed in a subordinate clause immediately preceding the argument to be established. The form here would be as follows:

I. Although America has great national wealth and high standards of living, yet the wealth is not evenly distributed, for
    A. Chronic employment is the child of the profit system, for
        1. In 1940, *Fortune* reported that 22 per cent of the American workers were outside the "going" economic order.

15. In the brief include the concrete evidence used in actual debate. The brief, as suggested earlier, is more than a chain of reasoning. It should include practically all the material to be used.

D. Rule for the Conclusion. 16. In the conclusion summarize the main arguments and follow with an impersonal affirmation or denial of the original proposition.

VI. The Skeleton Brief

The following skeleton outline will be of advantage in working out a brief:

Resolved, That .... (State the proposition.) ....

Introduction

I. The cause for discussion is as follows:
   A. ....
   B. ....
   C. ....

II. The history of the case is as follows:
   A. ....
   B. ....
   C. ....
   D. ....

III. The terms are thus explained:
   A. ....
   B. ....
   C. ....

IV. The conflicting arguments are as follows:
   A. The affirmative argue:
      1. ....
      2. ....
      3. ....
   B. The negative argue:
      1. ....
      2. ....
      3. ....

V. From this discussion is waived the question of ....

VI. It is admitted that ....

VII. The main issues are thus suggested:
   A. ....?
   B. ....?
   C. ....?
   D. ....?

VIII. The affirmative (or negative) will establish the following arguments:
   A. ....
   B. ....
   C. ....
   D. ....

Discussion Proper

The .... (Repeat proposition as you intend to prove it.) .... , for
I. .... , for
  A. .... , for
    1. .... , for
      a. .... , for
        (1) .... , for
          (*a*) ....
  II. (Here develop second main point.)
  III. (Here develop third main point.)
IV. .... , for
  A. The argument that .... is fallacious, for
    1. .... , for
      a. ....
  B. .... , for
    1. .... , for
      a. ....
  C. Although .... , yet .... , for
    1. .... , for
      a. .... , for
        (1) ....
    2. .... , for
      a. .... , for
        (1) ....

Conclusion

  I. Since .... ;
  II. Since .... ;
  III. Since .... ;
  IV. Since .... ;
Therefore, ... (Repeat proposition as you have proved it.) ......

VII. Briefing the Arguments of Others

In briefing articles, you may use either of two methods of procedure. You may compose an original brief on the basis of the material before you, or you may reproduce literally the arguments of the articles. In the first case, you select, omit, rearrange, and amplify. In the second case, you adhere closely to the methods, content, and sequence of the work under consideration. The first method is of course preferable if you wish to convince the reader of the truth or falsity of your proposition. The second method gives practice in analyzing and interpreting the argument of another; the reconstructed brief presumably reflects the mental attitude and mental process of the author in the construction of the argument.

VIII. Conclusion

To conclude, you need not be a slave to your rigid document. It should be for you a means to a practical end. Its construction, we hope, gives the facts, sharpens your mental processes, and creates a mental alertness which means a continuation of creative thinking. If you write your argument, you may and should push aside this elaborate outline. So may you shift the order of development, omit valueless statements, and include other persuasive material—in short, translate the dry structure into a living composition, vigorous, original, and spontaneous.

If you keep your mind alert both to argument and to original expression, if you follow the best standards of oral composition, and if you keep in mind the requirements of your audience and regard your speech as a process of communication, there is no reason why the brief, with its ten or twenty rules, should not be the basis for a speech effective in every detail.

EXERCISES AND PROBLEMS

1. Criticize the specimen debate brief in Appendix A. In what respects does it validate the rules for briefing as suggested in this chapter?

2. Construct the introduction to a complete brief on the affirmative of the current school or college question for debate as announced by a national speech committee.

3. Construct a complete brief, following the plan illustrated in Section V of this chapter.

4. Convert the following statements into a brief. Include each statement. Use proper indentations, symbols, connectives, and punctuation. Use each statement once only. Copy it exactly as printed below. Submit your project to the instructor and to the class for criticism.

a. The Frazier-Lemke Act decision denied Congress power to suspend farm mortgages for five years.

b. Our economic basis today is national rather than state.

c. Iowa has been unable to control corn-hog production when Illinois has been free to go ahead full blast.

d. The Supreme Court has by recent interpretations of the Constitution made national social and economic legislation difficult or impossible.

e. Edwin Corwin states that "the basis of our prosperity is national."

f. Congressional control of the Supreme Court decisions is necessary.

g. The decision in the Railroad Pension Act of May, 1935, denied Congress power to set up old-age pensions for railroad employees.

h. The Supreme Court has hindered desirable social and economic legislation.

i. The states through legislation have been unable to meet the situation.

j. Present conditions demand social and economic legislation on a national scale.

5. Criticize a printed brief in a current volume of the *University Debater's Annual.*

6. Brief an editorial from a recent newspaper.

7. Brief a representative speech from the current volume of *Representative American Speeches* or from a recent issue of *Vital Speeches of the Day.*

CHAPTER 8

Evidence: Principles and Types

I. Importance of Evidence in Argument, Discussion, and Debate

Argumentation rightly stresses evidence or facts as the basis of the logic. In the everyday world of affairs we make unnumbered inferences without evidence. We accept our own judgment as trustworthy; and in many cases our friends, when confronted with our conclusions, admit them good-naturedly or keep silent. The human mind is so organized, however, that different people fail to make the same inference from a given group of facts because their experiences differ or because their prejudices affect their points of view. Hence arises the necessity for argument.

The elementary principle behind all argumentative thinking and speaking is this: Whenever you make an assertion or advance any proposition which you wish others to accept, couple that idea with evidence sufficiently complete to convince "beyond a reasonable doubt." Because people have their prejudices and individual points of view, it is often necessary to justify to others what to you seems obvious.

President Franklin D. Roosevelt in his war message to Congress on Dec. 8, 1941, submitted the following facts (evidence):

1. Yesterday, Dec. 7, 1941, the United States of America was suddenly and deliberately attacked by the Naval and Air Forces of the Empire of Japan.

2. The attack yesterday on the Hawaiian Islands caused severe damage to American Naval and military forces. Many American lives were lost.

3. American ships were reported torpedoed on the high seas between San Francisco and Honolulu.

4. The Japanese government launched an attack against Malaya.

5. The Japanese forces attacked Hong Kong.

6. The Japanese forces attacked Guam.

7. The Japanese forces attacked the Philippine Islands.

8. The Japanese attacked Wake Island.

9. The Japanese attacked Midway Island.

With this evidence clearly before the American public, the President concluded, " The facts of yesterday speak for themselves. The people of the United States have already formed their opinion, and well understand the implication to the very life and safety of our nation." What was the implication? "There is no blinking at the fact that our people, our territory, and our interests are in grave danger." The President, on the basis of these facts and this inference, ended his message with, "I ask that Congress declare that since the unprovoked and dastardly attack by Japan on December 7, a state of war has existed between the United States and the Japanese Empire."

II. What Is Evidence?

A. What Are Facts? They are the concrete or abstract material out of which we attempt to weave conclusions or from which we try to draw inferences or between which we attempt to establish relationships. Facts are to be distinguished from theories. The latter are merely speculative statements, which by general admission may or may not be true. Facts, on the contrary, represent items which allegedly are to be accepted before further amplification or inference is to be attempted. Facts have to do with the existence of things, the occurrence of events, including their causes and results, the classification of data, and the character of phenomena. Facts are contrasted with general laws or principles, to which they give rise, and which in turn lead to the investigation of other concrete and related material.

To the scientist, for example, facts are laboratory material assembled for experimental purposes. Or they are matters of observation to be checked, verified by independent observers under similar conditions, and so collaborated and used as the basis of dependable conclusions.

B. *The Changing Character of Facts.* Facts or evidence are accepted only because those immediately concerned with them so recognize them. Observation and opinion rather than abstract theory interpret certain situations or items as "facts." I am not here concerned with the philosophical question of the origin of phenomena and of the nature of ultimate "truth." I am observing merely that you and I today accept certain facts which in the next decade or century may be regarded otherwise. Theological, astronomical, and other scientific information of centuries ago proved to be nothing other than superstition. The practical test, then, of evidence is its approval by lay and expert opinion. Both the layman and the expert, however, repeatedly demonstrate limitations in the evaluation of facts or evidence.

C. *Specific and General Facts.* Facts may range from the most concrete and specific items to those of the larger or general category. If we were to cast our alleged facts into a scale with the most concrete particulars at one end and the most abstract descriptions at the other, we should find it difficult to draw a line between the most tangible and familiar details and the more intangible and generalized statements.

III. Relation of Evidence to Argument and Proof

Thus the basis of argument is evidence—concrete illustration, quotations, instances, and figures. The process of advancing from evidence to conclusion is argument. The conclusion is proof. "Proof is the sufficient reason for assenting to a proposition as true."[1]

An illustration of the relationship of these terms is found in the following section of a brief:

I. The Nazi party in Germany, after Hitler became Chancellor in 1933, liquidated the German labor unions and regimented the German working class, for

  A. When Hitler came to power there were three large groups of trade unions, for

    1. The German Trade Union Confederation (ADGB) and the

---

[1] Francis Wharton, *Treatise on the Law of Evidence in Criminal Cases* (11th ed.), Vol. I, p. 5, Lawyers Co-operative Publishing Company, 1932.

General Employees Confederation (AFA) numbered more than 4,500,000 members.
2. The Christian Trade Union had over 1,250,000 members.
B. These groups were in general opposed to war, for
1. These workers of 1933 still remembered the heavy price German labor had paid in the First World War.
C. First the two larger unions were destroyed, for
1. On April 21, 1933, the Nazi party issued an order, under Robert Ley, that called for the destruction of the two larger unions, for
   a. It directed seizure of the properties and arrest.
   b. It ordered arrest of their leaders.
   c. It ordered the Nazi party organs to occupy the labor union properties and arrest of the personalities under question.
2. On May 2, 1933, the orders were carried out.
   a. All labor funds were seized.
   b. Ley was appointed leader of the German Labor Front.
   c. On May 19, 1933, "trustees" of labor, appointed by Hitler, were established to regulate the conditions of all labor contracts as a substitute for collective bargaining.
D. On June 24, 1933, the remaining Christian Trade Unions were similarly seized, pursuant to an order of the Nazi party signed by Ley, and destroyed.
E. In November, 1934, a decree provided that the owners of enterprises should be the fuehrers and the workers should be the followers (bait to the industrialists to their later ruin).
F. On June 26, 1935, a compulsory labor decree was issued providing that all young men and women between the ages of 18 and 25 should be conscripted for labor.[2]

In this brief the proof consists in the conclusion that the Nazi party in Germany after Hitler became Chancellor in 1933 destroyed the labor unions and regimented the German working class. The detailed enumeration of instances attending this liquidation constitutes the evidence. The source of the testimony here is Robert H. Jackson. The basis of every worth-while argument must be these instances, authorities, statistics, hypothetical examples, or other factual details that furnish the foundation for the superstructure of argument or inference.

[2] Briefed from Robert H. Jackson's "International Military Tribunal: Opening Address," to try Axis war criminals, Nov. 20, 1945, Nuremberg, Germany.

IV. Classification of Evidence

These facts, figures, instances, authorities, analogies, and other details that make up evidence are conveniently classified according to their (1) form, (2) source, and (3) relationship to the conclusion or proof. This classification, common in law, may also help the debater.[3]

A. Form of Evidence. What form may these materials take? They may be (1) objects or things themselves—material evidence; (2) verbal evidence, the statements concerning objects; (3) positive evidence, the facts that go to prove the existence of the alleged facts; and (4) negative evidence, that which draws conclusions from the absence of facts. Let us illustrate each.

Material, or real, evidence—that of the object itself—is illustrated by the exhibition to the jury of a bloodstained knife, the injured limb, the viewing of the premises, the production of a document. No logical process is presumably employed. All that is needed is apprehension of the thing as alleged. Debaters and other arguers in extralegal situations sometimes introduce maps and other aids to substantiate their case. Lecturers often use audio-visual aids (motion or still pictures) to establish a conclusion.

Verbal or testimonial evidence is the assertion of human beings about such objects or materials as the basis of inference to the propositions or conclusions.

Note that real and verbal evidence may be combined.   To

---

[3] Evidence as used in the courtroom has a restricted meaning not attached to the popular use of the term. Courts of law, for many reasons, have limited the application of evidence. The orderly conduct of trials, the unreliability of human senses, and various other factors have led courts to limit the kinds of evidence used. The laws of evidence, stipulating what shall be admissible, are made by legislature or inherited from English common law, and, of course, are followed rigidly. These rules stipulate, for example, that a man, after seven years of absence, shall be assumed to be dead; that facts of general knowledge do not require proof; that evidence must be confined to the point at issue; that the burden of proof is upon him who holds the affirmative; that hearsay evidence is inadmissible; that testimony in general should have to do with matters of knowledge rather than of opinion.

Outside of the court we refuse to be bound by these restrictions. In practical debate all evidence is admitted; the only question is the value of that evidence.

prove the increase in prices in 1947, Congresswoman Helen Gahagan Douglas, of California, appeared in the House Chamber with a shopping basket containing butter, eggs, and pork chops. She quoted prices: in June, 1946, these items as exhibited cost in the Washington, D.C., market $10.00; in March, 1947, these same foods cost $15.02.

Positive evidence was offered in the White murder case, Salem, Massachusetts, 1830, by witnesses who identified Frank Knapp as observed in Brown Street near the house of the murder about the time of the assassination of Captain White. With the aid of such testimony Daniel Webster succeeded in getting a verdict from the jury (in the second trial). Negative evidence consisted of the fact that Frank Knapp was apparently unable to verify his assertion that he was elsewhere at the alleged time of the crime.

Debaters frequently use negative evidence—sometimes without justification. The debater may say, "No evidence exists that the Communists are committed to the overthrow of the American government by force," or some similar statement. Almost invariably *some* evidence may be adduced. A less fallacious statement would be that "No evidence has been offered in this debate" concerning the disputed point. Negative testimony of this kind would have weight.

B. *Source of Evidence.* According to the nature of its source, evidence may be (1) original or (2) hearsay; (3) written or (4) unwritten; (5) ordinary or (6) expert.

Original evidence is any fact or statement of fact from the primary source without passing from mouth to mouth or from secondary printing to other secondary printing. Hearsay evidence is that transmitted from one person to another and then offered as essential fact. Written evidence is any fact derived from a recorded source. Unwritten evidence is that which springs from common knowledge or is of oral origin. Ordinary evidence is that of the layman or everyday witness without special knowledge. Expert evidence is that presented by an authority, one whose reputation and training lead others to accept his opinion on matters in his special field. Primary sources are the original documents, the first witnesses to the event or situation. The court stenographer's record or the newspaper reporter's account of a trial or speech is primary (the record of what a writer saw or heard). The editorial comment on the same event would hardly be classed as primary.

Original or primary citations the debater sometimes neglects. He says, "*Representative American Speeches for 1945–46* states that 'there is no defense against the atomic bomb.'" What the speaker means is that "Dr. Harold Urey stated in an address at Chicago, Illinois, on Feb. 25, 1946, 'there is no defense against the atomic bomb, and there never will be any defense.'" (Cited in *Representative American Speeches: 1945–46*, p. 103.)

Original evidence is exemplified by the statement, "Secretary of State (General) George C. Marshall stated that 'I cannot escape the conclusion that the possibilities of atomic explosion make it more imperative than ever before that the United States keep itself militarily strong and use this strength to promote cooperative world order.'" (Address to the *New York Herald Tribune* Forum, Oct. 29, 1945.)

Hearsay evidence would be, "The speaker said that it is reported that Secretary of State George Marshall testified that the possibilities of atomic explosion called for military strength and for use of that strength to promote a cooperative world order."

Written evidence would be that found in printed or typed argumentative articles; unwritten evidence would be these same facts incorporated in a speech.

Ordinary evidence is that given by the student debater who asserts that Federal income taxes should be reduced. Expert evidence would be similar testimony offered by the Secretary of the Treasury.

C. Relation to Conclusion. Evidence is further classified, according to the relation that the facts bear to the conclusion, into two types: testimonial, or direct, and circumstantial, or indirect. In the Carlyle Harris murder case the following statement was given in instructions to the jury:

Evidence is divided into two kinds, direct and circumstantial. It is direct when the witness testifies to the principal fact in issue, as when a murder is committed and the witness testifies that he saw the blow inflicted. . . . In such a case the truth of the witness is the main object of inquiry.

In circumstantial testimony . . . the circumstance must be proved to the satisfaction of the jurors and it is for them to . . . draw the inference.

For example, the shooting of Senator Huey Long in the rotunda of the state capital at Baton Rouge, Louisiana, on Sept. 9, 1935, by Dr. Weiss had at least a dozen witnesses. Their testimony to the principal fact would be direct evidence. The evidence in the trial of Bruno Richard Hauptmann in 1934 for kidnaping and killing the Lindbergh baby was circumstantial. No person saw that crime committed. Circumstantial evidence included among other things the handwriting of Hauptmann as compared with that used by the writer of the ransom notes; the possession by Hauptmann of marked money; the comparison of the wood in the ladder found near a window of the Lindbergh house at Hopewell, New Jersey, with that in the garage of the Hauptmann home in the Bronx, New York; the links of time; the accused man's occupation; and his activities before and after the crime. The general conclusion in such a case is based entirely on inference.

What of the relative value of testimonial and circumstantial evidence? The popular impression is that direct testimonial evidence is much more trustworthy than indirect or circumstantial. Seeing is believing, we are told, and the most reliable kind of material is obviously that in which the witness testifies directly to the truth or falsity of the proposition. The fact is, however, that circumstantial evidence, when properly dovetailed, is as significant and conclusive as the direct type. The eye and the ear are not infallible whereas a complete chain of circumstances may present the true account of the incident. Few murder convictions are based upon direct evidence. Circumstantial material need not depend so heavily upon human fallibility. "Witnesses may lie but circumstances cannot." Clothes, fingerprints, tools, typewriting, handwriting, chemical analysis of blood, and all kinds of materials become the clear basis for conviction. A classic illustration is the case of Professor Webster, of Harvard, found guilty of the murder of Dr. Parkman. The two had quarreled over a debt. It was discovered that Dr. Parkman had made an appointment with Professor Webster though no one had seen an interview. A search of Webster's laboratory revealed the charred bones and the identifying false teeth in the furnace, a sufficient basis for conviction.

One of the chief elements in the picture that convicted Hauptmann was the ladder. H. Koehler, wood technologist of the U.S.

Forest Service, testified that part of the wood used in the ladder found outside the Lindbergh house came from the flooring in Hauptmann's attic. The basis for the confession and conviction in the Loeb-Leopold case was the discovery of a pair of horn-rimmed glasses, found near the culvert in which the murderers had deposited the body of Bobby Franks.

Circumstantial evidence can be convincing. But all circumstantial evidence, of course, is valid only to the extent that it proceeds from sound reasoning. It is impressive in proportion to its cumulative character. In order that it may be valid, the representative facts must all point to the alleged conclusion, and no representative facts may indicate otherwise.

In short, each type is weak, and each is strong. The value of either type is to be measured only by the extent to which it convinces.

V. Representative Types of Evidence in Argument

In argument, evidence consists typically of (1) general or specific instances; (2) hypothetical instances, cases, or illustrations; (3) statistics; (4) analogous instances, situations, or objects; (5) authority or opinion.

Although evidence or fact crops out in many forms in argument, whether the argument is oral or written, the factual types most frequent are those listed above. Here may we merely refer to each. In the next chapter we shall outline methods of evaluating each form. In a later chapter on types of argument we shall view further these same factual details as they relate to the larger framework in argumentative discourse.

A. *General or Specific Instances as Evidence.* The instances may form the basis of a general inference. We may argue that "Present-day American civilization is robust because we have had in recent years representative philosophers, scientists, preachers, and statesmen as leaders." The philosophers and other groups enumerated are instances that support the proposition. These examples are general instances. More specifically, we may infer that "Present-day American civilization is robust because we have had as representative leaders in recent years John Dewey, Albert Einstein, R. A. Millikan, Harry Emerson Fosdick, Fulton J. Sheen, Franklin D. Roosevelt." The specific instances have thus been substituted for the general examples. The debater's arguments are filled with such illustrations or more concrete cases.[4]

B. Hypothetical Instances or Illustrations as Evidence. Sometimes the arguer, especially if factual items are not available, may resort to imaginary or hypothetical instances. The logical value of such materials may not be great. Certainly, as devices to create interest, such illustrations are to be encouraged.

C. Statistics as Evidence. Evidence is often composed of statistics. The word *statistics* is derived from *state* and indicates the methods used for collecting data and drawing inferences from them that will be of value in the conduct of the state, *e.g.*, we have statistics in regard to population, numbers of nationalities, immigration, births and deaths, disease, etc. The word applies especially to complex data involving large masses of material, the essential character and interpretation of which are ordinarily difficult to determine.[5]

D. Analogous Cases or Objects as Evidence. Sometimes the arguer, discussant, or debater will compare two cases or objects, or two groups of cases or objects and thus draw a conclusion. This is argument by analogy or comparison. Certain factors or conditions, true of a familiar case (case A), are also suspected of being true of a relatively unknown case (case B). Great Britain, for example, has nationalized some of its economic life, including railroads and coal mines. Should the United States also nationalize transportation and mining? We have relatively complete information about the British case (case A) because we can view the instance in operation. Although the United States (case B) is similar to Britain in many respects, the one factor about which we speculate (government ownership of railroads and coal mines), is unknown to us (unknown because at the time of this writing such public ownership does not exist here).

When the cases under comparison are so remotely related as to be in entirely different fields, we popularly call the comparison one of *figurative analogy.* The latter usage, like that of hypothetical illustrations, is chiefly effective as persuasion rather than as logic.[6]

[4] For tests see Chap. 9.
[5] For further treatment of statistics, see Chap. 10.
[6] For tests of analogy as evidence see Chap. 9.

E. Evidence from Authority or Opinion. All evidence, be it concrete fact or more general opinion about facts, leads in the final analysis to the human agent who originated the information or opinion. If we are listening to spoken argument, we peer back of the facts and assertions to inquire, Where did you get your data? What source will verify (or has verified) your facts? Thus we fully examine the individual who orally testifies to the event or situation (which in turn is recorded) or who himself puts on paper the alleged facts or the opinions about facts. If such source is a layman, we refer to him, by analogy of the courtroom, as a witness. If he is an authority, we give him special standing as an expert.[7]

VI. RECORDING OF EVIDENCE

Note taking, as we observed previously, is essential for any methodical preparation of term papers as well as arguments, discussion, or debates. A special phase of such note taking is the accurate recording of the facts, of the source of facts, and of opinions.

Decide, then, on a filing system, be it file boxes, large envelopes for each group of cards, loose-leaf pads in which the data can be constantly reorganized, or merely rubber bands to bind the 3-by-5-inch cards. Apply principles of thorough canvassing of the available sources. Don't copy everything, but be sure that the residue of your investigation is sufficient and that the source can be instantly quoted in detail for all who may be interested in verifying your materials.

VII. CONCLUSION

The aim of this chapter has been to remind you of the basic importance of facts or evidence; to classify evidence and to help you to become more observant of the representative types as they occur in argumentation, discussion, and debate; to suggest systematic ways of detecting and assembling concrete items that strengthen your argument; and to encourage you to ground these arguments in logic and fact rather than in assertion. In the next chapter I propose to outline the principles and tests for evaluating the quality of these facts as used by you and others in argumentation, discussion, and debate.

[7] For tests of source (or authority) as evidence see Chap. 9.

EXERCISES AND PROBLEMS

1. Illustrate the significance of a "fact" as it is regarded by a scientist, a historian, a college debater.

2. Brief one of the following speeches to illustrate the incorporation of "facts" as the basis of the argument: (*a*) Robert H. Jackson's "International Military Tribunal: Opening Address," Nov. 20, 1945, Nuremberg, Germany, in *Representative American Speeches, 1945–46,* pp. 60–73; (*b*) Philip Murray's "Strikes, Wages, and Industrial Profits," Nov. 18, 1946, in *Representative American Speeches, 1946–47,* pp. 177–189.

3. Classify evidence according to (*a*) form, (*b*) source, (*c*) relationship to conclusion or proof.

4. Evaluate the evidence in a contemporary speech as reprinted in a recent number of the *Congressional Record* or of *Vital Speeches of the Day.*

5. Discuss each of the following problems: (*a*) the relative importance of circumstantial vs. testimonial evidence; (*b*) general vs. specific instances as evidence; (*c*) hypothetical instances as evidence; (*d*) statistics as evidence; (*e*) analogous cases as evidence.

CHAPTER 9

Evidence: Techniques and Tests

How shall we select and present evidence and opinions so that they will have proper weight with readers or listeners? How can we discriminate between strong and weak evidence as presented by others? How shall we test the sources of evidence? What concrete criteria for using and evaluating facts (evidence) shall we apply?

I. The Use and Evaluation of Evidence: Its Content

A. Select and Present the Kind and Amount of Evidence That Will Most Effectively Convince and Persuade Your Readers or Listeners. Evidence should be sufficient to satisfy the readers or listeners. To be sure, you cannot satisfy every carping critic. Certain Socratic opponents will try to pinion you by insisting upon one detail after another until you may give up in despair. Your rhetorical problem, however, is to persuade and remove the inhibitions of those who are open to conviction and who expect only a reasonable sufficiency of material. In theory, however, you are to say to your audience, "Are the statements I have made and the logic I have presented and the data I have offered sufficient for your approval? If not, I shall try, subject to the limitations of time allowed me, to provide further argument and evidence until you are satisfied."

B. Collect and Present Abundant Evidence. Even though you

cannot have time or space for the amplification of each bit of supporting data, you should nevertheless be well armed with relevant facts. Every argument you develop should have a surrounding medium of factual detail. You should know more about your theme than appears on the surface. If challenged, you should be able to come at your proposition from fresh angles and with fresh information. Especially if you are to rebut and to reestablish your case, you are expected to reinforce your ideas with additional items. Let your speeches and writings, then, run to the concrete and loom large with figures, historical and other illustrations, concrete cases, and authorities.

C. Select and Present Representative Evidence. Your facts should not be selected in order to provide you with "special pleading." Such argumentative technique is resorted to, to build up your case by ignoring certain facts and featuring only those favorable to your side. When you generalize from instances, for example, your task is to assure yourself and others that your cases are typical. And when you examine others' arguments, you are counseled to check the facts to determine their representative character. Do the cases selected fairly represent the whole?[1] Fifty students, to cite a case, are examined to determine the physical and mental fitness of a thousand students. These fifty samples must not be the exceptionally capable physically or mentally, nor yet the comparatively inefficient ones, but rather those selected from the rank and file. Seven newspapers are examined as illustrating the tendency of the press to feature crime and scandal. The city-manager plan in three cities is reviewed to prove the efficacy of this type of government. Four cities are examined to demonstrate the lack of law enforcement in present-day America. In these cases typical newspapers, cities, and states must be selected.

It is difficult for some debaters to resist the temptation to select cases that are especially favorable—to magnify, for example, the single instance of some city that had an exceptionally bad record in juvenile delinquency.

D. Check Your Evidence and That of Others for Accuracy. The goal of absolute accuracy is most difficult to reach. Scientists, research students, investigators of all kinds, newspaper re-

---

[1] For further examination of the tests of argument by generalization, see Chap. 14.

porters, and others are continually in search of the facts. You, then, are to analyze carefully and recheck your own data and that of others to guarantee that complete reliance may be placed upon the materials dealt with.

In argument by generalization, for example, the entire superstructure falls if the evidence at the base is faulty.

If the conclusion is drawn that lynching is on the decrease in the United States because during the past year only eighteen cases were reported in the various states, is it true that only eighteen were officially recorded? Sometimes a careful scrutiny of the facts will reveal details or major features of a situation that are inaccurately reported. Many generalizations are based upon newspaper reports which, however zealous the reporters may be to "get the facts," include at times erroneous information.

Analogical reasoning, similarly, demands accuracy in the facts on which the total comparison hinges. The facts alleged to be true in regard to the factors under comparison must be verified. If it is asserted that compulsory automobile liability insurance should be adopted in my state because that program has worked well in Massachusetts, we should make sure that the law has worked well in that state.

No safeguard against false analogy is more necessary than a thorough knowledge of the underlying facts. The drift of the discussion or debate is usually (we hope) in favor of the one who has the most complete and accurate information of the subject matter. All temptation to yield to coloring of facts or suppression of unfavorable elements should be resisted.

E. *Check Your Evidence and That of Others by the Citation of Possible Negative Facts.* By negative facts I refer to instances or information that may conflict with your positive evidence. I refer to facts that are exceptions to your data. This suggestion is merely stating in reverse fashion our advice above to focus on representative evidence.

The method of formulating a generalization on the basis of a large number of positive instances, called the *enumerative* method, has so many weaknesses that some logicians condemn it altogether. Bacon called it "puerile, precarious, and exposed to danger from contradictory instances." Accordingly, we ask, Are there any exceptions or negative instances? Our constant tendency is to generalize as a result of observing a few positive instances without taking pains to see the exceptions that are observable. A householder has difficulty with the family plumber who belongs to a union and charges union wages. The householder's conclusion is that labor unions are unreasonable and unjustified. A physician evidently uses bad judgment in a certain case, and the patient dies. The bereaved ones conclude that doctors are stupid, unreliable quacks. The farmer denounces all book agents because one of them fleeced him. One dishonest lawyer, one drunken college student, one backsliding minister will call forth a series of sweeping generalizations that condemn the entire group to which he belongs. In each of these cases a further examination would no doubt bring to light many exceptions. And a single negative instance should go far to destroy the argument.

F. *Use the Most Recent Evidence and Check That of Others for Recency.* Since the world changes daily and the facts of yesterday quickly become dated and unserviceable, your continual responsibility is to arm yourself with up-to-date information. The facts concerning Middleton, Indiana, in 1890 no longer held when that city was examined by Dr. Lynd and his associates in 1924. The population, reading habits, leisure-time activities, and hundreds of other facts pertaining to that same city in 1950 will in turn be markedly different from the information concerning these things in 1924. Don't allow yourself to be caught and embarrassed by some critic or opposing debater who proves that your data are obsolete.

G. *Make Your Evidence Consistent with the Context.* Are the facts as stated to be reconciled with each other? Is the undesigned testimony offered by a witness directly contrary to other statements made by him? Sometimes, in his zeal to stress various arguments, a debater uses facts that apparently contradict each other. A student argued for government ownership of coal mines because it would mean cheaper coal to the consumer. In the next breath he argued in favor of such ownership because it would mean much better labor conditions in that the laborers would receive much higher wages. He did not dispose of the apparent inconsistency between the higher wages and the lower price of coal. The evidence may not be inconsistent, but if it appears so, your business is to make clear that the apparent discrepancies are to be reconciled.

H. Verify Your Evidence and That of Others by the Tests of Logical Argument. I refer here not so much to the argument as included in the debate or discussion itself as to the reflective process by which the speaker or listener can corroborate the details as submitted.

Here we touch upon a matter of causes and results. The principles and characteristics of argument as discussed in the following two chapters need to be applied as a final gauge of the validity of evidence. The laws of inductive and deductive reasoning are to be closely applied.

We should inquire, Is it reasonable to suppose that the evidence is as presented? A witness testified that snow fell in the state of Iowa in July. We ask, By what laws of causation could such a freak of nature be possible? Is the testimony consistent with argument from cause to effect? with the laws of analogy? with the argument from specific instances?[2]

I. Defend Your Evidence by Adequate Rebuttal and Refutation. Apply the methods of refutation and rebuttal as outlined in later chapters. Without pugnacity, you may reestablish your evidence after it has seemingly been undermined. Your facts are well grounded only when they will withstand the sharpest criticism.

II. USE AND EVALUATION OF EVIDENCE: ITS LANGUAGE

A. Couch the Evidence in Concrete Language Free from Possible Misinterpretation. Your phrasing of items and the fidelity with which you follow the laws of efficiency in using the English language are important in your introduction of figures, cases, and other underlying forms of support for your argument. Much will be said later in this book about language in argument. You are here reminded that the evidence itself, like the argumentative and persuasive elements, is to be clearly and simply worded.

B. Point Out to Your Listeners the Significance of Your Material. If, for example, you quote Harvey Firestone as an authority on rubber, it would be well to cite his particular qualifications and lead the audience thus to appraise rightly his opinion concerning the future of the rubber market. If you are using statistics, make clear that the averages on which your argument rests have

---

[2] Later chapters will deal fully with the tests of logical argument. See, for example, Chap. 12.

significance; or that you are using a median, to determine in what class you have the most representative number of cases; or that you have taken other precautions to conform to statistical tests.

C. *Avoid Presenting Evidence in Exaggerated Language.* Show your audience that the value of your evidence has not been exaggerated. Qualify your statements so that those who listen will have confidence not only in the items which you present but also in your judgment and integrity as an arguer. Never say "millions" when you mean "thousands."

D. *Simplify the Evidence So That the Auditors May Quickly Catch It.* This suggestion means that statistics should not be too numerous, that they should be expressed in round numbers, that they should be translated by means of analogous cases, and that the important items should be repeated.

E. *Show That Your Evidence Fits In with the Established Beliefs and Attitudes of Your Readers or Hearers.* Suggest how your facts coincide with the audience motives of self-preservation, profit, social convenience, ambition, duty, justice, and similar drives. This suggestion means that you will adapt your materials to persuasive ends. You will use lively and connotative language. Can you do so without violating the principles of well-balanced interpretation of your facts? I believe you can express yourself in attractive language without overstepping the bounds of accuracy and fidelity to truth. Vivid and persuasive language will identify your arguments and facts with imaginative and emotional concepts. Such identifications are justifiable if you make these appeals not substitutes for logic and facts but rather techniques to impress others with what you regard as stable and sound information and inference.

III. Use and Evaluation of the Sources of Evidence

In addition to the facts themselves viewed for their intrinsic accuracy, their internal consistency, and their accuracy of wording, the critic or the creator of argument should evaluate the source of the information or opinion.

All evidence, we are agreed, traces its origin to observers or others who have directly experienced the facts and recorded them—by utterance or by written symbols. In the courtroom these sources are *witnesses* or, where special fitness to testify is recognized, *experts*. Debaters and other lay arguers lump these

witnesses and *experts* under the general category of *sources.*
Sources, then, we use to refer either to a person who offers oral
testimony, or to the printed document in which the source appears.

How do we test such original basis of fact?

*1. Have you recorded accurately and completely the sources of
your evidence and are you ready for their citation in reply to any
requests?* Radio debaters, to my knowledge, have more than once
after a broadcast had telephone calls with requests for substantia-
tion of certain facts cited in the broadcast. It is not sufficient for
you to say, "Oh, that is a matter of common knowledge." Rather
you will be able to report that "My source for the statement that
'Woodrow Wilson at Princeton year after year was voted the most
popular professor by the students' was cited from Ray Stannard
Baker's *Woodrow Wilson, Life and Letters,* Vol. 2, p. 13."

*2. Is the alleged author of the evidence under examination actu-
ally the source or author of it?* We need to determine the authenticity of documents. A certain speech, let us say, is attributed to
Franklin D. Roosevelt. Some critics allege that Raymond Moley
may have written it. The investigator, as best he can, must try to
decide upon authorship in this case as in all other instances.

*3. Is the author or source of this evidence competent to express
a valid opinion or to supply accurate facts?* What of the special
or general training of the source? What of his opportunity to
observe and to interpret the event? What of his ability to recall
the details? What of his skill in using the English language so
that his terms may reflect his extended meaning? John Bassett
Moore and Elihu Root, for example, were authorities on international law; Charles A. Beard and A. Lawrence Lowell, on government. Later John Foster Dulles, Bernard Baruch, and Warren F.
Austin were authorities on America's relation to the United Nations.

Debaters often commit the fallacy, to be discussed more fully in
the chapters on "Obstacles to Straight Thinking" of assuming that,
because a man or woman is prominent, his or her opinions are
expert on every subject. If a baseball player achieves national
fame, he straightway is quoted as having declared that this automobile is more satisfactory than any other; that this brand of
collar wears better than all others. He may be quoted as an authority on any matter from political parties to the rehabilitation of

China. Automobile magnates are not always experts concerning racial problems; Congressmen are not always the best authorities concerning what types of jet planes should be built; internationally known business leaders are not always specialists in the field of drama or poetry and may be no better qualified than less pecunious citizens concerning the value of some freshly produced drama. Only men who have become specialists on a given subject are worth citing as authorities on that subject.

The obstacles to competency of witnesses are numerous. Powers of observation and judgment differ widely. Mary E. M. Splaine, the chief witness in the conviction of Sacco and Vanzetti for the payroll robbery and murder at South Braintree, Massachusetts, identified Sacco. Dr. Morton Prince, professor of abnormal and dynamic psychology at Harvard, thus commented on her testimony:

> I do not hesitate to say that the star witness for the government testified, honestly enough, no doubt, to what was psychologically impossible. Miss Splaine testified (though she had only seen Sacco at the time of the shooting, from a distance of about sixty feet for from one and one-half to three seconds, in a motor car going at an increasing rate of speed at about fifteen to eighteen miles an hour) that she saw, and at the end of the year she remembered and described, sixteen different details of his person, even to the size of his hand, the length of his hair (as being between two and two and one-half inches long), and the shade of his eyebrows! Such perception and memory under such conditions can be easily proved to be psychologically impossible. Every psychologist knows that—so does Houdini. . . . Why was not Miss Splaine asked to pick out Sacco from among a group of men? If this had been done, this unconscious falsification of memory would have been avoided.[3]

Note that errors appear in reporting, such as the omission of statements, or errors of addition or substitution. Note that many who testify are not in a position to observe; their observations are hearsay evidence. Similar is the testimony of children or of the mentally incompetent. Mental disease, senility, deafness, blindness, limited education, inexperience, lack of mental poise, weak memory, suggestion, or failure to understand the questions put to a witness—any of these may account for faulty evidence.

4. Is the authority or witness free from prejudice? The preju-

[3] Letter, "A Psychologist's Study," *Boston Herald,* Oct. 30, 1926.

dice growing out of racial, nationalistic, political, economic, military, religious, or purely personal interests will often explain the character of the testimony.

Men who bewailed a weak army and navy and the need of appropriations and were themselves naval and military officers would naturally have their testimony discounted.

5. *Is the authority reliable?* Is he given to bombast, exaggeration, and questionable assertions? The application of this test would lead to the rejection of the authority of certain prominent newspapers.

College debaters, like other people, often assume that because a statement is printed, it is necessarily an accurate and reliable statement. Whoever bursts into print, therefore, is freely quoted. Only through experience, sometimes disheartening experience, do we come to realize how much that is found in books and papers is utterly unreliable. Newspapers, although they are in the main laudable agencies for informing public opinion, necessarily gather their news quickly and from sources that frequently are open to question. Hence the false statements and the exaggerations that occur. Moreover, the human family is so eager to add to the world's libraries that books are hastily or ignorantly patched together. Students of argument will do well to scan with discrimination printed sources as well as oral testimony.

6. *Is the authority definite?* "Statistics show," "someone has said," "a prominent member of the National Manufacturers' Association said recently," "a British diplomat wrote," and similar expressions mean little. In argumentation, especially in debating, the source should be precise. In the body of the written forensic the references should be explicit; accurate and definite sources should appear as marginal notes or footnotes. In actual delivery of the debate the speaker need not bore the audience with elaborate recital of page and chapter; whenever it seems necessary, however, the speaker must be ready to cite his sources.

7. *Is the authority or source primary rather than secondary?* Debaters often say, "The *Congressional Record* tells us . . . ," without suggesting that, no doubt, some Senator or Representative is holding forth on the page cited. Or we may be told that the latest number of the *United States News* declares on page 43 that such and such a statement is true or untrue. The need here is to get the exact source and, if possible, the original one. Perhaps

the magazine is quoting Senator Smith in a recent speech in Congress. The student will ultimately substitute, for statements of the type above, such remarks as "Senator Smith, in his address in Congress on April 13, said so and so." If necessary, you can refer to the volume, number, date, and page of the *Congressional Record*.

Be sure that your record in each case is primary. A primary source of any information is the "oldest living record that furnishes that information, either explicitly or by implication, or an authentic copy of that record." Primary sources are either original documents or copies of original documents. Of course, an original document should be examined if possible, for example, the original letters of Lincoln rather than the copies. Secondary sources, for example, histories and biographies written long after the death of the subject, are often prejudiced and inaccurate. Primary sources, such as the Gospels, should be carefully examined from the angle of external criticism and from that of internal criticism. External criticism looks to the origin of the document, its authorship, and the source from which the information came. External criticism has been applied to documents. An instance is the scrutiny of a series of documents purporting to be orders from the president of Mexico for payment to the editor of *The Nation* for propaganda in favor of the government of Mexico. Another instance is the examination of an alleged decree of the Russian government, which appeared in the American press in 1918, ordering the nationalization of women. Both documents proved to be forgeries. Internal criticism examines the manuscript or printed source by any means available to decide whether what it says is really true. This type of criticism involves all the tests of evidence and of argument.

8. *Is the authority supported by other sources?* Superficial students often rely on one authority. Continued reference to one book is usually an index of limited preparation.

9. *Is the authority supported by argument from specific instances, causal relation, and analogy?* Evidence from authority, excellent as it is, should not be used exclusively. Students often make the mistake of trying to prove their case by a list of quotations from magazines and other sources. Authorities are mainly to furnish a source for verifying facts rather than for the voicing of opinions. A variety of evidence should be used, both

direct and indirect. Articles and other sources of information should be thoroughly digested so that the ideas as presented become fresh and original. As suggested above, testimonial evidence, wherever possible, should be combined with circumstantial evidence.

10. Does the authority testify contrary to his apparent interests?

11. Is the authority or source acceptable to the audience or reader? No matter how attractive your source, it (or he) may for some reason not immediately apparent to you be unacceptable to your listening or reading group. Constantly view your authority in view of his acceptability. In any case, your function is to show his significance and value (as we indicated above).

IV. INVENTORY OF THE TESTS OF EVIDENCE AND OF THE SOURCES OF EVIDENCE

To evaluate your own evidence and that of others, apply the following tests:

(1) Is the evidence acceptable to the audience? (2) Is the evidence abundant? (3) Is the evidence representative? (4) Is the evidence accurate? (5) Is sufficient account taken of negative evidence? (6) Is the evidence the most recent available? (7) Is the evidence consistent with the context? (8) Is the evidence confirmed by tests of logical argument? (9) Does the evidence withstand the test of counterevidence? (10) Is the evidence expressed in concrete, unambiguous language? (11) Is the significance of the evidence clearly indicated? (12) Is the evidence expressed without exaggerated language? (13) Is the evidence expressed simply? (14) Does the evidence offered support the established beliefs and attitudes of the hearers or readers? (15) Are the sources of evidence recorded accurately and can they be accurately cited? (16) Is the alleged source or authority of the evidence the true source? (17) Is the source or authority competent to express a valid opinion on the matter under examination? (18) Is the source or authority competent to supply accurate facts and does he do so? (19) Is the source or authority free from prejudice? (20) Is the source or authority reliable? (21) Is the source or authority definite? (22) Is the source or authority primary? (23) Is the source or authority supported by representative types of valid argument? (24) Does the

source or authority testify contrary to its apparent interests? (25) Is the source or authority acceptable to the audience?

EXERCISES AND PROBLEMS

1. Brief an argument from a recent legal, political, or business speech that contains a considerable amount of concrete fact. For examples, consult *Vital Speeches of the Day, Congressional Record, Representative American Speeches,* or similar sources of public addresses. Apply the tests of evidence summarized at the end of this chapter.

2. Apply the tests of evidence to each of the following examples:

a. "One of the most serious problems the insurance companies have to face right now is the driver under 25 years of age. Numbering only about seventeen or eighteen per cent of the nation's drivers, he causes twenty-five per cent of the accidents. His accidents are likely to be severe ones. And he is getting worse all the time. While there is no striking difference in the death totals for drivers under 25 between 1946 and 1947, it is discouraging to note that these drivers were involved in almost 62,000 more non-fatal accidents last year than the year before. There is no doubt that young drivers are involved in more than their statistical share of accidents."—Jesse W. Randall, speech of May 15, 1948, *Vital Speeches of the Day,* Vol. XIV, p. 515, June 15, 1948.

b. "LONDON, Dec. 6—Winston Churchill predicted today that under socialism 12,000,000 Britons 'will have to disappear in one way or another.'

"Delivering his most violent attack yet on the present Labor Government at a Conservative party rally in Manchester, Mr. Churchill said he was 'quite sure that socialism—that is to say, the substitution of state control by officials instead of by private enterprise—will make it impossible for 48,000,000 to live in this island.'

"At least a quarter of all who are alive today, Mr. Churchill continued, 'will have to disappear in one way or another after enduring a lowering of the standards of food and comfort inconceivable in the last fifty years.'"—Mallory Browne, *New York Times,* p. 23, Dec. 7, 1947.

c. "In the light of recent events, and until the Soviets stop their expansion moves, we must forget our desire for the limitation of armaments. Funds that are being sought for the construction of public works that are meritorious but are not urgent, must be diverted to the national defense. It is unfortunate, but true, that some people in this world respect only force. The strength of our arguments for peace depends in some measure upon the strength of our armed forces."—James F. Byrnes, speech of Mar. 13, 1948, *Vital Speeches of the Day,* Vol. XIV, p. 362, Apr. 1, 1948.

d. "It would be one of the greatest mistakes this country can make to put the Communist party in the category of a political party."—Rep. J. Parnell Thomas (R) of New Jersey.

e. "But we must face the facts.   This international unity which won the war—and which pledged these ideals—has fallen apart."—Senator Arthur H. Vandenberg (R) of Michigan.

f. "Our military forces will not be 'too little and too late' in the next national emergency, if the people understand the present world situation."—General Dwight D. Eisenhower.

g. "Management abuses are just as much against the public interest as labor abuses and what I want to see is a balance of power which will check the excesses of both."—Ira Mosher, chairman, National Association of Manufacturers.

h. In a recent article in a national magazine, Philip Wylie, who has made himself famous by being "agin" practically everything, declares that a college education is decidedly detrimental to women.

Mr. Wylie feels that a college education probably makes girls "less happy, more foolish, not very knowledgeable and of far less value to the human race."

i. "So far as the Russians are concerned, it would seem to me that the main use of the atomic bomb in their hands is as a propaganda weapon."—R. E. Lapp.

CHAPTER 10

Argument: Generalization

Proving your proposition involves not only the collection of facts and evidence but detailed reasoning about such data. Every effective debater and discussant will do well, therefore, to know the principles and techniques of assembling and using effective logic. Logic in argumentation concerns itself mainly with inference.

I. RELATION OF INDUCTION TO DEDUCTION

How do we generalize? To answer this question, we may now examine in more detail the inductive process. Just how do you make these mysterious transitions from datum to proposition, so swift, so difficult of objective description? Tracing deliberately your experience in "reflective thinking," you differentiate one aspect of it as that by which you start with concrete objects or details and end with a general "idea," principle, or proposition.

This approach you call *inductive*. The other aspect of your thinking occurs when, in reverse fashion, you concentrate first on the general concept or conclusion and then proceed to the specific event or object. This logical mode you label *deductive*.

Just how do these forms differ? Suppose you are to deliver a five-minute speech on the proposition, *The representative South American nations are unprepared for a major international war.* Your first speech is inductive. It unfolds as follows: Brazil is

115

unprepared for international war (in equipment, finances); so is Argentina; so is Chile; so is Columbia. Therefore (concluding statement), "The representative South American nations are unprepared for a major international war."

Your second speech is deductive. You begin thus: "The representative South American nations are unprepared for a major international war." You then accumulate specific details: Brazil is unprepared for such war; so is Argentina; so also is Chile; so also is Columbia.

The types are thus graphically illustrated:

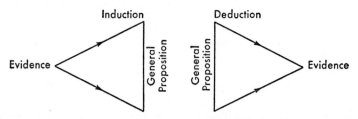

The two modes, although superficially quite different, are in reality closely articulated: they are complementary. To begin with an enumeration of concrete instances of South American states that are unprepared presupposes or assumes that the speaker or thinker is working from an assumption, later to be verified, that these countries are unready for war in case Russia and the United States should presently enter World War III and the nations of the Western Hemisphere should be expected to line up with this nation. The deductionist, in turn, sets forth his preliminary propositions only after he or somebody else has already established, or partly established, the supporting evidence (inductive materials) of these premises. Thus the inductionist, like any thoroughgoing scientist, charts his way by aid of assumptions, hypotheses, or general premises. The deductionist, likewise, concedes to the demands of science that he validate out of experience (concrete data) the premises and hypotheses which are his starting point. The two modes are opposite faces of the same coin. For you to treat the two as if they were antagonistic, widely separated, or for you to regard either one as unnecessary, is to fail to understand the role of the inferential process. Whether you tag your argument as *inductive* or *deductive* depends merely on your point of view.   In either case, if you are a careful reasoner, you will demonstrate both modes.

The two charts above should be merged:

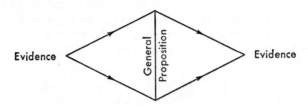

II. Generalization from Specific Instances

I now propose to discuss with you the typical modes of inference from induction: (1) generalization from specific instances; (2) generalization from statistics; (3) generalization from circumstantial detail.

Reasoning from specific instances to a general proposition or conclusion is the typical expression of induction—argument by generalization.   Genuine inference is called for—not just a simple counting of cases.   The conclusion extends beyond the immediate data before you so that some originality or insight is needed.   You are asked to make an *inductive hazard* and yet one that turns out to be sensible and well justified.   To do so you will keep in mind several obvious tests of such examination and interpretation of instances or cases: (1) Are the instances examined sufficient in number to warrant the generalization?   (2) Are these instances representative or typical?   (3) Are negative instances discoverable?   (4) Are the instances actually "true" or what they appear to be?   (5) Does the generalization conform to the requirements of the laws of probability and causation?

These tests of validity obviously overlap; for example, the first three are merely your cue to scrutinize carefully the number and character of the cases you are dealing with—whether or not they support your point.   The fourth one is merely to remind you that the facts themselves should be checked—not taken for granted.   The fifth test suggests that you have the role of a "scientist" and that a larger view of your materials is essential if you are to avoid hasty generalization.

A. *Are the Instances Sufficient in Number?*   The starting point is to examine the instances offered to support the general proposition. What number is necessary before we can draw a conclusion? Certainly, the number varies according to the kind of material under observation. Can we prove that all members of the freshman class at the State University of Iowa are over seventeen years of age by examining a hundred of the two thousand cases? Obviously, the assertion cannot be made until the age of each is checked. On the other hand, we can conclude that these freshmen are *in general* readers of *Life, The Reader's Digest,* or other magazines though the questionnaire supplying the data might be filled out by only four or five hundred. Multiplication of numbers should give more accurate results, but it is unnecessary in this case to have a thousand cases before a safe generalization can be made. It is one thing to generalize concerning the assumption that each one is at least sixteen and another to infer that the group in general reads certain magazines.

In natural science the bases of generalization may be that of a few cases. The material studied is uniform, *e.g.,* the specific gravity of a diamond, the character of an equilateral triangle, the speed of falling bodies. In the social and political realm, however, such homogeneity of materials or instances is not quite so apparent.

Collectors of data in the fields of social and political science must observe a relatively large number of instances. A thousand apples or potatoes may prove a fair sample of a hundred thousand, but mankind varies so markedly in individual differences as to require a much more complete survey before an inclusive statement concerning the whole can be ventured. If you study the incomes of farmers in the United States, of schoolteachers, or of steelworkers, you should cover thousands of cases.

Such an extensive survey, however, is obviously costly and often impossible. To secure data, even on such items as those included in the United States census, has not always been easy. Many men and women have stoutly resisted the invitation of the census taker for them to reveal their ages, income, and other personal facts. Not all who should be enumerated are included; inaccuracies in fact are bound to creep in; and the collectors of data are not always careful, intelligent, and open-minded.

Necessary though this method of induction is, it thus has its limitations and must be supplemented by other tests. Its limitations are so striking as to lead critics like Lord Bacon to condemn it as "puerile, precarious, and exposed to the danger from contradictory instances."[1]

B. *Are the Instances Representative?* Accordingly, we look to the character of each specimen as well as to the number of cases. Why all college freshmen need to be examined before we can conclude whether they are over seventeen years of age is evident. It is impossible to select those who are typical of the total number with respect to the item of "seventeen years." It is highly important, therefore, to find individual members who incorporate those characteristics of the group as a whole, characteristics directly related to the factor or item under dispute. If you conclude that "college graduates in general have larger incomes than noncollege men in business," you must select for your two groups of cases those who have in common all factors except college training. Those grouped under the two classifications should be alike in intelligence, age, and social environment. The generalization would be warranted, then, if the one causal element of college training affected one group and not the other. If college men in business had higher incomes at the age of thirty years, the inference would be that college training did make the difference. The conclusion would, of course, be unwarranted if the investigator had attempted to generalize from college graduates with high intelligence in contrast to the rank and file of the noncollege group.

So we resort to the method of sampling. This principle assumes the use of a considerable number of items, chosen *at random* from among a very extensive group. Thus, if we interview a score of the students of Williams (or Bowdoin) College and find them splendid examples of college men, we conclude that the students of Williams (or Bowdoin) College are excellent collegiate types. For the conclusion to be reliable the samples should be chosen at random. Random sampling is that which is done independently of the prejudices or attitudes of the sampler. Cases so selected are fair representatives of the whole. They reflect the general character of the total group, as determined by careful analysis and observation. The assumption is that the entire lot will be of the same nature as the selected cases. This assumption holds

[1] Quoted from D. S. Robinson, *The Principles of Reasoning*, p. 206, Appleton-Century-Crofts, Inc., 1924.

whether the instances inspected are homogeneous (essentially alike) or heterogeneous (different in marked respects).

To further validate the sampling method, statisticians sometimes sample the samples. Thus we can take as samples of college students every tenth undergraduate out of a student body of 5,000; we may thus have some 500. We can determine fair instances of these 500 and can then attend to the hundred chosen for detailed study.

To further ensure the validity of these examples, care is often taken to control the character of the selections, especially when the statistical unit is heterogeneous, *i.e.*, when it is made up of dissimilar elements unevenly distributed throughout the group.

Such controlled sampling is illustrated by the Gallup poll technique.[2] Dr. Gallup's attempts to sample public opinion were complicated by the fact that the American voting public is not a homogeneous group but rather is one in which there are "significant differences of interest and outlook." Considerations of geography, occupation, age, sex, political affiliation, race, religion, and general cultural background are the basic determinants of their experiences and opinions.

The public is made up of men and women living in different geographical sections and earning their daily bread as farmers, mechanics, coal miners, doctors, housewives, businessmen, bankers, merchants, salesgirls, teachers, industrial workers. It is constituted of separate economic classes, age groups, and political parties. Its component individuals represent different racial, religious, and linguistic backgrounds. Human beings are not identical units, for their attitudes and opinions are formed within the circumference of the everyday life experiences and activities which they share with their fellows.[3]

Gallup thus tried to include in his sample the differing types representing the manufacturing East, the Middle Western farmer, the urban millions, the one-fourth of all American families that live in villages, towns, and cities under 25,000 population; the third of workers in the skilled and unskilled groups; the fifth that work on the land; the fifth who compose the white-collar group; the one-twentieth who make up the professional class; the small

[2] George Gallup, *The Pulse of Democracy*, pp. 60*ff.*, Simon and Schuster, Inc., 1940.
[3] *Ibid.*, p. 61.

number of multimillionaires; the lower one-third, many of whom are below the minimum subsistence level; the one-half under thirty years of age; and the one-tenth over sixty.

Gallup also found it necessary to distinguish the group from which he sampled American public opinion in general (social cross section) from that unit representing the voting population (political cross section). Many Southern Negroes, for example, were in reality disfranchised as were other groups lacking age or property qualifications, citizenship, ability to read or write, or civil rights.

It is significant that this investigator stressed the character of the sample rather than its size. As Gallup put it, "no major poll in the history of this country ever went wrong because too few persons were reached."[4]

Criticizing his own technique, Gallup concludes,

Of these two major determinants of reliability—the character and size of the cross section—the former is, by all odds, the most important. If the cross section is carefully selected, a sample of only a few thousand will give accuracy within 3 or 4 per cent. On the other hand in a cross section which is badly chosen, no amount of mere case piling will eliminate the error.[5]

C. Are There Negative Instances? An obvious weakness of the simple enumeration method of induction is its undue stressing of the positive case to the exclusion of contradictory examples. Any generalization that results from "uncontradicted experience" relies too fully on limited knowledge of the field. Businessmen in 1936 and 1940 and 1944 who moved in an economic stratum in New

[4] *Ibid.*, p. 68.

[5] *Ibid.*, p. 71.

The extensive criticisms of the Gallup, Roper, Crossley, and other polls immediately after the presidential election of November, 1948, hardly invalidate the significance of the comments cited here concerning sampling techniques. The obvious unreliability of those predictions in that campaign should encourage the student to examine more sharply those methods of gathering and interpreting data. Note for example, that such samplings are of consequence, assuming that they are accurate, *only at the time they are collected.* Public opinion may shift rapidly. Apparently it did so in the later stages of that campaign. The shift was striking in the United States a few hours after Pearl Harbor. Furthermore, "undecided attitudes" need to be heavily reckoned with in any attempt to interpret and *predict* on the basis of such reports.

York concluded continually that "Americans are almost unanimously opposed to Franklin Roosevelt as President." A certain university freshman, who was thrown into a pond by the members of a college fraternity, concluded that "all fraternity men are brutal snobs." Many Americans, reviewing the testimony of the Nuremberg trials of Germans for war crimes, concluded that "*All* Germans are barbarians."

The inductive leap is more fully established if, in addition to an enumeration of the cases in which the generalizations hold, full account is taken of the failure to find cases in which it does not hold. Men of wealth did help reelect Roosevelt; many fraternity men have no trace of snobbishness; many individuals in Germany and Japan doubtless did have qualities of idealism and could not all be classed as "barbarians." The addition of negative cases strengthens the enumerative method of induction.

Propositions are not proved by your citing the selected cases for "our side"; neither is the proposition disproved by the opponents who select instances favorable to their case. Rather the dovetailing of the data and the addition of any other details with respect to the units under consideration are the only sensible means of pointing the way to the real truth.

D. Are the Instances "Accurate" or "True"? In many argumentative situations the conferees are prone to assume that instances brought forward for proof are what they purport to be. You should have healthy skepticism, however, here as in other aspects of the reasoning process. If it is asserted that the state of New York has no sales tax, we need to explain what such tax is and inquire whether it is not true that that state levies taxes of the essential nature of that type. Here, as in other forms of argument, we need to check the veracity of the specific statement before venturing the inductive hazard.

Thus to check each fact we revert to the tests of evidence and ask again, What is the character of the witness? Did he observe clearly and accurately? Was he prejudiced? Was he in a position to observe? Does the fact have the earmarks of authenticity? Obviously the modes of reasoning are no stronger than the accuracy of the underlying facts.

E. Does the Generalization from Instances Conform to the Requirements of Scientific Analysis and of Causal Connection? Observation and experience are often insufficient as tests of inductive reasoning. Our experience, as we indicated above, is too limited, and our means of covering the entire sphere of a given order of objects is not available. How, then, can we justify the voyage from the known to the unknown? In addition to the assembly of numbers and of representative samples, in addition to the inclusion of exceptions, in addition to the verification of the facts thus arrayed, we need to recognize and state the laws of causation implied in every generalization.

Our method is that of the scientist. He tests the instances by complete analysis and experimentation. He weighs the results until he recognizes the general law or principle that explains the cases. He compares and studies the results "until the underlying system, of which the instances and their elements are all fragments, is finally brought to light and formulated as a law."

Our problem—and it is not beyond even the alert high-school pupil—is in the realm of social thinking to do what every inventor or even an immature experimenter does in investigations in physical science. Our task is to relate segments of knowledge concerning totalitarian governments, Federal powers, a single six-year term for the Presidency, the American theater, tactics of labor unions, Federal aid to education, state medicine, a Federal Press Commission, or other social, political, or artistic questions. The details fall into systematic patterns. We have not at hand the material to piece out a mosaic, but we have assembled sufficient bits to describe with confidence the character of the undeveloped area. The jumble of meaningless events and objects, as we toil over them, takes on a consistency and homogeneity that bring to us immense satisfaction. We use the method of enumeration of typical instances and of examination of negative cases; but in so doing we attempt to place the items or fragments into an "order system," or orderly arrangement in a given field. Insight comes to our aid in the process and gives the procedure the stamp of genuine induction or the inference of valid generalization.

III. Generalization from Statistics

Generalization from statistics involves the tests of specific instances. Because, however, of the complicated character of the statistical items, we here suggest the special criteria.[6]

[6] For fallacies of statistics in argument see Chap. 14.

How shall we decide whether the statistics have been properly compiled? If we are properly critical of figures, we should ask:

1. *Has the material been accurately collected?*

2. *Has the material been properly classified?* The method of classification will, of course, be determined by the purpose. The same material can be classified in different ways. Suppose, for example, you propose an investigation to determine the standing of intercollegiate athletes in comparison with college students in general. You will need one classification of the athletes; another, of college students in general; another, by college subjects; another, by college terms or semesters; another, by sexes.

3. *Is the sampling properly done?* Because it would be impracticable to gather statistics from every institution and every student since the beginning of intercollegiate athletics, average grades relating to sample or representative situations would need to be used.

You would apply the tests of classification suggested above; you would consider exhaustiveness of the division and mutual exclusiveness of the items.[7]

4. *Does the statistical process conform to the tests of evidence and of generalization?* Was the evidence obtained from more than a single observation? By more than one observer? Were the collectors reliable? Was the evidence obtained from more than one source? Was the evidence secured from a random selection? Were the cases sufficiently numerous? Was the evidence derived from typical cases and at typical periods? Was the evidence obtained over a time spread? Was due account taken of negative cases?

5. *Are the units properly defined?* In the illustration cited above, what is an *athlete*? A *sport*? A *game*? Against what institutions? The criteria applied here are those discussed above on definitions.[8]

6. *Is the quantity measured by the statistics an index of that about which we want knowledge?* What are we attempting to prove when we draw inferences from figures? Does, for example, the number of aircraft in an air force indicate the strength of the aerial arm of defense? The size of a nation's army, the power of that army as a fighting unit?

[7] See pp. 72–73, 169.
[8] See p. 172.

7. Are the data ordered in a series? After the classification is properly done, each class is to be arranged in some array or series. This step is in reality a more detailed classification within each of the original classes. For example, in the illustration above, in which students are classified for purposes of comparison between intercollegiate athletes and other groups, the athletic groups would in turn be arranged in an orderly series to show their grades in general, their grades with respect to a year in the university, with respect to type of athletics engaged in, and with respect to studies pursued.

8. What correlation, if any, exists between two or more series or sets of data thus arrayed? What differences exist in percentages between, for example, the grades of intercollegiate athletes and of students in general? The assumption is that certain events or conditions appear together or are associated with each other. Sometimes the connection is purely accidental and imaginary. Sometimes, however, the association is genuine. Height of a man and weight, maturity and intelligence, favorable environment and health, opportunity for learning and ready skill, and long lists of other paired items have a real relationship. When the phenomena thus vary together, that fact is described as "correlation" between the matched series.

The discussion of statistical methods as given here is suggestive only. You probably are not interested in penetrating into the complexities of those applications of mathematics. Nevertheless, you, as a debater and discussion speaker, will be constantly quoting figures or listening to them. Some knowledge of these principles of statistical procedure, therefore, is helpful. For further insight into such methods you are advised to examine an elementary text in this field.

IV. ARGUMENT FROM CIRCUMSTANTIAL DETAILS

The problem of generalizing from particulars is sometimes not so much that of counting instances or statistical accumulation as it is that of noting accompanying circumstances or details. We attempt to put together isolated items much as we work out a jigsaw puzzle. Typical illustrations are those of methods of detectives in solving crimes and of courtroom trials based on circumstantial evidence. For example, Daniel Webster attempted to show that Joseph White was murdered not by a single person but by several conspirators. Webster called the attention of the jury to the "appearances" in the White home on the morning after the murder. Joseph White was found murdered in his bed. Apparently, no stranger did the deed because no one unacquainted with the house could have carried it out. Webster tried to show that somebody in the house had cooperated with somebody outside. The window, he pointed out, had been opened so that the murderer could enter. A window was unbarred from within, and the fastening was unscrewed. The key to the door of the chamber in which Mr. White slept was gone. Webster noted that the footprints of the murderer were visible outdoors and that they led toward the window; he stressed the fact that a plank remained by which the window had been entered. Webster enumerated similar details; they converged and so established the general proposition that the murder was the result of a conspiracy.

Generalization of this type, or scientific induction, to be valid, requires that the assembled circumstances be sufficient in number to permit the completion of the picture. Moreover, none of the items should lend themselves to an interpretation otherwise than as enabling us to solve the puzzle. Furthermore, the tests of causation, analogy, and authority should support the attempted inference.

To establish the validity of inference from circumstantial detail, then, we apply the same criteria suggested above for inference from specific instances. We need to establish the validity of the facts (Was there a "plank"? Was the window really "unlatched"?) to be sure that a sufficient number of details are presented to warrant the inference; we need to recognize the significance or insignificance of each detail; and we need to apply the tests of causation, analogy, and authority. Especially are we to take account of the relationship of the phenomena under examination to the "implicative whole" or "general system" into which we attempt to fit each detail.

EXERCISES AND PROBLEMS

1. From one of your own written arguments, or from a debate printed in the latest volume of the *University Debater's Annual*, cull out two or three examples of argument by generalization or specific

instance, including the use of statistics. Explain the strength and weakness of the argument by applying the tests of generalization. Be sure to view your examples in the light of the context.

2. Write an argument (maximum 400 words) for delivery before your group or over the local radio station. Incorporate several examples of sound reasoning by generalization.

3. Read an extended argument by one of the older speakers (*e.g.*, Webster, Clay, Calhoun, Lincoln, Douglas, Bryan, Beveridge). Without reproducing passages, you will write a one-page criticism of the speaker's use of argument by generalization.

4. In each of the following cases of alleged reasoning by generalization point out (*a*) whether the example is one of argument by generalization—either fully developed or implied; (*b*) whether, on the basis of your own knowledge and on the basis of the argument as presented, it meets fairly well the tests of valid generalization; (*c*) what, if anything, needs to be done to make more satisfactory the argument by generalization in this case.

(1) "College women are alert to the problems of the times and are well educated concerning current affairs. The Wellesley women, for example, have a chapter of the National Student Association and a well-developed system of student government."

(2) "If you bear the name of Smith, the chances are that you will be a successful person. We have only to cite Alfred Smith, Captain John Smith, Logan Pearsall Smith, Goldwin Smith, Joseph Smith, Sydney Smith."

(3) "The salaries of college teachers are quite adequate. A recent analysis of such salaries shows that the average college teacher receives annually $2,600."

(4) "The new near-miracle of surgery in getting people out of bed the first or second day after operation and so curing them faster was described Tuesday to the American College of Surgeons.

"The speed-up, partly a war development, was told by four physicians—Howard Rusk, New York, N.Y.; I. S. Ravdin, Philadelphia, Penn.; John H. Powers, Cooperstown, N.Y., and Henry H. Kessler, Newark, N.J.

"Dr. Powers told of 238 civilian patients, operated on for appendicitis, hernia and several other abdominal operations. They got out of bed the first or the second day. They were compared with another group, of 120, who stayed in bed 12 days.

"Those who got up left the hospital five days to a week quicker. They required less morphine, and had less gas pains. They ate good meals sooner.

"They had no reduction in post-operative pneumonia, but the danger of blood clots was much reduced.

"Dr. Ravdin told of a Chinese soldier whose heart stopped beating during an operation.

"The surgeon opened the chest and massaged the heart back to life. Eighteen hours later the Chinese soldier walked two miles to a bazaar to buy fruit.

"Dr. Ravdin said that the Chinese have been practicing post-operative ambulation—the technical name for getting out of bed—for a long time."

CHAPTER 11

Argument: Analogy

I. ANALOGY AS COMPARISON OF PARTICULARS

Inference, as I suggested in the previous chapter, often reasons from one instance or particular to another. The logical method is one of comparison, resemblance, or analogy. Here the basis for inference is matching of two individual objects in a given number of points. The inference is that they are in all probability alike in some other respect, known to be true of one, but not authenticated in the case of the other.

Let us illustrate: "The senior students of Brunswick University rank high in the test of literary appreciation and skill as given by the National Foundation for the Advancement of Learning; it is therefore probable that the seniors of Portland University will also rank high in this same test." The comparison is between two universities, about each of which much is known. We have the data to prove that the seniors of Brunswick have given a good account of themselves in literary knowledge. We know nothing of the results of similar testing in the other institution. Before such testing takes place we can only conjecture. We do know, however, that Portland has a senior class population of about the same size and character (with respect to social and economic status and sex distribution) as that of Brunswick. We know, too, that the institutions are similar in other important respects, such as endowment, faculty rating, location, and educational perspective. We, therefore, conclude that the proposed examination as administered at Portland would have results essentially like those reported for the Brunswick seniors. Expressed syllogistically, the pattern or reasoning would be somewhat as follows:

1. The seniors at whatever school is similar to Brunswick University, in numbers, location, endowment, educational outlook, and related items, would possess a high rating in the National Foundation test of literary appreciation and skill.

2. The seniors at Portland University are similar to the seniors of Brunswick University in those factors mentioned in proposition 1 above.

3. The seniors of Portland University, therefore, may be predicted to score as high in the proposed test as did the seniors of Brunswick University.

II. ANALOGY AND IMPLIED GENERALIZATION

Although argument from resemblance concentrates upon specific relationships and its conclusion is a specific one, it nevertheless assumes a general proposition which makes possible the reasoning. The arguer who resorts to analogy really places his concrete items for comparison in a general field or order system. He then assumes that all objects in that field have certain characteristics in common. Thus the development of his argument, if fully examined, would involve first, induction (specific to the general), and second, deduction (general to the specific). In the illustration cited above the reasoning is—all institutions that have conditions essentially like those of Brunswick University would be expected to react similarly when given academic tests. The reasoner, then, accepting and assuming this major proposition, turns again to concrete cases one by one and either accepts or rejects them as belonging to the category thus formulated. In argument from resemblance we merely suppress the full-fledged line of reasoning, implied or taken for granted. Thus:

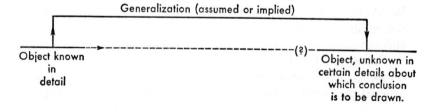

Generalization (assumed or implied)

Object known in detail → - - - - - - - - - - - - - - - - - - -(?)- Object, unknown in certain details about which conclusion is to be drawn.

III. ANALOGY, A COMPARISON OF EITHER OBJECTS OR RELATIONSHIPS

Analogy, I suggested above, may deal with things. "Two things," states John Stuart Mill, "resemble each other in one or more respects; a certain proposition is true of one; therefore it is true of the other."[1] Richard Whately, on the other hand, conceived of analogy as dealing with a "resemblance of ratios," or relationships. "Thus an egg and a seed are not in themselves alike, but bear a like relation to the parent bird and to her future nestling, on the one hand, and to the old and young plant on the other, respectively; this relation being the genus under which they both fall."[2]

A. Analogy of Relations (Mathematical Analogy). The Whately approach is often described as *mathematical analogy.* The resemblance or similarity is between the two relations. Thus, comparisons are made between the captain and his ship and the President of the United States and his country; between the legs of an animal and the four supports of a chair; between the protection to a country afforded by a large standing army and the protection to a city offered by a fire department. Because certain things are involved in one of these relations, it is assumed that the fact of a general similarity carries with it the same things in the other relation. But this concept of analogy is too narrow for actual purposes. Debaters every day, to say nothing of scientists, are using arguments based on a similarity of the objects themselves.

B. Analogy of Things (Logical Analogy). Accordingly, we refer also to *logical analogy,* that which deals with the direct comparisons of objects. In this category is the familiar comparison between the earth and Mars to furnish us with possible conclusions concerning life on that other planet.

C. Literal and Figurative Analogy. Sometimes we distinguish the comparisons between objects in the same field and those in a different class by labeling the first *literal analogy* and the second *figurative analogy.* A comparison between two students,

---

[1] J. S. Mill, *System of Logic* (8th ed.), Book III, Chap. XX, par. 2. Longmans, Green & Co., Inc., 1872.

[2] Richard Whately, *Elements of Rhetoric* (new and rev. ed.), p. 115, Sheldon and Company, 1871.

two universities, two cities would be a *literal* one. When the comparisons are identified with agencies or objects so remotely related as to fall into obviously different order systems, then we view the resemblances as *figurative.* To illustrate, "The present system of declaring war by vote of Congress is sound and strong, like a trestle over which twenty trains have passed." Here Congress is the trestle; the rumbling trains are the declarations of war by Congress. We know—assume—that the trestle has withstood the strain; so do we conclude that Congress—and America —will continue to stand the stress of this method of deciding whether we should declare war—as Congress did on Dec. 8, 1941. Here the comparison is that of a *resemblance of relations,* or figurative analogy.

D. *Comparison and the Principles of Continuous Variation and Similarity.* These comparisons, simple or complex, all follow the law of continuous variation and of continuous similarity. We simply start with familiar and uncomplicated categories and then add wider and wider groupings. Who is to say where one sharply demarks itself from its closely related areas? We simply stop at whatever point suits our purpose. Obvious resemblances we call *literal;* those which are more distant we may refer to as *figurative.*

Thus have been compared the United Nations, war, and leprosy ("It is proposed to give us perpetual peace by tying us up with the United Nations and so engulfing us in every major war; it is like trying to exterminate leprosy by turning the lepers loose in the country and encouraging the mingling of lepers with the general population."); the farmer, the ballot, and a shepherd's crook ("The farmer uses the ballot effectively just as Moses used his shepherd's crook to perform miracles and to free his people."); national defense and a dike ("National armaments keep out invaders just as the Holland dikes keep out the sea— or did so before World War II.").

Most of these remote comparisons provide pleasure rather than logical conviction. They are explanatory, or they have persuasive more than argumentative value. Their function is important in enabling us to break from narrow areas of thinking and application and to explore more distant regions. In any case whether the comparison is of things or relations, literal or figurative, the same criteria of validity should be applied.

How, then, shall we justify as logical reasoning the various forms of analogy?

IV. Tests of Analogical Reasoning

May we now examine in some detail the separate steps of the analogical method and summarize the criteria of logical validity.

A. *Are the Two Objects or Relationships under Comparison Alike in Significant Details?* Just as generalization must be based upon representative or significant cases, or upon details that furnish a consistent picture, so must inference from comparison result from observation of important or significant details of the respective cases.

In 1947 and 1948 many representative Americans argued that the United States and fifty-odd other members of the United Nations should merge into a world government. The analogous case, according to these reasoners, was that of the organization of the American Union from the colonies. Just as in 1775 to 1787 the colonial government emerged into the government of the United States, so the freedom-loving nations of the world could and should get themselves together in a kind of world organization comparable to that which took place on the Atlantic seaboard in 1787. The question involved in this comparison was whether the two historical cases would be parallel in those significant matters having to do with the success or failure of such supergovernment. The factors included education, cultural affinity, common economic and political outlook, power to survive external attack, and a willingness to abandon the traditions of separate nationhood and national sovereignty. It was difficult for many impartial readers and auditors of this proposal for world government to accept the validity of the analogy. Many of the particulars under comparison were significantly different.

When are the points of resemblance basic or significant? Obviously, the likenesses are essential when they are necessary to prove the case at hand. The validity of such tests must, of course, be decided by the particular analogy under consideration.

B. *Are Points of Resemblance Sufficiently Numerous?* And are these points of resemblance significant in relation to the conclusion? Again, as in argument from generalization, account should be taken of the number of the points involved. Certainly in valid analogies resemblances should be reasonably numerous just as is the case with valid generalization. A comparison between the state legislature of Iowa and that of Wisconsin, for example, would yield many important details common to both organizations. To argue, however, that directing the destinies of the United States is similar to navigating a ship may be an illuminating figure; nevertheless, the comparison involves institutions which have practically nothing in common. A logician would be hard put to it to list any number of items common to the Federal government and an ocean liner. Both numbers and representativeness of the items must be considered.

C. *Do Significant Differences Occur?* Just as in any valid generalization full account must be taken of the exceptions, so in establishing an analogy examination must be made of the differences in order to decide whether any of them may be crucial. In a Town Meeting of the Air debate on the question, "Would a union of democracies promote world peace?" one of the speakers, arguing against the proposal, pointed out that Britain or France would not work with the United States in any common government because there were essential differences between these three countries. Said the speaker, "The primary difficulty with the union of democracies, as I see it, is that Britain and France are really not democracies, in our sense, in spite of their Parliaments and Trafalgar Squares. They are Empires first; and whenever the interests of Empires and Democracies clash, Democracy goes down."[3]

D. *Do Tests of Similar Instances Confirm Ordering the Validity of the Comparison?* Still another test that you may apply to argument from analogy is the *test of similar instances and of negative instances.* Your investigation at this point is not so much a scrutiny of the two cases or relations immediately under examination as it is an examination of other related cases. If, for example, you are comparing the legislatures of Iowa and Wisconsin, you might throw further light upon the argument by comparing the Minnesota legislature with that of Wisconsin or Iowa.

E. *Does Examination of the Underlying Generalization Confirm or Deny the Validity of the Analogy?* Inherent in every analogy is the process of generalization. The character of each

[3] *Bulletin of America's Town Meeting of the Air,* "Would a Union of Democracies Save World Peace?" Vol. 4, No. 18, p. 9.

unit under consideration needs full definition and classification. The question before you, therefore, is "Does example, or case A, correspond to the general description you have offered of a field?" You may reason, for instance, that Sinclair Lewis's *Babbitt* is a worth-while novel of contemporary American life. His forthcoming publication, *Kingsblood Royal*, Lewis followers in 1947 reasoned, would, therefore, be a promising book. The reasoning was that the forthcoming book would be like its predecessor. The reasoning from analogy failed on several counts. What was the basis for the generalization that *Babbitt* was a successful novel of contemporary American life? In stating that conclusion, did we take sufficient account of the literary elements of the book, including characterization, dialogue, setting, plot, atmosphere, and similar items that enter into a successful piece of fiction?

In addition to the implied generalization involved in a description of each case or each relationship, we also must recognize that *every comparison is in reality the product of an inference from a particular case to the character of the general field,* from which general proposition we in turn proceed to the other concrete case. To illustrate: In the comparison of the two novels, *Babbitt* and *Kingsblood Royal* the implied generalization apparently was that Sinclair Lewis was an excellent novelist, and therefore whatever he produced would be of high quality. We weighed not only the character of his book *Babbitt* but also the quality of his other fiction as a basis for our assumption that he was a writer of genuine literary skill. *Every case of inference from analogy, therefore, assumes or implies a general statement. This proposition, often assumed without warrant, we should examine as a further check on the analogy.*

F. Does Argument from Causal Relation Confirm or Deny the Validity of the Analogy? Still another criterion of valid analogy is the test of causality. Definite causal relation should exist between the items involved in analogical argument. A general principle or law must be stated and tested. Or a series of propositions must be constructed to show the causal relationship between the terms. In 1945 many observers were arguing that "France was crushed in 1815 and arose again from her defeat; so will she after 1945." Were the conditions soon after 1815 similar to those after 1945? Not only do we attempt to array specific items relating to those respective periods which might justify the comparison, but more significantly we look to the possible causes which might operate in both situations to explain common results.

Argument from analogy is in the ultimate analysis similar to the argument from effect to effect, in which a common cause is sought which explains the coordinate effect. What factors were at work for the revival of the French nation after the fall of Napoleon, factors that continue to operate in these later days? The genius of the French people? The tradition of liberty which no foreign aggressor could stifle? Perhaps the genius of the Frenchman (common cause) that rehabilitated France after 1815 (one effect) would restore that nation again after 1945 (another alleged effect). The readers of this book may judge for themselves the validity of the argument in the light of history after 1945.

G. *Are the Facts on Which the Analogy Is Based Reliable?* Finally, we may ask, are the facts upon which the comparison is based accurate? If we infer that the scholarship of the student population in a given university must be high because that institution won a national football championship, we must be sure that facts underlying this comparison between football performance and scholastic performance are accurate. Is it true that the university under consideration actually won a "national football championship"? If so, how would that splendid result be determined and announced?

Here, as in testing other types of inference, we ask whether the source of the information is competent, free from prejudice, reliable, definite, and supported by other authorities. Such testing will inject into the discussional situation something of an objective attitude and will be a healthy check upon those extended arguments grounded in half-truths or unsubstantiated facts.

V. Strength and Weakness of Analogy

The method of analogy can at best produce only probability. Resemblance in itself is insufficient for satisfactory deduction but must be followed by classification, correlation, and other logical procedures that penetrate fully into the respective divisions that are under comparison. Therefore, many critics treat this type of argument as chiefly explanation rather than as inference.

We need not go so far as to ignore this mode of reasoning. Whether we like it or not, analogy has been employed widely in physics, chemistry, and every other branch of science, including the social sciences. The diagnosis of diseases, historical interpretation, discoveries in chemistry, physics, and astronomy —all have applied with excellent results this comparative method. The debaters, too, are constantly—and with justification—citing analogous cases where a proposal has or has not worked. We should continue to respond to such forms of proof, however, with prudent reference at every point to the requirements of logical validity.

EXERCISES AND PROBLEMS

1. Write an argument (300 words) in some phase of a debate subject on which you are at present working. Feature argument by comparison or analogy.

2. Apply the tests of analogical reasoning to the analogies or comparisons noted by you in a recent Congressional or political debate. Summarize in a page or so your criticism.

3. Comment on the following alleged examples or argument by analogy. (a) Indicate whether such reasoning is used here; (b) give reasons for your opinions; (c) apply the typical tests of such reasoning, and expound at some length each test as it relates to this example; (d) suggest how the analogy might be strengthened to be more acceptable as applied logic.

(1) "Give your daughter music lessons. My girl studied piano for four years and developed much skill."

(2) "Take Mrs. Mercer's Elixir of Wild Root for your arthritis. I have been told that Rudolph Reimer did so and found later that his trouble diminished."

(3) "Why not give complete independence to Puerto Rico as we have given it to Cuba?"

(4) "Baseball is the national game of this country. Why should it not become the national sport of Great Britain?"

(5) "Our University has had a splendid record in intercollegiate debate. We should certainly do as well in athletics."

(6) "Communism apparently works well in Russia. Therefore, should it not succeed equally well in Czechoslovakia?"

(7) "I advise you not to take that history course. I got into it and practically flunked."

(8) "It might have helped Mr. Truman a bit to recall that he was not the first president who found himself with his two strongest cabinet officers seriously at odds at a moment of great international danger. President Washington had to ride out a conflict about American policy in Europe between his secretary of state, who was Jefferson, and his secretary of the treasury, who was Alexander Hamilton. Like Henry Wallace and James Byrnes, they and their followers differed not only about foreign affairs but about internal, and then as in Truman's administration this clash deeply embittered the controversy."

(9) "It is a waste of time to search for the intention of Congress in adopting many laws after 1933 because Congress had no intention. The record throws no more light than might be obtained on a difficult passage in Hamlet by inquiring of Yellow Kid Weil what Shakespeare intended when he wrote it."

(10) "Others may boast larger cars, costlier homes . . . but nobody can smoke a better cigarette!"

(11) "I wish scientists would stop fighting the common cold. The cold is a blessing as it teaches humans to take care of themselves. People are by nature careless and would not protect their bodies from exposure or sudden change in temperature if it were not for the unpleasant effects of a cold. Removing the cold germ would be like removing traffic cops and traffic fines. You could go on pleasantly driving through red lights until the day of the crash."

CHAPTER 12

Argument: Causal Reasoning; Authority

1. Characteristics of Argument from Causal Relation

A. Argument from Causation a Relation between Particulars. A form of reasoning more explicit and fundamental than that of argument from specific instance, authority, or analogy is argument from causal relation. Your problem here is to determine the relationship between two items or phenomena. As in the case of analogy, your thinking concentrates on particulars. But whereas in analogy your conclusion or "leap in the dark" relates to one of these facts or relationships only, in causal relation your inference concerns both factors. You say, "These two elements are related; one affects the other (or they are mutually affective)."

Reasoning from causal relation illustrates clearly our assumptions concerning the consistency and permanence of law. The universe, according to this theory, acts consistently and uniformly. Our experience with nature confirms our early experience; events do not just happen, but rather "certain sequences in events take place over and over again." Lightning is followed by thunder. The warm days of spring are inevitably accompanied by violets in the ravine back of my house. A football, after soaring 40 or 50 yards, falls to the earth. Jet planes, overcoming gravity, rush through space at a speed of 600 miles an hour. Day after day in summer, rain refuses to fall. The inference is that dust storms will come and crops will wither. The government develops a program of strong national defense with universal military training. One deduction is that the United States will plunge into war. Billions of dollars are spent on rehabilitating postwar Europe. One conclusion is that the general price level in the United States will soar (as it did after 1945). The national debt rises and rises. One prediction is that money inflation will inevitably follow. The child of a wealthy businessman suddenly disappears. The inference is that the case is one of kidnaping. The Republican party was defeated in the campaigns of 1932, 1936, 1940, 1944, and 1948. Many Democrats predicted the demise of the Republican party. A certain Senator filibustered against a bill popular in his home state. One deduction was that this Senator would lose his seat in the next election.

B. Argument from Causal Relation a Form of Induction and Deduction. What relation to generalization or induction has inference from causation? The process of causation is partly inductive because the phenomena examined, like those of analogy, are regarded as instances or details or segments of a given area or field. In every case of causal reasoning a generalization is implied. If, for example, the conclusion is drawn from a hot, dry summer that the region may become a dust bowl and that the crops may wither, the conclusion is based upon an implied generalization, namely, that whenever rain fails in Iowa, Nebraska, Oklahoma, or related regions, during June or July, the corn and other crops shrivel, and the warm wind blows up a dust storm. Whenever the children of rich men are carried away, the motive is usually a ransom to the kidnaper.

This generalization becomes a major premise of a syllogism, the conclusion of which is made up of a specific statement, the consequent or effect. For example, (1) All great imperialistic nations have their rise, decline, and fall. (2) The United States is allegedly a great imperialistic nation. (3) The United States is having, or will have, its rise, decline, and fall.

C. Causal Relations as Interaction. For convenience we describe causal relation as existing when a single act or phenomenon acts upon another phenomenon. This activity we describe as occurring in chronological order. One event succeeds another in time, and we have the connection of dates. Causality, however, as a logical concept cannot be explained quite so easily. It is hardly sufficient to say, for example, that sulfanilamide cures pneumonia. It is hardly accurate to say that there is power or energy in the drug itself which somehow released produces the effect of health. The truth is that the action of the drug on the human body cannot be explained merely in terms of that chemical; the change attributed to it as cause must be decided also in part by the condition of the pneumonia victim. Certainly, if an organism of the patient did not react in some reciprocal fashion to the compound, there would be no cure. "Action and reaction are equal and opposite," Newton's third law of motion, conveys somewhat the idea of mutual activity. "Causation, then, is interaction; cause and effect are simultaneous; the effect is not contained in the cause; there is a passive factor."[1]

In addition to this notion of interaction, our concept of time and space renders obsolete the idea that causation is merely a chronological demonstration. According to our later notion of the universe, time and space are united in a four-dimensional world made up of events. Every event is correlated with a unit of time. "In connection with every point is a fourth coordinate or time coordinate." We are familiar with the illustration that when one looks from the window of a moving railroad car, objects in the landscape seem to be moving in the contrary direction. We are reminded that, if we are floating down a stream, we cannot see beyond the bend. If, however, we are in an airplane the boat and the river become a unit. The apparent rest or motion of an object is relative to the rest or motion of the observer. If time is a relative concept, it is only for illustrative purposes that we speak of cause and effect as indicating a temporal relationship.

D. Causation and Continuity of Events. Not only does this later idea of time or duration lead us to question the simple chronological description of sequence, but the notion of *continuity* of events or phenomena also makes it impossible to draw a sharp distinction between cause and effect. Does the murderer's bullet produce death? Between the penetration by the

[1] F. R. Tennant, "Cause," *Encyclopedia of Religion and Ethics*, James Hastings *et al.*, editors, 12 vols., Vol. 3, Charles Scribner's Sons, 1911.

bullet and the ending of life, scientists would mark out many successive events, each one of which might be put forth as the explanation of the result. Every event, according to the philosopher and logician, may be divided and subdivided into a complete system or series of systems. Thus the treatment of cause in its relationship to fact resolves itself into an analysis of continuum or system, or an "inferential whole."

Moreover, both causes and effects are so numerous that it is impossible to describe these relations in terms of sharp separation between single cause and single effect. The diphtheria germ may cause death, but the group of circumstances operating in this case is too complicated for us to describe causes and results in such simple terms. We are really dealing with a system of events, and this system moves within a larger system, the whole making up a vast pattern. We single out one unit and call it a *cause;* another, and call it an *effect*. We need to test carefully these relationships before drawing a hard and fast conclusion.

Argument from causality is usually classified as from cause to effect, from effect to cause, or from effect to effect.

II. TYPES OF CAUSAL REASONING

A. Inference from Cause to Effect. Inference from cause to effect (*a priori* reasoning) draws a conclusion concerning the effect of an observed phenomenon. Such reasoning focuses upon a known fact, event, or phenomenon and argues that it is of such character as to influence another fact, event, or phenomenon.

Here the chronological concept of causation will help us. Argument from known cause to an unknown effect is based upon the examination of a situation which occurs before the alleged fact or phenomenon. Our starting point here consists of an examination of antecedent circumstances, which we set out to prove are sufficient to determine or modify certain circumstances of a later date. We may thus argue from past to a more recent past (Was the Webster-Hayne debate, 1830, the major cause of the Civil War?); from past to present (Was the Civil War a major factor in the present expansion of centralized government in the United States?); from the past to the future (Has the Russian record of expansion in Central Europe and Asia since

1945 resulted in a chain of events that will spell the rise of that nation as the dominant world power?); from the present to the future; or from one future event or circumstance to a more remote event or circumstance (When television becomes widely applied to the United States, will the result be a sharp decline of interest in attendance at motion picture theaters?).

In each case we point to a known situation or group of antecedent circumstances which we attempt to show are sufficient to produce the alleged result of the consequence. The *known cause* in one of the propositions considered above is present-day scientific civilization as illustrated by the radio, airplane, and atomic bomb. The alleged *effect* is the increase in national vulgarity and regimentation through the medium of bad propaganda, and perhaps destruction from the air by invaders.

B. Argument from Effect to Cause. When we focus upon an observed result and attempt to set up possible or probable causes, we reason chronologically from the known facts of the present to the past, or from the past to a more remote past. Certainly, the best illustrations of the difference between reasoning from cause to effect and from effect to cause can be seen in those problems in which we speculate concerning the future. In such case we proceed only from known cause to alleged effect. Examples of the reverse kind of reasoning can be cited from phenomena dealing with the present or with the past.

Causation, as we have stated, is a problem of interaction. Whether we proceed from cause to effect or from effect to cause is merely a question of our point of view. Reasoning from effect to cause is merely to attempt an explanation of certain relationships responsible for certain known or assumed circumstances. Reasoning from effect to cause views the situation from the angle of consequent rather from that of antecedents; we label the process *a posteriori* reasoning (reasoning *from that which comes after*). In 1940, in the face of Hitler's prophecy that England would be invaded "at an early date," the world beheld the British Isles free from direct invasion from across the channel (known effect), and concluded that the activity of the Royal Air Force of England and the might of the British Navy (alleged causes) were mainly responsible for staving off these attacks. The great stock-market crash of 1929 and the attendant depression in the United States (known effect) were explained variously as the outcome of the war of 1917, the "orgies" of uncontrolled capitalism, and the corruption or ineptitude of the Republican party in checking inflation (alleged causes).

C. *Argument from Effect to Effect.* Students of argumentation usually include in their classification of causal reasoning a third form, argument or inference from effect to effect. This mode argues from one effect to another effect of the same cause. The separate "effects" presumably do not directly influence each other, but both are dominated by a common factor or factors— a common cause. To illustrate: "This student was just graduated from college with high scholastic honors; therefore, his life's expectancy is longer than that of the average American." The complete argument assumes that the scholastic honors in college are the result of a degree of freedom from physical and mental strain. The cause thus assumed has another alleged effect—that of keeping its possessor young longer than those not so exempt and of increasing his chances to live to an old age. The presence of one of these phenomena, therefore, is presumably attended by the other.[2]

These illustrations of reasoning from effect to effect may be graphically shown:

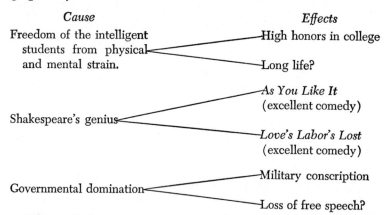

Cause	Effects
Freedom of the intelligent students from physical and mental strain.	High honors in college
	Long life?
Shakespeare's genius	As You Like It (excellent comedy)
	Love's Labor's Lost (excellent comedy)
Governmental domination	Military conscription
	Loss of free speech?

[2] This particular argument, is open to obvious question. A survey by the Metropolitan Life Insurance Company, under the direction of Dr. Dublin, showed that college honor men (whose lives were marked by moderation) exhibited "an extraordinary longevity"—three and a half years better than carefully insured lives. Whether any individual might conform to the statistical average is, of course, questionable.

Consider this example: "Any nation that adopts a permanent system of military conscription will lose both its liberty and its will-for-peace." One effect (the adoption of a permanent system of military conscription) is, according to the argument, due to an effort of the government to have complete control over the political, economic, and military life of the nation. This same cause (that is, governmental domination) will allegedly lead to the abandonment of free speech, free press, and other civil rights.

III. The Tests of Causal Reasoning

The validity of reasoning from cause to effect, from effect to cause, from effect to effect is determined by answering specific questions concerning the character of the alleged connection between antecedent and consequent: (1) Can a causal relation be established? (2) Is the alleged cause adequate to produce the alleged effect? (3) Is the result the product of a sole cause or of a plurality of causes? (4) Are other causes operating to prevent the known or alleged causes from producing the known or alleged effects? (5) Have the alleged facts been verified?

1. Can a causal relation be established? The causal connection, apparently assumed as present, often disappears under close analysis. Phenomena, for example, may be associated only by chance. Coincidences are often seized upon as explaining cause or effect. "Light three cigarettes from a single match, and you will have bad luck" and similar superstitions are cases in point. Reasoners often associate events in some causal connection merely because incidents take place at the same time or because they immediately succeed each other. Droughts, earthquakes, and even political parties in power have been connected in some mysterious fashion simply because these phenomena and institutions function simultaneously. The Volstead Prohibition Law operated in the United States during 1919 to 1934. Divorces per capita increased in the United States during this time. Was any causal relation between these two sets of facts discernible? Probably not. On the other hand, bank accounts increased during that time, and more telephones were in use. Those who tried to prove desirable results of prohibition sometimes argued that the law favorably affected the bank accounts and even increased the number of telephones. The starting point, then, is to be sure that the factors are causally connected.

2. *Is the known cause adequate to produce the alleged effect; or is the alleged cause adequate to produce the known effect?* This second test leads us to examine the complexity of phenomena and the multiplicity or plurality of causes. Often a given phenomenon may operate but without sufficient energy (to use the physical analogy) to become a controlling cause. For example, physical environment is alleged to be the cause of poverty (the observed result). But is that cause adequate to produce the outcome in the specific case before us? Too many examples may be cited of men and women who have risen above an unfavorable economic environment. If physical environment is the explanation, what shall we say of degeneracy, disease, intemperance, desertion, old age, indolence, and other factors that contribute to poverty? Obviously, when we begin to analyze events and conditions that explain riches, poverty, health, attitudes, choice of companions, and a hundred other social matters, we need to avoid oversimplifications of the forces at work and the overemphasis upon the influence of *one* cause.

In World War II it was alleged at the time of the French military debacle that the French army at Sedan and on the Somme collapsed because the German invaders used some mysterious weapon said to paralyze the opposing forces and literally to "freeze the French soldiers in their tracks." History, however, failed to confirm the use of a weapon or agency of this kind. On the contrary, the German White Book and French official reports together with subsequent testimony made it clear that real factors at work in the destruction or surrender of the two million Frenchmen, and the downfall of the 500 million dollar Maginot Line included (*a*) lack of French preparedness, especially in tanks and airplanes; (*b*) lack of "the will to fight"; (3) corruption in the French army and in civilian life; and (4) the activities of the "fifth column." Was any one of these antecedents adequate to produce the alleged consequent? A reasonable and systematic analysis of this historical instance would lead us to give full weight to the multiplicity of causes and to discount the dominant influence of a single factor.

3. *Are other causes operating to prevent the alleged cause from producing the effect?* Our problem, again, is that of sepa-

rating one cause from many and of eliminating all others as possible factors in determining the result. Let us grant that general prosperity in the United States produced a rise in the stock market. Certainly a causal connection between such prosperity and a rising market is easy to establish. But countercurrents may be effectively at work, such as the activities of the Federal Reserve Board, presidential or other influential statements designed to halt a rising trend. It was argued that England would starve Germany in 1940 through an economic blockade. Critics of this prediction pointed out, however, that other factors were at work to neutralize the effect of such naval imprisonment of the Nazis. Subsequent events verified the critics. It was pointed out that Germany had really been at war since 1935 and that that nation had been preparing against such starvation. It was further indicated that Germany had such complete control over its own people that, if necessary, the followers of Hitler would face starvation without revolt. It was also pointed out that the followers of Hitler for a long period of years had been saving up materials and had relatively more reserves in 1940 than they had in 1914. It was further observed that, in spite of the blockade, goods were coming into Germany through Spain, Russia, Turkey, and other neutral sources. Russia and the Balkans, for example, were open to German commerce whereas in 1914 and 1917, or during part of that period, these avenues were closed to the Teutons. Thus at the outset of the war a situation which threatened to strangle Germany was largely defeated by a combination of events and conditions hardly foreseen by many pro-British prophets. The factors at work in 1914 to 1917 were largely negative in the events in Germany in 1939 to 1945. We need caution in asserting that "history repeats itself."

4. *Does the argument from causal relation meet the test of valid scientific induction?* Reasoning, as we suggested in a previous chapter, is a process of ordering a set of circumstances and grouping them in a given system. Each event or circumstance fits into its part in the general pattern. A recent illustration of how this method works is illustrated in the discovery of the planet Pluto. Astronomers noted that the gravitational pull of Neptune was found to be inadequate in explaining the aberrations of Uranus. It was later noted that both Neptune and

Uranus were moving irregularly in their orbit and that another undiscovered planet more distant than Neptune must be the explanation. Dr. Percival Lowell computed the orbit in which the hypothetical new planet should move and named it "planet X." Finally, the astronomers of Flagstaff Observatory in 1930 announced to the world the discovery of Pluto. Thus did these investigators of the solar system place together their fragments of knowledge to complete the puzzle by adding the ninth planet. Thus can we, in relations of social and political experience, summon the "circumstantial evidence," the "attendant circumstances," to describe an "implicative system" in such a way as to confirm the causal agencies at work.

5. *Have the alleged facts been verified?* Finally, as in the testing of generalization and analogy, the accuracy of the facts in causal reasoning must be checked. In the discovery of Pluto, the first task of an investigator was to verify the irregularities in Uranus and Neptune. Upon the character of the evidence— the exact nature of the facts under observation—will hinge the nature of the causal inference.

IV. ARGUMENT FROM AUTHORITY

A. *The Method in General.* Many inferences are based upon direct reference to facts established by authority. The assertion is made that life is immortal. The reason for the assertion is advanced: "Dr. Arthur H. Compton, Nobel prize winner in physics, holds that biologically speaking, life is essentially immortal. The apple may decay, but the seed grows into a new tree, which flowers and begets new seed. It is because we concentrate our attention upon the tree that we say the end of life is death. Life, whether it be of an apple seed or the germ cells of man, is essentially continuous and eternal."[3] Here the induction is made that because one authority testifies about a circumstance, that testimony justifies the generalization. The inference is based upon the assumption that whatever the authority, in this case Dr. Compton, says about a specific matter is true. Expressed in complete form, this argument would read:
1. Life is essentially immortal, for
   a. Dr. Arthur H. Compton so states, and

[3] H. Gordon Garbedeian, *Major Mysteries of Science*, p. 60, Garden City Publishing Company, Inc., 1933.

b. Dr. Compton's statements are to be accepted as true.

B. *Tests of Argument from Authority* (*Tests of Inference from Authority*). The tests applied here are those discussed in connection with direct evidence: (1) Is the authority competent? (2) Is the authority prejudiced? (3) Is the authority reliable? (4) Is the authority definite? (5) Is the authority supported by other sources? (6) Is the authority supported by argument from specific instances, causal relation, and analogy?

Let us apply these tests to typical cases. Is Dr. Compton competent to express an opinion on immortality? (For his general competence, including training, see *Who's Who in America.*) Is he prejudiced? Reliable? Definite? (See the source of this quotation.) Is he supported by other authorities? Is he supported by argument from causation? Why should life be essentially immortal? Is it not that we are talking about the body or hull that surrounds the living germ? Or is it the mental and emotional processes to which we refer in describing immortality? What, scientifically speaking, are some of the conditions which make for life without end? Can we condition life and growth, for example by gaining control of electrical charges? What are the chances, if any, that man may gain power to supply new electric charges to dying cells or dying bodies in order to perpetuate their life?

Compare Dr. Compton's argument with those of Dr. Fisk and Dr. Dublin. "The cycle of human life may be extended indefinitely," states Dr. Eugene Lyman Fisk, Director of the Life Extension Institute. "That there is a limit to the period of life a man may enjoy and that the idea of time having an effect on aging and decaying is as baseless as the jargon of a Hoodoo savage."[4] On the other hand, it is contended that the prediction of a span of life longer than eighty years is vain. Dr. Lewis I. Dublin, of the Metropolitan Life Insurance Company, testified that, "Nothing has happened to encourage the hope that the span of human life may be extended."[5]

Are these authorities quoted above competent in their fields of statistics? Are their statements the highest form of scientific judgment? What research experience lies back of these statements? Does Dr. Fisk overstate the case in the statement

[4] *Ibid.*, p. 80.
[5] *Ibid.*, p. 82.

quoted above? What reasons may be advanced for believing that the span of human life may extend beyond seventy years in the next decade? To what extent can we create an environment more favorable to longevity? To what extent may we improve in the direction of "race hygiene?" Thus our testing of argument from authority will lead us (1) to survey in detail the fitness of the witness to testify and (2) to analyze the logic of his statements. Testing of inference from authority, like the weighing of arguments from analogy and generalization, becomes a matter of tracing cause and effect and of scientific verification of ex-cathedra remarks.

EXERCISES AND PROBLEMS

1. Explain each: (*a*) Argument from causation is a relation between particulars. (*b*) Argument from causal relation is a form of induction and deduction. (*c*) Argument from causal relation is a demonstration of interaction.

2. Illustrate the difference between argument from cause to effect, argument from effect to cause, and argument from effect to effect.

3. Comment on the following examples of alleged argument from causal relation: (*a*) Indicate whether the example is one from causal relation. (*b*) Give reasons for your opinion. (*c*) If causal reasoning, identify the exact type. (*d*) Apply the typical tests of such reasoning. (*e*) Suggest how the reasoning might be made sound (if it is weak or unsound).

(1) "Our family of six rode out the 1918–19 flu epidemic with nary a sniffle—due, my mother still believes, to her wisdom in making for each neck a little bag of asafetida. Fact is, down our way those who wore asafetida bags buried those who didn't."

(2) "Soviet Russia, in attempting to dragoon Norway into surrendering Spitzbergen and Bear Island for use as military bases, has made clear that it proposes in good season to attack the United States. The Arctic bases which the Russians demand are capable of being used for rocket and long range bomber attack upon American cities."

(3) "A blanket so heavenly-soft, so snugly warm, so feather-light, you'll never want to leave it!"

(4) "General Marshall looks at universal military training as a means of providing training in all the techniques of warfare. He says, in effect, that it is even more seriously needed than ever before in our history for two reasons: (*a*) because warfare has become so much more complicated and therefore requires longer to learn and (*b*) be-

cause we will never again have as much time as we have had during the first two world wars to get ready for decisive action."

(5) "The worst depression on record immediately followed the attempt to boost the American standard of living by enacting the highest tariff schedules on record (the Smoot-Hawley bill).   Since then under the Trade Agreements Act these subsidies and barriers have been reduced 30 per cent—and (a) no industry can show that it has been damaged and (b) the standard of living, and our export trade, have increased prodigiously."

(6) "The only certain defense against the long-range offensive weapons of the next war—whether they be atomic, bacteriological, chemical, or of some other type—may be the capture of the launching sites and productive facilities of the enemy.   Likewise, an aerial or stratospheric surprise assault against the United States might well be followed quickly by an invasion."

(7) "The United States is in a strongly advantageous position with respect to atomic bombs.   The first Russian bomb explosion occurred in the summer of 1949, four years after our first atomic bomb explosion on July 16, 1945."

CHAPTER 13

Argument: Deduction

I. Assumption and Hypothesis in Argument

If you examine almost any argument, spoken or written, you will notice that it is developed deductively. The speaker or writer states certain ideas, illustrates them in detail, and draws conclusions. The usual advice of teachers of communication is to organize the speech deductively. They suggest that you proceed with an introduction including a statement of your thesis; a main body in which propositions and subpropositions are in turn unfolded; and finally a conclusion or summary and further enforcement of the ideas. This conventional order of treatment is, I suppose, followed chiefly for clarity. Listeners more readily grasp what you are driving at if you tell them what you intend to do, if you remind them that you are doing it, and if you advise them finally what you have done.

In discussion, too, the deductive framework is closely followed. It consists of a (1) statement of the problem, (2) outlining of goals to be followed in any solution, (3) statement and examination of the representative solutions, and (4) further examination and verification of the preferred solution.

For persuasive purposes, it is often preferable to begin the speech with concrete details and point the way to general conclusions. Thus did Thomas Huxley lecture on "A Piece of

Chalk." He focused the attention of his Norwich, England, audience first on the chalk itself; then on the English cliffs from which it came; then on ancient sea bottom and the forms of ancient life evidenced in the deposits; and finally on the general principle and method of evolution. Not so often do we follow this commendable inductive method. Rightly or wrongly, we usually adhere to a deductive method of development.

What is this deductive pattern? It is a series of assumptions, opinions stated and not proved but rather taken for granted, and of general propositions that are concretely illustrated or proved.

For example, Winston Churchill, at Fulton, Missouri, on Mar. 6, 1946, proceeded on the assumption, which he stated but did not amplify, that "The security, safety and welfare, progress and freedom of all peoples will depend upon the destruction of war and tyranny."

Sometimes, as in discussional situations, we label these assumptions *hypotheses*. How does a hypothesis differ from an assumption? The hypothesis is a preliminary suggestion at a solution, to be verified by appropriate reasoning and fact. It is a proposition that the scientist may use for assembling his data and for securing a fruitful result of his observation and analysis. For hundreds of years the Ptolemaic theory or hypothesis of planetary motions prevailed until the more plausible Copernican theory succeeded. The hypothesis is identical with the tentative conclusion that the student of discussion or debate sets up to prove or disprove. For example, the problem is, What shall we do to increase the production of coal in the United States and at the same time guarantee the workers maximum wages and satisfactory living conditions and the public maximum fuel at satisfactory cost? Tentative solutions (hypotheses) would be (1) Federal regulation of the coal mines, (2) government ownership and operation of the mines, (3) continuation of programs of labor laws, NLRB, temporary coal commissions, and similar policies.

II. CHAINS OF REASONING IN ARGUMENT

Many arguments are complex, made up of a series of abbreviated syllogisms or elliptical arguments. The conclusion of one syllogism becomes a premise for the next one, so that the result is a chain of reasoning. The problem is to organize the assertions into full syllogisms and to test each one separately. These chains, and the syllogisms into which they are converted, may be categorical, disjunctive, or hypothetical.

To illustrate, a speaker develops his ideas in the following sequence: (1) Only if we preserve our democratic system will the United States government survive. (2) Only if we preserve free expression of opinion will we preserve the democratic system. (3) Only if we have adequate public discussion and debate will the free expression of public opinion be preserved. (4) Only if we provide adequate training in discussion will we have adequate public discussion and debate. (5) Only if we have capable teachers of discussion in schools and colleges, will we have adequate training in discussion and debate. Therefore, connecting (5) and (1), only if we have capable teachers of public discussion and debate in schools and colleges, will the United States government survive.

You will find interest and profit in casting these statements into syllogistic form and testing each one, both in terms of meaning and of logic. Probably no chain of reasoning, stated in these severe, unqualified forms, is sound. Qualified by the language of probability (in the chain above, substitute "usually" for "only") and presented to the audience in this consecutive fashion, such chains of reasoning may please the listeners and satisfy their sense of orderliness and logic.

III. DEDUCTIVE REASONING AND THE SYLLOGISM

How shall we test these assumptions and hypotheses and these broad sweeps made up of chains of reasoning? The logicians reduce many of these patterns to the syllogism, a series of three propositions so related that the third constitutes a deduction from the first two.

For example:

(*Middle term*)

Major premise   1. Whatever program for dealing with the coal problem in the United States will best serve the interests of the American people
(*Major term*)
should be adopted.
(*Minor term*)

Minor premise   2. Government ownership and operation of the
                          (*Middle term*)
                        coal industry   would be for the best
                        interests of the American people.
                                (*Minor term*)
Conclusion   3. Government ownership and operation of the
                          (*Major term*)
                        coal industry   should be adopted.

This categorical syllogism of the "first figure" contains three propositions and three terms. They are arranged as follows:
  Middle-major
  Minor-middle
  Minor-major

IV. DEDUCTIVE REASONING IN PRACTICE: THE ENTHYMEME

A. Enthymeme. Arguments are seldom stated fully. One premise at least is usually taken for granted or may be considered too obvious for statement as a formal proposition. Both in speechmaking and in writing, syllogistic argument emerges from the midst of a series of details, bits of evidence, citation of cases, and from a setting which is designed to illuminate as well as convince. A speaker, including the discussion leader, assumes that listeners can usually supply missing propositions and premises. If the techniques of formal logic were followed, speechmaking and writing would become a humorous or dull recital of syllogistic premises and conclusions.

When a premise or conclusion is absent from an argument, we call the telescoped syllogism an *enthymeme*. For example, a speaker declares: "Trade wars between the Latin-American countries threaten dissension, and should therefore be suppressed." Another replies, "Whatever nation has a corner on the world's gold will be dominant in world affairs, and the United States has that gold." And a third concludes: "Whatever program we adopt to purchase the Western Hemisphere surpluses, will surely benefit the American farmer; and therefore we need to cooperate with Latin America." These speakers may not know or care whether their statements are enthymemes. If we choose, however, we may expand each proposition into a full-fledged syllogism for purposes of further survey of the logic.

Enthymemes are of the first, second, or third order, according to whether the major premise, the minor premise, or the conclusion is absent.

These enthymemes can easily be converted into a categorical syllogism of the "first figure" for purposes of testing. The first step is to put down the conclusion. It is usually obvious, even if absent. If present, the conclusion is usually introduced by such expressions as "therefore," or "for." This conclusion has for its predicate the major term; for its subject, the minor term. Each term is then placed in its appropriate premise. The minor term is the subject of the minor premise; the major term is the predicate of the major premise. The middle term may be supplied from the context. To illustrate, let us convert the statement, "The United States will go bankrupt, for it is headed toward a debt of more than 500 billion dollars." First, we place as the conclusion, "The United States will go bankrupt." Next we place "The United States" as the subject of the minor premise and "will go bankrupt" as the major term, in the predicate position in the major premise. Thus we have the terms as follows:

"will go bankrupt"

"The United States"

"The United States will go bankrupt."

"Has a national debt of more than 500 billion dollars will go bankrupt" becomes the middle term. Stated as a universal (an inclusive statement) we have the completed major premise, "Whatever nation has a national debt of more than 500 billion dollars is headed for bankruptcy"; and the completed minor premise, "The United States is such a nation." (In the major premise above, "probably" or equivalent language should be inserted.)

V. Types of Syllogisms

Syllogistic inferences are usually classed as (1) categorical and (2) conditional. The latter form in turn is made up of disjunctive and hypothetical types. Each type differs from the other by the character of the major premise or initial proposition. Note the syntax of the major premise in each case as a clue to the type.

A. *The Categorical Syllogism.* The categorical type has for its major proposition an unqualified or categorical assertion. Such proposition defines, classifies, or asserts without qualification, such as "America is a democratic country" (classification); "Democracy is a form of government in which people rule" (definition).

B. The Disjunctive Syllogism. The disjunctive construction has for its major proposition one in which alternative possibilities are stated. Symbol of such syllogism is "either . . . or." Examples of such disjunctive statements are "Either we will establish international control of the atomic bomb or our Western civilization will perish"; "Either we should own and operate the railroads of the United States or we should regulate them more efficiently"; "We should either suppress the labor unions or license them under Federal law."

C. The Hypothetical Syllogism. The hypothetical syllogism has for its initial statement a statement in which the chief assertion is a condition. The symbol of such a proposition is "if." The sentence is a complex one, in which the dependent clause, preceding the main one, expresses the condition. The conditional clause is the *antecedent;* the main clause, the *consequent.* To illustrate: (1) If the United Nations controls the atomic bomb (antecedent), we shall escape destruction (consequent). (2) If we were able to unite the entire transportation system of the United States under a single highly regulated agency (antecedent), the cost of living in this country would be reduced (consequent).

VI. Tests of Syllogistic Reasoning

What constitutes valid inference through syllogistic construction? Formal logic sets up exact tests for establishing the validity of a syllogism. In general these tests aim to examine the consistency and structure of the reasoning rather than its validity as measured by evidential and inductive tests. Our purpose, *as students of discussion and debate, requires that we scrutinize syllogisms (or enthymemes, chains of reasoning), not so much as severe and isolated samples of logic, but as living expressions of opinion and reasoning on the controversial problems of our world.*

Debaters and discussants interested in understanding the nature of syllogistic reasoning and false reasoning resulting from violation of the rules should review an elementary text on logic and enroll in a course in that field.

The debater, casting his thinking or that of others into these referential forms of deduction for testing, should ask, (1) Are the propositions arranged in acceptable form? (A hypothetical syllogism should conform to the organizational pattern for that type.) (2) Are the terms used free from ambiguity and vagueness, and are they definite, clear, and accurate? (3) Is the major proposition or premise logically and factually satisfactory? Is it, for example, free from all-inclusive terms, such as *all* or *every*? (4) Is the minor premise or proposition also clearly established through tests of evidence and argument? (5) Does the conclusion follow logically from the preceding statements? And does independent examination by evidence and argument confirm its validity?

VII. APPLICATION OF SYLLOGISTIC ARGUMENT TO DISCUSSION AND DEBATE

What practical applications, then, shall we make of deduction, as framed in syllogistic forms, to argumentation, discussion, and debate? The syllogism, as a pure demonstration of logical formula, is of doubtful value to students of discussion. Formal logic apparently assumes that the premises are "either true or false." The syllogistic methodology puts down conditions under which the conclusion inevitably follows. The assumption is that of *"absolute truth and certainty."* Argument, on the contrary, concerns itself with the *probability* of a given proposition. Your attitude is that of a pragmatist. That is, you propose continual reference to experience, to a continual reshaping of premises that you and your fellow discussants have framed, and to a continual testing of your hypothesis. Your goal is the continual verification of certain propositions or suggested conclusions rather than the logical pursuit of inferences categorically set up at the outset.

Furthermore, you are concerned with a universe that is an organic unity rather than a series of separate structures. Syllogisms and formal logic imply that ideas can be neatly compartmentalized. But terms and items with which we grapple merge with each other in a continuous pattern. We apply the principle of continuous variation to such concepts and so reject the rigid classifications imposed by proponents of strict syllogistic procedure. Our propositions are of the complex fabric of human experience. Each argument lies in a network of surrounding circumstances. The specific argument is to be viewed in this complicated background.[1]

If you will grant the restrictions as here indicated and if you will regard deduction as the expression of a framework into which a given argument normally falls, you may use with great profit the syllogistic patterns. They will serve as a check on your thinking and as a guide to the clarification and simplification of your meanings.

What then is the conclusion?

1. Much of your argumentative speaking and writing and that of others will be deductive. Therefore you will need to examine it logically.

2. You should frequently reduce the reasoning to syllogistic form to test its validity and to clarify the thinking.

3. These syllogistic forms are to be applied practicably and are not to be treated merely as abstract exercises in "logic chopping."

4. You will avoid the fallacy of *allness* in your use of syllogisms. You will use *some* or equivalent qualifying term in the so-called categorical statements.

5. You will examine each statement in the light of the context and attendant circumstances.

6. You will apply to each premise the unlimited use of scientific and inductive techniques.

7. You will verify all facts stated or implied in the inferences.

8. You will test the *either-or* statements by the principles of division and classification.

9. You will test the *if-then* statements by the requirements of logical reasoning from causation.

10. You will apply the principle of *probability* rather than of *absolute certainty* to each proposition.

11. You will apply the principle of *continuous variation* to the terms and propositions.

12. You will examine each term according to the requirements of satisfactory definition.

[1] The statements above are condensed from A. Craig Baird, *Discussion: Principles and Types,* p. 166, McGraw-Hill Book Company, Inc., 1943.

With such an approach to syllogistic reasoning and deduction in general, you will find these forms a genuine aid in preventing or revealing superficial thinking.

EXERCISES AND PROBLEMS

1. What is distinctive in each of the following: (a) assumption, (b) hypothesis, (c) premise, (d) theory?

2. List the asumptions you would make in arguing in favor of, or in opposition to, government ownership and operation of the basic industries of the United States.

3. Develop a chain of reasoning on some recent subject you have recently debated or discussed. Follow somewhat the method suggested in Section II of this chapter.

4. Frame an example of the categorical syllogism; of the hypothetical syllogism; of the disjunctive syllogism.

5. Convert into a series of syllogisms two or three representative arguments of one of your recent debates. Test the validity of these syllogisms.

6. Write two short speeches (each 200 words) embodying the same subject matter, one developed inductively, the other, deductively, on one of the following topic statements:

a. The American citizens should (or should not) endorse the principles of the Socialist party.

b. Congress should enact legislation sharply curtailing installment buying.

7. Explain the validity (or invalidity) of the following arguments (cast into syllogistic form if the example is not already so constructed):

a. In the last war we made the mistake of disarming unilaterally. We should not make that mistake again.

b. If the United Nations repeals the veto powers of the Security Council, that organization will have more permanency. Such repeal offers little prospect of enactment.

c. Either we must support Great Britain to the hilt, or we will be unprepared for the next war. Therefore, let us effect a close military alliance with that nation.

d. A nation cannot exist divided. This nation is now much divided —with Republicans and Democrats ranged against each other. Therefore, this nation cannot endure.

e. Democracy is based upon the belief that the individual comes first. I am an individual. Therefore, I come first.

f. The representatives at Washington should each vote as inde-

pendents. Mr. Thomas is a representative at Washington. Therefore, he should vote as an Independent.

g. The American press is free. The *Daily Iowan* is one of the
American press. Therefore, the *Daily Iowan* is free.

h. You should join the greatest body of parliamentary workers anywhere in the world. The Congress of Industrial Workers is the greatest parliamentary body of workers anywhere in the world. Therefore,
you should join the Congress of Industrial Workers.

i. We should adopt a program of peace at any price. Surrender to
the Russian Communists represents peace at any price. Therefore,
we should surrender to the Russian Communists.

8. Reduce the first affirmative (or other) speech in a recent number of the *University Debater's Annual* to a series of deductive statements (perhaps couched in syllogistic form). Comment on the validity of the deductive reasoning.

CHAPTER 14

Obstacles to Straight Thinking

I. Importance of Straight Thinking in Argumentation, Discussion, and Debate

Argumentation, discussion, and debate, as we have repeatedly reminded you, are primarily demonstrations of straight thinking. Discussants, especially, are supposed to think in an atmosphere free from prejudice and therefore are less likely to exhibit illogicality. Whether or not in practice these discussants fare comparatively well, we are agreed that debate and persuasive speaking and writing, by their very purpose of introducing persuasive elements, encourage fallacious tendencies. The round-table or panel participants, in theory at least, calmly unearth each other's loose thinking and mutually try to build up their sound foundations. Debaters need to be especially careful of their own performance, for the other side has ample opportunity to expose weaknesses of their adversaries. Whatever your motives for sound reasoning, you will be continuously alert to the pitfalls at every turn.

What are they? They are stumbling blocks of language, definitions, facts, analysis of the subject, statement of hypotheses, arguments from generalization, analogy, causation, and deduction.

Why these violations? Sometimes misguided debaters or "shyster" politicians resort to stratagems and deliberate twisting of facts.   Their ways are the Hitlerian ways of spreading confusion by vicious propaganda.   The educational philosophy of students of argumentation rejects all sharp practices designed to confuse other speakers or writers or to gain an unfair advantage with a judge in a debate contest.

Why then our weaknesses?   Partly because we lack adequate information on the subject; or because we are unfamiliar with the logical principles called for in applying those facts; or because our own prejudices lead to rationalization rather than to clear reasoning; or because we have a streak of gullibility and swallow as "gospel truth" others' assertions.

II. Classification of Fallacies

Any complete classification of fallacies is probably impossible. The errors of the mind are so numerous and so unpredictable as often to leave us in the dark as to how the illogicality actually occurs.   The logician De Morgan concludes, "There is no such thing as a classification of the ways in which men may arrive at error: it is much to be doubted whether there ever can be."[1] For practical purposes of argument the following representative group classification is offered.   I propose to explain briefly each example and to suggest ways of correcting it.

I. Misuse of definitions
   A. Lack of definitions
   B. Vague definitions
   C. Inaccurate or equivocal definitions
II. Misuse of language
   A. Abstract language
   B. Verbalisms
   C. Emotional meanings
   D. Loose grammar and syntax
   E. Illogical parallel structure
   F. Excessive coordination of ideas
   G. The fallacious or complex question
III. False division, statement of issues, and partition
   A. Suppression of important issues (partial division)
   B. Cross division
   C. Stressing a minor issue
IV. False use of facts (evidence)
   A. Unsupported assertion

[1] A. De Morgan, *Formal Logic*, p. 237, Taylor and Walton, 1847.

    B. Inaccuracy of facts
    C. Inconsistency of facts
    D. Partial evidence
    E. Ambiguity in statement of facts
    F. Incompetency of authorities
  V. False argument from generalization
    A. Insufficient number of cases
    B. Instances not typical
    C. Ignoring negative instances
    D. Inaccuracy of instances cited
    E. Faulty causal connections
  VI. False arguments from statistics
 VII. False argument from analogy
    A. Too few resemblances
    B. Comparison based on insignificant particulars
    C. Ignoring important differences
    D. Lack of causal connection
    E. Inaccuracy of facts
VIII. False argument from causal relation
    A. Assumed connection between phenomena
    B. Assumed connection between phenomena and antecedent
    C. Inadequate cause assumed to be a sufficient cause
    D. Ignoring of counteracting causes
    E. Inaccuracy of facts
  IX. False argument from authority
  X. False reasoning from general propositions
    A. Faulty construction of syllogistic forms
    B. False reasoning through vague or ambiguous phrasing of the proposition
    C. False assumptions in the major propositions or premises
    D. Misstatement of facts in the major or minor premises and conclusions
    E. Begging the question
      1. Arguing in a circle
      2. Assuming a more general truth which involves the point at issue
      3. Assuming that what is true of the whole is true of each unit
  XI. False argument from ignoring the question
    A. Slanted or emotionalized language
    B. Substitution of irrelevant argument
    C. Repeated affirmation
    D. Substitution of questions for argument
    E. Invective or name calling
    F. Vindication of self and colleagues (prestige appeal)

G. Eulogy of the people
H. Substitution of authority for argument
I. Appeal to humor, sympathy, fear
J. Appeal to tradition and custom
K. Appeal to ignorance of the opposite side

III. Misuse of Definitions

How do arguers err in the use of definitions? (1) Needed definitions are not given; (2) even when they are inserted, they may be vague; (3) or they may be ambiguous or equivocal or fail to take account of the context.

A. Lack of Definitions. Initial fallacies occur in these failures of clear interpretation. The confusion continues throughout the argument.

B. Vague Definitions. Even when explanations do occur, they are often vague or abstract. To define a Republican as "one who supports the principle of free government," as a speaker did at a recent National Republican Convention, contributes nothing to the clearness of the thinking. Similarly, in a discussion of "How can we put the unemployed to work?" the "unemployed" were defined merely as "those who want work and cannot find it." The "out-of-workers" cannot be so easily classified.

C. Inaccurate or Equivocal Definitions. Hardly more satisfactory are those definitions that are specific and yet are inaccurate. Equivocation is often used as identical with ambiguous construction, discussed below; but the latter fallacy is reserved for those cases growing out of syntax or grammar. To illustrate: "A democrat is a person who hates kings and believes in the rule of the people; therefore vote for Jones, a good Democrat." A "democrat" is obviously used in a different sense from a "Democrat."

To avoid these fallacies of definition you will examine every term, confer with other discussants and especially those who have a different approach than your own and thus clarify whatever needs explanation. In so doing, you will follow the principle and procedures for correct definition.[2]

IV. Misuse of Language

Aside from the problem of accurate definition is that of semantic accuracy in general. Words should tell us precisely what

[2] See Chap. 5.

they mean. Negatively, they should avoid confusing our reasoning. Fallacies of language appear, and terms are vague when the language is technical or emotionally freighted; when the argument is cluttered up with verbosities or jargon; when slang or pedantry impedes the clarity of thought. I have in mind here language in written argument as well as in discussion and debate.

A. *Abstract Language.* Abstraction, particularly, because it becomes an easy substitute for concrete information, is the bane of discussion as well as of other controversial speaking. A debate on "Shall the United States further centralize the powers of government?" gave over the session to the consideration of the subquestion, "Are there factors of sufficient emergency to warrant the adoption of a program of further concentration of Federal powers?" In the first thirty minutes the following terms were bandied about, each unchallenged and each undefined: *social control, individualism, New Dealism, monopolistic industry, liberalism, regimentation, propaganda, social change, agricultural surplus, Americanism, civil liberties, consumer power, social unity, the American way of life, dictatorial control, industrial democracy, resistance to,* and *invasion.* I do not suggest that each word uttered should invite the vocal response, "What do you mean by that term?" But in the case cited (a typical one, I believe), the panel group of six apparently committed themselves through their silence to various ideas which later in the discussion they apparently repudiated.

B. *Verbalisms.* Like the use of abstract terms, including these with ambiguous or equivocal meanings, is the tendency of some speakers and writers to be guilty of "verbalism," the substitution of language for thinking or the undue use of language, or to resort to technical vocabulary. Great thinkers, like John Dewey, often write or speak in abstractions so that occasionally we need a translator of the academic or technical vocabulary.

Some speakers are like Mr. Pecksniff in Dickens's *Martin Chuzzlewit,* who "was in the frequent habit of using any word that occurred to him as having a good sound and rounding a sentence well, without much care to its meaning."

C. *Emotional Meanings.* The fault of technical, profound or repetitious language, however, is minor compared with that of resorting to emotional meanings. We may, for example, describe objectively the party of former President Franklin Roosevelt as the Democratic party. Or we may label it as the party of "radicalism incarnated." Youngsters may be children or they may be "brats." A prominent industrialist may be the president of the Votex Company or he may be a "big shot."

Are we then to abandon these pictorial or interesting qualities of style in order to have discussional directness and simplicity? My suggestion is that each speech occasion has its own stylistic requirements. Some situations in which the primary aim is to entertain or impress will call for this more moving style. The principle to be applied is that of audience adaptation in view of the occasion and of the purpose of the speeches.

How will you avoid illogical reasoning through bad language usage? (1) You will be sure that your verbalizations correspond to your thinking; (2) that your words are explicit, precise, concrete, simple, clear-cut; (3) that definitions are framed in accordance with the principle of continuous variation; (4) that definitions are consistent; (5) that your connotative language at all points is based upon a background of logical thinking so that your heightened vocabulary is more than a substitute for argument itself.

D. *Loose Grammar and Syntax.* Sentence structure will often result in logical confusion. All loose grammar and syntax may be put down as involving fallacies. Sentence elements, for example, may be out of logical harmony with the context. To illustrate, "America is more powerful on the ocean than any nation," compares members of the same nation. If you intend such meaning to be logical, your standard of comparison in the *than* clause should be restricted to *other* or equivalent words. More logical is the statement: "America is more powerful on the ocean than any other nation." Note this confused statement: "Churchill is the best of all other present-day speakers."

E. *Illogical Parallel Structure.* Mistakes in parallel structure within the sentence also interfere with the continuity of the thought. Sentence elements that have the same logical office should be grammatically parallel. Infinitives should match infinitives; relative clauses should correspond to relative clauses. Otherwise logical uncertainties may result.

F. *Excessive Coordination of Ideas.* But even excessive coordination of ideas may lead to loose thinking. Untrained speakers fail to indicate differences in the relative importance of their ideas. Every thought is cast into an independent clause. The series may be strung together by "and" or "so." The result is a monotony of ideas, with little opportunity for the listener to discriminate between important and unimportant context. The remedy is, of course, to frame your ideas into short sentences, to express minor ideas in subordinate clauses, phrases, or single words, and to make more prominent the significant propositions.

Dangling modifiers, words, phrases, or clauses without proper grammatical construction, lack of grammatical agreement between subject and verb, and similar errors are familiar illustrations of bad grammar and of inadequate education. They are also examples of carelessness or inadequacy in thinking. In any formal conversation or orderly discussion we can usually make ourselves understood despite these oral slips. Nevertheless, trivial though they are, they interfere with the communicative process and cannot be ignored in any orderly treatment of right and wrong thinking.[3]

G. *The Fallacious or Complex Question.* Sometimes a question is to be phrased so as to imply a statement that needs proof. The question may invite a "yes" response. For example, "Shall we not join the Republican party?" Sometimes the question is so worded as to imply a question that needs proof. An unwarranted premise is implied. Consider the well-known question, "Why are college professors more absent-minded than other people?"

To keep your phrases, clauses, and sentences comparatively free from "crooked" thinking, be sure that your word agreements, cases of pronouns, tenses, moods, grammatical constructions, coordination, and subordination of ideas express exactly what you have in mind. Let your questions be impartial ones; and let the hidden terms ("question-begging" ones) be eliminated.

V. FALSE DIVISION, STATEMENT OF ISSUES, AND PARTITION

A. *Suppression of Important Issues (Partial Division).* Debaters and others, although justified in selecting from many

---

[3] The student is advised to review any standard handbook of composition. Review also Chaps. 5, 15, and 17.

points those that deserve stress, are often guilty of ignoring important arguments. The debater, for example, may argue by the method of residues that the problem is an "either-or" one. He may contend that in dealing with large industries the issue is, "Shall we have nationalization, or shall we continue competition?" He ignores the obvious third ground of analysis and discussion, "Private ownership and operation with government regulation," as in the case of railroads.

B. *Cross Division.* The principle of exclusiveness as well as inclusiveness must control the selection and framing of the main issues or points to be developed. For example, in one discussion of the question, "Shall the United States adopt a program of military intervention in Central America?" the following issues were developed: (1) Is intervention morally justified? (2) Is it economically desirable? (3) Will it be politically defensible? (4) Will it produce ill will in South America? (5) Is it necessary for the defense of the Panama Canal? (6) Will it return to the United States added trade in that region? Questions (3) and (4) obviously overlap since they both deal with politics. Questions (2) and (6) overlap, for they both stress economic security. The logical error is in the assumption that we are developing a new issue whereas we are merely returning to one already analyzed under another caption or heading. Incidentally, we may further complicate the confusion of cross division by asking what is meant by "economically desirable," "morally justified," "politically defensible."

C. *Stressing a Minor Issue.* Debaters, for motives of strategy or otherwise, may concentrate on a minor issue and play it up as the all-important question.

How then can we present an analysis of the problem by a statement of issues and constructive points that satisfactorily cover the case (partition) and yet avoid the charge of fallacious reasoning? Obviously, we shall analyze and develop those leading propositions that the subject and the audience demand. We shall avoid *special pleading* (used here as playing up a minor issue). We shall make this division according to the principles of exclusiveness and inclusiveness of materials. And we shall translate stock issues and corresponding propositions into specific questions and statements that are unmistakable in meaning.

VI. False Use of Facts (Evidence)

The reasoner's initial problem of judgment is to decide what is a fact. Discussion and similar forms of intellectual explanation and discovery begin with the phenomena that challenge our feelings of satisfaction. Observation and reporting of facts are done by two chief sorts of agents: witnesses and authority. The real difference between the two groups is that the authorities are witnesses who have had so much experience and training in observing certain phenomena that their word (*i.e.*, of these witnesses) is accepted without insistence that they prove at every point their fitness to testify.

A. *Unsupported Assertion.* Arguers of all kinds, those who merely write and those who speak, fill their discourse with bold or fairly subdued remarks that ring with confidence but fail to echo facts or sustained arguments. Mere assertion is probably the commonest fallacy in argument and may be technically put down as argument without evidence.

B. *Inaccuracy of Facts.* Sometimes the debater will flood his communication with facts. Upon examination, however, many of these items turn out to be distorted or unauthenticated.

C. *Inconsistency of Facts.* One method of demonstrating the inaccuracy of facts is to show that two sets of evidence in a given speech or article are inconsistent with each other. One set must, therefore, be wrong.

D. *Partial Evidence.* Speakers frequently will cite only part of the evidence needed or introduce a part quotation from authority. Thomas Dewey, in debate on Sept. 25, 1944, to prove that the Democratic party had not been sufficiently active in preparing for World War II, cited Senator Alben W. Barkley of Kentucky, as saying, "When Pearl Harbor came, we were not ready." Dewey failed to quote Barkley's later sentence, "And though unready for it when it came, we had gone further and faster and with more profound temporary adjustments in our lives than was true of any other nation on earth in all the history of mankind."

E. *Incompetency of Authorities.* The source of the fact or authority cited may be subject to any one of the many weaknesses of such evidence. A witness or authority may be incompetent in knowledge, in ability to report accurately, in intellectual honesty, or in prejudice.

How may we avoid such logical weaknesses in the use of facts? We need (1) to check and double check the accuracy of the statements on which we rely; (2) to examine carefully the primary source from which facts come and to weigh without prejudice the strength and weakness of that source; (3) to square each set of facts we use with others that we cite or may cite; (4) to guarantee consistency of evidence; (5) to shape the facts in concrete language free from possible misunderstanding; (6) to verify the facts by applying tests of causation and of multiple (added) evidence.

VII. False Argument from Generalization

In the search for fallacies of generalization the tests which have already been suggested should be applied. Hasty generalization, perhaps the most common sin of all who argue, appears (1) when the number of specific instances relied upon to support the conclusion is too small; (2) when negative instances appear; (3) when the specific instances are not fair examples of the whole; (4) when the facts upon which the induction is made are unreliable; (5) or when faulty causal connection is evident.

To avoid hasty generalization, then, (1) include a sufficient number of cases; (2) be sure they are typical; (3) give full weight to the negative instances; (4) check carefully the facts which compose the instances; (5) check your generalizations by the supplementary tests of other types of argument, including tests of causal reasoning.

VIII. False Argument in the Use of Statistics

Argument from statistics is usually faulty in the same respects as is reasoning from specific instance.

(1) The material may not have been accurately collected. Compilers may have been faulty or deficient in any one of the tests indicated above for valid use of testimony or authority. (2) The material may have been improperly classified. The sampling may be improperly done. The evidence may have

been obtained from only a single observation or by only one observer, by unreliable collectors, from only one source or a selection other than random, from an insufficient number of cases or a nontypical case. (3) The unit may have been improperly or carelessly defined. (4) The quantity measured by the statistics may not be an index of that which we want to know. Does the number of students enrolled in a given college, for example, indicate the intellectual leadership of that institution? (5) The data may not be ordered in a proper series. The series may be done according to unsound statistical procedure. (6) The correlation between the two or more series of data thus arranged may be extremely low. (7) There may be a low degree of reliability of the coefficient of correlation.

If you are to compile and use statistical materials or if you are to examine the statistics presented by others, you will be sure that the facts are determined; that cases in sufficient number are involved; that the samples are fair, that the data have been collected by proper tests of authority; that the data as collected represent the proper kind; that incomplete evidence is used only as incomplete proof; that negative data are properly noted; that the units are properly defined; that the classification of items has been logically carried out; that the data have been arranged in proper series; that the correlation has been determined between two or more series of such data thus arranged; that the assumptions or hypotheses have been properly stated; that the testing of computations for probable error has been accurately done; and that the conclusions are in line with the data.

IX. False Argument from Analogy

In our examination of argument from analogy we apply the tests discussed earlier for such reasoning.

False argument from analogy usually occurs when (1) too few resemblances are observable; (2) when the comparison is made on a basis of insignificant particulars; (3) when important differences are ignored: (4) when a lack of causal connection is obvious; (5) when the facts cited are inaccurate.

To assure your analogies of reasonable acceptance (1) check the facts on which they are based; (2) examine the causal connections involved; (3) take full account of the differences as well as the likenesses; (4) assure yourself that the resemblances are numerous and representative in relation to the conclusion you are attempting to draw.

EXERCISES AND PROBLEMS

1. Point out any fallacies involved in the following. Describe specifically the type of fallacious reasoning and indicate how the weakness may be corrected.

a. The Republican party should continue in power; for the country has prospered.

b. School tests are a useful preparation for life; for life is made up of a series of tests.

c. Indiana is the best state for farming. Montgomery County is the best farming county in the state. My uncle's farm is the best farm in the county. Therefore, my uncle's farm is the best in the United States.

d. If anyone doubts the importance of an acquaintance with the principles of physiology as a means to complete living, let him look around and see how many men and women he can find in middle or later life who are thoroughly well.

e. Whatever civilization is in Japan is almost entirely due to Christianity, for wherever Christianity has gone it has brought about higher standards of living.

f. Robert Burns, Christopher Marlowe, Edgar Allan Poe, and many other literary geniuses were intemperate. It is only natural that this student with his literary gifts should be somewhat dissolute.

g. The thorough preparation that Green College gives for public speaking is shown by the honors won in the last twenty-five years in forty out of fifty-one intercollegiate debates.

h. Your college education will pay you well; statistics show that five years after graduation the income of the college man is $2,500.

i. Mr. Blank will be a fine preacher; for his father and grandfather were both successful clergymen.

j. I believe that municipal ownership and operation of bus lines is advisable because it will do away with civic corruption in that there will no longer be a private company to bribe the city officials.

k. The interests of the employers and employees are identical; for both are to be classed as laborers, one laboring with his hands, the other with his brains.

l. The alumni will no doubt contribute the money for the erection of a new gymnasium because we know how generously they have responded to the call for funds to erect other buildings.

m. If prices are too high—in relation to wages—people can't buy what they'd like to buy.

If they can't buy, business will have to slow up production of goods.

A slowup in turning out goods would throw people out of work.

The more people out of work, the fewer goods can be bought.

And so on—with this circle getting wider all the time and the country slipping into a depression.

n. If we really want to prevent the spread not only of "Soviet imperialism" but also of the communist idea, whether for the sound purpose of enabling the two systems to get along together in an organized and peaceful world or for the desperate one of having supporters in a test of destructive power, our foreign policy must indeed provide substitutes for the gravitational attraction of Sovietism.

2. In a brief written report criticize the representative fallacies of (*a*) language, (*b*) facts, (*c*) statistics, (*d*) generalization which you may observe in a recent printed student debate, or in a recent debate in Congress. Name the fallacy and explain both what is obviously wrong and how the error in reasoning might be corrected.

CHAPTER 15

Obstacles to Straight Thinking (*Continued*)

I. FALSE ARGUMENT FROM CAUSAL RELATION

A. *Assumed Connection between Phenomena.* Probably the most prevalent form of this fallacy or error is the attempt to identify logically those items or phenomena that are associated only by chance. This fallacy is that of *non sequitur*, "it does not follow." Coincidences are regarded as cause and effect. Examples of such pseudo reasoning are the popular superstitions such as, "Don't occupy Room 13; it will surely bring you bad luck!"

B. *Assumed Connection between Phenomenon and Antecedent.* The same fallacies or errors occur when the argument is advanced that a causal connection occurs by reason of the fact that one event precedes another. This is the fallacy of *post hoc ergo propter hoc*, "after a fact, therefore, because of it." We too easily assume that events that antedate other events must somehow produce the later phenomena. Because of the general acceptance of this naïve method of reasoning, untold errors creep into historical, social, economic, and political thinking. During the summer of 1934, for example, a season of unusual drought developed, with grasshoppers and dust storms throughout the

175

Middle West and Southwest. Some members of this region connected this catastrophe with the Roosevelt administration and with the Secretary of Agriculture, Henry A. Wallace.

C. *Inadequate Cause Assumed to Be a Sufficient Cause.* Here the causal connection may be fairly well established, but the disposition of the reasoners to oversimplify leads to the magnifying of the importance of associated factors. To illustrate, "Ingersoll will succeed as teacher of speech, because he was a distinguished interscholastic debater." Experience in speaking of that type would no doubt help in preparing for teaching, but certainly other factors are essential. Ingersoll, to get on in the teaching world, would certainly need to have (1) a knowledge of the theory of speech in general, (2) sufficient brains to secure a college degree, (3) ability to meet the minimum requirements for a teaching certificate, (4) personality, interest, and other factors that mark a successful teacher.

D. *The Ignoring of Counteracting Causes.* Even though a single cause or group of causes may be singled out as controlling in this continuum or series of causes and results, the significance of countercauses is not to be overlooked. Just as a scientist gives validity to his generalizations by giving full place to the exceptions, so does he trace adequately negative or counteracting causes. Will, for example, the United States finally absorb Mexico? (1) Some military critics might argue that the United States would ultimately do so to guarantee full protection of this country in World War III. (2) The possibility of Russia or her allies seizing Mexico and so threatening this country and the Panama Canal might require our taking over Mexico. On the basis of these arguments it has been concluded that the history of 1848 would repeat itself and that the United States would absorb its neighbor to the south. The counteracting factors in such argument might be utterly ignored: (1) revulsion and opposition of the American citizens to the seizure of any weak neighbor, (2) American interest in retaining good will in all South and Latin America, (3) little fear of aggression from Mexico, (4) absence of marked communistic or Russian ascendancy or influence there, (5) the extension of loans to Mexico, (6) a program of economic cooperation with that country, (7) the Treaty of Chapultepec and later Latin-American agreements that would make unwise such a move. These and other factors might be cited to illustrate how counteracting causes need to be weighed before a conclusion is warranted.

E. Inaccuracy of Facts. Faulty reasoning from causation constantly appears when the facts are erroneous. A familiar statement reads, "A great peril is arising to cast its shadow across the power of America. The name of this peril is physical deterioration. The origin and explanation of this physical deterioration is lack of calcium in the present-day diet." Before we accept such argument, we may well decide just what is meant by "a great peril" and by "physical deterioration"; and we may ask whether "lack of calcium" lies at the bottom of our "physical deterioration." Plenty of evidence can be mustered to throw doubt upon the accuracy of the statement above.

To avoid the pitfalls of loose causal reasoning (1) verify the facts; (2) establish a causal connection between the phenomena; (3) make clear the effectiveness of the cause you single out; (4) take full account of the multiplicity of causes and results operating in the area with which you are dealing.[1]

II. FALSE ARGUMENT FROM AUTHORITY

A. Errors of Reasoning in Relation to Inference from Authority. We have stressed the more obvious ways by which both oral and written sources violate the canons of sound inference.[2]

How shall we correct bad testimony or weak authority? Be sure that the sources or witnesses are competent to observe; that they are properly trained for observation; that the facts or opinions are accurately and clearly stated; that the results are not the expression of bias, general or specific mental or emotional instability; that sources cited are first hand rather than secondary; that the documents cited are genuine; that evidence is corroborated by other sources; that the inferences from authorities are enforced by argument from deduction and induction.

[1] The student is advised to examine John Stuart Mill's canons of causality: (1) phenomena are causally related when they occur in a sequence; (2) they are not so related when an antecedent is invariably absent; (3) they are causally related when any variation in one phenomenon has a corresponding variation in the other. Cf. R. W. Sellars, *The Essentials of Logic*, pp. 226ff.; D. S. Robinson, *The Principles of Reasoning*, Chaps. 20, 21; John Stuart Mill, *Logic*, Book III, Chap. 9.

[2] See Chaps. 10 and 11.

III. FALSE ARGUMENT FROM GENERAL PROPOSITIONS (DEDUCTION)

Typical forms of crooked thinking in argument from deduction include (1) fallacies growing out of faulty syllogistic forms, (2) vague or misleading phrasing of the propositions, (3) false assumptions in the major premises or propositions, (4) misstatement of facts in minor premises, (5) begging the question by argument in a circle, (6) begging the question by assuming a more general truth which involves the point at issue.

A. *Faulty Construction of Syllogistic Forms.* The syllogistic forms may be so organized as to result in confused deductions. Logicians cite and illustrate the many illogical moods of the categorical syllogism. Scrutiny of these sixty-odd moods, many of them illogical, is obviously beyond the scope of this volume. In the construction of the disjunctive syllogism, too, the alternatives named in the first proposition may not be exhaustive or may not be mutually exclusive. Hypothetical syllogisms may be so framed that the minor premise denies the antecedent or affirms the consequent. The conclusions, in such cases, are probably fallacious.

B. *False Reasoning through Vague or Ambiguous Phrasing of the Propositions.* The remedy is to review each term to assure ourselves and others that it means what we intend it to mean.

C. *False Assumptions in the Major Propositions or Premises.* Here we need to be especially careful, for we are dealing with one of the most frequent fallacies of the debater. Assumptions in debate are often not clearly stated; or they are not factually grounded; or they may be based upon prejudice or bias that reflects itself in the wording. These assumptions may be all-inclusive, couched in "allness" language. The "either-or" (disjunctive) or the "if-then" (hypothetical) propositions may likewise violate the canons of proper division or of sound causal reasoning.

Frame clearly your assumptions; check and verify them to make sure that mature reasoners will accept them.

D. *Misstatement of Facts in the Major or Minor Premises and in the Conclusions.* Those who resort to deductive reasoning are not less obligated to rely on facts at every turn than are the inductive reasoners.

E. *Begging the Question.* Begging the question (*petitio prin-*

cipii) assumes without evidence or argument a conclusion to be proved. Characteristic ways of begging the question include arguing in a circle and assuming a more general truth which involves the point at issue. Note each:

1. *Arguing in a circle.* A common form of begging the question is found in the fallacy of argument in a circle (*circulus in probando*). Here two or more unproved propositions are used to establish the validity of each other. This argument may be expressed in at least two syllogisms, the conclusion of one being used as a premise to prove this same assertion. Examples are the following:

Fighting should be prohibited, for it is morally wrong; we know it is morally wrong because it is a practice that should be prohibited.

These statements arranged as syllogisms would be as follows:

a. Whatever is morally wrong should be prohibited.
b. Fighting is morally wrong.
c. Fighting should be prohibited.

The minor premise is thus proved:

a. Whatever should be prohibited is morally wrong.
b. Fighting should be prohibited.
c. Fighting is morally wrong.

2. *Assuming a more general truth which involves the point at issue.* In this fallacy the conclusion to be proved is used to establish itself by being stated in a more general or inclusive form. (This is sometimes called the *fallacy of synthesis.*) The fallacy is in reality one of repetition; a generalization is implied. The fallacy is illustrated by the following example: "The students of Bridgewater University should be put on probation, for all such students should be placed on probation." The fallacy here grows out of the fact that a generalization is implied and yet is not proved. To expose the fallacy, the argument may be expressed as a syllogism:

a. Whatever students burn signboards, assault policemen, injure parking meters, storm motion-picture houses, should be put on probation.
b. The students of Bridgewater University did these things.
c. The students of Bridgewater University should be put on probation.

3. *Assuming that what is true of the whole is true of each*

unit. In the same way we often assume that what is true of the whole is true of each part. (This fallacy is the converse of the fallacy of synthesis.) The fallacy of division is illustrated by the following arguments:

a. The soldiers of Company F were superior fighters in World War II, for the Seventh Army was a superior army.

b. Brown County is a rich county. Mr. A lives in Brown County. Therefore, he is a rich man.[3]

What shall be done to avoid the more typical faults of argument from deduction, including the use of syllogistic forms? (1) Avoid the "allness" propositions; substitute language that expresses probability rather than absoluteness. (2) Express the deductive propositions in the simplest, clearest language of which you are capable. (3) Test and double test all facts incorporated in these propositions. (4) Apply the principles of division and classification to the disjunctive forms. (5) Apply to the hypothetical forms the tests of argument from causal relation. (6) Substantiate all propositions by adequate argument and evidence. (7) Avoid using the same term with different meanings in related propositions. (8) View the rules of syllogistic reasoning, principles, and processes in the light of contemporary "scientific" methods. (9) Regard deductive reasoning as for practical application rather than for abstract theorizing or logical hairsplitting.

IV. False Argument from Ignoring the Question

The error of ignoring the question (*ignoratio elenchi*) in reasoning occurs when the debater jumps the track in the argument and arrives at an irrelevant conclusion or at the logical conclusion through illogical reasoning. Begging the question sticks to the problem but merely asserts what needs to be proved; ignoring the question usually leads the disputant and audience away from the problem. Ignoring the question is likely to follow when one is unable, through ignorance, to relate premise to conclusion or when, through intent, he sidesteps the argument. The proper method of refuting such fallacy is to state the argument clearly and show that the assumed conclusion is irrelevant or illogical.

[3] The fallacies of begging the question should also be regarded as falling under "False Assumptions in the Major Propositions, or Premises."

The representative forms of this fallacy are (1) slanted or emotionalized language, (2) substitution of irrelevant argument, (3) repeated affirmation, (4) substitution of questions for argument, (5) invective, (6) vindication of self and colleagues (prestige appeal), (7) eulogy of the people, (8) substitution of authority for proof, (9) substitution of humor for proof, (10) substitution of appeal to tradition and custom for argument, (11) appeal to ignorance of the opposite.

A. *Slanted or Emotionalized Language.* Our previous discussion of language has made clear the common and highly objectionable device of flooding your argument with words and phrases that are charged with bias and high emotion. Such language is slanted. One Congressman, opposed to world government and other international commitments, spoke as follows (I have italicized the more obvious emotionalized or slanted terms):

Mr. Speaker, in my opinion, the Members of the House of Representatives should not remain silent while a large number of international *moon gazers,* who seem to be floating around in a *pink cloud of sublunar radiation,* attempt to destroy the Government of the United States or make it subordinate to UN, which has been compared to an *International Sanhedrin.*

I am opposed, and I believe nine tenths of the American people are opposed, to setting up any *supergovernment* over the United States.

These speeches that were made yesterday, especially by Mr. "Corn" Wallace, former Secretary of Agriculture, and others I could mention, *demanding* that we subordinate this Government to *this outfit* in New York, *this Tower of Babel* if you please—that behind-the-scenes talk mostly about what they are going to get out of the United States or what they are *going to do to us*—do not reflect the sentiments of the American people.

It is time for *real* Americans to *wake up* and say to the world that we are not going to destroy the United States or subordinate it to the will of *an outfit* dominated by Joe Stalin, Molotov, or Gromyko.[4]

B. *Substitution of Irrelevant Argument.* This controversial strategem is deliberate or unintentional diversion. The strategy is to shift the discussion to another proposition which is not directly related to the point at issue but which gives the strategist

---

[4] *Congressional Record* (daily edition), Vol. 93, p. 3062, Apr. 1, 1947.

stronger ground on which to argue. This fallacy occurs in debate when a disputant, apparently cornered, diverts the argument to another field. Such extraneous argument is exposed by reminding the debaters and audience what is the real issue.

A kindred strategy is to refute—intentionally or otherwise—an argument in debate not advanced by another speaker. Frequently in debate, especially in high-school debate, where rebuttals are carefully prepared and often memorized, an argument is refuted that has not been advanced—nor presumably will be—by the other side. The debater's duty is immediately to point out to the audience that discussion of an irrelevant argument has taken place. This remedy, of course, is to bring the argument back to pertinent issues.

C. Repeated Affirmation. This fallacy occurs when, in lieu of an argument methodically unfolded, the speaker or writer merely repeats, again and again, his own proposition. This technique is the familiar one of sinister propaganda. Hitler used it with telling (if momentary) effect in 1937 and 1938. It is also the technique of brisk advertisers via the radio and press. The strategem is based upon the fact of human suggestibility. Repetition, we are told, will make hearers tend to believe that statement.

The only protection is to expose the lack of factual argument and to insist that independent judgment should not be abandoned in the face of the tricks of suggestion.

D. Substitution of Questions for Argument. The ambitious and enthusiastic speaker may develop a veritable avalanche of questions. They may be on or off the subject. The purpose is to overwhelm the opposition. Such deluge of questions may give the questioner prestige by the implication that he himself can easily answer each one. The one questioned, on the other hand, may have so many ideas thrown at him that adequate answer seems impossible. Observers may easily get the impression that he is ill-informed and logically unprepared.

Legitimate questions to point an argument or to enforce it persuasively are in order. Every good parliamentary debater uses questions effectively. But to make the entire argument a parade of major and minor interrogations is clearly a demonstration of ignoring the issue.

The protection against such bombardment is for the follow-up debater to say, "Mr. So and So has invited me to answer a wide range of questions, some of them pertinent, some of them inconsequential and irrelevant. In my argument I shall deal at appropriate points with those that have importance."

E. *Invective or Name Calling (Argumentum ad hominem).* Invective played a prominent part in British parliamentary oratory. Burke, Chatham, Pitt the Younger, Fox, and many another leader interspersed in their parliamentary debates the castigation of political foes. In contemporary American political speaking, however, the denunciatory type of speaking has not been so prominently used either in Congress or elsewhere. Invective, as a rhetorical form, has largely disappeared (note as exceptions, Churchill's castigations of the enemy in World War II). Name calling continues to be a means of destroying an argument without directly attacking it. In recent years, the labels of "Democrat," "Republican," "Nazi," "Communist," and their equivalents have been hurled back and forth as a substitute for analysis and appraisal of the ideologies for which these names stand. "Atheistic view," "communistic views," "money-changers," "international bankers," and similar epithets have been launched against men and movements. The logical assumption in such denunciations is that it is unreasonable for a sound proposition to be identified with an individual whose personality may be condemned.

F. *Vindication of Self and Colleagues (Prestige Appeal).* The reverse of invective is the glorification of oneself, colleagues, and cause. Just as a typical courtroom speaker breaks down the authority of his opponents, so does he exalt himself, friends, and clients.

In his speech accepting the nomination, delivered at Elwood, Indiana, on Aug. 17, 1940, Wendell Willkie justified himself as a presidential candidate by showing that he belonged to the common people. He told of his humble ancestry and of his father and mother, who had lived in Central Europe.

They were humble people—not members of the ruling or wealthy classes. . . . As their descendant I have fought from boyhood against all these restrictions, discriminations and tyranny, and I am still fighting. My grandparents lived in Germany; they were supporters of the Democratic Revolution in that country, my father was three or four years old when his parents settled in Northern Indiana. . . . **As a** young man he helped clear the forest. . . . They hated oppression, hypocrisy or arbitrary control of any kind. They lived in the qualities that made America great—an independent spirit, an inquiring mind, and a courageous heart.

There is no objection to the enhancing of oneself, or friends, or ancestors. The practice is common in political speaking. The only question arises when these laudatory techniques become a substitute for argument. The fallacy rests upon the false assumption that any proposition is logical which is identified with an individual who is faultless.

G. *Eulogy of the People* (*Argumentum ad populum*). Fallacious reasoning arises when the speaker praises the people rather than analyzes the argument. Such eulogy is similar in effect to denunciation of opponents, the vindication of oneself and friends. The speaker may glorify the people by calling them "plain folks" or "common people" or he may identify an argument with them because they allegedly believe in it. Again the criticism of such form of proof arises when it obscures or leaves out the logical material.

H. *Substitution of Authority for Argument.* A third fallacy closely related to the preceding one occurs when the talk refers not to the truth or falsity of a proposition but to the fact that some alleged authority supports it. We must make clear the distinction between the legitimate use of authority as one of the methods of supporting an argument and the identification of the authority with some idea in order that the prestige of the speaker may carry through successfully the given proposition. It is one thing to use authority as one of several forms of proof; it is quite another, and fallacious, to devote a speech or written statement exclusively to the stressing of such authority with little or no attempt to analyze the arguments themselves.

I. *Appeal to Humor, Sympathy, Fear* (*Argumentum ad misericordiam*). Still another illustration of ignoring the question by resorting to emotional substitution lies in the use of humor, sympathy, and fear. Humor, we agree, is almost necessary for effective presentation before an average audience. The lighter mood is certainly not out of place in a discussion or debate situation. It is when the discussion or debate degenerates into a series of jokes or anecdotes and becomes a substitute for analysis and reasoned argument that it is to be condemned. For

example, one speaker argued that the wage-and-hour law as put
into effect by the New Deal administration was justified because
it was a means of withstanding technological unemployment.
Technological unemployment, so ran the argument, was part and
parcel of the scientific age. The wage-and-hour law was, therefore, justified because we are living in a scientific age. To prove
that point the speaker proceeded as follows: "One man on a
farm today with power machinery can do the work of five men
or twelve men, depending upon how far back you wish me to
go to make the comparison. Electricity? By our laws we are
foretelling the progressive movement of science—everything today is being done by electricity. Why, they even have an electric polling machine in New York, where a candidate is elected
and his opponents electrocuted at the same time. A young
woman called up her husband and said, 'George, you had better
come home.' He said, 'What is the matter, honey?' She said,
'I don't know; I must have got the wires crossed or the plugs
mixed or something, our radio is all frosted over and our refrig-
erator is giving a fireside talk.' "[5]

*J. Appeal to Tradition and Custom (Argumentum ad vere-
cundiam).* Auditors are often stirred through appeal to their
loyalty to tradition and custom. The speaker implies that cus-
toms or traditions that have persisted are therefore to be continued, and that the things that are untried are therefore not to
be accepted. This weakness in the argument occurs when the
line of reasoning does not point to the truth or falsity of a proposition but assumes that tradition or custom justifies the conclusion. A typical example of such reasoning argues that, "America
ought to go slow in centralizing its government because from
the beginning of this republic we have been careful to preserve
the Federal system by which states' rights have been fully pro-
tected." This argument, stripped of its oratorical accompani-
ments, is merely a warm emotional assertion that we should not
have undue centralization because our forefathers seemed to
prefer otherwise.

In addition to the emotive appeals enumerated above, such
typical sentiments as those of self-preservation, profit, personal

---

[5] Joshua Bryan Lee, "Technological Unemployment and Relief," in *Representative American Speeches, 1938–39* (A. Craig Baird, ed.), p. 111,
The H. W. Wilson Company, 1939.

and social convenience, indignation, and duty become the chief material of many speeches or written addresses. Each argument or proposition will carry with it strong emotional stimuli. To the extent that the emotions which stimulate approval are aroused will a speech or point of view be regarded by its sponsors as successful. Discussion, however, minimizes these emotional drives. Although we agree that the appeal to one's pocketbook, to the motive of self-preservation, of profit, of opportunity to make personal and social progress are all highly acceptable in persuasive argument, these forms of *pathetic proof* are not to replace sound reasoning.

K. *Appeal to Ignorance of the Opposite (Argumentum ad ignorantiam).* Still another characteristic mode of departing from the question through emotional appeal is that of appealing to ignorance. In this case the speaker attempts to prove not the truth or falsity of the proposition itself but the fact that people are ignorant of it. Such reasoning assumes that whenever information to prove a proposition is lacking, that proposition is false. For example, "There can no longer be any doubt that some of these members of the Communist party are in the pay of the Soviet government. None of them can prove they are not."

These various departures from solid line of argument and analysis are here listed not because they often crop out in discussion but because they pervade the popular speechmaking and form the backbone of much propaganda with which we are beset!

V. Conclusion

How shall we fill our speeches with logic and inject also effective persuasive elements without guilt of these and other characteristic fallacies of ignoring the question? Our problem is one of integrating motivative elements with straight thinking. The two orders of expression (if, indeed, we may suggest such dichotomy) may be compatible if we approach properly the entire enterprise of logical thinking. We can avoid illogical diversions, name calling, and the other manifestations of crooked thinking if we divest ourselves of prejudice and hollow rhetoric; if we inspect our language so that it is both precise and accurate; if we commit ourselves first of all to frank and full exposition of facts and accompanying logic. Freedom from these fallacies of emotional-

ism and propagandistic trickery should be best practiced by those
who possess disciplined minds and character.

EXERCISES AND PROBLEMS

1. Point out any weaknesses in each of the following. (*a*) Label
specifically the fallacy or logical weakness according to the list of "obstacles to straight thinking" mentioned in this chapter. (*b*) Show how
the difficulty may be corrected. (*c*) Hand to the instructor your
written comment on those exercises (or from the list below those the
instructor may designate).

(1) The younger generation is entirely too cocksure in its ideas.

(2) Said head football coach Houser to his squad, "If any of you
smoke, off the team you go. Smoking ruins your health."

(3) Babe Smith, in an advertisement, states that "I always smoke
Que-Ebs cigarettes to give me a lift."

(4) Said the student to his friend, "Last year in Maine we enjoyed
the tiled roofs and stucco walls. Don't you admire those Colonial
houses with such tiled roofs and stucco walls?"

(5) "Have you read Upton Sinclair's *Babbitt?*"

(6) "That Smoot-Hawley tariff was the direct cause of the collapse
of 1929."

(7) "If you have abdominal pain take Beeman's Pain Remover. It
is guaranteed."

(8) "He's a whiz, and so popular with the Pi Gees. He'll surely
get there after he gets his sheepskin."

(9) "I limp. I'll probably never get a job."

(10) "If you want to be well educated, I advise you to read many
books."

(11) "Redheaded people have bad tempers. Joe is redheaded."

(12) "Dark-haired girls are usually good students."

(13) "Undergraduates who play football make poor grades. Niles
Norris plays football. Therefore, he makes poor grades."

(14) "Why is it that girls never understand football or baseball?"

(15) "All spiders have eight legs."

(16) "Haste makes waste."

(17) "Good literature should be read by our college students. The
Bible is good literature. Therefore, the Bible should be read by our
college students."

(18) "Why is drinking coffee more injurious than drinking high
balls?"

(19) "Why does going to bed early make us wiser than going to
bed late?"

(20) "Why are Americans more humorous and sociable than Europeans?"

(21) "Why does fright turn the hair white in a single night?"

(22) "The youngest child has less intelligence than the eldest."

(23) "Inflation, once started, cannot be controlled."

(24) "Join the crowd at Duffy's, for there you'll find food you'll like and the drink you'll enjoy. Everybody so advises you."

(25) "Consider our schools. The hidden costs of poor education, lost opportunity, and poverty resulting from inadequate schools are costs the nation can no longer afford. Federal aid to education will be a lot less expensive than ignorance and illiteracy."–President Harry S. Truman, September 5, 1949.

(26) "If the Chinese communists take over that nation, the entire Orient is bound to come under the domination of communism."

(27) "Compulsory arbitration and judicial settlement of labor disputes mean the substitution of law and order for war and lawlessness. If civil disputes are to be settled in court, why is it not reasonable for industrial disputes to be settled in a similar way?"

CHAPTER 16

Argumentative Composition: Divisions of Discourse

I. Function of Composition in Argumentation, Debate, and Discussion

Three basic elements underlie the preparation of a successful argument: (1) content or invention; (2) structure or organization; and (3) composition, style, or language. Certainly, content, which we have reviewed at length in the preceding chapters, is central in your skill. With nothing much to say you cannot get far in argumentative or any other kind of speechmaking or writing. These materials, however, as we have repeatedly noted, need shaping into coherent, relevant, and impressive order. Hence we work at outlines, briefs, and systematic structure of talk or written communication. Ideas and their structural effectiveness, nevertheless, involve the application of vocabulary. Therefore, early and late we must attend to words and their combination as the effective agents in the interpretation of this well-ordered content.

Language or style, then, is no extraneous or decorative feature of such communication. Rather, it is closely integrated with thought itself. All forms of discourse, including argumentation, must concern themselves at every turn with the use of words.

Words and sentences cannot be separated from thinking. Logic is inextricably interwoven with word symbols. Facts, it

189

is true, are not words; nevertheless, as far as practical results are concerned, facts *are* words. The language by which the fact is interpreted to the listener—whether we like it or not—largely determines our notion of what is "fact" or "event." Preceding and succeeding chapters of this book make clear the close association of thought and language.[1]

II. Composition and the Speaker's or Writer's Purpose

Your purpose in argumentative speaking or writing, whether discussion, persuasion, or technical debate, will strongly affect the character of your composition. Each occasion will suggest to you special compositional techniques.

In round-table discussion, for example, you have merely to be clear and accurate. When you take the platform for a panel, symposium, or lecture-forum, you will obviously shape your language not only for such clarity but for added interest and attention.

Debaters, more decisively committed to persuasion and audience conviction, adopt a more typical forensic style. Often this style is hopelessly trite and conventional. At its best, in Congressional debates or in the courtroom, the composition is original and colorful.

When the occasion calls for important decision and when the speaker is deeply moved and capable of profound expression, oratory in the best sense results—logic pervaded with imagination and emotion.

Woodrow Wilson before Congress asking for a declaration of war against Germany, Franklin D. Roosevelt before his microphone asking the nation to support his policies against Germany twenty-five years later, Winston Churchill before the wrecked House of Commons in 1941, asking the Englishmen to support a war that meant only "blood, sweat, and tears,"—these arguments called for language of high emotion. In the speeches of these great orators, therefore, you will find figures of speech, invective, parallel structure, rhetorical questions, climax, vivid word style.

III. Three Methods of Composition

This text aims to guide you in both written and oral argument. Some of your creative work may take the form of short or ex-

[1] See Chaps. 5, 12, and 14.

tended written argument. Your term papers, letters to the editor, editorial and similar contributions will usually reflect argumentative and persuasive aims and methods. This text aims to suggest principles and specific aids for such composition.

Oral argument, discussion, and spoken debate, as contrasted with these typical written forms, may be composed according to one of three methods: (1) oral composition before delivery, (2) oral composition on the platform itself, and (3) written composition.

A. *Oral Composition before Delivery.* According to the first method, you will draft a few notes from your brief or discussional outline. With these before you, you will rehearse the speech until the ideas or even the exact words take definite form in your mind. This process is in effect the composition of a number of speeches, for it is evident that each rehearsal will yield an address more or less different from those that precede. Whether composition of this type is effective will depend partly upon the definiteness with which the outline, or brief, has been worked out; partly upon the thoroughness with which the oral rehearsals are conducted; and partly upon the composer's previous training in oral and written English.

B. *Oral Composition at the Time of Final Presentation.* Oral composition that is done only as part of the final presentation has the same advantages as oral composition prior to delivery: it develops a colloquial style usually associated with the most satisfactory form of popular address. The oral method, however, too often develops a speech which is discursive, thin in thought, superficial, mechanical, and repetitious. He who waits until the moment of delivery itself is usually guilty of all the compositional faults identified with impromptu speaking. Only he who by training and temperament has wide command of the English language and ability to think with clear penetration should resort to this method. Woodrow Wilson in his later political campaigns, especially in his Western tour supporting the League of Nations in 1919, was able to compose in this way with skill. His speeches, many of them extemporaneous, have the finish of carefully prepared manuscripts.

C. *Written Composition.* Shall you, then, write your speeches before delivery? Usually, you should do so. Only thus will you develop the relevancy, the force, and especially the compactness which are essential in debate. Only thus will you be able to clarify, simplify, and express those finer shades of meaning which characterize the superior debate. Debaters under my observation have frequently rewritten a speech five or six times.

"But," it may be objected, "to speak of a written debate is to misuse terms, for a genuine debate is filled with rebuttal and other impromptu elements that can never be fully prepared beforehand." Such criticism is sound. Written debates are dangerous; for the composer, even in the heat of the contest, may rely too much upon his manuscript or his memory. The result will be stiffness, a literary rather than an oral style, a general failure to adapt the argument to the audience and to the contentions advanced by opposing speakers. *Nevertheless, if you are to do well in a debate or with a persuasive or discussional speech, you will write it beforehand—at least until you become a veteran speechmaker.*

May I add that practice in actual speaking must receive an equal amount of attention. The writing must be freely supplemented by oral practice. The result will be an oral rather than literary style.

IV. Composition and the Brief or Outline

Since the brief is a formal statement, made up of a complete list of arguments with evidence, the resulting debate will in many particulars differ from the outline. So will a discussant take wide liberties with his preliminary outline. In the more persuasive forms of argument, many emotional elements will, of course, be added that have no place in a mechanical statement of the case to be developed.

V. Principles for the Composition of the Argument as a Whole

The general framework of your discourse will be governed by the same principles applicable to structure or organization. Structure requires (1) selection of materials to ensure unity, (2) arrangement of ideas in effective sequence, (3) relative extensiveness of treatment. These same qualities of style should determine your management of the composition as a whole.

A. *Unity*. As the brief or outline is relevant, so should the speech itself be. Avoid digressions. Preserve unity of tone.

Debaters often attempt a curious blending of the dignified style with undue informality, frequently in the form of humor. Avoid also discordant notes and unexpected change of level which to the audience sound artificial.

B. *Order.* Arrange the ideas in the order that will be the clearest to the audience. This order may be chronological, from the simple to the complex, from cause to effect, from the less important to the more important, from the abstract to the concrete, or the reverse. Unite the paragraphs and the larger divisions of the speech by means of connective words, phrases, and sentences. Link together the larger divisions by announcing each division and by the frequent use of summaries. Apply also the principle of variety. Mix the inductive method with the deductive.

C. *Proportion or Emphasis.* Consider also the principle of force or emphasis. Each idea should have that amount of space and position which its importance indicates. Secondary ideas may be dismissed in a few words; more significant arguments need more space and should be placed first or last. The opening section or the final position may be given to the most impressive idea.

D. *Interest.* Observe likewise the principle of interest. Use freely illustration, humor, narrative style, direct dialogue, and the other devices that hold attention (interest). In general, the writer-debater should visualize clearly an audience—not a hard thing for the average college speaker who appears only before a college audience—and construct the speech so as to impress that audience.

VI. Composition of the Introduction

The work of writing will be more systematically managed if you regard the composition as divided after the conventional plan of introduction, discussion proper, and conclusion and if you regard each of these sections as a complete composition in itself. The purpose of the introduction is to attract favorable attention and interest and to give the necessary preliminary information. Cicero said that the purpose of an introduction is *reddere auditores benevolos, attentos, dociles,* "to render the hearers well disposed toward the speaker, attentive, and open-minded." Negatively, the aim is to avoid arousing inhibitions, as is often done when the note of denunciation or belligerency is sounded at the outset. Positively, the material should be so selected and expressed as to place speaker and audience upon common ground and to keep them there. The principle of persuasion should govern the method of composition. The introduction should serve as a true approach to the argument proper. You have your choice of several methods, according to your discussional or other purpose and according to the occasion and audience.

A. *Personal Introduction.* You may begin with a personal introduction in which you appeal for sympathy or confidence, for fair play, sense of duty, or responsibility, or in which you compliment your audience. Because reference to yourself may seem unduly laudatory or insincere or because your reference to your audience may likewise seem too calculated, you must use with extreme caution this form of approach.

Consider the direct simplicity, humor, the compliment to President Truman, and the assumption of personal authority in the opening of Winston Churchill's Address at Fulton, Missouri:[2]

I am glad to come to Westminster College this afternoon and am complimented that you should give me a degree. The name Westminster is somehow familiar to me. I seem to have heard of it before. Indeed it was at Westminster that I received a very large part of my education in politics, dialectic, rhetoric and one or two other things.

It is also an honor, perhaps almost unique, for a private visitor to be introduced to an academic audience by the President of the United States. Amid his heavy burdens, duties and responsibilities—unsought but not recoiled from—the President has traveled a thousand miles to dignify and magnify our meeting here today and give me an opportunity of addressing this kindred nation, as well as my own countrymen across the ocean and perhaps some other countries too. The President has told you that it is his wish, as I am sure it is yours, that I should have full liberty to give my true and faithful counsel in these anxious and baffling times. I shall certainly avail myself of this freedom and feel the more right to do so because any private ambitions I may have cherished in my younger days have been satisfied beyond my wildest dreams. Let me, however, make it clear that I have no official mission or status of any kind and that I speak only for myself. I can therefore allow my mind, with the experience of a lifetime, to

[2] A. Craig Baird, *Representative American Speeches: 1945–46*, p. 21–22, The H. W. Wilson Company, 1946.

play over the problems which beset us on the morrow of our absolute victory in arms; and try to make sure that what has been gained with so much sacrifice and suffering shall be preserved for the future glory and safety of mankind.

B. *Striking Question.* Begin with a striking question. William J. Bryan begins his address on "The Value of an Ideal"[3] by raising questions: "What is the value of an ideal? Have you ever attempted to estimate its worth? Have you ever tried to measure its value in dollars and cents?"

C. *Narrative or Dramatic Method.* Use the narrative or dramatic method. It gives vividness and emotional power to the speech.

Note the personal deed narrative technique in the opening of Ben Kuroki's "The War Isn't Over at Home," given before the *New York Herald Tribune* Forum on Oct. 27, 1945. Kuroki, the son of a Japanese seed-potato farmer of Hershey, Nebraska, part of a crew of a B-24, flew thirty missions in the European zone and twenty-eight more against the Japanese home islands, and was twice awarded the Distinguished Flying Cross. His argument was one for racial tolerance.[4]

The town I came from is called Hershey, Nebraska. It's near the Platte River, between Cozad and Ogallala, about twelve miles down the road from North Platte. We've got a farm there—my father and mother and my brother George and I. We raise sugar beets and seed potatoes. Dirt farming isn't a very easy life, but it suits us fine.

I never traveled much. I'd go down to North Platte for feed, or go fishing up in the mountains over in Colorado or down to Chicago to see my sister. I figured some day I'd get to New York, but I didn't plan on visiting Tokyo. Japan is the land of my ancestors, but I never had any desire to go there. And yet, one morning like a lot of other American boys, I started out down the road from my house and I was headed for Tokyo. And like a lot of other American boys, I got there the hard way.

D. *Significant Quotation.* Begin with a significant quotation. Dr. H. F. Harding, at that time Colonel and Chief of Staff, Headquarters, Replacement Training Command in the Pacific

[3] *Selected Speeches of William Jennings Bryan,* Vol. II, p. 239, Funk & Wagnalls Company, 1911.
[4] Baird, *op. cit.,* p. 209.

Ocean Areas, opened his address on "New Directions for Higher Learning," at Honolulu, on May 25, 1945, as follows:

"In one of those brilliantly illuminating passages of *The Republic* Plato tells us that 'The direction in which education starts a man will determine his future life.' This is the text I want to take to discuss with you tonight some 'New Directions for Higher Learning.'"[5]

E. Reference to the Occasion. Refer to the importance of the occasion or to the significance of the surroundings.

General Douglas MacArthur, Commander in Chief of the United States Army in the Pacific Area, immediately after the formal and unconditional surrender of Japan, aboard the battleship *Missouri* in Tokyo Bay on Sept. 2, 1945, began his radio address to the American people and to the world as follows:

My Fellow Countrymen: Today the guns are silent. A great tragedy has ended. A great victory has been won. The skies no longer rain death—the seas bear only commerce—men everywhere walk upright in the sunlight. The entire world lies quietly at peace. The holy mission has been completed. And in reporting this to you, the people, I speak for the thousands of silent lips, forever stilled among the jungles and the beaches and in the deep waters of the Pacific which marked the way. I speak for the unnamed brave millions homeward bound to take up the challenge of that future which they did so much to salvage from the brink of disaster.[6]

F. Striking Statement. Sometimes, when the facts justify it, you may startle your audience by a striking statement at the outset. Bernard M. Baruch, United States Representative to the Atomic Energy Commission, opened his address before Hunter College, on June 14, 1946:

My Fellow Members of the United Nations Atomic Energy Commission, and My Fellow Citizens of the World: We are here to make a choice between the quick and the dead. That is our business.

Behind the black portent of the new atomic age lies a hope which, seized upon with faith, can work our salvation. If we fail, then we have damned every man to be the slave of fear. Let us not deceive ourselves: We must elect world peace or world destruction.[7]

[5] *Ibid.*, pp. 229–230.
[6] *Ibid.*, pp. 13–14.
[7] *Ibid.*, pp. 120–121.

G. Steps of Analysis in Discussion, Debate, or Formal Argument. The suggestions above refer for the most part to the opening of the introduction, or preliminary approach. If you follow the pattern of a more formal argument, you will include some or all of such steps as (1) cause for the debate or immediate interest to an audience, (2) explanation of terms, (3) brief history of the case, (4) brief suggestion of the conflicting arguments, (5) statement of issues, and (6) contentions to be developed.

In debate, the first affirmative may (according to the time at his disposal) give several of these steps. Usually, he opens with suggestions of the immediate importance of the problem, explanation of terms, outlining of issues, and an explanation of what he intends to attempt to prove. Each of these steps, it goes without saying, should be not an end but a means. The history, for example, need not refer to every root of an institution in the period before the Christian Era. This step means the selection of those items that relate most strikingly to the immediate discussion. Again, the definition of terms should be more than a dry and severely technical description. Rather it should be brief, popular, interesting, and, if possible, a general explanation, personal rather than academic. The conflict of opinion, like the history and definitions, should be free from the technical, mechanical, or lifeless style usually present when the brief is closely followed. A general comparison of the rival points of view rather than a catalogue of arguments on each side will be sufficient. The issues, however, should be clearly, even mechanically, stated. The composer must not run the risk of having the audience fail to understand these pivotal questions.

A discussional speech, by contrast, might enlarge on each of these steps so that the entire talk becomes one of analysis. In such performance the cause for discussion or immediate importance of the problem to this group might be regarded as the introduction.

Other speakers, primarily interested in a persuasive address and not much concerned with formal definitions and the other elements of forensic analysis, might state immediately the theme and the partition of the subject.

Dr. W. N. Brigance, in discussing "The Backwash of War," an

address delivered more than forty times between 1943 and 1945, stated his theme:

After nearly four years of war the shooting is over, and now the backwash has begun. I want to inquire what this backwash will do to the emotional responses, the conditioned reflexes, and the behavior patterns of the American people. Let us look first at the effects on the men in the armed forces, then later we shall consider the effect upon American civilians.[8]

H. Transitional Introduction. A transitional introduction is often desirable. Such approach (1) makes an assumption based upon previous remarks, (2) refers to a preceding speaker, (3) states an argument to be refuted, or (4) summarizes what has preceded.

An Oxford speaker in an American college debate hurried at once into his discussion with the following sentence: "I will try to show how much I appreciate the honor that has been accorded to me and my associates from Oxford by going straight on with the debate where it has been left by the last speaker."

VII. COMPOSITION OF THE ARGUMENT
PROPER OR MAIN BODY

Each issue will be developed as a separate and complete argument, often with its own approach or topic ideas, its discussion, and its summary or enforcement. Here the principle of clearness needs application. Likewise the principles of identifying beliefs and of keeping on common ground with the audience must be applied at every step in the writing. Remember that in writing, as in actual delivery, fixed beliefs can scarcely be changed—at least in a single speech! Therefore, you will, as far as possible, identify with the fixed opinions of the audience the proposition which you wish them to accept. This point of view will lead your style to take on a persuasive oral quality characteristic of your style in speaking. Arguments will be advanced inductively or deductively as the occasion suggests. Now you will proceed boldly, now cautiously, now admitting, now expounding, always trying to keep on common ground and yet always advancing to your goal of securing the complete response.

[8] *Ibid.,* p. 76.

In the development of the argument specific methods should be kept in mind.

1. Explanatory materials. Although analysis belongs primarily to the introduction, it is obvious that such materials also find a place throughout the discussion proper. These elements which explain and supplement the purely logical statements are composed of (*a*) definitions, (*b*) general explanations, (*c*) repetition for clearness and force, (*d*) summaries, (*e*) topic propositions.

2. Argumentative materials. The specific types of argument (whether you are engaged in constructive discussion or in refutation) will be used, including argument (*a*) by specific instance, (*b*) by analogy, (*c*) by causal relation, and (*e*) by authority.

3. Persuasive materials. The well-developed argument includes a considerable amount of motivating material, designed to embellish, reinforce, apply, and interpret these expository and argumentative or explicit materials in such a way as further to establish belief and lead to action. This material will be composed of (*a*) rhetorical questions, (*b*) figures of speech, (*c*) imperative and exclamatory sentences, (*d*) parallelism, (*e*) analogies, (*f*) euphony, (*g*) rhetorical rhythm, and similar language techniques. Naturally the extent to which you rely on each of these types of materials will depend on whether you discuss, debate, or persuade.

VIII. COMPOSITION OF THE CONCLUSION

Since the conclusion marks the true climax of the speech, establishing fully the grounds for accepting the argument, giving the grounds for accepting the argument, giving the audience once and for all the final impression of the speech and speaker, it is highly important that this section be intelligently planned. Sufficient but not too much space (or time) should be allowed for an adequate conclusion. Many school and college debaters time their speeches poorly and leave the platform with the final part of the speech unsaid. Other public speakers conclude and reconclude. In composing your speech, you have the simple problem of calculating the probable number of words at your disposal and apportioning the number given to each general division. A speech of ten minutes would represent some twelve hundred words. Not more than two hundred would be reserved for the conclusion and hardly that number for the introduction unless your address is a debate and is that of a first affirmative, in such instance three or four hundred words would perhaps be reserved for the analysis of the question. In oral composition for the public occasion, you will watch and check the distribution of your time and words. Whether the conclusion be written or oral, it should be painstakingly prepared so that it forms a true climax to all that precedes. This observation applies especially to radio scripts.

A. *Simplicity and the Conclusion.* Public speakers of earlier generations often made the conclusion a genuine peroration, in which lofty terms and sentiments were uttered in tones and words that were highly artificial. The contemporary speaker, especially the debater, cultivates sincerity and simplicity in the conclusion as in other sections of his argument.

B. *Methods of Developing the Conclusion.* Since the purpose of the conclusion is to make clear what has been stated, to reinforce the argument, or to ensure the desired emotional response from the audience, the content will consist of a summary, a vivid picturing of the whole problem from an emotional and imaginative angle, or an appeal reinforced by illustration, quotation, or other rhetorical device.

1. *Summary.* Make the conclusion a summary. This may be a review of both affirmative and negative arguments, recapitulation of one's own case, or a summary of both one's own case and that which will be presently discussed by one's colleagues. A discussional speech may content itself with a simple summary.

The greatest weakness in the conclusions of student debates is that the final summaries are mechanical echoes of the brief—clear but dull. Such phrases as the following have been used until they have lost their effectiveness: "since we have proved," "therefore, we maintain," "let us now sum up the case on both sides," "to summarize briefly the case for the affirmative," "we believe that we have proved," "I shall detain you but a moment longer," "let us see what we have proved," "one word more and I am done."

2. *Series of questions.* End the speech with a series of questions put to the audience or to a succeeding speaker. This de-

vice usually looks forward to a later speech by the questioner. Such final questioning is worth while only if the framer knows his ground.

3. *Suggesting a solution.* Sometimes conclude the speech by suggesting but not proving a solution. The statement would be, of course, subject to the criticism of any unproved proposition and is justified only when the speaker has already established his case.

4. *Reinforcing the argument by rephrasing the main ideas in dignified and different terms.*

5. *Personal ending.* Occasionally use the personal ending. It is often effective in the mouth of some individual whose motives have been assailed. Ben Kuroki closed the speech referred to earlier in this chapter, alluding again to his experiences, background, and motives thus:

Back in high school in Nebraska, one of the things they taught me was that America is a land where it isn't race or religion that makes free men. That's why I went to Tokyo. I went to fight for my country, where freedom isn't color, but a way of life, and all men are created equal until they prove otherwise. That's an old idea we have in Hershey, Nebraska, just down the highway from Cozad, which is near North Platte.[9]

6. *Prophecy.* Occasionally, the speaker may suggest his preview of the future, a future suggested by his previous argument. Winston Churchill, addressing Congress on Dec. 26, 1941, concluded his eloquent speech by such prophecy:

It is not given to us to peer into the mysteries of the future. Still I avow my hope and faith, sure and inviolate, that in the days to come the British and American people will for their own safety and for the good of all walk together in majesty, in justice and in peace.[10]

7. *Resolution.* The method of formulating a program of action is often couched in the form of a final resolution. Thus, Wendell Willkie, in his address on "Lidice," on Sunday, July 12, 1942, in the ceremonies at Stern Park Garden, Illinois, during which that city was renamed Lidice, Illinois, in honor of Lidice, Czechoslovakia, destroyed by the Germans, concluded:

[9] *Ibid.,* p. 212.
[10] Baird, *Representative American Speeches: 1941–42,* p. 29.

Let us here highly resolve that the memory of this little village of Bohemia, now resurrected by the people of a little village in Illinois, will fire us, now and until the battle is over, with the iron resolution that the madness of tyrants must perish from the earth, so that the earth may return to the people to whom it belongs, and be their village, their home, forever.[11]

8. Quotation, anecdote, striking statement. End with a quotation, citation of authority, anecdote, or striking statement, or some combination of these elements.

In general, the conclusion must fit the audience. Sometimes it is preferable to frame the closing remarks only when under the spell of the occasion. The exact situation may inspire the speaker to a type of utterance at once spontaneous and persuasive, more effective than anything that might have been previously set down and reproduced. Don't ramble, don't expand, don't introduce new elements. Select the type of conclusion, or the combination of types, that will bear home most impressively your points. When you have finished, stop.

EXERCISES AND PROBLEMS

1. Write a five-minute argument for public presentation (specify the type of audience you address, *e.g.,* classroom, radio). Incorporate the suggestions of this chapter concerning methods of developing each section of your discourse. Read or give extemporaneously this speech before your group.

2. With the suggestions of this chapter in mind, offer constructive suggestions for the reconstruction of the arguments delivered by your course mates in their fulfillment of exercise 1 above.

3. Analyze the appropriateness (adjustment to speaker, audience, subject, and occasion) through vocabulary, as illustrated in one of the following arguments: (*a*) Clarence Darrow's "Closing Argument for the Defense of the Loeb-Leopold Case," Aug. 22, 23, and 25, 1924; (*b*) Robert Crowe's "Closing Argument for the Prosecution in the Loeb-Leopold Case," Aug. 26, 27, 28, 1924.

4. Criticize a recent argumentative speech as reported in *Vital Speeches of the Day* or in *Representative American Speeches* (an annual since 1938.)

(See next chapter for other exercises on oral style.)

[11] Baird, *Representative American Speeches: 1942–43,* p. 167.

CHAPTER 17

Argumentative Composition: Language

I. PRINCIPLES OF LANGUAGE USAGE

In this chapter we are concerned with language as an important tool in argumentation, discussion, and debate. A few principles of language usage we here summarize before we outline concrete applications to debate and discussion.

(1) Words are not the same as the referents or things which such symbols represent. The word *America* is not the same as the continent for which the noun stands. (2) Words are not always the same as the thought process from which the language emerges. Obviously, it is easier to *think* than to translate these mysterious mental activities into equivalent language. (3) The words, however, should correspond to such thinking. (4) The words as uttered or placed on paper should enable the reader or hearer to construct a thinking pattern that duplicates that which you, the composer, may have in mind and try to impart. (5) How successful this transfer is will depend to a large degree on the experiences, interest, intelligence, and similar factors possessed by the auditor or reader. (6) Words have both denotative or literal meaning and connotative effect or suggestion beyond this actual or immediate meaning. *House* may imply all sorts of suggestions to those who listen to the word. (7) In argumenta-

tion, discussion, and debate we use language both to transfer literal meanings and to stimulate response through the emotional-imaginative elements conveyed by these same words. (8) Words are to be understood not in isolation but in their context. (9) We need to define or explain repeatedly if our communication is to achieve the results we hope for. (10) Language constantly changes. We need to be alert to meanings of the present date. (11) Since one word (again consult your dictionary) may have many meanings, we need to make clear which one we are using. (Definition is a problem of abstracting or selecting the elements of the object or idea we are attempting to define or explain.) (12) The use of synonyms will enable you, by comparison, to set forth more clearly the concrete meaning you are attempting to convey.

With such principles, familiar to the semanticist, in mind, may we now turn to concrete applications of language to discussion or debate.

II. LANGUAGE APPLICATIONS

A. Adapt Your Language to the Audience. Sooner or later in your progress as an arguer you will grapple with the problems of English composition. Language, you agree, enlivens or deadens much of what you say. Energetic delivery and ingratiating personality will supplement ideas and forms of expression. How much more forcible and persuasive becomes your effort, however, if you couch it in expressive and appropriate words, terms, and sentences.

In composition shall you follow closely the precepts of grammar and rhetoric? Or is Herbert Spencer right when he says, "A clear head, a quick imagination, and a sensitive ear, will go far towards making all rhetorical precepts needless."?[1]

Your principle, to provide for you a guide in effective direction of words and combinations of words, is that of audience adaptation. What language devices will most economically and efficiently appeal to your audience of either auditors or readers? As Spencer puts it,

A reader or listener has at each moment but a limited amount of mental power available. To recognize and interpret the symbols presented

[1] Herbert Spencer, in *Representative Essays on the Theory of Style* (W. T. Brewster, ed.), p. 167, The Macmillan Company, 1905.

to him requires part of this power; to arrange and combine the images suggested requires a further part, and only that part which remains can be used for realizing the thought conveyed. Hence, the more time and attention it takes to receive and understand each sentence the less time and attention can be given to the contained idea; and the less vividly will that idea be conceived.[2]

Just as ideas of the speech (or written argument) and even delivery must be adapted to the learning level, cultural standards, mental and emotional attitudes of an audience on a given occasion, so must language be selected and modified to secure maximum audience acceptance. Whether your sentences are clipped, your words abstract or concrete, your phrases nicely balanced will depend largely on your purposes with a specific group of listeners or readers and on the receptivity of your listeners (or readers) to audience demands and interests.

The ability of listeners (or readers) to give only limited attention should be reckoned with. The sustained attention-span, capacity of only a few seconds at a time, for example, affects the matter of sentence length and complexity.

B. Use Accurate Language. Use the word symbol that effects most closely the idea you would communicate. Your previous experience—both in writing and speaking—has made you continually conscious (I hope) of the need for precise statement. How refreshing it is to shape and pronounce vividly (or write) the word or term that exactly fits. How disastrous, on the contrary, it is to content yourself with loose, vague, or limited vocabulary.

Select, then, from the related meanings, the synonym that fits the mark. With a thesaurus or book of synonyms at hand, explore the details of vocabulary. Not only will you bring comfort to your reader or hearer, but you will clarify your own thinking and will enlarge your stock of ready words.

Avoid, then, ambiguity of expression. As I write this paragraph, "economic planning" is prominent in national speech-making. One group of contemporary economists uses the term as describing merely the technical process of mapping systematically a program for dealing with prices, wages, and other aspects of the industrial process. Another group, however, with an eye to the totalitarian record, assumes by the term *economic*

[2] *Ibid.*, p. 169.

planning state manipulation of the economic order, regimentation, and the destruction of all liberties!

In securing accuracy, repudiate every disposition to fall into exaggerated and all-inclusive usages. Many enthusiastic speakers and writers fall into a quandary of such extreme word mongering. We assert that "the plan is absurd" when we mean that "the plan is ineffective," or "inoperative." The radio speech or the printed page abounds in such fast and loose declarations as, "All Southerners would trample the Negro"; "English socialism is really totalitarian"; "Contemporary American novelists have sold out to the book-of-the-month promoters."

The statements here quoted obviously need qualification and in every case need more accurate phrasing.

To avoid such word habits you will examine your attitudes, check your statements with facts, and, certainly, refuse to sacrifice precision to emotional fervor.

As a further guarantee of accuracy, define carefully. Avoid piling up words about words. Make your explanation in terms, function, or purpose of your term to be defined; use history, etymology, or other means of explication. Redefine; be sure that the context enforces your definition.

C. Use Objective Language. A subtle but well-defined difference exists between language that conveys thought and "truth," and that which conveys bias and, therefore, distorts "truth." Those writers or speakers given to name calling are far from objectivity (language which reflects facts without emotional cloudiness).

If you condemn Russian expansionism, put it, "Russia has systematically expanded since the time of Peter the Great so that in 1950 she commands more territory than ever before," rather than "Through history Russian aggression rolled over alien races until today she threatens to engulf all civilization." The latter statement is more picturesque but in deliberative discussion, moderation of statement is to be encouraged.

Without weeding out all colorful expression, we propose that you scrutinize the nouns, verbs, and adjectives that may be freighted with demagoguery.

D. Be Concrete. Whether you write or speak, you will usually link together too many generalities. These confusing abstractions occur in sentences, and in words. A good psychological and rhetorical principle as old as the first Grecian rhetorical records and as new as the latest semantic cautionings, is that of specificity in language. Whether you are composing for radio, newspaper, scholarly journal, debate, or extempore speech, you will at every point work for definiteness of terms. Concreteness is largely a matter of a condensed illustration or example for general statement.

Contrast the examples of the abstract style in the first column with more concrete illustrations in the second:

Great Britain has strategic areas which must be defended.	The British Commonwealth of Nations depends for its life upon the Suez Canal, Gibraltar, Iran, Turkey, and the Malacca Straits.
The British Commonwealth of Nations and the United States are economically drawn together.	Prior to World War II, 40 per cent of the United States' foreign trade went to the United Kingdom, 16 per cent to Canada, and 20 per cent to the Pacific, including Australia, while one-third of Britain's exports came to the United States.

For concreteness, use individual names of people or places: omit colorless phrases; insert specific dates, days, hours; give figures and statistics; include instances, illustrations, analogies, direct quotations. In general, make each word and term conjure up concrete association. Your meaning will be clearer and more interestingly expressed.

E. Be Concise. Conciseness is a matter of expressing the subject with the greatest economy of words. Formal school debate especially encourages brevity because of the time limits. When the debater realizes that he must unfold his entire argument in a ten-minute speech, he practices the art of concise statement, perhaps the chief glory of the debating style. The amateur stylist sometimes lingers unduly over each idea to make it clear and significant; he elaborates each illustration; he quotes authorities at length; he expands his summaries, his appeals, and his introductions. Genuine economy necessitates discrimination in the selection of these ideas and illustrations.

F. Use Unhackneyed Language. Like colorless or vague language is the continual resort to platitudes and triteness. Speeches abound in clichés. Terms originally fresh and meaningful lose their appeal through mere recurrence. Just as popular songs or slogans by and by bore the listener, so words often repeated become meaningless. Successful appeals should be varied. The same stock of terms permits endless combinations. Originality depends upon the turns of phrases or words in fresh combinations.

To obtain freshness and originality you will avoid, for the most part, mechanical and formal expressions. It is, of course, necessary to make the material absolutely clear; in addition, it should be attractive. The method of enumeration will leave the listener cold.

Use also as sparingly as possible the technical terms of debate, such as "origin of the question," "honorable opponents," "worthy opponents," "honorable judges," "judges," "I have proved," "I have proven," "we still maintain," "debate," "discussion," "we defy our opponents," "conflicting opinions," "main issues," "first," "secondly," "thirdly," "we challenge our opponents," "our friends of the negative," "well," "consequently," "extraneous matter," "waived matter," "in summary let me say," "I thank you."

As the customary style of the college debater is charged with mechanical and trite terms, so is it highly repetitious. Something is to be said in favor of repetition as a rhetorical device to secure force. Burke, Webster, Chatham, and Erskine were masters of force through their ability to reinforce an idea by repetition. You need, however, to guard against repetition of another sort, the result of a narrow vocabulary or of carelessness. Such repetition makes student debates monotonous and weak. If the subject happens to be *Resolved, That the government should own and operate the coal mines,* the terms *need, ownership and operation,* and *coal mines* are used over and over. The remedy lies in a determination to use a varied vocabulary.

G. Use Illustrative or Figurative Language. Concreteness often takes the form of illustration, comparison, analogy, or figure of speech. The use of such connotative language is sometimes regarded as artificial and ornamental. Figurative language, however, is fundamentally justifiable as a means to accomplish the practical ends of argument. Illustrations and figurative terms make the debate clear, vivid, emphatic, impressive, and interesting. Moreover, they often have value as evidence and so further directly the establishment of conviction. Thus when Burke, in his discussion of conciliation with the colonies, wished to make clear that by a natural law the power of a large empire is comparatively slight in its more remote colonies, he used figurative language: "In large bodies, the circulation of power must be less vigorous at the extremities. Nature has said it." Speaking of the right to tax America he proceeded, "Their love of liberty, as with you, fixed and attached on this specific point of taxing." He added, "Here they felt its pulse, and as they found that beat they thought themselves sick or sound."

A number of suggestions, most of them obvious, are here offered as aids in use of illustration.

1. Let the illustrations be sufficiently numerous. An abstract style and literal phrasing should in every case be translated into concrete language.

2. Illustrations should be pertinent. Be sure that your language emphasizes what you wish to emphasize. Select the figures that best express your ideas.

3. Analogies and figures of speech should lie well within the experience of the audience.

4. Illustrations, analogies, and figures of speech should be well within your own experience. Let each definite detail come not from artificial collections of information but from your personal observation or your reading of history or other sources. Occasionally, debaters will refer to books of humorous selections as means of embellishing their speeches with humor. The effect is often pathetic.

6. Worn-out illustrations and hackneyed figures should be avoided. "No plan is perfect. Even the sun has spots," made a strong impression on debate audiences. But this metaphor has run its course. "You cannot break up the trusts any more than you can unscramble eggs" also had its day with debate teams. "The plan is a dangerous weapon" is also worn out.

H. Use Oral Language in Speech Composition. The principles above refer to oral and written compositions. The debater and discussant or persuasive speaker must be alert to use oral language. Your speaking style should be that of idiomatic conversation. It should avoid the stilted vocabulary of textbooks and the discussion style of other written literature. It should possess those peculiar word inflections, order, and combinations of any oral exchange. Good conversation is elliptical, *i.e., phone, movie, coed.* Contractions are frequent, as *got* (to have), *hike* (to walk), *pull* (to influence). Undue informality is in bad taste before an audience that expects dignity of language. Equally ill-advised is an elevated oratorical style or a technical vocabulary before untechnical audiences. Make your style personal, *i.e.,* "I," "we," "you." Use simple words as does Winston Churchill.

The oral style also calls for more repetition of words, phrases, and larger elements of composition than is necessary in written work.[3] If you say a thing once, your hearers may not get it at all. Important facts and ideas, therefore, should be repeated. How many times? Obviously, much depends on the character of your audience, the occasion, and your vocal skills. To overdo repetition may deaden interest.

Jersild conducted an investigation to determine the effectiveness of modes of emphasis in public speaking. He tested the effect of repetition on causing ideas to be remembered by those who listened to a simple speech. He concluded that "several repetitions distributed through the speech seem to have the higher values than fewer distributed repetitions."[4]

Such repetitions may be either the exact words or equivalent phrasing.

I. Use Variety in Language. Change in language to maintain maximum attention is also necessary. "To maintain attention we must have diversification of stimuli."[5]

The wide use of synonyms, the diversification of sentences, the duplication of ideas in different language, and the incorporation of varied types of evidence and illustrations—all contribute to such effectiveness.

III. Sentence Usages

A. Importance of Sentence Structure. The greatest economy of the listener's attention, the greatest appeal, and the most complete response, as I suggested above, result from proper consid-

[3] See Gladys Borchers, "An Approach to the Problem of Oral Style," *Quarterly Journal of Speech,* Vol. XXI, pp. 373–375, June, 1936.

[4] A. T. Jersild, "Modes of Emphasis in Public Speaking," *Journal of Applied Psychology,* Vol. XII, pp. 611–620, December, 1928.

[5] Jon Eisenson, *The Psychology of Speech,* p. 214, F. S. Crofts & Co., 1938.

eration of sentence structure. What I have said about the principles and methods of word usage applies also to the larger units of composition—to phrases, clauses, and sentences. It is assumed that you have had considerable training in English. It is nevertheless worth while to review types of sentence structure that are most appropriate in the composition of an effective debate or argumentative speech or article.

B. *Types of Sentence Forms.* Usually prefer short to complex or compound sentences. But be sure your style is not choppy and thin. Alternate loose with periodic structure. The balanced sentence emphasizes through contrast and comparison. It impresses through its cadence, and it aids in recall of the ideas. Numerous transitional, summarizing, and introductory sentences are also necessary to clarify meanings and to keep the listener on the trail of your thinking. Debaters often neglect to use sufficiently such helps to compositional coherence and unity. Inject frequently imperative, exclamatory, and interrogative sentences when your emotional reaction to your thinking needs adequate expression. Don't, however, overdo such forms—especially the interrogation. Continually check the internal structure of the sentence so that grammar and syntax are acceptable. You are concerned not simply with your prestige as an educated person but with your success in clarifying and convincing through sentence forms unmistakable in their meaning.

IV. Methods of Improving the Composition of Oral
and Written Argumentation

By way of summary of these specific compositional principles and methods, we here revert to the methods characteristic of successful speakers.

A. *Reading.* Most outstanding speakers, including Edmund Burke, Daniel Webster, Woodrow Wilson, and Winston Churchill, have been wide readers and conscious students of language.[6] For language proficiency I know of no substitute for wide and continued reading in representative literature, including the best speeches of older and present-day debaters and persuasive speakers.

[6] For further illustrations see W. N. Brigance, ed., *The History and Criticism of American Public Address,* 2 vols., McGraw-Hill Book Company, Inc., 1943.

B. *Writing.* Case histories of important platform arguers and orators will make clear that they wrote and rewrote their discourses for presentation. Both in school days and later they habitually put their ideas on paper and subjected themselves to the discipline of repeated revision of a text.[7]

C. *Listening.* Listen to superior lecturers and debaters, including the radio speakers; note their language skill.

D. *Logic and Semantics.* Elect courses in semantics, logic, argumentation, and public speaking. Test arguments. Your examination and correction of fallacies will add to your facility in effective usage of words.

E. *Study of Words.* Finally, I would endorse the traditional advice of teachers to study words, their history, and present meanings. Study systematically synonyms and antonyms. Work continually with the dictionary. I know of no formula more necessary than that of writing and rewriting with a dictionary within reach. Continued experience with words will no doubt give you a wide vocabulary and thus strengthen your ability to extemporize effectively—the *summum bonum* of every debater.

EXERCISES AND PROBLEMS

1. Rewrite (or write) one of your recent debates with special attention to oral style. Read it or otherwise submit it for class criticism.

2. Criticize the style of a printed student debate. (See any recent volume of the *University Debaters'* series.)

3. (*For advanced students.*) Make a précis of one of the following treatments of oral style. Comment on the point of view and conclusions of the writer: (*a*) H. L. Ewbank, "Four Approaches to the Study of Speech Style," *Quarterly Journal of Speech,* 17:458–465, November, 1931; (*b*) Gladys Borchers, "An Approach to the Problem of Oral Style," *Quarterly Journal of Speech,* 22:114–117, February, 1936; (*c*) W. N. Brigance, "The Use of Words," in *Speech Composition,* pp. 120–196; (*d*) Lester Thonssen and A. Craig Baird, "The Style of Public Address," in *Speech Criticism,* pp. 405–433.

4. Evaluate the oral style of a representative American debate as delivered during recent months and as printed in the *Congressional*

---

[7] For examples of methods of speech composition see the testimony of Robert H. Jackson (*Representative American Speeches: 1945–46,* p. 61); A. H. Compton (p. 109); and Lewis M. Brown (p. 134).

Record, Vital Speeches of the Day, or as recorded and transcripted by the investigator.

5. Evaluate the oral style as illustrated by one of the following (or similar prominent political speakers of recent decades) in a speech delivered since 1941: Franklin D. Roosevelt, Winston Churchill, Arthur H. Vandenberg, Thomas E. Dewey, Herbert Hoover, Robert Taft, Harold E. Stassen.

CHAPTER 18

Persuasion: Techniques of Motivation

I. ARGUMENTATION AND PERSUASION[1]

Argumentation, as we explained at the outset of this book, is a process of influencing the belief and conduct of a hearer or reader by supplying him with reasons and motives for action. Such aim suggests that successful argumentation results from securing the desired response from the audience. The specific end of argument is affecting belief and conduct. How do we supply reasons and motives for action?

The arguer, we are told, does so by (1) catching the attention of the potential hearer, (2) holding his interest through effective selection and presentation of ideas, (3) convincing him through logical argument and evidence, (4) persuading him through proper motivating materials, and, finally, (5) securing from him definite action.[2]

These purposes clearly involve more than cold reasoning and objective demonstration. Such goals call for persuasion as well

[1] Strictly speaking, we should not include persuasion as one of the principles of discussion. Because, however, discussants should know their audiences and the ways of propagandists and other persuaders, we are retaining this chapter in Part II.

[2] H. L. Hollingworth, *The Psychology of the Audience*, pp. 12–13, American Book Company, 1935.

as logic. Why? Because man is an emotional personality. Even his reasons are a solvent of facts, inferences, beliefs, and desires. His emotions are to be heavily reckoned with.

What is persuasion? It has to do with any "verbal method of influencing human behavior."[3]   In this chapter, however, we shall limit it to the special method of influencing an audience through emotional appeals or the art of motivation by means largely nonlogical. What techniques as persuaders shall we use?

II. Techniques of Persuasion

A. *Analyze the Audience as Individuals and as a Group.* Your "audience" may sometimes be a single listener. What are his characteristics that will govern our methods of appealing to him? Although individuals vary widely, some tendencies are markedly apparent. What differences exist between the individual who composes your one-man audience and the same individual merged with several others assembled to hear you? Much, of course, depends upon the numbers of hearers, their contiguity to each other, the skill of the speaker in "polarizing" the group (establishing a close response between speaker and audience), the degree of circular response (response between speaker and audience, and audience interaction). Certainly, if we may generalize with respect to the average member of that audience, the tendencies analyzed below are also prevalent—in certain respects may sometimes be intensified—when hearers as a fairly homogeneous group are responding. As Oliver observes, "The sense of identity diminishes and inhibitions are weakened. . . . As a consequence crowds tend to act as units, to go to extremes in their emotional expressions, to subordinate their judgments even more readily than do individuals to their emotions."[4]

1. *The individual and the audience as a group are affected by basic emotional responses and desires.* Although the more sophisticated individuals whom college students often address direct their thinking into more reflective channels and follow primarily an intellectual pattern, the emotional thinking is at all points active. Although training, tradition, and personal experiences modify and curb these elemental responses, the drives,

[3] Robert T. Oliver, *The Psychology of Persuasive Speech,* p. 10, Longmans, Green & Co., Inc., 1942.

[4] *Ibid.,* p. 172.

wants, desires, and the marks of emotional thinking and acting continually assert themselves.

Audiences, as a group, are also basically emotional. Their reflective thinking becomes relatively less operative as they unite under speaking leadership. To cite Hollingworth,

> The members of an audience are more alike in their instincts and emotions than in capacity to follow logical reasoning: hence emotional appeals or topics will move uniformly and generally influence them. The beliefs of an audience do not depend on evidence alone; they are definitely warped, even against the evidence, by desires and hopes.[5]

Charles Bird concludes that "With few exceptions crowd behavior is a regression to the uncontrolled and destructive activities or to the volatile, superficial, and uninhibited happiness of childhood."[6]

2. *The individual and the audience as a group tend to believe what satisfies their primary and secondary needs and wants.* "Each one believes what he wants to believe." What are the basic (primary, physiological, biological) and secondary (derived, psychological, social, learned, habitual) wants? They include food and drink, escape from persons and things that threaten our security, sexual satisfaction, self-preservation, association with (or avoidance of) others, assertiveness, accumulation of goods, comforts, personal and social convenience, social approval and popularity, social dominance (or submission), control or other disposition of opposing persons or things, realization of personal or social aims, conformity (or nonconformity), change (escape from boredom, reality), intellectual and aesthetic satisfaction (*e.g.*, problem solving, creativeness). These items obviously overlap. They are not readily classifiable.[7] They do illustrate the representative reactions associated with our actions. We tend to reject those propositions and ideas foreign to these motivating constituents of our personality and experience and

---

[5] Hollingworth, *op. cit.*, pp. 137–148.

[6] Charles Bird, *Social Psychology*, p. 357, Appleton-Century-Crofts, Inc., 1940.

[7] See for classification and discussion of emotions and drives, Carl E. Seashore, *An Introduction to Psychology*, pp. 302–337, The Macmillan Company, 1924; Edwin G. Boring, Herbert S. Langfeld, Harry P. Weld, and collaborators, *Introduction to Psychology*, pp. 183–222, John Wiley & Sons, Inc., 1939; Bird, *op. cit.*, pp. 78–100.

appropriate those beliefs that promise immediate and enduring satisfactions. Audiences, like individuals, want arguments and appeals that assure them of security, economic and social satisfactions, and other drives.

3. *The individual and the audience as a group tend to respond to connotative language.* The emotional and figurative associations of words affect strongly our decisions and conduct. Our conditioning experiences accompanied by word symbols later call forth the emotional responses identified with the original reactions. Thus the whole pattern of word symbols produces an emotional current inextricably interwoven with the so-called intellectual movement. Certain words and terms, obviously, more quickly and powerfully stimulate than do others. These are the characteristic "loaded" words. Some of them produce approval and cooperation, such as *American, expert, celebrity, sponsor, he-man, angel, Abraham Lincoln, scholar, lover, grandmother, debutante.* Others invite repulsion, such as *enemy, demagogue, traitor, informer, cheat, deserter, liar, hypocrite, seducer, slut, defaulter, assassin, gunman, roughneck, upstart, scatterbrain.* How is it with the crowd? "Crowd language is often language of desire. Not argument and proof but usually bold affirmation are the forms of expression. . . . Most action-compelling words succeed because vague and unanalyzed feelings are aroused by them."[8]

4. *The individual and the crowd tend to be suggestible.* Suggestion is the automatic response to a stimulus or the acceptance of a proposition without deliberation. The approval is direct, immediate, apparently without motivation. When without reflection you yield to the common "Support Gallagher for mayor," you are governed entirely by suggestion. When you submit to the injunction "Support Gallagher" only after you have concluded, "With Gallagher as mayor, taxes will be better enforced," you are acting from reason or from expressed motives rather than from suggestion. Suggestion furnishes the case of an apparently incidental stimulus touching off "responses quite disproportionate to its inherent strength."[9]

[8] Bird, *op. cit.*, p. 357.

[9] See also E. B. Titchener, *A Textbook of Psychology*, p. 499, The Macmillan Company, 1910; W. D. Scott, *Psychology of Advertising*, p. 80, Small, Maynard & Co., 1921; William McDougall, *Social Psychology*, p. 97, John W. Luce Company, 1921; Bird, *op. cit.*, pp. 258–259.

In crowds, the imitative impulse, the lowering of the barriers of individual leadership and direction help to explain the release of emotional controls and the yielding to suggestion. To cite Bird again, "Marked suggestibility and an intensification of emotion have been stressed as outstanding features of crowd behavior."[10]

Argument, to be effective, will furnish, in addition to logical grounds for proof, statements which reinforce the ideas so that although sheer logic or obvious exhortation may fail, direct or indirect suggestion may succeed.

5. *The individual and the crowd tend to rationalize.* Your average listener or reader no doubt honestly believes that he is usually governed by reason and good sense. He likes to hear speeches that have the earmarks of logic. He prides himself on his ability to sift idea from idea and to stamp as acceptable those that conform to common sense. To his friends, especially his family, he justifies his actions by reciting good and sufficient reasons. Even to himself, he probably recites arguments that enforce his wish to follow a given course of thinking and acting. This practice of aligning dominant desire with insufficient reasons and of formulating pseudo reasons to give an air of rationality to an irrational position or action is rationalization.[11]

Rationalizing has its source in a strong desire in conflict with another desire. Let us suppose, for example, that Jane, a college sophomore, is a good student and, in fact, is headed for Phi Beta Kappa rank. She, however, is much interested in a young man at a neighboring college. He has invited her to a week-end dance and carnival at his institution. She has impending examinations the following week and term papers due, but she wants very badly to have that wonderful week end. The conflict between this social release and the social prestige of scholarship (to say nothing of the approval of her parents) is tremendous. She finally decides to go. She deceives herself as to her real reasons. She convinces herself that she can do a better job of writing a term paper if she has the three-day change from academic pressure. She assures herself that she can grind for those exams if

<hr>

[10] Bird, *op. cit.*, p. 356.

[11] *Cf.* Percival M. Symonds, *The Dynamics of Human Adjustment*, Appleton-Century-Crofts, Inc., 1946. Edwin Arthur Burtt, *Right Thinking*, pp. 63–66, Harper & Brothers, 1946.

she gets up fresh and alert by the alarm clock early on Monday. Even if her grade point average falls, she reasons that her social success will outweigh these scholastic losses. Such is the technique of rationalizing.

Jane is like the fox who lost his tail and told himself (and the world) that tailless foxes are much more in the vogue. The fox was honest in his line of reasoning. It was nevertheless sham reasoning for him to conceal his disappointment at parading before fellow foxes attired with splendid tails.[12]

The rationalizing of predetermined attitudes and activities underlies much thinking in interpretations of current philosophy, history, and political science. Conclusive positions in any of these fields may reflect the mind of those who have a special stake in the given area. Their conclusions may first of all be largely unreasoned and emotionally determined. When their principles or formulas are critically questioned, these philosophers or social scientists will rise in defense with elaborate arguments. Thus knowledge and its description become stereotyped. The explanations, to a large degree, represent rationalization. Thus do we erect logical skyscrapers on foundations of wishful thinking and desire.

Why do we so rationalize? Partly to resolve our private conflicts with ourselves and thus escape confusion; partly to retain or establish social approval of actions otherwise appearing as stupid; partly to gain satisfaction through such proof to ourselves that we are men of reason rather than children of emotion.[13]

Crowds are probably more open to the rationalizing process than are the individuals in isolation or free from group influence. Their collective tendency to prefer the less intellectual appeals and their ready response to slogans and conclusions that coincide with their stereotypes would point to their adoption of group rationalizing. They are delighted to hear and amplify for themselves reasons that appear to confirm their earlier opinions. Their response to group pressure would make them less conscious of individual responsibility.

6. *The individual and the crowd tend to think and act from prejudice.* Debate implies the use of argument and evidence as

[12] *Cf.* Oliver, *op. cit.*, pp. 182–196.
[13] Hollingworth, *op. cit.*, pp. 112–118.

the basis of judgment. Its atmosphere is judicial. The prejudicial person, however, forms a judgment or opinion without proper examination of the facts or reasons "essential to a just and impartial determination."[14] His mental decisions are on grounds other than those of reason. These decisions, moreover, are shaped before the argument and evidence are presented. Prejudice grows out of motives well developed before the controversial situation arises that reveals the bias.

Prejudice may or may not be socially harmful. Certain biases may be socially useful, as when a child is biased against going with strangers encountered on the street.[15] Other prepossessions or motives influencing judgments may be highly harmful, as was the bias of Cavalier against Puritan, or Irishman against Englishman, of Yank against Southerner, of Jacksonian Democrat against Whig, of Latin American against the "Yankee pig." In 1949 and after in the United States, prejudice, strong or otherwise, continues to occur between rural and urban citizens, whites and Negroes, Americans and Russians, corporation leaders and labor unionists, Republicans and Democrats, Methodists and Presbyterians, Harvard and Yale, Iowa and Minnesota, public and private colleges, teachers and businessmen, boys and girls, school debaters and athletes, philosophers and scientists, Old Guard and New Dealers, college graduates and noncollegians.

Why these prejudices? They are traceable to such external, social forces as influence of parents, other children, sports, rhymes, celebration of holidays, books, newspapers, cartoons, motion pictures, radio, Sunday schools and churches, teachers, textbooks, songs, speeches, occupations, and similar experiences. Behind these social forces lie inner motives of the individual referred to above—his self-interest, self-esteem, dislike of change, and desire for novelty. The point is that whether biases may or may not be harmful, their expression is frequent. Every human being possesses them in larger or smaller degree.

7. *The individual and the audience tend to accept fallacious arguments.* High emotion and bias become fertile agencies for the spread of fallacious argument. However thin and crooked

---

[14] Webster's *New International Dictionary of the English Language,* 2d ed., unabridged, 1949.

[15] Edwin L. Clarke, *The Art of Straight Thinking,* pp. 9ff., Appleton-Century-Crofts, Inc., 1929.

may be the reasoning, it stands a good chance of acceptance if it feeds these emotional attitudes. The person may confuse many words for genuine argument, he may generalize from a single, untypical example, draw false conclusions from false analogies, may mistake antecedent facts for genuine causes, or subsequent facts for genuine effects, may mistake correlation or coincidence for causal relation, may succumb to any one of the many fallacies of argument or evidence discussed above.[16]

Hollingworth concludes that

The average man prides himself on his rationality, but his conception of evidence and of the nature of proof is naïve and easily satisfied, even by specious and invalid argument. In a group situation susceptibility to cheap and fallacious modes of persuasion is by no means limited to the average man.[17]

Scholars, college students, business executives, and others composing sophisticated audiences are by no means exempt from acceptance of fallacious reasoning.

These, then, are at least seven factors in the human personality and in individuals assembled as audiences with which we are to reckon in framing our arguments—the tendency to react emotionally rather than rationally, to believe what satisfies primary and secondary needs and wants, to respond to connotative language, to be suggestible, to rationalize, to reflect prejudice, and to yield to specious argument and evidence.

C. *Analyze the Specific Audience.* In addition to an analysis of the intellectual traits of the individual and of the group tendencies, we shall make as complete analysis of a specific audience as may be practicable.

1. *Analyze the occasion.* Review the aim of the meeting. Is it an audience gathered to see and hear you give a typical college debate? Is the atmosphere largely educational, an occasion for demonstrating good argumentative technique? Is it a radio speech? If so, what manner of audience is to tune in? Are they to be businessmen, school administrators, housewives, a civic organization; or are they members of some "college of the air"?

What of the rules for the occasion? Is it to be cross-examination? Panel forum? Examination by audience? Direct-clash

---

[16] See pp. 171*ff.*
[17] Hollingworth, *op. cit.*, p. 138.

procedure? If so, what reactions are you attempting to obtain from the audience?

Even the size of the room and the other physical details are important. Any attempt to frame your speech with these physical limitations and requirements of the occasion in view should make your success more certain.

2. *Analyze the audience in terms of the arguer's purpose.* The purpose of the arguer is to (*a*) catch the attention of the potential hearer, (*b*) hold his interest through the selection and arrangement of ideas, (*c*) convince him through logical argument and evidence, (*d*) persuade him through proper motivating materials, and (*e*) secure from him definite action.[18]

Not all persuasive or argumentative speeches need to stress these five steps. The final step, for example, will, of course, be omitted in situations where the speaker's aim is to secure only the most general agreement with his ideas. You will note, too, that these steps or aims need not be developed in chronological succession. Rather these aims overlap at every point. The speech is a unit, in which attention, interest, conviction, persuasion, and action (as we define these terms) parallel each other and merge. The action step and the motivating elements are in reality identical; the fivefold differentiation is largely one for convenience in treating aspects of this highly complex problem of audience control.

Audience and speaker may have a number of mutual relations. The individuals of the audience will have definite relationships to one another, and the speaker will bear a relation to these individuals.

Note the differences in typical audiences in the relations of the members to each other and to the speaker. The public-square crowd, for example, which you may sometime address if you are politically ambitious, has little homogeneity, common interest, or purpose. In this situation you will apply the entire formula and may spend most of your time in trying to get attention. Your sales talk to an individual prospect often presents a similar problem in applying at length each phase of the complete process— a problem hardly less difficult to solve than that of speaking in a municipal park. Your process of orienting a typical college-debate audience is relatively easier. The group arrives in the

18 *Ibid.*, pp. 12–13.

auditorium with a fairly well-established pattern of attention; they know something of the speakers, the subject, and the general situation into which they voluntarily fit. If you address a college mass meeting, you may have some of the elements of the soapbox occasion; but with the aid of a common collegiate enthusiasm, cheers, and music, you should quickly polarize or orient the group toward your purposes. The discussion occasion represents still another type. You have no great need to secure attention; you can concentrate on unfolding your ideas and creating an intellectual solidarity.

The radio audience is particularly difficult to orient because it is an "absent audience," largely to be dealt with on the basis of its supposed character. Thus, while the materials can be prearranged, you have no instant assurance either of success or of failure.

3. *Analyze the specific interests, intelligence, and cultural level of the audience.* In addition to this understanding of the general action tendencies which challenge and hold attention, the debater will analyze the specific interests of the audience and their attitude toward the question. The salesman, before approaching his prospect, finds it desirable to make a fairly complete inventory of the interests and special traits of the prospect. If the person interviewed is interested in golf or tennis, is a member of a well-known country club, president of some service club, a radio fan, a college graduate, a banker, a reader of Joseph Conrad and Stevenson, a Republican, or a Methodist, these and similar facts are significant in determining the type of argument to be presented.

Even the college debater who hopes for a decision from the critic judge has his audience. The contest debater will doubtless modify his presentation in the light of the educational and other experiences, interests, and attitudes of the judge. If it is known that the critic judge discounts humor and relishes plain statement reinforced by abundant evidence, the arguer in his presentation will not ignore such information. Every good contest arguer, however, speaks to the larger audience as well as to the judge.

4. *Analyze the prejudices of the audience.* Picture to yourself the individual backgrounds that partly explain possible audience prejudices. Better still, examine your own modes of thinking.

You form a pretty fair sample of the college group. How many of your own ideas were really implanted in you by older, more dominant boys or girls? By your kindly parents? Consider the influence upon you, in childhood and since, of books, newspapers, magazines, cinema, radio, teachers, preachers, parents, school, popular songs, public speakers, and friends. Not all these acquired prejudices are objectionable. Many of them, however, do guide you and with little critical evaluation by you; and many of them need inspection and rejection. As an experiment, test yourself for prejudices and persuade your colleagues to do so. Make an extensive list of your biases, religious, racial, economic, political, social, physical, literary, scientific, and educational.

Such self-analysis will encourage you to analyze the group before whom you are to debate. With such insight into your group, you can capitalize on rather than combat these deeply grounded emotional sets; your arguments will be shaped in the light of such audience determinants.

5. *Analyze the attitude of the audience toward the question.* Again, the attitude of the listeners toward the subject largely determines the selection of material and order of presentation. Toward the proposition the audience may be (*a*) strongly favorable, (*b*) slightly favorable, (*c*) undecided or indifferent, (*d*) slightly opposed, or (*e*) strongly opposed.

Those who are strongly favorable to the speaker enthusiastically applaud each sentiment. Such an audience may be a group of Republicans listening to a defense of the policy of high tariff or an audience of World War II veterans listening to an argument in support of more adequate national housing.

In a distinct group are those who are doubtful about the proposition or indifferent to it. To this section of an audience your chief energy will be directed. Your real victory comes not so much in quickening the enthusiasm of those favorably inclined as in persuading those who have been open-minded and genuinely deliberative.

The greatest problem, of course, lies in influencing the hostile, or opposing, group. Such listeners may pretend to be open-minded or think that they are receptive to logic. In reality they reject whatever argument fails to coincide with their established beliefs. A lifelong Republican, after hearing a twenty-minute speech urging him to vote the Democratic ticket, is not often converted to Democratic doctrines. Nevertheless, advance knowledge of the audience's attitude will surely help you to shape your speech effectively. Favorable auditors become more favorable, deliberative minds incline to vote for you, and even an occasional opponent will relent as you suggest new beliefs that may be linked up with set attitudes.

6. *Analyze the knowledge and experience of the audience with the problem.* How much do the auditors and audience participants know about the immediate problem? As best you can, you should know definitely their information as well as the extent of their experience in participating in, or listening to, previous discussions and debates on this subject.

7. *Analyze the attitudes of the audience toward the speaker or speakers.* An important factor in the persuasive process is the attitude of the audience toward the speaker. If it has confidence in your intelligence as a speaker, your good will toward them, and your high moral character (your honesty of purpose and sincerity), your argument is half won. On the contrary, if the group dislikes you, rates low your reputation, and listens with suspicion to your every idea, you can accomplish little, be your logic and argument ever so sound and well expressed. Even though these adverse audience attitudes toward the speaker may be utterly unjustified, the fact of their existence must be faced and properly dealt with. A third attitude, neither favorable or unfavorable, often exists. The listeners may know absolutely nothing concerning the speaker. They did not catch his name over the radio or as he was briefly introduced on the platform. Whatever these attitudes, you the speaker will aim to establish or further establish your (a) good sense and competency to handle the topic, (b) cooperative and generous attitude toward your group, and (c) ethical and moral integrity.

The following questions you may use as criteria for audience analysis:

I. The audience traits, beliefs, attitudes
   A. Age differences?
   B. Numbers?
   C. Nationality?
   D. Sex differences?
   E. Intelligence?
   F. Education?
   G. Occupations?
   H. Cultural interests?

    I. Economic status?

    J. Economic, social, political, religious, and other attitudes and interests?

    K. Representative needs, wants, and desires?

    L. Audience type—heterogeneous or homogeneous?

II. The audience and the subject

    A. Knowledge of the subject?

    B. Experience with the subject?

    C. Stake in the subject?

    D. Attitudes toward the subject?

III. The audience and the speaker

    A. His reputation and prestige?

    B. Audience impression of his knowledge?

    C. Audience impression of his social interests, humor, and good will?

    D. Audience impression and knowledge of his experiences, training, and other background?

    E. Audience impression and knowledge of his honesty, sincerity, and moral responsibility and leadership?

IV. The audience and the occasion

    A. Size, shape, acoustics, and other elements of the auditorium?

    B. Platform arrangements, number of speakers, and abilities of chairman?

    C. Length of speech or speeches and similar details relating to the speaking program?

    D. Appropriateness of the speech or speeches?

    E. Purpose of the meeting?

D. Select and Frame the Subject with a View to the Needs and Requirements of the Special Audience.   In an earlier chapter we suggested principles to govern the selection and framing of the subject.   Here we merely remind ourselves that you will simplify your problem of influencing an audience if you light upon a topic of peculiar interest to them.   If you happen to elect that side of the problem that coincides with their beliefs, you will also help your case.   Naturally, both subject and side will be determined by the purpose of the gathering.   We are not implying here that you will happen to defend whatever position most of your prospective audience holds.   Most of your subjects, including the intercollegiate debate topics, are selected by others.   Often, however, before campus and community meetings groups, you can pick your question.

E. Select, Arrange, and Proportion the Arguments with a View to Persuading Your Audience. Your technique with a brief before you is to select those arguments that will best accomplish your purpose. Arrange the ideas in the most effective sequence to appeal to your audience, and give to each idea the proper proportion. The brief thus becomes not a speech plan but a logical survey to be adapted to the particular audience. You ask, What arguments best attach themselves to the established beliefs of the audience? What arguments will best enable you to keep on common ground with your listeners and lead them to your conclusion? To illustrate, suppose you, the speaker, are to develop the argument in support of the proposition, *Resolved, That Congress should immediately appropriate an additional four billion dollars for the Air Force during the next two years.*

Suppose you are talking to a group of students, the large majority of whom intend to vote against your proposition. You would probably stress the arguments that

1. War still threatens.
2. Our national defenses must be sufficient for any emergency.
3. The existing international agencies for peace are unable to prevent a conflict.

By tying up these arguments to the established beliefs that "War is a terrible calamity," "War will destroy my individual happiness," "A nation should be prepared for defense," you may overcome the opposition (although many will not be moved by your contentions).

Again, assume that your audience is a woman's club of some church. Most of them presumably have a strong distrust of the powerful military and might have an idealistic conception of the times when "war shall be no more." For this group you will probably argue that

1. A larger military machine would foster international peace.
2. Other countries would hesitate to quarrel with us.
3. Our strength would lead us to become more active in promoting world peace.

Again, you are invited to address a group of businessmen, most of whom have indicated their opposition to your position. Here the third section of your brief will perhaps be used:

1. Continued support of a vast military machine would be a desirable expenditure of money.
2. It would be cheap insurance.
3. The sum involved would not be sufficiently large to prevent the reduction of national taxes.

Other arguments would be necessary to the completion of a logical case, such as,

1. War threatens.
2. Our national defenses are inadequate.

But complete response from each audience necessitates the stressing of those special arguments that fit in most readily with the mind patterns of the listeners. In no case have you been inconsistent with your own logical stand. You have simply attempted to select, arrange, and emphasize those aspects most likely to secure approval.

What about the order of emotional and of logical proofs? Should argument come first and persuasion follow? It is impossible to answer without understanding of each audience (and the requirements of the same group will vary from meeting to meeting). Sometimes you will first present ideas that strongly align themselves with the hopes, desires, and beliefs of the hearers. But you will couple these emotional drives or follow them, with such arguments as you can muster. Thus your auditor will not only receive strong emotional stimulus to follow your bent but will be quickened to rational appeals that confirm and make permanent the program to which you have committed him. Your procedure here takes account of the auditor's interest in being rational.

Sometimes the emotional (motivative or persuasive) proofs will come first. This occasional priority of so-called appeals to logical materials will be no mere trick to engulf your hearer in a sea of false argument.

A similar principle will govern you in unfolding inductive and deductive argument. Shall you proceed from the limited to the more general? It all depends. Often you can gain your point by moving in from one concrete item to a wider series of ideas until the logical goal is accepted. The deductive plan, on the contrary, may be followed (and usually is) when your time is limited, when your audience wishes logic rather than merely interesting treatment, and when persuasive results may not be so necessary.

What of the position and amount of rebuttal in persuasion? Not only will you protect your lines of reasoning, but you will make clear the possible fallacies of counterargument and evidence. Such refutation usually occurs after your own arguments, but may precede or accompany them.

Your job is to remove the inhibitions of auditors and to anticipate fallacious objections. For example, you will be alert to point out that vigorous assertion or volubility should not supplant proof; that dogmatism or mysticism should not supersede logic; that mere coincidence is not to be confused with causal relation; that assault upon a man's character is not to be substituted for logical criticism of his arguments; that reliance upon hearsay testimony, generalization from exceptional cases, arguing in a circle, or begging the question constitutes unsound technique. Thus you will provide a logical pattern of your materials; your auditor's distrust of demagoguery will thus be heightened and his respect for his own mental processes increased.

F. *Develop the Motivative Elements with a View to Persuasion of the Audience.* At this point in our treatment of persuasion we deal most directly with the representative drives of the listeners: self-preservation, accumulation of goods and comforts, personal and social satisfactions, social recognitions and power, overcoming of opposing persons and situations, adherence to duty, justice, self-sacrifice, and cooperation.

These appeals, as I indicated above, are merely suggestive. Others will occur to you as you deal with practical situations. At any rate you will give other names and classifications to these drives. All are based upon the primary emotional states, usually limited to fear (anger) and love (sex) and hunger. Based upon such elementary division is a category of emotions, which include sympathy, gratitude, hope, pride, friendship, good will, pity, and similar terms under love; and hatred, indignation, contempt, revenge, shame, jealousy, and various others under fear or anger. These emotions become drives or motives. We will illustrate a few of these motives as addressed through argument.

1. *Self-preservation.* "Abolish the atom bomb by international agreement." "Vote for the bill to require all autoists to have liability insurance."

2. Accumulation of goods and comforts. "Buy an endowment policy with the West Insurance Company and spend your old age in ease." "Keep the state income tax at its present level and so lower your high property taxes."

3. Personal and social satisfactions. "The state of Texas should further increase its appropriation for public instruction." "The city of Lewisville should build and support a municipal dancing pavilion."

4. Social recognition and power. "Subscribe to the Union fund, for we must have the finest university center in America." "Let us build a million-dollar high-school building so that our city will have a reputation for educational progressiveness."

5. Resistance to opposing persons and situations. "Support the Bruner-Holmes antilabor law, for unionists are getting a monopoly of labor and are dictating to management." "Declare war on Russia at once so that our international leadership for peace and democracy may not be destroyed."

6. Adherence to duty and justice. "Vote for the bill extending Federal aid to education, for such a bill will provide for more equitable educational opportunities to the pupils of backward states."

7. Self-sacrifice. "This national emergency calls for every citizen to do his full duty in military enlistment and in keeping high civilian morale behind the front."

8. Appeal through the personality of the speaker. The emotional drift of any speech will be governed not only by the specific lines of appeal suggested above but by that vague factor we call the speaker's personality. If the audience has confidence in the speaker, in his intellectual competence, his good will, and his moral leadership, and if his personality so dominates that all opposition is for the time broken, then the proposition will be accepted, attention held, and the decision reached.

a. TACT. Tact, positively considered, is the ability to say those things which impress the listener favorably; negatively, it is the good judgment to avoid saying those things that create inhibitions. Many a debate, otherwise quite satisfactory from the point of view of delivery and of argument and of evidence, has fallen flat because of the speaker's failure to say the appropriate thing or his disposition to say the highly inappropriate thing. It has been said that nine-tenths of the art of public speaking lies in the tactful statement of ideas. The proper method of procedure in developing or exercising tact is to understand your audience. Tactlessness usually results from failure to understand human nature in general and, specifically, the people composing the immediate audience.

b. SINCERITY. More confidence is given to that arguer who evidently believes what he states and who is genuinely concerned that the audience holds similar beliefs. Nothing so ruins the effect of good argument as a suggestion of insincerity.

The only way to succeed in giving the impression of sincerity is to be sincere. Under no circumstances should a speaker allow the public to have a false impression of what he thinks. If he opposes military training in the American universities, then he should never allow an audience to assume that he is for such tactics and training. As Demosthenes declared, no one has a license to misrepresent his real convictions.

c. EARNESTNESS. Sincerity means earnestness, seriousness of purpose, determination, alertness, and a moral stamina that commands from the audience if not agreement at least profound respect for the ideas of the disputant. Earnestness grows out of the speaker's faith and begets faith. Smartness of style, flippancy, and cynicism may for the moment hold the attention; but the hollowness of the speaker's purpose shows through, and the audience loses contact with the argument because of the loss of confidence in the spokesman for the argument.

d. HUMOR. Debaters are often solemn without being in earnest. Either solemnity or earnestness, and the two are often the same, is not inconsistent with humor. Genial humor, whether quiet or broad, is almost necessary for the effective persuasion of the average audience. The lighter mood breaks down hostility, puts the speaker on common ground with his audience, creates a common emotion—and so a psychological crowd—and thus becomes a great ally to sound argument. School and college debating especially need the element of humor, for the discussions are usually upon heavy subjects. The content of most debates is a compact assembling of statistics that for many people means downright dullness. He who can lighten the serious and thoughtful passages with spontaneous wit has a great advantage.

How can a debater who has *no humor* acquire that quality? The answer is that every student, as well as practically every other human being, does possess a sense of the comic. The spirit needs only release.

Humor in debate need not consist of a series of jokes. Anecdotes may be introduced, but they should be brief and appropriate. Neither should humor be a substitute for sound argument. Quaint asides, unexpected turns of language and ideas, and sharp reply to thrusts are the stuff of the debater's wit.

e. SELF-CONFIDENCE. The audience will have far more respect for that speaker who has the courage of his convictions— who is sure of his facts and his position. No audience will develop enthusiasm for the debater whose voice has the note of uncertainty or query or who seems to be apologizing for his ideas. For a debater to rise in the face of a strong attack and to proceed calmly, sure of his position, self-poised, self-controlled, will engender that same spirit in the attitude of the listeners. It is a quality which excludes loss of temper, nervous excitement, and cloudy thinking. To have this confidence the speaker must, of course, be well prepared. Only a mastery of every fact and only previous experience in talking over these points will give that ring of confidence and that platform poise essential to the good impression.

f. FREEDOM FROM PUGNACITY. Since a debate is an intellectual combat, the participants sometimes become heated and feel that they must literally exemplify the tactics of the prize fight or the medieval tournament. A degree of unpleasant aggressiveness sounds in every line and furnishes the basis of every argument. The attacks are touched by such expressions as "Our opponents would have you believe," "The gentlemen have failed utterly to establish their contentions." The whole attitude reflects a determination to destroy the opponent utterly. And many a member of the audience may feel that such aggressiveness amounts to egotistic arrogance. Judges and audiences have often voted down a good debater solely because he set out to whip all who stood in his way.

g. MODESTY. Far more effective is the quality of modesty. School and college debaters sometimes develop egotism. Something about the type of discussion and the firmness with which convictions must be held develops that quality. And the rewards of the game sometimes produce that result just as occasionally athletes acquire conceit. School debaters, in particular on winning teams, become heroes to parents and community—a dangerous situation indeed. The most effective speakers, nevertheless, have a natural modesty. No superciliousness, strut, or pompousness may be detected. Proper cultivation of modesty is a matter not of dissembling, or of cultivating a sense of inferiority, but rather a matter of understanding one's limitations in life and of giving all things their proper value. The boastful and vain speaker needs direct criticism, and sometimes severe joltings, before he has this almost fatal handicap removed. Do not parade your knowledge. Don't insinuate that you have made a clever point. Avoid apologies that will suggest that you are insincere.

h. COURTESY. He who is modest will have also good breeding. The spirit of courtesy is highly necessary, especially if the occasion be a genuine contest. Audiences will turn in disgust from the speaker who shows bad temper toward his opponents and who engages in ill-timed invective or insolence. Courtesy is necessary, not only toward the opponents but toward an audience.

G. Persuade through Selection and Arrangement of Words, Phrases, Clauses, and Sentences. Above we suggested the power of loaded or connotative terms. Since the arguments and motivative appeals are expressed through words (in addition to vocal and visual aids in oral expression), the manipulation of language becomes a central medium in determining the persuasive results. You will here review the discussion of language in the preceding chapter. What are these language characteristics that have persuasive value? Accuracy and clearness of words and terms, concreteness, conciseness, colloquial quality, variety, freedom from hackneyed phrases and triteness, figurative terms, illustrations, parallelism, repetition of words and ideas, interrogative, interjective, and imperative sentences, balance, periodic structure—all (if used with good judgment and without resort to the excesses of style for its own sake) will enhance mightily the motivative force of your discourse.

III. CONCLUSION

Dogmatic rules and arbitrary devices for winning and controlling audiences "do not always work as predicted by the experts, who themselves disagree in many of their recommendations."[19] Since no two audiences are the same (nor yet the same

[19] *Ibid.,* p. 18.

audience on successive occasions), since the speaker, his speech, and the occasion always contain variant factors, and since speech-making is an art and not a science, only principles and approximate suggestions for persuasion can be laid down. It is hoped that the principles and suggestions of this chapter, however, will sharpen your interest in audience adaptation and your skill in persuading that audience. Certainly, you will use these skills with proper regard for your responsibilities as a speaker of the highest ethical standards.

EXERCISES AND PROBLEMS

1. Differentiate persuasion from logic as *purpose* and as a *mode of affecting audience attitudes and behavior.*

2. Discuss the following propositions: (*a*) The individual is strongly affected by basic emotional responses and desires. (*b*) The individual believes what satisfies his primary and secondary needs and wants. (*c*) The individual tends to respond to connotative language. (*d*) The individual tends to be suggestible.

3. Explain rationalization and prejudice as factors related to individual and group attitudes and behavior.

4. What differences exist between the individual who composes a one-man audience and the same individual merged with many others in an audience situation?

5. What factors in the occasion are to be noted by the speaker for his help in audience adaptation?

6. With the aid of the series of questions given in this chapter as criteria for analysis of the audience, explain in detail the characteristics of the audience and factors affecting the audience situation for a given speaking situation in which you have recently participated.

7. Analyze a face-to-face audience addressed recently by the President of the United States.

8. Criticize a recent speech (consult *Vital Speeches of the Day* or any current daily, reprinting the speech in full) with respect to factors of audience adaptation.

9. Rewrite, to increase audience appeal, one of your recent debates or other arguments.

10. Prepare a five-minute argument for presentation over the radio. Give special attention to factors of audience appeal.

11. Give a five-minute persuasive speech to your group, in which you stress factors of "ethical proof" (such as personal qualities of humor, tact, good will, sincerity).

CHAPTER 19

Delivery

I. The Argumentative Speaker's Problems of Delivery

In judging the efficiency of an oral argument you should, of course, give chief consideration to the material or ideas rather than to delivery. In reality, however, audiences put much stress on voice and other elements of presentation. Even the most logical auditors, we must admit, are susceptible to forceful speech. Though your arguments are a bit flimsy, you will often carry weight with an audience, if not with the judge, by means of your superior delivery. On the other hand, though you recast your argument, though you select the phrases that illuminate your ideas, and though you give clear reply in rebuttal, you may fail if your voice is weak and your attitude is hesitant or uncertain.

What are the chief criticisms of discussants and debaters? Here are comments of judges given after observing the delivery at the outset of a beginning course in discussion and debate (general trends only are indicated):

Rate: Too fast.
Pitch: Too high and in monotone.
Audience contact: Little projection; ignoring the audience.
Reference to notes: Too frequent reliance on notes.
Emotional behavior: Random muscular activity; lack of enthusiasm; undue severity of attitude toward the subject and audience; absence of humor or pleasantry; nervousness; aggressiveness.

Intellectual behavior: Doubtful motivation of strong conviction or belief.

Conversational mode: Absent-mindedness; lack of communicativeness; undue memorization; impromptu speaking; too much reading.

Platform manners: Failure to address chairman or audience; lack of poise.

Bodily action: Slouchy posture; rigid and fixed position; monotony of gesture; gesture without meaning; bodily jerkiness; continual movement; waving of arms.

Voice: Breathiness; unduly fast rate; monotony of rate; pitch unduly high; undue loudness; indistinctness; hesitancy, many "and—uh's."

Pronunciation and enunciation: indistinctness of vowels and consonants; slovenly pronunciation.

Considerable time in your preparation should therefore include practice in delivery. In the distribution of the debater's time for preparation, he usually spends so many hours—and so much energy—on collecting and organizing his case that he has only last moments for drill in delivery. One-third of your time, as a rough estimate, should go to training in oral presentation, preferably in practice debates and discussion.

II. Suggestions for the Improvement of the Delivery in Argumentation, Discussion, and Debate[1]

A. Improve in Your Pitch Flexibility and Get Rid of Unfortunate Pitch Patterns. A competent speech person should help you diagnose your individual problem. You should know whether you have an abnormally high or low pitch; whether you are unable to discriminate pitch sounds; whether there is lack of variation in your pitch; whether you have undesirable pitch patterns. Your adviser will then outline a remedial program for you.

Some of these principles and correction will include the following: You will see that your breathing is well controlled as you speak. If you have physiological defects of throat, nose, or mouth, the clinical advice is important. You will see that your voice mechanism is thoroughly relaxed as you speak. You will learn to hear your own tones as recorded, to study pitch dis-

[1] This chapter assumes that you have had training in the fundamentals of speech or equivalent course. For further review of these principles, consult one of the texts on delivery listed in the Supplementary Readings, Appendix C.

crimination, and thus to minimize pitch monotony (either within the general pitch range or within the syllable).

You will even resort to a piano or other musical instrument and with its aid determine what is your normal pitch level. You will work to break the singsong pattern and your habit of continual rising inflection. You will practice reading aloud and will go about that experience intelligently. The habit will become for you a permanent one. Emotional and mental adjustment will accompany your program. Your intonations, inflection, "pitch shifts," will register emotional activity in accordance with the meanings you are attempting to communicate.

B. *Control Your Vocal Intensity or Loudness.* Just as many discussional students need voice improvement with respect to pitch, so do they need to concern themselves with the loudness of their discourse. The degree of loudness depends upon several factors, including the amount of energy or force with which the air is expelled, the amplitude of vibrations of the vocal bands, and the "amount of amplification of the tone by the resonators."[2] Obviously, loudness, pitch, and other elements of tone production are closely related or, in a sense, aspects of one process.

What are the chief violations of proper standards in tonal loudness? Many debaters are too noisy, especially those who have built up a concept that good speaking consists of adopting a platform "grand manner" reminiscent of Chatham or Webster. Public-address systems and other products of this exciting age have rendered less necessary the straining for vocal *volume.*

Most speakers, especially beginners, are too soft-spoken. The factor of "audience projection" in the sense of vocal energization is almost entirely lacking.

Still another disorder or defect in the debater's delivery lies in loudness monotony. As variation in pitch is necessary to keep the listener awake (or in the room or on the dial of your radio program), so is variation in loudness. A continuously loud or persistently weak tone shows poor adjustment to the speaking situation and lack of mental and emotional appropriation of the ideas as they are uttered.

What are obvious procedures for correction of defects in speaking loudness? Adjust your voice to the size of the room.

[2] Grant Fairbanks, *Voice and Articulation Drill Book,* p. 191, Harper & Brothers, 1940.

Keep your eyes on those in the rear. Decide whether they can hear you (when in doubt, you are justified in asking them); also decide whether you are too noisy (although you will hardly wish to interrupt your speech with, "Ladies and gentlemen, am I shouting?"). Your instructor and fellow speakers will usually give you helpful tips at this point.

Be sure you are not breathy. The old-fashioned advice to inhale and exhale deeply several times before speaking and to relax completely your jaw and throat muscles before beginning your speech is not bad. At any rate, you need to see that your resonance cavities give maximum reinforcement to the sound.

Be sure that your degree of loudness corresponds to the emotional, imaginative, and intellectual content of the ideas you are uttering. If you vary your pitch to correlate with the emotional and mental phrasing of your meanings, then your loudness or intensity will no doubt be more acceptable to your hearers.

Your real trouble, in many instances, is not that you lack intensity but that you do a bad job of phonating your vowels and consonants. Your defect is lip laziness. Here the instructor can guide you in matters of articulation. It is well known that adequacy in force (loudness) often resolves itself into a problem of efficiency in articulation.

If you address a college graduation dinner or a student "pep" meeting, you will fortunately have before you a public-address system. With such an instrument one problem of loudness for you will end, and another will begin—a new problem of vocal adjustment. You will rehearse before this loudspeaker, at least to the extent of "one, two, three, four," and will modulate your tones so that the audience will find pleasure in your vocal directness and simplicity.

C. Control Your Speaking Rate. Most debaters and many discussants speak too fast. Read aloud one of your speeches at your normal rate, and time it to the second. Better still, record it on a phonograph or dictaphone, or have someone else time you. Or otherwise discover your rate per minute. Is it less than 125 words or more than 185? Then you are probably reading too slowly or too rapidly. Whether a given rate is best for you depends on whether yours is a normal one for you, whether it is slow enough to make your ideas intelligible, whether you are reading or extemporizing, or whether you are adjusting your total speaking to the immediate occasion and audience. Before large audiences the rate is usually slower. According to King, Roosevelt in fifty speeches had a rate per minute (with time out for applause) of 108 (nearest whole number).[3] When you are especially eager to secure total comprehension of your ideas, the rate will be retarded. Obviously, the rate varies according to the meaning and emotional content of the material.

D. Improve Your Voice Quality. Bad voice quality results in voices that are characterized by nasality (when the nasal opening at the point of the soft palate allows disproportionately large amounts of air to pass into the nasal chamber), denasality (when the closure of the nasal opening is largely blocked as in the case of those with severe head colds), harshness, or hoarseness (when the vocal bands are inflamed or temporarily paralyzed or otherwise rendered inoperative in their complicated functioning), muffled tone (when too much throat resonance develops and the partials of higher frequency have been deadened); metallic sharpness (when too much mouth resonance occurs).

E. Articulate Carefully. What program or principles may you follow for articulatory improvement? (It is assumed that you will be supervised by competent teachers.) (1) You should cultivate a flexible, active voice and articulatory acceptability. Are your teeth properly occluded and developed? Your tongue free in its movements? Your palates, hard and soft, free from disease or abnormalities? Your lips normally shaped? Your jaw and face muscles functioning properly? Your throat and nose free from inflammation? (The answer to some of these questions may lead you to a speech clinician and to a physician.) Usually, your difficulties are those of bad speaking habits. To establish desirable habits, you will initiate and continue exercises for the lips, jaw, and tongue.

(2) You will practice correct formation of vowels and consonants. Get a drill book on voice and articulation and rehearse to yourself the proper ways of correct phonation and articulation. Avoid, for example, the omission of consonants ("goin'" and "comin'"), unnecessary additions ("idear" for "idea"), substitutions ("w'ich" for "which"), and the "hissing" or "lateral" "s." (Your instructor will help you.)

[3] Robert King, *A Text Analysis of Representative Speeches by Franklin D. Roosevelt,* Purdue University, January, 1946.

F. Pronounce Acceptably. 1. Carry with you a dictionary. Many collegians regard the dictionary with suspicion—a "symbol of pedantry." Even so, if you intend to make headway with pronunciation, you will thumb your dictionary. A convenient edition of *Webster's New International Dictionary* will serve.

2. Record samples of your own speaking and check the pronunciation. Get the advice of your instructors and faithfully resort to pronunciation drills. Listen to your own speaking. Check the speech of others, including the enunciation and pronunciation of radio speakers.

3. Avoid the use of incorrect vowel and consonant usages. (Avoid pronouncing "a" as in "say" like "i" as in "die" in such words as "day" and "may"; avoid using "haf" for "have"; "bran" for brand"; "reconize" for "recognize.")

4. Include the necessary syllables and give every syllable its full measure. Avoid dropping necessary syllables ("annihilate" not "anni'late"; "barrel" not "bar'l"; "boisterous" not "boistrous"; "boundary" not "boundry"). Avoid adding unnecessary syllables as "ath-e-lete" for "ath-lete."

5. Other suggestions concerning pronunciation by discussant, persuasive speaker, and debater include (*a*) avoid misplacing accents; (*b*) recognize and apply strong and weak forms of pronunciation so that you will not sound artificially precise; (*c*) modify your pronunciation to meet the requirements, including physical conditions, of the immediate occasion (do not before one person prolong your vowels as much as you will in addressing 500); (*d*) within limits conform to the acceptable speech standards of your region, and respect the pronunciation habits of those of other sections; (*e*) above all, do not use affected pronunciation or attempt to remake your speech in imitation of Eastern, or Oxonian British, or other pattern foreign to your culture.

G. Have Proper Control of Bodily Activity. Visible behavior is almost as decisive as audible expression in conveying impressions to an audience. Most people are primarily visual-minded. They follow bodily movements more easily and readily than they do the vocal tones. Furthermore, such activity aids the speaker to interpret his meanings. Moreover, bodily action, as a complement to speaking, is natural. It is an attribute not limited to

the Websters, Clays, and Bryans. It originates in the impulse
of the speaker to project his ideas to an audience.

Because, then, action contributes in such great degree to effective delivery, the aspects of bodily control, posture, movement, and gesture cannot be ignored by students of discussional
speaking.

Be sure that your posture is natural and easy. Your body
should be relaxed, your breathing functioning normally. Some
occasions will lead you to assume a somewhat dignified posture
as when you are delivering a speech at graduation. In other
situations, you may even perch yourself on the corner of a
school desk (as instructors sometimes do) to put everybody at
ease. Your posture will express your vocal expression. Ordinarily, if err you do, you will do so on the side of dignified
bearing. You will avoid standing at military attention; planting your weight almost entirely on one foot; rocking on your toes
and heels; leaning over the footlights (or platform) toward your
hearers; or clutching your arms, or keeping them continually
hid behind your coattails (figuratively speaking). Your posture
will convey self-control, energy, and a real friendliness toward
your group.

Discussants and debaters are often guilty of two violations of
proper movement. In one case they "anchor" and develop in-
ertia that destroys their effectiveness. This school of speakers is
victim of the bad speech philosophy which teaches that "movement is a sign of bad form and that cultured speakers have a
minimum of bodily display." The other fault lies in excessive
movement. Audiences become bored by the monotonous rhythm
of a speaker, his uneasy shifting from one side of the rostrum to
the other, or his uneasy clutching at the back of his chair (if he
happens to be behind it). Immobility kills speech; excessive
movement is even worse. In general the amount and character
of the movement can be determined only by the temperament
and cultural habits of the speaker, by the character, size, and
physical surroundings of the audience, by the occasion, whether
it be informal panel, public forum, or radio speaking. To fall
into the speaking situation, familiarize yourself with the physical
surroundings of your speaking scenes. Physical exercises, athletic experiences, dancing, and gymnasium drills should all make

your body more flexible and responsive to your emotional and mental attitudes.

The effective discussion student proceeds with his arms at rest and at ease. His arms will be at his sides (unless he happens to be taking notes); his hands may even be in his pockets. Mostly they are available to interpret his ideas. When the impulse comes, he will release his arms. These gestures may be emphatic, descriptive, or suggestive. In any case, they will be forceful, well controlled, impressive.

Bodily activity should be adjusted to the speaking situation. Avoid the annoying mannerisms that interfere with your effectiveness (such as jingling coins or keys over the radio). Bodily action will be an aid to what you say. You will overcome emotional instability, self-consciousness, inferiority illusions, and you will speak as if the subject possessed you. With friendly critics to call your attention to your more obvious faults of action, you will render your speaking personality more and more pleasing.

H. Adopt the Conversational Mode of Delivery. Effective delivery, speech teachers remind us, is conversational. Wendell Phillips has often been cited as a "gentleman conversing." Fiery abolition orator and supreme public lecturer, Phillips nevertheless retained a speaking style characteristic of those who use few of the formalities of platform oratory.

Conversation is the norm. Discussion speakers seated around a table are likely to have these characteristics of genuine talk. These same contributors, however, when they get on their feet, especially if they happen to be on a platform, sometimes adopt an oratorical inflection.

What then, do Wendell Phillips, the table talkers, and the conversational orator have in common that sets them off from the unconversational performer?

1. The conversational speaker is more likely to have as his goal the message or idea itself rather than the oral method of expressing it. Something of the exhibitory is there in all of us. But for us to assume on a platform the role of a public speaker is fatal to the end or goal before us, which is to convince or inform somebody about something and not to impress them with our voice, gestures, and inflections. The difference is a subtle one, but it can usually be noted by listeners and corrected by speakers.

2. The conversational speaker has instant and complete intellectual and emotional reaction to the words he is uttering or is about to utter. He constantly asks himself (before he begins talking), What do I mean by this idea? and in the course of this argument he continues to focus upon his meanings and their relation to his auditors.

3. The conversational speaker has a "lively sense of communication."[4] He is in complete communication with his audience as he is with his theme and its details. He is active, enthusiastic, and alert to every audience reaction. He establishes eye-to-eye contact and talks to each as if these two were the only ones present and the whole business were a highly personal one.

The converse of this communicative spirit is absent-mindedness or indirectness. The speaker is unduly conscious of his appearance, voice, and gestures, or he may be lost in contemplation of ideas regardless of the people before him. In either situation he is looking at his hands, wondering where to put them, or he is gazing out of the window, perhaps seeing nothing there because he is lost in reverie. Audiences should never be spectators. The response should be circular, with the speaker stimulating the audience, and it, in turn, transferring to the speaker its own enthusiasm.

The genuinely communicative debater or discussant has bodily animation, openness and ease of voice, active mentality, qualities that will generate mutual understanding between the speaker and his group.

I. Project to Your Audience. The conversational speaker has excellence of voice control, including variety in pitch, rate, intensity, and pleasing articulation and pronunciation, just as agreeable conversationalists in educated society have these things. *Amplification, however, is needed if proper projection is secured.* When the speech teacher advises a student to be "much more conversational," the result is often passivity and deadness. The speaking manner must be sufficiently vigorous to hold the attention. Just as in private conversation we continue to look at the other member of the dialogue and unconsciously become annoyed if he shows that his mind or attention is wandering, so in public discourse should we tolerate no listener

[4] James Winans, *Public Speaking* (revised ed.), Chapter 1, Appleton-Century-Crofts, Inc., 1927.

apathy but should energize our speaking to ensure complete "polarization" of speaker and auditor.

J. Speak As Often As You Can before People. This suggestion means that you will perform oftener than once every two months in your campus or other club and oftener than the classroom assignment permits. Before your classmates you may be able to give a two-minute speech at each meeting—three times per week; or you may engage in a classroom discussion once a week. This schedule is satisfactory as far as it goes; but to get the maximum speaking development, you need to "go in" for whatever other opportunities your school or college speaking program offers. Many college debaters, for example, engage in scores of debates, in the tournaments and elsewhere. This writer has just seen the conclusion of a tournament of eighteen colleges and universities in which for three days, one hundred students engaged in original oratory, extempore speaking, debate, discussion, and dinner speaking. Most institutions have an extensive program of intramural speaking. The trend is more and more to set up opportunities not simply for five or six debaters but for larger groups. No matter how busy you may be, your waking schedule will include many such experiences. In addition to these formal programs, you should seek out conversations with interesting collegemates. Note how they talk, and in your part of these dialogues try to improve in your own readiness.

Mere repetition of speaking, if you have proper guidance, will develop you, much as such constant repetition has converted third-raters into those who have great audience acceptability. Prominent senators, extempore radio commentators, preachers, and facile business speakers have become so after weeks, months, and years of constant speaking experience have given them this facility.

It goes without saying that supervision by speech experts helps tremendously. Webster, as an apprentice lawyer, gained much, both in the construction of a legal case and in its presentation, from his advisers, Jeremiah Mason and Christopher Gore. Mrs. Franklin Roosevelt, who made excellent progress as a public speaker, had the counsel of a speech instructor.

K. Read Aloud Systematically. Bryan, Beveridge, Woodrow Wilson, and many another speaker early formed the habit of reading aloud. Lincoln was another who profited by such practice. W. H. Herndon, his law partner, reports, "When he [Lincoln] reached the office about nine o'clock in the morning, the first thing he did was to pick up a newspaper, spread himself out on an old sofa, one leg on a chair, and read aloud, much to my discomfort. Singularly enough Lincoln could never read any other way but aloud. The habit used to annoy me almost beyond endurance. I once asked him why he did so. This was his explanation: 'When I read aloud two senses catch the idea; first, I see what I read; second, I hear it, and therefore I can remember it better.' "[5]

Read aloud your own productions and those of others. Have a given fifteen-minute period each day for reading as if you were before an audience. The experience will enable you to put into practice every principle of good delivery. Especially active will you be in rehearsing these speeches of yours which you intend to read over the radio or before audiences.

L. When You Speak, Be Yourself. Good vocalism is more than an exercise in mechanical manipulation of tones and gestures. It is an art based upon the functioning of many physiological concomitants. Many facts and suggestions concerning the principles of good speaking will help you. But the details of your delivery will vary with the occasion and with your total personality. Your posture, bodily movements, and gestures, for example, will be those best adapted to you as an individual. Rules cannot be arbitrarily set down. For you to succeed in delivery does not require that you have certain types of locative gestures; nor that you move at certain angles on the platform; nor that you take your position invariably "with one foot about seven inches in front of the other, with your weight resting on the ball of the left foot"; nor that your articulation and pronunciation be those of Forbes Robertson, Gielgud, or other important English actors; nor that your platform tones be those of a John Barrymore or Helen Hayes. Although you will adhere closely to the principles of good speaking, you will use those practices that best accomplish your immediate speaking objective. Within the limits imposed on you by nature and your environment, you will express with maximum effect your ideas, and always through the medium of your own individuality.

[5] W. H. Herndon and Jesse W. Weik, *Abraham Lincoln*, Vol. II, p. 1, Appleton-Century-Crofts, Inc., 1928.

M. Develop Skill in Extempore Speaking. Your skill in discussion will depend partly on your facility in extempore speaking.

Extempore speaking is not impromptu talking. The latter experience takes place when you draw a strange topic out of a hat and start talking without a moment's reflection. Or when you are enjoying your dessert, only to have the chairman say, without any warning to you whatsoever, "I note that at the other end of the table is our fellow townsman, Mr. Harrington. We welcome him home and will be glad to have a word from him concerning 'What my town needs most.'" Such crisis no doubt encourages freedom of speaking. But it is not to be encouraged; it usually fosters rambling, the multiplication of words, superficial thinking, and factual inaccuracies, and (perhaps in school and college) "bluffing."

Extempore speaking, on the contrary, occurs in those situations in which the speaker has made thorough preparation. He may talk directly from an outline. He memorizes ideas rather than words. With a few notes the speaker is able to talk freely and forcefully. He always is in contact with his audience, always alive to the situation. His material he continually adapts to the occasion.

The shortcomings of extempore speaking are similar to those of impromptu address. Overstatement will creep in. In a speaking type, such as discussion, in which accuracy is at a premium, the extemporizer may resort to hasty generalizations, voluble assertions, and may commit similar fallacies of inference and evidence; and he may repeat phrases and words endlessly. His outline may stand out like a house without roof or boarded walls.

The remedy lies in rigid speech preparation; writing and rewriting to strengthen the vocabulary; oral rehearsals sufficiently numerous to get rid of a mechanical English style; oral practice, again, to add extempore ease. The command of ideas and words and the easy expression of them before an audience is an art of slow development. High-school and college students who excel in extempore speaking are those who have had much early training in such style. Five years from now you will no doubt be a more effective extempore speaker—if you persist in the practice of the art.

N. Use Notes and Other Mechanical Aids Judiciously. Good delivery requires audience projection, a full realization of the words as they are uttered. Any interfering mechanism, whether it is a speaker's brief, a manuscript, blackboard, or speaker's stand, should be avoided. If you can refer to your notes so that your audience scarcely realizes what you are doing, we certainly cannot criticize you. Outlines are to be condemned only when they interfere with the directness of the delivery and impede the speaker's thinking. Such notes do enable the speaker to refer to detailed statistics, exact sources, and other information that would tax the memory and lead to bad guessing.

In your rehearsal you will familiarize yourself so fully with the outline that you will simplify it more and more until presently the gist of a twenty-minute connected talk may be compressed to a few scattered items on a single 3- by 5-inch card. Platform notes, of course, are not to be confused with a full-fledged brief or discussional outline. Such subject-outline becomes the background for the the more meager platform outline. The former is for all to read; the latter should be sacred to the speaker alone.

Shall charts, blackboard illustrations, and similar visual aids be used? By all means. Any organized information, presented in form easily understood by the audience and left in full view of them for the hour, is to be welcomed. Again the delivery should be rehearsed. Don't move uncertainly toward your blackboard, wave your chalk about, pause lengthily as you look around the board for certain figures. Plan carefully, set up your chart or blackboard statistics before the audience assembles. Familiarize yourself with the ways of the pointer (if you are to use it) and otherwise show that you can handle without self-consciousness or hesitancy these aids.

O. Develop Acceptable Personality Traits. Personality affects or determines speaking effectiveness. The total physical, mental, and emotional resources must be well organized if the speaking is to have proper impressiveness. Physical and emotional disturbances, for example, result in nervousness, bad bodily activity before audiences, unsatisfactory phonation, with violations of proper pitch, loudness, rate, and tone quality. Passive, uncertain tones reflect a personality purposeless, emotionally unstable, perhaps introvertive.

1. Self-inventory. The starting point in developing satisfactory delivery is to begin with you yourself. Know yourself as a person and a speaker. Instructors will help you to make a proper diagnosis and inventory of yourself. Welcome criticism—both of your speaking and of your social and other attitudes.

2. *Emotional control.* Seek to establish emotional control and balance. Rely on yourself. Prepare your ideas so carefully that you can present them under all circumstances. Get rid of the forebodings, the self-indictment, the suggestion that you are a poor speaker and that you have nothing worth while for people to attend to.

3. *Self-confidence.* Refuse to allow the impressiveness of the occasion, the number of people present, the celebrity of the chairman or of those who happen to listen, the severity of the critics, the power of the opposing team if the situation happens to be that of debate, or the superiority of your auditor if the occasion is that of a personal interview, to overwhelm you. Confidence grows out of a conviction that you are well prepared and that you have the stamina and ability to handle any situation. Undue self-esteem is, of course, unfortunate, but most debaters and speakers suffer from underestimation rather than overestimation of their powers. Act as if you were confident and courageous; and confidence will in most cases result. The audience will instinctively have more faith in you. Their faith will reinforce your own.

4. *Intellectual and moral stability.* Only those who have or who are making a vigorous attempt to have sincerity, open-mindedness, genuine social outlook, real interest in the problems of others, modesty, tact, level social outlook, and the other virtues of a pleasing personality are prepared to speak. Those who do attain this desirable condition of emotional balance and of intellectual and moral stability will undoubtedly manage far better the technicalities of delivery than will the maladjusted. Or such is the assumption of this writer.

EXERCISES AND PROBLEMS

1. (*Suggestion to the instructor.*) Make a recording of a fifteen-minute class discussion. Have the members criticize the recording in regard to pitch, loudness, rate, voice quality, articulation, and pronunciation.

2. Record one of your debates by a dictaphone or other recorder.

Note your own vocal problems. After the use of exercises for a month take another recording and make comparisons.

3. (*Suggestion to the instructor.*) Have the class listen to a broadcast by the President of the United States or by some other prominent speaker and make systematic notes on the delivery. Let each member in a one-minute speech offer his comments.

4. (*Suggestion to the instructor.*) Play a recorded speech by any prominent speaker and have the class criticize the delivery.

5. Read one of your prepared speeches (four minutes in length) in a hall as if before several hundred people. Persuade one of your friends to sit in the back seat and criticize you.

6. (*Suggestion to the instructor.*) Invite each member of the section to write briefly his criticism of each debater's delivery. Do not have the criticisms signed. Distribute to each these comments and confer with each about his performance.

Part III

Discussion

CHAPTER 20

Discussion: Aims, Relationships, Techniques

I. WHY DISCUSS?

Much of your argumentative or controversial speaking will be discussional. Some of it will be casual and informal—at dinner or in "bull sessions." Some of it will take place in so-called discussion groups in courses. Discussion, too, is continually scheduled as adult education and as community programs, for example, the Des Moines (Iowa) community forums, established by John W. Studebaker, later of the U.S. Office of Education. A powerful agency in bringing discussion to millions has been the radio, with the University of Chicago Round Table, America's Town Meeting of the Air, and a long list of similar programs, many of them limited to local stations. Even the military forces in World War II sponsored systematic discussion for the GI's and the "gobs." Discussion has been widely applied as a learning tool. As we have often been reminded, ours is a government by talk. Debating and discussion have been a necessary practice of free speech, free assembly, the secret ballot, and nationwide voting. For our government to function effectively the rank and file as well as top executives and legislators in office must be alert to the public problems and must weigh and settle them through group discussion and debate.

At the outset of this book, I reminded you how argumentative study and practice should serve you as education. What results should you expect for your own development after a school year or so of discussion?

These should be some of the educational outcomes: (1) You should have progressed in the art of reflective thinking. (2) You should have strengthened your personal qualities of open-mindedness, tolerance, self-control, and emotional stability. (3) You should have strengthened your habits and techniques of testing facts and arguments. You should have made progress in distinguishing straight from crooked thinking, the noting of fallacies and of bad propaganda. (4) You should be able to define more accurately and weigh language in its constantly changing character and in its connotative and denotative implications (semantic skills). Discussion continually deals with meanings. (5) You should have improved in your application of the scientific method. The scientific method includes (a) recognition and statement of a problem, (b) focusing on facts, (c) the setting up of hypotheses, (d) the stressing of logic and evidence, (e) the minimizing of emotional judgments and the preservation of objectivity, (f) the testing of various solutions, (g) the reexamination and further testing of the preferred solution, (h) the statement of conclusions limited by your data and analysis. (6) You should have made progress in socialized thinking, teamwork, consciousness of audience relationships and group solidarity. (7) You should have developed in your understanding of the method of problem solving by consensus and group judgment rather than by silent acquiescence, by compromise, by the methods of suggestion and propaganda, by intimidation, decrees, mere legalism, or force. (8) You should have improved in your ability to communicate both by speaking and writing. (9) Because discussion concerns itself with live issues, you should have become much better informed concerning the contemporary events and problems. Wherever contemporary economic, political, and social problems are under consideration, you should—after a year—be more at home as an articulate and competent contributor. In short, you should be on the way to a broad education and, incidentally, to occupational competency. (We assume that the skills and abilities listed above are important for economic efficiency.)

II. What Is Discussion?

So many varieties of speechmaking—conversation topped off with a few questions, general public speaking, debate, propagandistic speaking, lecturing—have been labeled *discussion* that we find confusion in knowing what is expected of us.

A. *As a Discussant You Are First of All Confronted by a Genuine Problem.* You find yourself in what John Dewey calls an "indeterminate situation," one that is "uncertain, unsettled, disturbed." You become conscious that you are out of harmony with your surroundings or that your environment has somehow changed so that you have lost your equilibrium. Hence this "indeterminate situation" becomes, as Dewey calls it, a "problematic situation." You inquire about the "felt difficulty." It may be a problem of fact as when you read the headlines and ask, "Are we about to have a war with Russia?" or "Am I paying too much Federal income tax?" Or the problematic situation may be one that arouses you to possible action. You ask, "Shall Congress lower the personal income taxes?"

B. *As You Initiate Your Inquiry and Attempt the Answer, You Are Engaged in Reflective Thinking.* Reflective thinking, as here interpreted according to John Dewey, is a description of the factors in the situation that arouse the inquiry and an analysis of the "felt difficulty" that produces the perplexity.

The discussant lines up clearly the factors (facts)—obtained by observation or otherwise—that make up the difficult situation. He traces the causes of these phenomena; formulates the hypotheses or tentative solutions or "ways out"; weighs each in the light of the data available; and after a comparison of the choices as formulated and tested, determines the wisest and most practicable outcome and further verifies that preferred conclusion.

This is the formula of orderly thought, the problem-and-solution technique carried out under conditions that involve the collection and testing of evidence; the application of representative modes of reasoning, both inductive and deductive; the full and fair examination of counterargument and evidence; the dispassionate inference from the argument; and the shaping of conclusions that are clearly within the bounds of the data. This is the essence of reflective or critical thinking.[1]

[1] Review Chap. 4.

Such thinking is in contrast to random, emotional, or habitual thinking. Emotional thinking, as I indicated in an earlier chapter, is relatively disorganized and undirected. The more intellectual or "cortical" reflection, by contrast, rather than yielding blindly to impulse or stimulus, identifies the critical thinker with mental rumination. Psychologists, we are agreed, are by no means unanimous concerning the exact character of emotional, as contrasted with intellectual, reactions, but they are in substantial agreement concerning the fact that emotional behavior is much more disorganized and uncontrolled. The student of discussion proposes to exalt these more highly organized mental processes and to minimize the more discursive and impulsive ways of viewing a problem. Discussants are on the side of logic, scientific method, and dispassionate review. Our assumption is that valid judgments, whether they pertain to the definite aspects of natural or biological science or to the more intangible problems of social science, are more dependable when evolved in an atmosphere of intellectual dominance.

C. *As a Discussant You Are Engaged in a Cooperative Activity.* You will quickly find that your problem is that of others; that two heads are better than one; that you are a part of the social scene; that you comprise part of an audience; and that the group tendencies and spirit underlie your discussional efforts. Social adjustment, then, becomes the key to productive discussion. Each contributor casts aside his isolationist tendencies and his high individualism. He recognizes and practices the social principle of balancing individual with social needs and interests. Individual intellectual achievement is apparently more marked because group wisdom reinforces it. The open-mindedness of the group in turn breeds insight into the approach of each who has a stake in the controversy. Thus both the group and the individual presumably make more progress than would be probable otherwise. Perpetual antagonisms and judgments taken under such conditions offer little hope for the settlement of social problems. Simply put, discussion is based upon group cooperation. Your starting point is to learn the art of integrating with the thinking of others.

D. *As a Discussant You Are Engaged in Oral Communication.* Obviously, intelligent encompassing of the subject and cooperative examination of it through a meeting of minds free from hostilities and prejudices produce best results if the communication is effective. Whether the conferees are about a table or in a large forum, the occasion calls for unimpeded exchange of ideas. You need to be a pleasant, fluent speaker. The more articulate and effective this communication, the better for the cause of discussion. Not only should each know the techniques of analysis and solution, the skills of testing argument and evidence, the selection of proper words to convey these ideas, but speechmaking itself should be effective. The situation is that of oral speech —the interaction of speaker, speech, audience, and occasion. Acceptable standards of voice, bodily control, and proper functioning of the personality are essential to the success of the undertaking. As an effective discussant, then, you are an effective communicator, both in oral and written discourse.

These, then are the essentials of discussion: the recognition of a problem and its attempted solution; reflective thinking; group participation and adaptation; and oral communication.

III. What Is the Relation of Discussion to Other Speaking Types?

A. *Discussion and Conversation.* Discussion is not mere conversation. Many critics and even some textbook writers, especially writers for secondary schools, identify discussion with conversation. But conversation is usually without direction, without the analysis of a specific problem, without mature scrutiny of the definitions involved, without other of the somewhat exacting features necessary to orderly treatment of the question. Do not, then, assume that if you and several others converse interestingly for thirty minutes or an hour you have carried out a "discussion." The American scene is filled with talk, but a good deal of it is bad talking, and certainly a large amount of it is poor discussion. Only when conversation is stripped of its sharp partisanship, its pseudo levity, its aggressiveness, and its nonintellectualism does it approach the communicative act we here have in mind.

B. *Discussion and Persuasive Speaking.* Discussion is not persuasive speaking. Sometimes the program of a group, *e.g.*, those often represented on the American Forum of the Air, has been labeled a *discussion-symposium*. Each participant, however, is obviously bent on influencing others to think and act as he wishes. Each has injected into his organized discourse a considerable emotional and prejudicial appeal. Until such speaking, whether it is on a radio round table, before a court, or in a college classroom, abandons largely such mood and mode, it cannot be named *discussion*.

Just how does discussion differ from persuasive speaking? It has more in common with informative speaking than with the more impressive argumentative type. In common with argumentative speaking, discussion normally looks to the immediate causes of the discussion, the history of the problem, the definition of terms, the formulation of the issues, the mustering of argument and evidence, and the careful evaluation of each proposed solution. The differences lie mainly in the aim of each type of participant. The arguer, with his mind already firmly set, tries to persuade and convince others to accept his beliefs. The discussant is still in the exploratory stage. His speaking is a joint endeavor to throw further light on the problem. Tentatively, he may be on the affirmative or negative, but he retains a flexible position.

I am not here decrying the advocate. He has his goal. After he has properly followed through the analytical definitive and evaluative steps of discussion, he may have confirmed or newly established a given conviction, which in turn leads him in all sincerity to abandon the role of the discussant for that of the strong defender of a proposition. Our condemnation of him derives chiefly from his early and summary stand to which he arrives with little preliminary diagnosis. Such a pseudo arguer is really unfolding a series of rationalizations. His premises or foundations are not established as would be the case if he followed the method of discussion.

C. Discussion and Debate. What I have said of argument applies also to debate—argumentation under special rules. Debate is typically in progress on the Senate or House floor whereas discussion is usually the communicative technique of the committee chamber. Debate is chiefly a technique of expediency. In the world in which we live, it settles issues that cannot be weighed indefinitely, as, for example, whether we are to declare war on an enemy that has attacked us without warning.

Debate and discussion, as I view them, are complementary. Debate is, or should be, a phase of discussion. To make clear the relationship, consider the pattern of thinking of discussion. Discussion investigates and analyzes a question, defines terms, sets up possible outcomes, and determines a conclusion. The debater proceeds more or less similarly. As I remarked above concerning persuasive speaking, the difference is chiefly one of aim. But the good debater, like the discussant, often lingers over the proper understanding of terms and over the elements of analysis. Furthermore, he sometimes debates one side as freely as the other, not because he is a mere dialectician, but because he has not made up his mind. Most of us evolve our beliefs. We are not, most of us, of the die-hard debate school. For the moment we may defend eloquently a proposition but later veer to another platform. In view of such a long-range point of view we may correctly posit debates as merely a stage in the larger framework of discussion. It is really that stage in discussion represented by the weighing of alternative conclusions. The best debater, as I understand him, has much of the open-minded cooperative spirit of the discussant. In general, discussion may terminate at any stage in the five or six steps of the reflective pattern. When the thinking, properly operating, becomes crystallized for the time, honest conviction emerges and so debate. By and by the fixed position may be abandoned, and discussion again occur.

To illustrate the relationship, consider the following diagram:

DISCUSSION

(More likely points of conflict, variant conviction, and so of debate are indicated by asterisks.)

1. Explanation of terms.	Discussion may end and debate ensue.
2. Goals in analyzing and solving the problem.	Discussion may end and debate ensue.
3. Analysis of the "felt difficulty" or problem—including description of the disturbing phenomena, their causes, and results.	Discussion may end and debate ensue.
4. Statement of hypothesis or probable solutions to be listed.	Discussion may end and debate ensue.
5. Weighing of solution A.	*Discussion may end and debate ensue.

6. Weighing of solution B.	*Discussion may end and debate ensue.
7. Weighing of solution C.	*Discussion may end and debate ensue.
8. Validation of the preferred solution (A or B or C).	*Discussion may end and debate ensue.
9. Determination of a program to implement the solution preferred.	Discussion may end and debate ensue.

IV. What Are the Limitations of Discussion?

Discussion, as we here conceive it, becomes a technique wholly acceptable as an ideal but hardly realizable in this world of experience. Like religious freedom, peace, and other laudable ends, discussion apparently breaks down when introduced into any practical setting. How, we ask, can you hope to have a meeting of minds and an objective attitude when John L. Lewis and his colleagues, representing four hundred thousand miners, are seated with the mine owners and operators to negotiate wages and other aspects of employment? How can you have open-mindedness and honest cooperation when Molotov and his Soviet backers discuss with the Western Powers the age-old problem of Russian expansion in the Mediterranean, Middle East, and Far East? At best, so you suggest, the solid front of labor and the equally adamant management can only negotiate, arbitrate, and perhaps escape strikes and other threats of force. But arbitration is not discussion. It is only compromise that may settle nothing in principle and may serve only for an armed truce.

These practical instances, I admit, illustrate the difficulties of applying successfully this technique. Specifically, what are these limitations? (1) To discuss, you must lose—or minimize as best you can—your prejudices. Such self-discipline is hard to realize under conditions that affect your pocketbook and your security. (2) Furthermore, you must be pretty well informed on the problem. Intellectual skill—general education—are necessary. Only in groups that have such training and equipment, both in the problem itself and in the techniques of cooperative thinking and acting, can the procedure succeed. (3) Moreover, for discussion in larger groups you have the increasingly difficult task of creating crowd homogeneity and group reflection. Successful discussion probably varies in inverse ratio to the size of the audience, other factors remaining constant. (4) In addition to the necessity for proper personality adjustment to the group and intellectual and educational competency, you are confronted with the limitations of time and place. If discussion calls for many hours or days of deliberation in defining terms, analyzing the issues, pursuing the various panaceas or "ways out" and if, on the other hand, the problem is so insistent as to require early settlement, you face a dilemma. Discussion would seem to run counter to efficiency and to a world calling for action. If the enemy, without warning, should drop a bomb on Washington, D.C., the government obviously would have little time in which to weigh the issue. In such cases debate—and that extremely terse—would be called for.[2]

Despite these limitations, discussion, as I suggested at the outset of this chapter, has been adapted to practical situations. Committee sessions of our Federal and state governments, main and subcommittees of the United Nations, conferences between employers and employees are daily conducting what we agree are genuine discussions. Our assumption and hope is that more and more the formula of cooperative problem solving will be applied. Meantime in schools and colleges and in adult education we shall train ourselves in this art.

V. What Are the Techniques of Discussion?

What, then, are you to do in order to participate effectively in discussion? (1) You will understand your role as a member of a group and will divest yourself of those personal qualities that impede your participation in group thinking and decisions. (2) You will join with others in the clear formulation of the issue or problem in which you are mutually interested. (3) You will concentrate with others on the meaning of the major terms of the controversy and on all language causing confusion. (4) You will unite with the group in formulating goals or common objectives, referents to which the concrete problem and its solution will be related. (5) You will cooperate in diagnosing the difficulty or problem itself—in its expression, its cause, and results. You will give proper consideration to the points of view of all participants.

[2] See Irving J. Lee, "Why Discussions Go Astray," etc., Vol. IV, pp. 81–88, Winter, 1947.

(6) You and your colleagues will frame and interpret the proposed solutions. (7) You will test each outcome with full development of sound arguments and evidence. (8) You will join with the others in concentrating on that outcome that seems most rational and workable. (9) You will adapt yourself as well as you can to the exact procedure set up as the discussion medium —whether round table, forum, or panel. (10) You will be an attentive and cooperative listener. (11) You will organize your contribution and aid in the organization of the discussion as a whole. (12) You will use acceptable language in your contribution. (13) You will speak with acceptable standards of speech. (14) If you are chairman or leader, you will demonstrate the high standards expected of you. These are the representative goals before you in this field of oral discourse. The following chapters treat in detail these suggestions for effective discussion.

EXERCISES AND PROBLEMS

1. Present a short (two- or three-minute) oral comment on one of the following excerpts:

a. "Discussion is more than a means of generating thought and of sharing information. These worthy purposes are valuable concomitants. The thinking that follows a discussion may magnify greatly the value of the initial meeting of minds, and the sharing of information may form a valid end point for certain meetings. Yet, both of these objectives are the results of discussion and are not discussion itself."[3]

b. "We know that in most instances the product of the group is superior to that of the average individual working alone."[4]

c. "Discussion and debate, to be consistent with liberal educational ideals, should not foster a sort of predatory attitude—an attitude based upon a driving desire to beat the other fellow. Unfortunately that attitude is being developed in some quarters. As long as it exists, one phase of our subject will not be above suspicion."[5]

2. Report briefly from your own experience or observation the strength and weakness of discussion.

[3] Wayne N. Thompson, "Discussion and Debate: A Re-examination," *Quarterly Journal of Speech*, Vol. XXX, p. 290, October, 1944.

[4] William M. Timmons, "Discussion, Debating and Research," *ibid.*, Vol. XXVII, p. 417, October, 1941.

[5] Lester Thonssen, "The Social Values of Discussion and Debate," *ibid.*, Vol. XXV, p. 117, February, 1939.

3. Listen to a program of America's Town Meeting of the Air, or read the text of a recent one. Evaluate for the class the program as discussion.

4. Report to the class concerning the strength or weakness of a selected program of The American Forum.

5. Evaluate as discussion a recent program of the Chicago Round Table.

6. Report to the class concerning the success or failure of a recent campus discussion in which you participated or which you attended.

CHAPTER 21

Discussion: Patterns and Outlines

Your successful discussion will depend largely upon your understanding of the discussion pattern or structure. The thinking and speaking of the group, whether it consists of a round table behind closed doors or a large community forum, follows a well-defined formula of organization. Not every participant in his individual talk incorporates all steps of the pattern, but the group in their united performance are supposed to do so. Just as on a problem of policy a debate as a total performance runs the entire sweep of argument from *need* to *practicability* and treats the issues both affirmatively and negatively, so does the discussion of policy attempt similar comprehensive treatment. The individual debater will usually argue one phase only and, if he follows convention, will stick to one side of the argument. Similarly, if the discussion is cast into the symposium form, each speaker will present a single aspect of the problem. What is the general framework of discussion?

The structure, as we have explained in previous chapters, is that of logic, that is, *problem* and *solution*. This logical pattern resolves itself into several stages:

First is the initiation of the inquiry (recognition of preliminary facts or factors that give rise to the problem). Second is the analysis of the problem by viewing the specific facts that chiefly bear upon it, including the causes and results (as nearly as may be determined) of those phenomena. Third is the stage of theory, deductively formulated, as to the solution of the problem (the setting up of hypotheses by which to gauge possible solutions). Fourth is the stage of testing and comparing each hypothesis for its validity as a solution. Fifth is the final verification of that hypothesis selected as most tenable.

II. Pattern of a Discussion of Policy

Let us assume that you are engaged in a discussion of policy on the issue, "Shall strikes be prohibited in basic American industries?" What steps will you follow? (1) You will need to define terms. (2) You will expound the goals or aims to be considered in any solution to the problem. (3) You will analyze the data, phenomena, or situation giving rise to the problem, together with the background causes and alleged results of this problematic situation. (4) You will weigh the representative solutions as proposed by those interested. (5) Your next step will lead to the weighing of each tentative solution, with full evaluation of the arguments and evidence pro and con. (6) You will present a full diagnosis and verification of that solution allegedly preferred by the group after this full deliberation. (7) Finally, you will frame and justify a program to carry out the conclusions arrived at.

Applied to the strike problem, our discussion would revolve somewhat as follows: (1) We would first explain what compulsory arbitration means, its relation to mediation, conciliation, voluntary arbitration, and other types of labor negotiation. (2) We would frame certain goals of our labor-management economic system, such as full production, stabilization of the economic cycle, economic justice to the manager, employees, and to the consumers. (3) We would diagnose the industrial situation as it exists—the strikes, threats of strikes, the lockouts, and other facts of labor wars; the causes of these disturbances and possible results (if unchecked); the failure (or nonfailure) of existing legislation to cope with the alleged disturbances. (4) We would weigh in order the advantages and disadvantages of the representative solutions, including compulsory arbitration, socialization of industry, voluntary arbitration, and other legislation to deal with specific difficulties. (5) We would work out a given solution, review it again in relation to other proposals, and justify it in relation to the goals established above. (6) We would construct a working program to ensure the general acceptance and operation of our proposals or conclusions.

Discussion, by its very nature, must be relatively free from machinery. Therefore, such formula, like the *stock issue* in debate, must be used with much discretion. *Goals,* for example, may either precede or follow the analysis of the *felt difficulty,* or may even be omitted. Similarly, any one of the other phases may be telescoped, expanded, or omitted. The group, for example, may agree that the problem of strikes is an acute one and may move quickly to the two major solutions in which the group is interested: socialization of industry or compulsory arbitration.

III. Pattern of a Discussion of Fact

Suppose your question, one of fact, is, "Is the liberal arts college fulfilling its function?" (1) We should consider an explanation of terms. What is meant by the liberal arts college? What is its function? (2) We should set up *goals,* in this case, criteria of validity for determining what the function is. (3) We should examine the data, arguments, and evidence that bear upon the alleged fact, *e.g.,* the evidence concerning the functioning of the college in providing satisfactory training in social sciences and in political responsibility; in its training for intellectual growth; in occupational efficiency; in social adaptiveness; in moral and character development. (4) We should classify, synthesize, interpret, and evaluate these types of argument and evidence and thus attempt to arrive at some judgment concerning the extent to which the liberal arts college is succeeding or failing in its mission.

Thus the pattern for a question of fact ends with the weighing of the fact itself. Policy-determination questions culminate in a program for action. All issues of the latter embody, as subissues, these questions of fact. Most subjects of interest to discussion groups fall into the category of those of policy. The suggestions above should guide you in adapting your analysis to either type of problem.

IV. Principles and Methods for the Development of the
Discussion Pattern

A. Scope of the Discussion. Regard the discussion as successful even though only a limited part of the field has been covered.
Time may not permit you to treat the entire agenda. Honest
divergence of opinion may necessitate the exclusive concentration, for example, on definitions.

B. Meanings. At the outset clarify all terms under question
and continue to explain all words that block maximum communication. Discussion, because it puts a premium on clear thinking, is especially sensitive to meanings. The best discusser is a
good semanticist (one interested in the science of meaning). Regard the definition agreed upon as tentative and exploratory.
Look with reservation to dictionary or other categorical explanations. Definitions are complete or sufficient only when you have
ended the conference. Aim to reduce abstract terms to concrete
equivalents. Prefer operational interpretations. Define in terms
of purpose, history, contrast, authority, and analogy.[1] This
exactness, one of the goals of the discussant, is no mere exercise
in dialectics or casuistry. Alertness to word meanings and systematic definitions as agencies in communication are basic in
education.

C. Goals. State the principles by which you will evaluate
your facts and determine your solutions. This step is one of describing the larger milieu into which the immediate facts fit. As
a discusser you are called upon to establish and explain standards of value by which the testing of concrete items is to be accomplished. This description of objectives or goals, I agree, requires mature thinking. You must be a philosopher. The task,
however, is not always difficult. You and your colleagues often
find yourselves in substantial agreement concerning your aims.
When the broader vistas remain dim, you can only defer until
the facts and implications have been fully explored. Sometimes
the goals emerge only at the end. Occasionally, the entire problem can be disposed of in the concrete without reference to
wider concerns. Since *goals* call for deductive treatment and
more abstract thinking and since their analysis sometimes carries
the group into fruitless speculation, we can only suggest both the

[1] Review Chaps. 5 and 6.

importance and limitations of attempts at stating objectives. As *definition* in discussion is educationally important, so is the framing of desirable outcomes that remain to be tested.

D. *Analysis of the Problem.* In analysis of the irritating situation, you will set forth both the facts of the problem and their causes and probable results. Discussants often err in such analysis. Their view of the disturbing phenomena is too general. They may talk of strikes or high prices or threatened war or juvenile delinquency. They often fail to cite the details that make it a major controversy. If the problem is a grave one, certainly the full unfolding of the facts, gruesome though they are, is in order. I am not here advocating dramatic treatment but do urge concreteness as well as accuracy.

The second weakness of the discussant's diagnosis is the neglect of tracing causes of the problematic situation. Granted that these antecedent forces are many, not easily distinguished, and often lost in the shadowy past, it is nevertheless decisive to your "way out" to understand and explain the genesis and growth of the problem. Such penetration into the causal connections is the method of the philosopher and of the creative thinker. In such analysis you are on sound educational ground.

Equally imperative is it that you attempt to gauge the probable results of the disturbing situation. With what logic you can muster, you are called upon to predict. If the friction will automatically cease, and soon, then your discussion of what to do is simplified. If, on the contrary, the evolution means ultimate disaster to your interests, your choices must be sharply discriminated.

E. *Tentative Outcomes.* In proposing and examining representative solutions to the problem, give full weight to each proposal. Superficial logicians and discussants are likely to approach the solution phase with a limited notion of "what to do." The disposition is to obscure certain important avenues of "escape" and to oversimplify and narrow the choices. The amateur may conclude that "this single proposition is the solution." Most complicated issues demand complicated correctives. The labor troubles in the United States prior to 1946 resulted in a legal mosaic—the Taft-Hartley law. That legislation, whatever its merits or demerits, did embody a considerable number of specific correctives for the allegedly bad situation in industry.

Well-balanced discussants will include all the representative choices, will prefer "multiple hypotheses," and will avoid an early and overzealous defense of a given solution.

F. *Validating the Preferred Outcome.* In the validation of the solution that seems most promising the testing process should be complete. The advantages and disadvantages should be completely aired as well as the practicability and impracticability.

V. THE GROUP DISCUSSION OUTLINE

A. *The Principles and Rules.* Outlines are especially needed to give unity and direction to group discussion. In theory each member of the round table visualizes the issues so clearly that the common core on paper is unnecessary. In practice such a map is a minimum requirement for relevant and expeditious progress. Students in intercollegiate discussion programs organize and distribute the outline some weeks previously. More progress is thereby made in the one- or two-day conference. Student radio discussions' have similarly found a preliminary group outline indispensable. Certainly, the questions on paper need not be adhered to, but such organized material for reference minimizes occasional confusion in the program itself.

This group outline follows the general rules and principles for the argumentative brief.[2]

Essentially it is an analysis *in question form* of the explanation of terms and of the issues. (1) These questions should each be impartially worded. (2) Each should represent a complete interrogation rather than a topic. (3) Each should be couched concretely. (4) Enough subquestions should be inserted to provide specific clues to the answering of the more general queries. (5) The questions should be those that reflect differing points of view. (6) The questions should bring out the chief steps in the discussional pattern. (7) Both main and subquestions should be so selected and worded as to be answerable. I admit that discussants and all others inquire about problems or facts for which answers are impossible. Nevertheless, questions will be raised. Circumstances compel us to give such replies as we can, *e.g.*, we face many problems of policy that demand tentative answers: "Will we fight another war at an early date?" "Will our economic system presently collapse?" No man can answer such social-political questions that are of the future. But we need to give the best explanation we can as a basis for policies that must be shaped before time runs out. (8) Proper symbols and indentations should be observed to indicate the successive steps of the analysis and the logical partition of ideas. (9) Usually the questions should be worded to invite a yes or no response (or a qualified yes or no). It is more satisfactory, for example, to inquire, "Shall we adopt a program of compulsory arbitration of labor disputes?" than merely to ask, "What shall we do about the labor war?"

The framing of the group outline, in short, requires skill in the art of questioning as well as accuracy in the mechanics of outlining.

B. *Examples of Group Outlines.* The following group outline was prepared for an intercollegiate discussion, with some sixteen colleges and universities participating.

WHAT POLICY SHALL THE UNITED STATES FOLLOW
FOR FEDERAL CONTROL OF INFLATION AND
DEFLATION?

I. What do the principal terms involved in this problem mean?
  A. What is meant by *inflation?*
  B. What is meant by *deflation?*
  C. What is meant by *business cycle?*
  D. What is meant by a *policy of Federal control* of inflation and deflation?
II. What goals suggest themselves as regards an equitable economic order?
  A. Are periodic fluctuations in prices and living costs a "healthy" aspect of our competitive economic order?
  B. Would a leveling off of "peaks" and "valleys" in the so-called business cycle operate to the benefit of our society?
  C. Does the government have a responsibility for guaranteeing an adequate living standard for all citizens?
  D. Does the government have a responsibility for promoting a program of full production, full employment, of reasonable (but not excessive) profits, and of prices, wages, and living costs that give maximum economic justice to all citizens?
III. Do fluctuations in the business cycle constitute a major problem today?
  A. Does the evidence indicate that we are in a period of inflation today (as we defined inflation above)?

B. Does the evidence indicate that we are in a period of deflation today (as we defined deflation above)?

C. Does the evidence indicate that we are in a period of practical equilibrium of the business cycle today, with no well-defined trends?

D. If business cycle fluctuations, as analyzed in A, B, C above, constitute a major problem, what are the primary causes?

  1. What are the major causes of *inflation*?

    a. Are certain primary factors operating to reduce the *supply* of goods and services available for the consumer?

    b. Are certain primary factors operating to increase consumer buying power (*demand*) in proportion to the supply of goods and services available?

    c. Have certain government policies, *i.e.*, lifting of price and credit controls, and aid to Europe, operated to increase inflationary trends?

  2. What are the major causes of recent *deflationary* trends?

    a. Have modifications of previous estimates of the supply of goods and services available, coupled with a decrease in consumer demand due to depletion of incomes and credit restrictions, resulted in commodity market downward spirals?

    b. Have recent governmental policies, *i.e.*, grain purchases, Federal Reserve actions, been responsible for dips in prices?

E. Are results of current trends likely to be disastrous to national and world economies unless some positive program is taken to control inflation and deflation?

  1. Are we headed toward a severe business recession or depression?

  2. Are certain income groups, *e.g.*, farmers, salaried workers, laborers, likely to be affected adversely by continued fluctuations in the business cycle?

  3. Are we headed toward inflation?

  4. Are certain factors operating to insure greater stability in the business cycle? (Are present methods for dealing with inflation and deflation adequate?)

IV. Are representative solutions for dealing with this economic cycle problem satisfactory?

  A. Would a program of "voluntary" controls by consumers and producers adequately solve the problem presented by the business cycle?

    1. Are consumers in general willing to adopt buying habits designed to regulate consumer demand?

2. Would the manufacturers of consumers' goods cooperate in a program designed to speed up production to the point of eliminating scarce materials and thereby satisfying consumer demand?

3. Is labor willing to cooperate in such a program?

4. Does precedent indicate the success of such a program?

B. Should the Federal government alter its spending policies so as to reduce the flow of capital into commercial channels?

1. Should we reduce the amount of supplies and money being sent to Europe and other foreign countries?

2. Should the Federal government further reduce its budget by eliminating such expenditures as those for public works, military preparedness, and all other expenditures not essential to general administrative operating expenses?

3. Should all government subsidies be eliminated?

C. Should the Federal government institute a program of "economic controls" designed to regulate the fluctuations of the business cycle?

1. Should a program similar to the Office of Price Administration of World War II be revived, either with or without rationing?

2. Should there be more stringent Federal control over speculation on securities and commodities markets?

3. Should Federal regulations on credit and installment buying be imposed?

4. Should the Federal Reserve banks be required to restrict further credit by increasing rediscount rates and decreasing the number and size of loans?

5. Should the Federal government place ceilings on all prices and wages?

V. In view of the preceding discussion, does solution IV *A* or *B* or *C* or a combination of these or some other program appear most satisfactory?

A. Is the preferred outcome more advantageous than the others?

B. Is it more practicable?

C. Does it give more "social justice"?

VI. What program for putting this solution into operation is proposed?

VI. The Individual Outline

In addition to the group outline, each participant will need to construct an individual outline for his own treatment of the subject. This skeleton of the thinking incorporates some of the features of the argumentative brief.[3] The analysis or introduction as indicated there you will follow closely, except for the omission of the final step, "points to be proved." As I suggested for the construction of the brief, you will include in detail the definitions, issues, history of the case, and limitation of the discussion to the problem under examination. You will phrase every idea as a complete sentence, will use symbols and indentations, and will clearly differentiate the successive steps to be used in the analysis.

Your discussion proper in this individual outline will require you to examine fully the arguments or point of view of those who have a stake in the problem, but you will retain the approach and method of an expositor or analyst. To achieve a degree of objectivity you will brief in detail the representative sides of the problem. Your discussion proper will thus have both expository and argumentative sections. At those argumentative points, you will use *for* to indicate the logical connections. You will insert the concrete evidence and will cite sources, preferably in the margin.

This individual discussion outline is for your convenience only. If this preliminary method of preparation puts you in a strait jacket of thinking, you had best avoid the procedure. I am confident, however, that such expositional treatment of the problem will minimize your prejudice on the subject and equip you to enter the discussion with considerable knowledge of what is to be talked about.

A skeleton outline (much abbreviated) for an individual outline would be somewhat as follows. (The treatment is merely suggestive. Three solutions, for example, are here assumed although seven or eight might be presented in a given question.)

The question is . . . ?
(Complete sentences are to be used throughout.)

INTRODUCTION

I. This question is of importance, in that . . . .
II. The terms are tentatively explained as follows:
  A. By . . . . is meant . . . .
  B. By . . . . is meant . . . .

[3] Consult again Chap. 7.

III. The goals in any analysis and solution of this problem would include consideration of the following tentative propositions:

    A. ....

    B. ....

    C. ....

IV. The history of the problem is as follows:

    A. ....

    B. ....

    C. ....

V. The chief issues are tentatively suggested:

    A. Does this problem constitute a major economic, social, or political problem that requires solution?

       1. What are the chief facts or events that give rise to the problem?

          a. What are the causes of these phenomena?

          b. What are the probable results (if unchecked)?

    B. What are the representative solutions for dealing with this problem?

       1. What are the advantages and disadvantages, the practicability and impracticability, of solution A?

       2. What are the advantages and disadvantages, the practicability and impracticability, of solution B?

       3. What are the advantages and disadvantages, the practicability and impracticability, of solution C?

    C. In view of the discussion above, shall solution A (or B or C) be preferred?

       1. Does this preferred solution have advantages over the others?

       2. Is it more practicable than the others?

DISCUSSION PROPER

I. Differing interpretations of the problem of .... are as follows:

    A. Those who believe that the problem is a major one and calls for a solution present the following propositions, arguments, and evidence:

       1. They argue that the situation is disturbing economically, for

          a. ....

          b. ....

          c. ....

       (In each subdivision throughout this outline detailed evidence is inserted with the exact sources indicated in the margin.)

2. They argue that the situation is disturbing politically, for

    a. ....

    b. ....

    c. ....

3. For this situation certain causes are largely responsible, for

    a. ....

    b. ....

    c. ....

4. These causes are so significant as to make the problem inherent in the existing system (organization, institution), for

    a. ....

    b. ....

    c. ....

5. This situation, unless checked, will lead to disastrous outcomes, for

    a. ....

    b. ....

    c. ....

B. Those who believe the problem is not so serious as alleged above present the following propositions, arguments, and evidence:

1. The situation is not very disturbing economically, for

    a. ....

    b. ....

    c. ....

2. The situation is not so disturbing politically, for

    a. ....

    b. ....

    c. ....

3. The alleged causes that affect the present situation are not so significant as to be inherent in the present system (organization, institution), for

    a. ....

    b. ....

    c. ....

4. The alleged results of the present situation give no (or little) indication of disastrous outcomes, for

    a. ....

    b. ....

    c. ....

II. Those who prefer solution A present the following propositions, arguments, and evidence:

A. Solution A is necessary to correct the evils analyzed above, for

1. . . . ., for
   a. . . . .
   b. . . . .
   c. . . . .
2. . . . ., for
   a. . . . .
   b. . . . .
   c. . . . .

B. Solution A will be an advantageous solution, for
  1. It will result in benefit X, for
     a. . . . .
     b. . . . .
     c. . . . .
  2. It will result in benefit Y, for
     a. . . . .
     b. . . . .
     c. . . . .

C. Solution A will be a practicable solution, for
  1. It will be workable, for
     a. . . . .
     b. . . . .
     c. . . . .
  2. Precedent exists for it, for
     a. . . . .
     b. . . . .
     c. . . . .

D. Solution A will be preferable to the other solutions, for
  1. It will be more satisfactory than Solution B, for
     a. . . . .
     b. . . . .
     c. . . . .
  2. It will be more satisfactory than Solution C, for
     a. . . . .
     b. . . . .
     c. . . . .

(Other solutions are omitted from this sample outline.)

In case you wish to extend this individual outline by working out your own preferred solution, you may do so. We are sure, however, that any outline carried into the discussion itself should resemble more the skeleton form above than a debater's brief. After your discussion is completed and your views are further stabilized, you may resort to the construction and presentation of an argumentative brief.

EXERCISES AND PROBLEMS

1. Construct a group outline for the following (or some similar) question: Shall the American colleges abolish all the foreign language requirements for entrance or graduation?

2. With another student, exchange group outlines on a proposition of policy. Criticize each other's outlines according to the suggestions given above.

3. Construct a group outline for the question: Shall the citizen casting his first vote in the next Presidential election support the Republican (or Democratic) ticket?

4. For the question dealt with above, give a brief oral explanation of the goals or aims to be considered in any analysis and solution of the problem.

5. (*For the instructor.*) Assign to the class a local, state, national, or international problem of current importance. Assign six or seven to each discussion group. Each unit will submit its outline for preliminary criticism by the members of the other groups.

6. (*For the instructor.*) Have the class as a whole discuss at some length the definitions in the problem assigned above. Be sure to use varied methods of definition making.

7. (*For the instructor.*) Each group will discuss the problem outlined in exercise 5. The instructor and other observers will comment concerning the relationship of the discussion to the outlines previously prepared.

8. (*For the instructor.*) Assign to each an individual outline. The entire class may use the same subject. A class hour will be spent in commenting on the experiences and results of such individual outlining.

CHAPTER 22

Discussion: Special Types

Discussion is often regarded as the experience of a few people seated about a table and talking at random. Discussion, on the contrary, covers a wide range of occasions, audiences, and methods. Although the common frame of reference is the problem-solution aim, the type variations are numerous. You may, for example, be one of an unorganized group, diligent in discussion, uninhibited by outside listeners. You may accept an invitation to join in a round-table broadcast. You may work as a committee member to frame a resolution to be passed on to the larger organization. You may serve as a committee member or visitor in a legislative hearing. You may participate in a panel as one of the platform speakers or as one of the audience. You may help make up a symposium. You may attend a forum, either as the lecturer or as one of the audience who become vocal during the question-and-answer period. You may engage in a public dialogue with a colleague, bringing to the audience a lively but fairly objective view of the problem. You may participate in a "forensic experience progression," organized for intercollegiate performance. These discussional experiences suggest the wide application of the discussion principle. The adaptability of the technique to the needs and interests of a specific audience indicates the practicability of this kind of controversial speaking.

I. Round Table

The discussion type most widely practiced is the round-table or informal discussion. People around a table just start talking, and perhaps ideas will evolve and coalesce. The physical setup symbolizes the democracy and cohesion of the group. In theory no chairman is present, no dominant speechmakers, no formality of procedure. Despite the casual atmosphere of the occasion, the group demonstrates an orderly evolution of reflective thinking. Round-tablers aim to increase their knowledge and to shape ideas.

Where are round tables found? In a sorority or fraternity house or a dormitory. They take place in a high-school social-science club, in a college course based upon two lectures per week and one discussion period, in a classroom, in discussion or other speech courses, in some church organization, in a community club such as the League of Women Voters.

These informal discussions succeed best when not more than ten (preferably six or seven) are included. Your group, moreover, had best talk on a subject about which they are informed. *Fruitless, furthermore, is the discussion likely to be if the participants know little of discussion techniques.* Vigorous debaters should be excused—or muzzled. All other voluble talkers should be warned that the hour is short. The deliberations should be neither hurried nor retarded. In short, a good discussion should be—a good discussion.

II. Committee Discussion

If you want more formal treatment of the problem, you should convert your group into a committee. Your aim then is not primarily knowledge getting but rather legislative results. You want action. A chairman is assigned, and the others have official status. This committee may be that of a college class; of a men's honorary society, of the Mortar Board, of Delta Sigma Rho, Tau Kappa Alpha, Pi Kappa Delta (these three are honorary forensic societies), of the athletic association, musical club, or journalism staff. These committees may be those of the Kiwanis, the Chamber of Commerce, the Speech Association of America, the National Manufacturers' Association, the CIO, the Federal Council of Churches of America, or the Democratic National

Committee, the Senate Committee of Foreign Affairs, or the House Committee on Military Affairs.

How will your colleagues and you make a "go" of committee discussion? You will wield parliamentary law, but will use it not for obstruction but for expedition. Your group will pervade the room with the spirit of discussion rather than with that of bilateral debate.[1]

III. COMMITTEE HEARINGS

Public hearings, conducted, e.g., by legislative committees of either House of Congress or of a state government, aim to collect information on a proposed measure and to register public sentiment. The speakers may either volunteer or be subpoenaed. The speaker faces the chairman and gives a prepared statement containing facts and his views on the proposed bill. Prolonged searching questions and answers follow. The audience has no voice (sessions are often closed). The atmosphere is judicial. The entire performance should make clear the problem, clarify arguments, and set forth the various points of view. Notable in recent history were the hearings before the Joint Congressional Committee on Atomic Energy in 1947, prior to the appointment of David Lilienthal, chairman of the United States Atomic Energy Commission, and his five fellow commissioners.[2]

Somewhat similar public hearings are held by national, state, or municipal governments, to sound out sentiment concerning proposed legislation or policies about to be inaugurated, for which authority has already been given. Such an issue would be, Shall the City Council build a municipal swimming pool in the West Side City Park, or shall the pool be erected on land already available near the East High School?

In such hearings, after opening statements by the public officials, it becomes a general forum in which anyone may ask questions and, under certain conditions, give short speeches. These hearings may continue for several sessions.

[1] For more detailed suggestions for participation see Chap. 23.

[2] See A. Craig Baird, *Representative American Speech, 1946–47*, pp. 150–152, for a statement by Mr. Lilienthal.

IV. PANEL

How does a panel differ from a round table? For a panel an audience is added that contributes questions and short speeches. This type has one audience (the panel) within a larger one. If the two audiences can be welded into a single body for united thinking and communication, the panel is highly successful.

Panels are chiefly set up as occasions for learning. They were first introduced by Dr. Harry Overstreet at the conference of the American Association of Adult Education in 1932.

This type will be more effective if certain obvious conditions are maintained.

1. See that the physical conditions are favorable. The room should not be too large (or too small). The panel should remain seated directly before the audience so as to be both visible and audible. The panelers should talk directly to each other and yet address also the other listeners.
2. The panel should be limited to about five in addition to the chairman.
3. The audience itself should be 100 rather than 500.
4. The panel should proceed informally for thirty or forty minutes. The chairman should then summarize briefly and call for audience comment. This free period continues for another thirty minutes. The collective sense of the group and of the panel is then interpreted.
5. The question should be a limited one. (Almost invariably it is stated too broadly.)
6. The chairman should have geniality. He should know his fellow talkers and see that each is repeatedly tagged by name. He should know the subject; should have an outline and see that the others also possess copies. He should keep the conferees on the subject; should summarize frequently, interpose questions; should not talk too obtrusively; should have a sense of humor; should constantly keep the larger audience before him and bring them constantly into the cooperative experience.
7. The panel members, like the chairman, must know the subject and the techniques of discussion. They should have had a "warm-up" period before the public session; should have shared in constructing the group outline; should talk only briefly and do so distinctly and vigorously; and should accommodate themselves to the audience. They will abstain from debate. Each paneler will listen closely to all questions from the audience and,

if asked to answer, will respond briefly (not more than one minute). The audience period belongs to the audience.
8. The audience participator should also know the subject and the techniques of discussion. He will do a reasonably good job if asked to join the panel. When participating, he should rise and when recognized, announce his name. He should feel free to speak up and should do so during his period. Like the paneler he should not debate or talk at length (or even more than once). He should offer brief remarks as well as ask questions.

V. SYMPOSIUM

How does the symposium differ from the round table and the panel? It is marked by the set speeches assigned to each leader. Whereas the more informal types are made up of conversational exchange, the symposium consists of three or four prepared speeches related to the common problem. The entire symposium occasion would include (1) these prearranged talks which together would reflect the representative approaches to the problem, (2) a panel of these same symposia leaders, and (3) finally, audience participation as in the panel and forum. In the symposium, as contrasted with the panel, the audience has a better opportunity to gain a systematic and authoritative presentation of the entire problem. Unfortunately, these lecturers sometimes betray a biased viewpoint. Moreover, the individual speech of ten minutes may treat only superficially a broad aspect. Furthermore, the formal speeches and the subsequent speaker panel often take up practically all available time. Audiences may not have a chance.

How shall you direct and participate in a successful symposium?

1. Make the analysis of the problem complete before assigning the topics.
2. Limit the subject.
3. Organize the individual talk. Adapt the subject matter, however, to what has preceded.
4. The chairman must be especially alert to summarize the speeches and to show their common relationship.
5. Prepare the audience by assigning readings and—if possible— by a warm-up period before the symposium begins.
6. Time each speaker and stop him.
7. Reserve at least half of the time to the audience.

8. Speeches from the floor should be brief (one minute).

9. Stand to get recognition and remain so in speaking.

10. The chairman will restate the question often for the audience.

11. At the end the spokesman will summarize clearly the entire course and significance of the conference.

VI. Forum

The forum is a large gathering, often under community sponsorship, in which designated leaders present an important problem. The audience later questions the speakers and makes brief remarks. Often the meeting is one of a series. The forum, therefore, implies either one assembly or an organization that embraces a series of topics.

The community forum dates from colonial days and the New England town meeting. The Lyceum lectures after 1826 and the widespread Chautauqua movement after 1874 were later developments of the forum. John W. Studebaker, Commissioner of Education, who had previously experimented successfully with a forum at Des Moines, Iowa, initiated forums in 1936 and 1937 in some nineteen communities in as many states.[3]   During World War II, community discussions were encouraged as means of informing the community and of strengthening civilian morale. In postwar America these community gatherings have persisted.[4]

What is the usual procedure of a forum?   Usually a well-known lecturer talks, and either he or the local chairman leads the audience in remarks and questions. It may, however, make use of the round table, symposium, panel, or debate. These devices are not an end but a means to give the audience information and stimulus for the initiation of its own participation. Whatever the introductory type, the platform leaders must talk with balance and open-mindedness.

How will you organize the forum?   First, you will determine the desires and objectives of your sponsoring organization.   Are you to provide a learning medium?   If so, to what age and cultural groups will you appeal?   On what aspects of learning will

[3] For an excellent brief summary of the forum movement, see J. W. Studebaker, *Fifteen Months of Forum Demonstrations, Choosing Our Way,* Chap. 1, pp. 1–8, Superintendent of Documents, U.S. Government Printing Office, 1938.

[4] For later history of the movement see H. D. Hopkins, "The Public Forum," *The Debater's Magazine,* Vol. II, pp. 209–212, December, 1946.

you focus? Upon local, or state, national, or even international problems? You will need to interpret the needs and wishes of your clientele—Parent Teachers Association, Farm Institute Organization, World Federalists, or League of Women Voters. President Hopkins states, "The most satisfactory forum of which I know was one in which a fine cross section of the whole community made up the audience, and in which all groups took active participation."[5]

Second, you will select the subjects in consultation with representative opinion. Audiences should be invited to list preferences. Each subject should be more than one-sided and should require deliberation rather than mere exposition. Representative topics would include local government, labor disputes, taxation, juvenile delinquency, propaganda, prices, and housing.

Third, you will select the most feasible discussion type. The lecture presented by an experienced and expert speaker is the easiest solution to program arranging. Unfortunately, the superior speakers are expensive, or they are too busy. The panel is likewise satisfactory if you can get the three or four who combine good delivery with knowledge of the subject. The symposium, too, will often make a lively introduction to the subject, provided always that a stop watch is used.

Fourth, each speaker should be carefully chosen. He should know discussion, have force of personality, have geniality and cooperative attitude, with patience and tact. He should be unpedantic and able to deal with the rank and file. He should be free from prejudice and have sympathetic understanding of the purposes of a forum. He should be able to present a unified, unpartisan speech, weighted with information but interestingly composed and presented.

Fifth, with your committee you will select a suitable time and place for your forum or forums. College students are more likely to respond to your invitation if the meeting is scheduled for Tuesday, Wednesday, or Thursday evening. Obviously the date and hour are selected after examination of the congested listings of meetings already made.

Sixth, having selected your subject, speakers, type of program, and date and place, you will call on your public-relations member or committee to develop early and often details of the pro-

[5] *Ibid.*, p. 212.

posed meeting. Especially helpful mediums for publicity of college forums are campus and community newspapers, personal announcements before classes and organizations, printed (mimeographed or otherwise) invitations, campus posters professionally prepared and strategically planted personal letters, the telephone, personal calls, and above all, the radio. These details all involve administration and energetic and cooperative promotion. In our complex society, however, systematic presentation of your meeting is necessary if your cause is to have a proper hearing.

Seventh, with your speakers, subject, and audience assembled, you will need a chairman or discussion leader or coordinator. As we have stated many times, the elaborate foundation you have laid for a fruitful discussion will collapse unless this chairman is effective. He will map out his procedure and give copies to the colleagues on the platform. He will attend to the public-address system, ushers, timekeepers, and similar details. He will know how to summarize ideas, ask questions of the audience, supply knowledge and even wit. In short, he will be an efficient chairman, as has been George V. Denny, of America's Town Meeting of the Air.

Eighth, your audience will need education before the meeting. Suggested readings will be posted, pamphlets circulated, and other devices to supply motivation for further study. The library will cooperate. Also small groups should be organized to study and apply discussion techniques.

What is the possible contribution of the forum? President Hopkins lists these:

Promotion of thoughtfulness among our own people.
A curb to the influence of racial fermentation.
Replacement of propaganda with reason and judgment.
Rekindling faith in basic American institutions.
Reduction of the threat of growing class lines.
Stimulation for further study and investigation.
Correlation of new knowledge with past learning and experience.
Development of a critical attitude which demands validation of claims and assertions.
A growing sense of public responsibility.
Growth of the power to think straight and be vocally active in civic matters.
To be in a much fuller sense, a functioning and responsible citizen.

VII. INTERCOLLEGIATE DISCUSSION

Since 1930 discussion has been added to interscholastic and intercollegiate (and intramural) speaking contests. Special types of discussion, to enlist a considerable number of college students, have been introduced experimentally. A representative type is the *logical-pattern* or *forensic-experience progression* type, first sponsored by Dr. Elwood Murray, of the University of Denver. With minor modifications, such discussion is carried out in six or seven stages over a period of two days. These steps correspond roughly with the successive steps of the *reflective pattern* of a problem of policy. Theoretically, the six or seven assigned to each group will give a separate period to each of the following: (1) definitions, (2) goals, (3) analysis of the problematic situation, (4) discussion of solution A, (5) discussion of solution B, etc., (6) synthesis of the thinking and interpretation of that solution (or solutions) preferred, (7) framing of a program or implementing the conclusions. Since the speaking time of intercollegiate visitors is limited, these seven phases are usually condensed to about four or five meetings: (1) definition, goals, and analysis of the problematic situation, (2) discussion of solution A, (3) discussion of solution B, (4) discussion of the preferred solution (each to give a short statement of his individual conclusions in the light of the previous group thinking).

The evaluation or judging is done by a member of the faculty or other "expert" or group of critics. The critics rate the speakers as "superior," "excellent," "good," "fair," or "below standard," with critical comments to be passed on the discussants explaining the evaluations. These scores are translated into numerical equivalents. The score for each speaker in each round (with different judges for the separate rounds) and the cumulative rating of the discussant can be announced.

I recommend the following principles and methods be kept in mind:

1. This forensic program can be either intramural or intercollegiate. If restricted to home speakers and if the four or five rounds are adhered to, the program will obviously need to be carried on in out-of-school hours. As an intercollegiate contest, it can include as many schools and discussants as may be accommodated. Enough discussion quarters for the simultaneous

conferences of small groups must be lined up. On my campus we have had about one hundred participants (in units of six or seven) carrying through the successive stages.

2. The number in each group, as we have repeatedly observed, should be limited.

3. For the first round a skilled chairman should be assigned. Often he may be from the home institution. At the end of any round the group may nominate a leader from the following meeting. The rating of this leader may or may not be included in the comparative rankings in the tournament. (It is often held that this chairman is more likely to be given a "halo" rank although our Iowa experience does not so indicate.)

4. The subject should be limited. Usually the discussants attempt to solve a problem too broad for adequate treatment in the four hours of deliberation usually allowed. The topic should be one other than that on which these same speakers have recently debated. The debating point of view in such cases may mar the discussional aims.

5. To have valid results the performers must be well prepared. The topic should be announced early; a tentative outline of the alleged issues and points of view should be distributed early to the various colleges; a fairly complete bibliography on the problem should be handed out; the speakers should be selected early and systematically trained.

6. Those who participate should have had much training and experience in discussion. On the subject assigned, they should have joined in several sessions that duplicate the logical pattern proposed for the intercollegiate conference.

7. The chairman or leader of each group can easily make or break the group performance. He should be hand-picked. He will provide geniality, make the surroundings comfortable, keep to the subject, and synchronize the thinking.

8. Let each phase run uninterruptedly for an hour. Try to cover most of the ground allotted to that phase of the analysis.

9. See that the judges are competent, that they have proper instructions, that they spend a few minutes at the end to advise the group on discussion procedures and efficiency, and that during the discussion itself, they keep silent. Usually, one faculty judge is assigned to a group.

10. Bystander audiences are encouraged. If they are present,

group discussants need not ignore them.   The group, both for the sake of the judge and for the others present, should speak distinctly.

11. The *preferred-solution* stage should be carried out with individual speeches for each of the six or seven discussants. Each should stand, address the audience (if present). The general conditions of public speech should prevail.   The judges should rate each as speechmaker as well as discussant.   Those who direct these forensic progression programs are reminded that discussion often takes place in public speaking mediums as well as via an informal round table.

12. If it is desired, the first stage may also incorporate individual speeches—with each standing as he talks.

13. The implementation stage, reporting any resolutions or group recommendations, usually takes place in a combined assembly.   Here the character of the program moves toward debate.   A later chapter will review the procedures for such congress or senate.

The logical pattern is less rigid than competitive debate and offers more experience to a greater number of students than is ordinarily possible with the latter type.   This discussion apparently enlists the interests of a much larger number than does debate.   The logical progression type is a desirable educational experience and duplicates the situations of real life.

The critic, on several counts, may condemn these discussions. They are held to be demonstrations of loose talking without the thorough and accurate handling of facts and arguments as in debate.   Not enough incentive, we are told, is provided.   The best students, we are reminded, enter debate rather than discussion. Also the discussants are poorly prepared.   Also discussion is allegedly inconsistent with contest competition.   We doubt, however, whether the competitive factor affects strongly the situation.   The judge is merely a friendly adviser to help improve the quality of individual discussion.   The speakers appear to be little distracted by the critic.   If discussion contests arouse sufficient student interest to warrant intercollegiate gatherings and lead to improvement in discussion techniques, they are, in my opinion, justified.

VIII. Radio and Television Discussion

Discussion, more than hard and fast debate, seems acceptable over the air. The Chicago Round Table is a splendid example of the type. The People's Platform, in its earlier development duplicating conversation more than controversial speaking, has also a wide audience. America's Town Meeting of the Air, referred to previously in this book, is an example of the large forum. Sometimes it approximates true discussion; often it is a two-sided debate.

Radio discussion has much in common with discussion without the radio. The same patterns of thinking, the same weighing of alternatives, the same mental attitudes and cooperative expressions are present. The chief differences arise from the microphone and the invisible audience.

Radio discussion, I must admit, is hardly discussion in reality. It is rehearsed (or should be). Most of its details, even its conversational turns, have been carefully worked out. Such radio "show" is therefore artificial. Further, the planting of the microphone curbs spontaneity. Despite these restrictions the radio discussion becomes more and more an agency for the stimulation of public attention to a problem and a medium for the students and others to have training in discussion. The development of television promises to enhance the appeal of both round-table and forum types.

1. Have a clear understanding with your sponsors concerning the audience you are supposed to address.
2. Your subject must be limited. Nine-tenths of the radio topics are unduly broad.
3. Your purpose ought to be at least to stimulate interest in the problem. You must, therefore, be alive and interesting.
4. You will organize your speech. If your allotment of speaking time (symposium plan) is only three minutes, you will nevertheless shape your statements to conform to the highest standards of speech construction.
5. All speeches must be short whether they are of the set pattern or of the panel sort.
6. Prefer informal discussion to set speeches.
7. Have enough summaries to clarify the progress.
8. Radiate a pleasant personality. Reflect humor but not sarcasm

or belligerency. Show your courtesy, tact, and the other virtues that make you an agreeable companion and talker.

9. Write and rewrite your speech. Often the stations require a manuscript. Make your sentences short, concrete, oral, personal. Chop out the clichés and threadbare language.

10. Follow all the announcer's clues and advice. Start and stop exactly when you are supposed to do so.

11. With your manuscript before you, avoid reading or giving the effect of reading. Extempore ability is necessary. Listen to other programs. Note the rate, pitch changes, pauses, and other elements of satisfactory delivery. Record on a mirrorphone or dictaphone samples of your own performance and so improve.

EXERCISES AND PROBLEMS

1. Attend a classroom discussion (presumably one in the course in which you are enrolled) and draft a written criticism of the program.

2. (*For the instructor.*) Record a classroom panel discussion and play it back for criticism by the class.

3. Organize and lead a classroom round table. Report (on paper) your reactions as to your experience and your suggestions of how the program might have been improved.

4. (*For the instructor.*) Have the class organize and carry out a forensic progression program according to the suggestions given in this chapter. Spend a later class hour commenting on the strength and weakness of the discussions as a whole and that of individual performers as their records are shown in the reports by you and your fellow critics.

5. (*For the instructor.*) Arrange for a series of public forums, held in the class but following as best you can the details of a genuinely public forum. At a class period following each forum, have the class each present for you a short criticism of the forum. Discuss the physical arrangements, the delivery and discussional attitude of each platform leader, the success or failure in the following through of the discussion principles, and the discussional conduct of the audience.

6. (*For the instructor.*) Assign a series of ten-minute lectures to be delivered by selected student representatives. Follow each lecture with a thirty-minute discussion under the chairmanship of the "lecturer."

CHAPTER 23

Discussion: Leadership, Participation, Evaluation

Discussion, if it involves more than three or four informal con-
versationists, requires leaders. The larger the group, the more
complicated the situation, and the more heterogeneous the audience, the more necessary is this chairman. Discussion leadership is of a special kind. This leader is not the autocratic personality, not necessarily an expert, not a great persuader. His
dynamism lies in his cooperative character. His goal is that of
aiding in problem solving. He is interested in the desirable social and individual ends. If he leads, the favorable response by
the followers is because they recognize in him this worthy motivation. Under his unobtrusive direction, wise contributors expound freely, timid counselors speak up, blatant orators acquire
an unexplained modesty, audience rapport mounts, thought supplants emotional dominance, and practicable solutions begin to
shape themselves.

I. QUALIFICATIONS OF DISCUSSION LEADERSHIP

Suppose you are to lead a round table, panel, or even a large
community forum. What is to recommend you? The discussion occasion calls for more than the perfunctory chairmanship.
The latter role may often fall to the president of an organization

or some distinguished citizen. Each may be impressive in his general reputation but almost entirely unfitted for the job of directing social thinking. Studies in social psychology list many traits of leadership, such as high intelligence, wisdom, catholicity of temperament and outlook, courage, wide experience, and strong character. While I agree that these virtues seem out of this world, we are assured that leadership can be taught; that many college students, for example, have sufficient ability and personal mental and emotional maturity in intellectual and social behavior to prove much more than adequate for such occasions. What shall you do to qualify for successful leadership?

A. *Know the Subject.* Observation and experience repeatedly confirm that knowledge is one key to earning audience respect and support. You cannot always assimilate every detail of the topic. But as far as your resources permit, you will think, read, and organize. At a critical point in the deliberations, even the expert may become cloudy. You will help to clear the atmosphere.

B. *Know Discussion Techniques.* Have a well-established philosophy of what discussion is; its aims; its distinction from debate and oratory; its applications of the thought process; its organization and group outline; its utilization of divergent points of view; its weighing of solutions; its modes of language usage and of delivery; its enlistment of logical behavior.

C. *Know the Methods of Testing Argument and Evidence.* Since the heart of the communication in discussion is definition, analysis, hypothesis building, inductive and deductive methods of inquiry and inference, and the weighing of facts, you will ground yourself in these marks of straight thinking. This growth in experience with applied logic is, I agree, slow and arduous. You will soon acquire, however, experience sufficient for most occasions.

D. *Know Your Discussion Colleagues.* Perhaps you have had little or no previous acquaintance with colleagues. At least you will call them by name, learn their backgrounds, special interests, and points of view concerning the issue and their equipment with which to discuss it.

E. *Know the Participating and Listening Audience.* In most cases the audience analysis is not so difficult as it might seem. If your assembly is fifty college students who, like you, are analyzing the problem of a threatened rise in the tuition rates, you automatically sense the experience and thinking of those assembled. You are one of them. If your listeners are mainly a mixed popular audience, gathered in a local church under the combined auspices of the American Veterans of Foreign Wars, the League of Women Voters, the Chamber of Commerce, and the Interdenominational Union, the analysis is more complicated.

F. Train Yourself in Extempore Speaking and in Making Rapid Decisions. As coordinator you will abandon your cut and dried remarks, your neat outline, especially as you steer a question-and-answer period. Practice extempore speaking. The classroom will be a good training ground. Aim at rapid thinking and decision making. Essential to leadership is decisiveness—without aggressiveness—in your direction of the program.

G. Avoid Assertiveness. Your restraint, your willingness to encourage your colleagues and to discount your own importance in the give and take—all help you. Your aim is to forget your thorough knowledge, ready speaking, and excellent vocabulary. Your achievement will be that of producing a roomful of worthwhile talkers.

H. Have an Open Mind. What does open-mindedness imply? Among other things, respect for the opinions and arguments of others. You will be a good listener. You will have patience to see that assertions and evidence are traced to their alleged sources; that arguments are fairly examined; that your own interpretations are free from bias and are not injected too often or too positively.

I. Demonstrate Your Ability to Get Along with Your Colleagues and with Audiences. Cultivate a sincere interest in the crowd, a sympathy for their attempts at expression even though you regard their arguments as often thin, control of your own reactions to irritating conditions bound to arise.

J. Demonstrate Geniality. The occasion may lose its purpose if you set out to be humorous. Your natural optimism, and even pleasantry, nevertheless, should pervade the room. Your sincerity need not preclude occasional lightness. All must be in good taste, without sarcasm. You can at least discourage long faces and unnatural stiffness.

II. IMMEDIATE PREPARATION FOR THE DISCUSSION

Whether you are merely to organize a campus round-table discussion limited to a single session or to promote and lead a series of public forums or smaller round tables, your preparation will involve, on smaller or larger scale, the same duties and methods.

1. Get a working committee and have patience and skill enough to enlist their help.

2. Get a subject or subjects that have interest and meaning to the audience. Canvass the leaders and others for their suggestions on the topic. Whether you use a "hot" local issue will depend on your good judgment. Almost anything that is worth major time and preparation is justified, provided its public discussion will not stir deep-seated animosities.

3. Provide information for the speaker-leaders and for the audience. Students and all others who enter the discussion chamber need information. They should be encouraged and even inspired by reading helps, bibliographies, books, papers, and other reading materials placed at their disposal. Librarians and faculty are glad to cooperate. Your committee should prepare representative recent references, mimeograph them, and distribute them far enough in advance to be usable. Your foresight will bring ample returns.

4. Choose speakers of the round table or discussion. Those elected should have had training in discussion, should have time to prepare, have interest in the subject, special knowledge or point of view that needs airing. If several are to serve, they should be of comparable ability. One genius and highly skilled speaker may otherwise stifle the others.

5. Prepare and distribute agenda of the meeting and a group outline. Especially is it worth while to do so if several speakers are listed, and a public forum is attempted over the radio. A blueprint of what is to happen is necessary. Time limits, for example, should be clearly understood and announced in advance. Furthermore, a group outline is needed. Such outline, as we have remarked, should be worked out jointly. Otherwise, you will need to do it yourself. This framework will be drawn up according to the purpose of the meeting and the speaking personnel. Certainly it need not be closely adhered to but will form a dependable basis for the leader and the led.

6. Properly publicize the meeting if you wish an audience.
For suggestions consult the previous chapter.

7. Plan for audience participation. If a forum is to be held, arrange in advance for certain ones to talk from the floor. Such key contributors need to function to forestall awkward silence. The leader's experience will usually lead to complete audience spontaneity.

8. Know your parliamentary law. In an emergency you may need a knowledge of parliamentary procedure.

III. CONDUCTING THE MEETING

In the meeting itself you will be the coordinator. Somebody else may be the nominal chairman to introduce you. The destiny of the hour, however, should be in your hands.

1. Introduce the problem. No hard and fast formula can here be set down for getting under way. As the active chairman, you will be direct and brief. You will state the subject, add a few words about it, explain briefly why it has been selected; explain the organization of the program and specify when and how the audience will join in; introduce each speaker by name and describe in a few words his qualifications.

If no set speeches or panel are included, you will address your audience at once with a series of searching questions, both general and specific ones. You may even use a motion picture or other visual aids to stimulate your group to immediate response.

2. Help develop the discussion pattern. Your responsibility is to see that terms are clarified and remain so; that the problem is adequately developed rather than sloughed off; that solutions are each developed fully, but not until antecedent steps have been explored. Students—and others—often wish to rush into a solution without knowing very clearly what is wrong. You are to perform the difficult feat of checking interesting vocal excursions into tangent problems and yet avoiding the close pursuit of a cut and dried outline.

3. Introduce sufficient transitional and summarizing remarks. Not only at the end do you summarize, but you will at each stage link ideas together. Again you will clarify without boring. Each summary should be accompanied with, "Is this statement the consensus of the group opinion?" You will handle such details of units and coherence without sounding like a college professor or other pedant.

4. Do not neglect the human factor. If time permits and any member of the panel suggests personal experiences that relate, by all means encourage him to testify, but briefly.

5. Test all information and argument.

6. Ask questions rather than dogmatize. Here are a few questions that illustrate the desirable strategy of leadership:

Not so good	*Better*
You gentlemen have overlooked an important phase of the question.	Have any of you a point of view concerning this phase of the question?
Your statement is interesting, but you have failed to cite either argument or evidence.	What is our basis in fact and inference for agreeing with Gulley?
It seems to me that your attitude is colored by your negative position.	Is our approach to this problem leading us to neglect other positions that we may now examine?
Mr. Gulley, your remarks, although interesting, remind of the Irishman who remarked of De Valera that "He approached Dublin at the head of 20,000 words."	Have those of you who have not spoken, points of view you may care to offer?
Mr. Gulley, you failed to cite the source of your figures.	Mr. Gulley, will you please cite the references from which your statistics came?
Mr. Gulley, in your remarks are you not pretty hard on Brandenburg?	Mr. Gulley, what is the relation of your statement to the issue of obsolete housing (or whatever is the immediate issue)?
I'm sorry to interrupt you, Mr. Blank, but others wish the floor.	Thank you, Mr. Blank. Who is next to state his point of view?
I agree heartily with your statement, Mr. Blank.	Do we agree with Blank's statement?
Jones, we haven't heard from you. Will you explain your position?	Jones, do you agree with Blakely's statement?

7. Control the overtalkative, the silent, and the vituperative members. Use discretion and tact, but avoid the usual charge of allowing the passive to remain so; or of allowing somebody to monopolize things; or of permitting the positive personality to have free rein.

8. Take a vote at the end if your committee has planned such register of opinion.

The suggestions above concerning leadership will, of course, be much modified as your experiences multiply. In the classroom or elsewhere opportunities, we hope, may come to you to apply most of the suggestions above.

IV. Participation as Contributor

Suppose you have the good or bad fortune to be assigned not as leader but merely as contributor. Your mission is to share in the informal discussion or panel; to give one of the symposium speeches with the panel added; to comprise one of the platform lectures of a forum; to comprise one of a hundred who attend a Town Meeting of the Air program and ask a question you have carefully worded; or to join the audience in a more turbulent gathering of young Progressives to discuss possible Presidential possibilities in the national campaign of 1956. How will you conduct yourself with credit to the subject, the occasion, the audience, and the discussional art? Below is a summary of whatever wisdom and methodology have been unfolded in the preceding pages.

A. The Subject and You. As paneler, committee member, or forum speaker you will rightly share in dictating what is to be talked about. The philosophy of discussion requires that you be consulted concerning these issues and their framing. This last mentioned chore, by the way, is rarely carried out with much skill. Use your influence to limit the problem. Reject, for example, the proposal to discuss "Guns or butter." That slogan was catchy about 1940 and was the title of a University of Chicago Round Table. But catchy titles are not the same as problems properly stated. In the example cited, the issue was "Shall the United States devote a larger share of the national income to military preparation than to the production of foodstuffs?" You the astute discussant, however, will restrict the question to, "Shall the United States Congress adopt a minimum budget of four billion dollars for the air branch of national defense?"

B. *Research and You.* Patronize the library. Put on your study desk nine books and eighteen pamphlets. Take diligent notes on paper and many more mentally.

C. *Group and Individual Outlines.* Work with the panel and leader on a group outline. Also work out independently a discussion-brief that plumbs the subject. With such basic preparation you can report to your instructor (if this project is under his tutelage) that you have analyzed the problem and know a bit about it.

D. *The Discussion Meeting and You.*

1. *Argument and evidence.* Present your information concretely. Cite sources but do so easily without too much detail. Repeat an issue often enough so that we can always connect it with your detailed comment. Avoid complicated figures or extensive use of statistics. Add illustrations and introduce suggestive analogies. Cite authorities and indicate their background as experts. Introduce causal arguments; explain *why* facts and situations are so. Enforce the facts offered by others. Express the specious arguments of others, but do so in no high argumentative mood. As the discussion develops, qualify your original stand (if you honestly have modified your views). Cite cases and invite others to generalize or draw their own conclusions. At times admit your own biases, but do not deprecate yourself unduly. Be genuine.

2. *Organization.* Dovetail your remarks with those of others to further the analysis and argument. If your contribution is a forum speech, see that it is well organized and that the speech structure duplicates that of a discussion pattern. Incorporate definitions, goals, and other thought units. Help the leader to integrate the entire performance so that any critic and all laymen can easily recognize the relevancy proportion and sequence of the speaking occasion.

3. *Language.* Adjust your oral style to that of the group. If you are supposed to be semiformal over the air, do so. In general, radio discussants are usually informal. Their recordings, as later examined, reveal the use of first names for identifying each other, generous use of personal pronouns, broken sentences, interruptions, and even doubtful syntax and grammar. The lan-

guage is oral. Even though you have this oral quality, you will have varied language, original turns, and certainly language precision. Use tentative language, in which you state that "It seems to me," or "the cases I have examined." Avoid "the *only* conclusion a sensible person can arrive at is" and similar expressions of finality.

4. *Delivery.* What are the peculiar weaknesses of the delivery of discussants? Round-table contributors often assume that their discourse is strictly private. Their tones are therefore low and muffled. The result is not even good conversation. Communication, here as in other types of speaking, is complete only if the delivery is effective. Voice quality, sufficient loudness, a lively sense of communication, clear enunciation and articulation— these fundamentals of good speaking are among the determinants of desirable discussion. When the discussers move from a private table to a public platform for organized discussion, the demands upon delivery become correspondingly more severe. To qualify for such assignments, you will, therefore, prepare through training and organized experience in representative speaking situations. Especially is it necessary for you to develop extempore ability. As the round table challenges you to relate your contribution to what has immediately preceded, so do the larger forums and public panels necessitate much impromptu utterance.

5. *Listening.* As fluent speaking is required, so is genuine listening. Listening is not silence. It means active cooperation. You are engaged in a dialogue. The speaker finds constant response from you (favorable or otherwise) even though you are inaudible. You are "talking back." Test yourself, then, on your ability to follow and reproduce what has been said. The test is, Are you able to summarize at any moment what has just been said? And are you able to comment adequately on it?

6. *Questioning.* Intelligent listening is followed by intelligent questioning. Examine any well-regulated program in which the question-and-answer period is recorded (*e.g.,* America's Town Meeting of the Air) to note the framing and timing of questions "from the floor." Such interrogations should be short (twenty-five words have been the official limit for the Town Hall meetings). They should be framed simply. Highly involved sentences are out of place. (It is better to prefix to your query a

preliminary exposition.) Such questions should call for (*a*) further information on a point, (*b*) repetition of an idea not clear, (*c*) explanation of seeming inconsistency in a speaker's interpretations, (*d*) inference from certain data, (*e*) specific solution, (*f*) explication or illustration of an abstract term, (*g*) additional citation of expert testimony, (*h*) personal opinion of the speaker, and (*i*) an invitation for the speaker to summarize the state of the controversy. The questions should not be couched in strong emotional language or "loaded." Sometimes you may write your interrogation as the meeting develops and deliver it from memory or even read it. Clearness, preciseness, and conciseness are marks of intelligent questioning.

V. Judging Student Discussions

How shall we evaluate the discussion performance of each participant? The aim of such judgment is, of course, to suggest methods of improvement and so train the discussant for successful application in "life situations." An incidental purpose is to determine the relative ability of performers in competition. A speaker may be rated as superior (5), excellent (4), good (3), fair (2), or below standard (1).

A more specific criticism blank can be used, somewhat as follows (underscore or encircle the rating in each item):

1. Analysis of the problem (including definitions, goals, explanation of the problematic situation, its causes and results).

Superior, Excellent, Good, Fair, Below Standard

2. Logic and evidence (including knowledge, extent, and accuracy of the facts; soundness of the inferences from testimony and instances, analogies, and causal factors; adherence to the discussion pattern).

Superior, Excellent, Good, Fair, Below Standard

3. Language (including accuracy of definitions, clear and interesting language and sentence structure).

Superior, Excellent, Good, Fair, Below Standard

4. Cooperative thinking (including cooperation with the chairman and colleagues in definitions, furthering the process of problem-

and-solution, airing all points of view, asking pertinent questions, securing major agreement and minimizing minor differences, providing summaries, pointing the way to the next phase, indicating the formulation of an integrated solution).

Superior, Excellent, Good, Fair, Below Standard

5. Delivery (including good voice quality, desirable loudness, clear enunciation, pleasing personality, communicativeness, extempore ability).

Superior, Excellent, Good, Fair, Below Standard

6. Total effectiveness.

Superior, Excellent, Good, Fair, Below Standard

Total Rating _____

In each of these items the speaker may be rated as superior, excellent, good, fair, below standard. The maximum score would then be 30. The student should not only be given this report but should be advised concerning ways and means of improvement. The blank is a learning tool and not a scientific measure.

VI. EVALUATION OF DISCUSSION PROCEDURES AND PURPOSES

How efficient is discussion? How efficient are the methods of measuring the results of a given discussion? What of the relative efficiency of the different types of discussion, for example, the panel as compared with the symposium or the lecture-forum? What of the relative effect of discussion as compared with debate? How does discussion compare with other methods of influencing public opinion? How shall we evaluate the subjects chosen for discussion? The relative reliability of judgments reached by individuals after group discussion as compared with those same judgments by the same individuals without this group experience? How effective is discussion as a means of securing information? What is discussion? How efficient is logic as a factor in discussion? How shall we evaluate language in discussion? How effective is delivery in discussion? What of the effectiveness of methods of teaching discussion? Does discussion affect study habits? Intelligence? Ability to listen critically? Ability to detect fallacies? Ability to debate? To speak persuasively? To develop leadership? What general pattern of problem solving is to be preferred?

Keltner, in 1947, concludes after a survey of studies on discussion:

1. Discussion seems to have practical value in teaching students to think critically and to grasp and retain factual material and general subject matter.

2. Discussion may be taught at the junior high, senior high, and college levels with varying degrees of success in reaching its objectives.

3. Problem solving in group discussion is closely related to individual problem solving. It is thus concerned with the factors of reasoning and thinking that apply to individual thought.

4. The on-the-spot methods of measurement and analysis of group discussion still lack the objectivity and accuracy of paper and pencil tests of individual skills in reasoning and problem solving.

5. In general, the research in discussion has only scratched the surface of a tremendous realm of problems that must be solved before we can say that we really know what the discussion is about. We will continue to train people to discuss and to lead discussions, but we must recognize that this training is still inadequate.[1]

Those students interested in full understanding of discussion and in its development will study the experiments and other investigations of the nature and methods of this art.

EXERCISES AND PROBLEMS

1. (*For the instructor.*) Arrange a series of classroom discussions with rotating leaders. Give special guidance to the successive leaders. Have each member criticize according to the suggestions given in exercise 2.

2. Criticize the leaders of classroom discussions. In your one-page report for the instructor, include consideration of the following items: (a) knowledge of the subject, (b) knowledge of the technique of discussion, (c) knowledge of the discussants and adjustment to them, (d) open-mindedness, (e) geniality, (f) favorable physical conditions for the discussion, (g) effective handling of the phases of the analysis

[1] John W. Keltner, "What Do We Know About Group Discussion?" *Debater's Magazine*, Vol. III, p. 163, September, 1947.

and solution, (*h*) handling of questions by audience, (*i*) skill in summary and other elements to integrate and further the discussion.

3. Evaluate your own preparation and participation in a role other than leader in a discussion. Test your skill with respect to (*a*) your reading, (*b*) note taking, (*c*) preparation of an individual outline, (*d*) cooperation in preparing a group outline, (*e*) open-mindedness, enthusiasm, tact, (*f*) cooperation in definitions, (*g*) cooperation in analysis and solution of the problem, (*h*) use of sound evidence, (*i*) use of valid inferences, (*j*) exposure of fallacies, (*k*) language, (*l*) delivery, including amount of your talk, (*m*) listening, (*n*) cooperation in summaries, keeping to the subject, allaying divisive spirit of others.

Part IV

Debate

CHAPTER 24

Debate: Principles and Techniques

I. Relation of Debate to Discussion

Discussion, we have made clear, often evolves into debate. Once the analysis is made and the examination of solutions begins, firm conviction may emerge. Debate thus becomes necessary. This shift in techniques may occur not only at points where the way out is faced but earlier, as in the definitions, framing of goals, hypotheses, and review of the problematic situation.

Discussion and debate are complementary. The former implies analysis and disinterested review of arguments and evidence; the latter, special argument arising at any stage.

Discussion, ideally, makes debate unnecessary. Human nature, however, and the demands of some early decision and action—all work against cooperative reflection. To state these limitations is not to condemn discussion. We simply use it as far as is practicable.

Debate, likewise, is not to be dismissed as "sophism institutionalized." When well-grounded convictions prevail, democratic action requires that the various positions be fully argued and that votes and action follow. Democracy declares that judgments, even far apart, are based on intelligence and reflection and are, therefore, all valid. To break the impasse, however, the majority vote is evoked. But the minority is not trampled upon. Constitutional and other guarantees proclaim that democracy condemns both the "tyranny of the majority" and the despotism of a usurper minority.

If debate supplants discussion at a given stage, is the latter technique shelved for the remainder of the over-all deliberation? On the contrary, as opinion matures through a succession of debates, hints of consensus begin to appear. The cycle may move through discussional analysis, then debate, and again may revert to discussion. Debate, properly handled, contains the elements of good discussion. The debater, I conclude, is a practical problem solver whose method is often called for in the world in which we live. And, in his own right, he may have many of the virtues of the discussant.

II. Debate and Argumentation

How does debate relate to argumentation? Both use the principles of analysis, argument, evidence, brief persuasive composition, and delivery. Debate is argument under specific rules. What are they?

1. Time limits are observed. Intercollegiate debaters, for example, include four speakers (two per side) who talk for about one hour. Thirty years ago teams included three speakers each and they argued for at least one hour and a half.

2. The argument is conducted under parliamentary rules. Although few rules are imposed in the debate itself, in theory speakers may be interrupted at every point by rules of order. The purpose of such rules is to guarantee to the two sides equal protection and opportunity. Back of this machinery of law is the assumption that the Anglo-Saxon principles of justice and fair play are operating in the debate.

3. As further guarantee of justice to all, each side has an equal number of speakers, an equal amount of time. The affirmative opens because it "assumes the burden of proof," but to compensate for such disadvantage it has the final speech.

4. To ensure further application of the legislative-parliamentary principle, the subject is couched in resolution form. This is good legislative procedure which requires that one subject only be under consideration at any one time and that it be framed as a motion, bill, or resolution to allow voting on a single proposition.

5. To ensure review of the arguments presented, the sides are allowed an equal amount of time for rebuttal. According to school and college custom, each speaker is given five or six minutes for his reply, the negative opening and the affirmative closing this second round of speeches.

6. At the conclusion a vote is taken on the "merits of the question." Decision making is thus secured. (In student debates for learning purposes, the judge often decides in favor of the team that does the most effective debating.)

Lay audiences are encouraged to attend. Either they, the equivalent of the members of a legislature, or of the twelve members of a jury, do the voting. Or one or more "expert" judges may do so—these officials corresponding to the courtroom judge.

7. Debating is usually oral, although W. J. Bryan and Albert J. Beveridge, for example, engaged in a series of written debates in 1907.

III. School and College Debate in History

American school and college debating continues a mental discipline widely exercised even before there were printed books. Protagoras (481–411 B.C.) was apparently the father of school debate.[1] Greek and Roman students were trained through dialectic (debate by question and answer) and debate. Dialectic[2] was foremost among the seven liberal arts. After the Reformation, power in disputation continued in high regard, especially among the leaders of Protestantism. The academies and universities more and more took over the practice from the monasteries. Edmund Burke, for example, at Trinity College, Dublin, in 1742, founded a debating club, the minutes of which make clear that he spoke on numerous occasions.

In American colleges debating was carried on from colonial days. The Massachusetts Historical Society[3] lists several hundred subjects debated by Harvard students from 1655 to 1790. These questions included, "Was there a rainbow before the deluge?" and "Is the voice of the people the voice of God?" James Otis at Harvard had training in dialectics. Fisher Ames, entering Harvard in 1770, was a member of a debating society.

[1] Bromley Smith, "The Father of Debate: Protagoras of Abdera," *Quarterly Journal of Speech,* Vol. XXIII, pp. 426–431, October, 1937.

[2] Everett L. Hunt, "Dialectic: A Neglected Method of Argument," *Quarterly Journal of Speech Education,* Vol. VII, pp. 221–232, June, 1921.

[3] *Proceedings of the Massachusetts Historical Society, 1800–1881,* Vol. 18.

When Gouverneur Morris was graduated from King's College (Columbia) in 1768, his debating club presented him with a silver medal.[4]

Until after the Civil War, literary clubs flourished throughout the American schools and colleges and in many a town and country center. Webster, Clay, Calhoun, Rufus Choate, Phillips, and many other orators developed their skill in debating clubs in either a collegiate or a community organization. After the Civil War, training of outstanding speakers through college literary society debates continued. William J. Bryan debated at Illinois College. Albert J. Beveridge was a frequent debater in the "Old Plato" Society at Indiana's Asbury (later Depauw) University.

With the rise of intercollegiate debating beginning with the Harvard-Yale contests of 1892, the rules multiplied. Colleges East and West took up the "sport" and evolved complicated rules to govern the contests. Secondary schools followed the lead of the colleges. State universities fostered state-wide high-school leagues that today include hundreds of schools in a single state.

College debate leagues were formed, e.g., the Mid-west Debate League, the Western Conference Debate League, and the Eastern Intercollegiate Debate League. Long trips by debaters were projected. A single subject for the college year was selected.

After 1925 debate tournaments (or tourneys) became popular. Pi Kappa Delta, the intercollegiate honorary forensic fraternity, took the lead in sponsoring such gatherings. A hundred or more colleges with chapters of that organization have sent their debaters, orators, and extempore speakers to a biennial national contest. Four or five preliminary rounds of debates have been conducted before the eliminations begin. Three or four days have been spent in the process of selecting the winners.

Many colleges and universities, in line with this popular program, have staged invitational tournaments. Because for a relatively small financial outlay the debate teams can meet many distant schools, the tournament plan has grown in popularity.

---

[4] For a review of disputation and debate in colonial colleges, see Ota Thomas, "The Teaching of Rhetoric in the United States during the Classical Period of Education," in W. N. Brigance (ed.), *The History and Criticism of American Public Address*, 2 vols., Vol. 1, pp. 193–210, McGraw-Hill Book Company, Inc., 1943. See also for debating in colonial legislatures, George V. Bohman, "The Colonial Period," *ibid.*, pp. 3–54.

Debating for women has also increased, especially since the passage of the woman suffrage amendment. Intercollegiate leagues for women and occasionally separate debate tournaments are maintained.

The average college has from twelve to thirty active intercollegiate undergraduate debaters, who in a single season engage in fifty or seventy-five debates on five or six questions. Those who achieve distinction are eligible to such honorary forensic organizations as Delta Sigma Rho, Pi Kappa Delta, and Tau Kappa Alpha.

In June, 1921, Bates College sent a team to debate Oxford, England, in the Oxford Union Society, organized in 1823. In the following October the Oxonians, in a return engagement, met seven eastern American colleges. Until World War II these international debates continued. Visiting speakers from Oxford, Cambridge, Scotch universities, Trinity College (Dublin), Wales, Robert College (Turkey), University of Sydney (Australia), University of Hawaii, University of the Philippines, and others toured the colleges. In 1947 the international contests were revived. Cambridge visited some twenty colleges, and Oxford, later the same year and early in 1948, met in debate more than fifty higher institutions throughout the United States.[5]

IV. PREPARATION FOR DEBATE

A. *Debating Technique.* Debating, as this volume makes clear, is a complicated art. It is worth doing well. To save debating from mediocrity and worse, you should so apply the technique that those who listen will respect this student activity. Through proper classroom instruction, study, and extra classroom discipline the best results come. Your basis for good argument will be a thorough understanding of the elements of subject matter, efficient means of gathering and tabulating material, effective methods of organizing argument and evidence, ability to discriminate between sound and unsound materials, skill in com-

---

[5] For the history of intercollegiate forensics, see Egbert Roy Nichols, "A Historical Sketch of Intercollegiate Debating," *Quarterly Journal of Speech*, Vol. XXII, pp. 213–220, April 1936; Vol. XXII, pp. 591–602, December, 1936; Vol. XXIII, pp. 259–278, April, 1937. See also Lowery Leroy Cowperthwaite, "A History of Intercollegiate Forensics at the State University of Iowa, 1874–1946," unpublished master's thesis, State University of Iowa, 1946.

position of ideas, and power in rebuttal and in delivery, including ability to persuade an audience. You will eschew all tricks and smart strategy. Your goal is to get at the facts and truth rather than to play a shrewd game.

B. Systematic Work under a Debate Director. Do your work in harmony with the program mapped out by the director of debate. Note that he is a director and not a "coach." The latter has been, by practice, a sort of intellectual football coach who often drives his debating teams vigorously and with a sure hand but who, in his determination to win, may overlook on occasion the educational elements involved and thus pervert the sport. The director, or adviser, will select teams and call them together for general advice on methods of gathering material and working up the case. His main function will be to inspire rather than to command. His work throughout will be that of a critic rather than that of a member of the squad. His teams, it is hoped, will work as enthusiastically and effectively as those of the old-style coach and will doubtless win an honorable share of victories. The difference, measured by the results, is that teams under the influence of an educational director should develop more self-reliance and a more intelligent conception of the ultimate end of discussion, *i.e.*, the presentation of sound thinking no less than the gaining of a technical point.

C. Selection of a Desirable Question. Not always can you, the debater, determine the subject. A committee representing the Speech Association of America has been selecting an annual proposition. In many cases, however, at least for early-season debates, you can help to select the subject. Get one that is interesting and untechnical. It may often be a local issue—one related to the experience of the speakers. It should attract an audience; for debaters find little inspiration in addressing empty seats. The success of the discussion, however, is not to be measured merely by the number of persons who are willing to attend; for college debaters thresh out many questions which, by general admission, appeal to relatively few. We need to get away from the impression that the success of the debate is to be measured by the number of heads to be counted. Demagogues depend to a degree for their crowds upon the sensational character of their subjects, as widely announced. School and university debaters are justified at times in selecting topics that will interest only a special audience.

D. Thorough Preparation. Insist upon your own thorough preparation. The proposed reforms in debating, calculated to make the speaker a more human and companionable person as he faces an audience, also encourage the emphasis upon persuasion to the neglect of genuine argument. The educational justification of argument has been the severe mental discipline offered, a type of intellectual expression that has led debating in some institutions to be regarded as the gauge of the intellectual efficiency of the college. The surest way to discredit college forensics is to present public debates, especially those over the radio, for which the contestants have made only shallow preparation. If in 1915 college teams spent too many weeks or months in preparation for a debate, today they often spend too few. You and your colleagues in debate should give at least six weeks to solid preparation for a public debate on some important question, and you should know your facts and arguments.

E. Informal Discussion and Thinking. Your first attack upon the proposition is to meditate, canvass your own ideas and knowledge on the proposition, and hold colloquy with student squadmates and the faculty director. Few tangible returns may result, but at least your enthusiasm will be stirred.

F. Reading. With the aid of references supplied to you and (or better still) which you and the squad may jointly prepare on 3- by 5-inch cards and transfer via mimeograph to duplicate copies, you will move on to the library. Your reading will at first be broad. You will dip into encyclopedias, recent yearbooks, and perhaps an authoritative article in a recent periodical.

G. Note Taking. From the outset you will be a note taker. Efficiency and real progress will result. Not recording notes means futility and repeating your labor unless your memory for facts and the details of printed arguments is phenomenal.

H. Briefing. With your well-ordered collection of notes, daily mounting, you are to begin briefing. Your outlining will, of course, be dovetailed with your succession of trial debates and will be more or less complete only at the end of the season. At first you will work out only the introduction—following closely the method of the skeleton brief. Later you will brief a first affirmative, or first negative (according to the side on which you find yourself). Still later you will do the rest of the case. Some good debaters have been known to escape almost completely brief making. You, may I repeat, will not so escape. Presently you will discover that briefing is not only not irksome but is a positive asset.

I. Analysis of the Issues. You and your squad will have preliminary sessions in which each will report to the group short summaries of representative readings. Chiefly, however, will your conferences aim at analyzing the issues. With much blackboard demonstration your conferees will diagnose the possibilities of the arguments. Such exploration may well start with the stock issues but will certainly go beyond general questions. As your ideas and reading accumulate, you will enter these analytical sessions with much interest. The most stimulating, even exciting, experiences in debating a problem may well lie in these opening conferences on definitions and examination of the area of debate.

J. Practice Debates. Let us assume that you are now assigned to a side for the "trial balloons" on these issues and arguments. Perhaps you have a partner, or maybe you are asked to defend the entire side. Whatever the setup, you are to start speechmaking as soon as the squad is selected, and you are to keep at it.

K. The Case. Presently you and a squadmate will find yourselves teamed together for a public debate, perhaps for debates in an intercollegiate tournament. Your problem of preparation is to frame a team case. What is this "case"? It is a series of propositions, the essence of what you want judges and others to accept as your argument. How does this organizational pattern differ from the brief? Principally, in that the brief, as suggested in a previous chapter, is a logical document that comprises the full argument and evidence. From such a storehouse the two debaters will extract their major propositions for or against the resolution. You will draft this case with an eye to (1) proof requirements inherent in the question, (2) requirements imposed by audience attitudes and interests, (3) requirements of rhetorical clearness and interest calling for relevancy, sequence, and proportion of materials.

1. The case for an affirmative proposition of policy. How will this draft be applied to a typical affirmative case for a proposition of policy? The framework of the stock issues will often serve. You and your colleague must show that (*a*) the present situation is unsatisfactory; (*b*) the defects are inherent in the system; (*c*) the proposal will remedy these defects; (*d*) it will produce positive advantages without introducing other major evils; (*e*) it will be a practicable proposal; (*f*) it will be preferable to other remedies.

This order of treatment consists of setting forth the problematic situation; its causes, and the insufficiency of remedies other than the one proposed; the beneficial results of the affirmative panacea; its superiority over other remedies; and its practicability.

More specifically, the case will be distributed somewhat as follows: In his introduction the first affirmative will indicate the immediate importance of the problem to this audience, will define terms, state issues, and indicate the lines of affirmative argument. In the main body of this ten- or twelve-minute argument he will treat concretely the present evils, their causes, and the inadequacy or objections to remedies short of that which the speaker espouses. In conclusion he will summarize his argument and make clear his progress. What should he accomplish in addition to definitions and analysis (introduction)? He should establish the *necessity of this proposition*. Often this first affirmative will demonstrate that "there is need for a change." Such point accomplishes little. The logical distinction between "need for a change" and "need for *this* proposal" is all-important. Unless this opening speaker has covered this entire territory, he has hardly shouldered his share of the case.

The opening speaker may sometimes prefer a more inductive development. He may present, first, the controversial situation; second, the causes; third, the inadequacy of other alleged remedies; and fourth (a kind of summary of what he has discussed), the necessity for his proposal. At the end he will explain his resolution and add analytical details otherwise included in the conventional order.

The second affirmative has the responsibility of establishing the *results* of the proposal. He will show (*a*) its workability, (*b*) the advantages that outweigh disadvantages, and (*c*) its superiority over other proposals. The order in which he treats these aspects is for him to decide. Usually practicability should come first before the more theoretical arguments. As these elements are developed, he may weave into the logic the comparison with other solutions—and thus save himself the time otherwise given to arguing the separate proposition that "this solution is better than others." *Practicability* too, may be ignored as a separate concept, provided that such arguments are adequately developed in the proof of *desirable results*.

The primary points suggested above, together with preliminary rebuttal of the first negative, preliminary summary of his colleague's argument, and the final review of the entire case comprise the material of this second affirmative argument.

To illustrate: In an intercollegiate debate in 1948 on the subject, *Resolved, That a federal world government should be established*, an Iowa University team in the Western Conference Debate Tournament (women's division) argued the following points:

First affirmative

   I. Under present conditions world peace is threatened.
  II. The cause lies chiefly in the expansionist policy of Russia.
III. Existing agencies short of federal world government are inadequate to deal with the international crisis.

Second affirmative

 IV. A federal world government would be practicable.
  V. A federal world government would promote political solidarity, economic security, and minimize wars.

Sometimes the affirmative case conforms more nearly to an elaborate syllogism. The pattern for the proposition, *Resolved, That the government should own and operate the railroads of the United States*, follows:

First affirmative

   I. The railroads should be operated in the public interest.
  II. Public interest requires maximum service at minimum cost.
III. Under the system of private ownership and operation the public interest is not being adequately served.
 IV. A program of government regulation would be inadequate.
  V. Under public ownership and operation service will be much improved and the costs to the public reduced.
 VI. Government ownership and operation in the United States is practicable.
VII. Government ownership and operation is in harmony with our principles of democratic government.

2. *The case for a negative proposition of policy.* The best procedure for composing the negative case is to map out counter-

argument to the affirmative case.   Harder is it to put down specific directions for the negative pattern and for order of presenting it.   What are the choices?

a. You may organize on the basis of total denial of the propositions.   This approach means that the negative arguments would
be: (1) There exists no need for a change of policy.   (2) The
affirmative proposal is unworkable.   (3) It will lead to economic,
political (and other) evils.   The conventional negative case is
so developed.   The *no-need* phase calls for a diagnosis and defense of *status quo.*   Minor remedies may be proposed.   The remainder of the case consists of a full-fledged attack upon the
theory and workability of the proposal.   Usually the first negative speaker handles the *no-need* arguments.   This order of arguments, however, is often reversed, with the first negative immediately launching into a presentation of the bad results of the
change.

b. The negative case, however, can content itself with a defense of any one major argument against the affirmative.   It may
pass by the entire *need* issue and concentrate, through two
speeches, on *impracticability,* or on *bad results,* or on both.

c. A third choice is for the negative to include a counterplan.
Consider several of these negative possibilities and their distribution between the two speakers:

CASE A	CASE B	CASE C
	First negative	
I. The proposal is not needed.	I. The proposal is impracticable.	I. The plan is un-workable.
	II. The proposal is detrimental.	II. The plan is detri-mental.
	Second negative	
II. The plan is im-practicable.	III. The proposal is not needed.	III. A better plan is proposed.
III. The plan is detri-mental.		

CASE D	CASE E	CASE F
	First negative	
I. A better plan is proposed.	I. The plan is detri-mental with re-spect to points A and B.	I. The plan is im-practicable.

Case D	Case E	Case F
	Second negative	
II. The affirmative plan is impracticable.	II. The plan is detrimental with respect to points C and D	II. The plan is detrimental (or further arguments to support "the plan is impracticable.")
III. The affirmative plan is detrimental.		

Several other combinations are possible. For example, the entire negative case may be a counterplan, to be unfolded by the first speaker and further defended by his colleagues; or the negative may be pure rebuttal of the affirmative, a "birdshot" negative case.

The prospective case builders should be warned that negative arguments attacking practicability or detrimental features of the change without themselves assuming any responsibility for either the *status quo* or for modified *status quo* are illogical. Implied throughout your attack on any system is its worth as compared with some other standard. All argument is based on *relative* and comparative conditions and factors.

3. *The case for an affirmative proposition of fact.* Here the propositions resolve themselves into a series of statements that usually reflect (a) causes and results or (b) classification of the arguments or evidence. To illustrate from the proposition, *Resolved, That the American college is a failure:*

I. The students fail to have sufficient training in critical thinking.
II. The students fail to have sufficient training in the social sciences.
III. The students fail to have sufficient training in oral and written communication.
IV. The students fail to have sufficient training in philosophy and ethics.

The first affirmative would cover the first two of these statements. Note that the division is based upon a classification of the objectives of liberal arts education.

To illustrate from the proposition, *Resolved, That Russia was primarily to blame for the failure to make an early peace after World War II:*

I. Russia violated her agreement at Potsdam to cooperate in the political and economic unification of Germany.

II. Russia vetoed more than twenty-one decisions of the Security Council of the United Nations.
III. Russia manipulated the communistic overthrow of Czechoslovakia.
IV. Russia seized control of the Balkan states.
V. Russia retained control of half of Korea.
VI. Russia attempted the domination of Greece and Turkey.

Here the material is a grouping of evidence according to a geographical classification. Each speaker would deal in detail with three of the topics.

4. The case for a negative proposition of fact. The negative would be worked out like the affirmative—an analysis of the argument and evidence and a classification of such materials. Some or all the affirmative points would be denied, and counter-arguments or points might be developed. Little advance advice can be given concerning the selection or the allocation of these materials to the respective speakers.

L. Written Composition. Write your debate speeches in order to practice condensation, clearness, accuracy of expression, and persuasiveness. The question continually arises, Should debaters write their arguments? I urge such composition. But leave your written documents at home. Certainly do not memorize them and certainly don't follow them slavishly.

Insert numerous (but not too numerous) questions to hold interest and bring forth the issues. Fill your speech with illustrations, examples, connotative language, and striking analogies. Make your authorities stand out and quote statistics so as not to flood the audiences with details. Use round numbers. Interpret them so that audiences can understand their significance. Cite the sources when you suspect that the figures may be challenged. But don't laboriously and continually refer to page and paragraph.

M. Practice Rebuttal. Prepare your rebuttal systematically and fully. See the next chapter for rebuttal and refutation techniques.

N. Delivery. Practice delivery daily. Talk to a vacant chair or to a colleague. Review the chapter on delivery and develop a direct, vigorous, conversational style, free from bombast or insincerity.

V. Presentation of Debate

A. Platform Conduct. In the public debate and in all practice debates, observe the amenities of the occasion. Be courteous. Your salutation will be "Ladies and gentlemen," rather than "Mr. Chairman, worthy opponents, honorable judge, ladies and gentlemen." Welcome (in unhackneyed and sincere language) your guest speakers; thank the other college, the Rotary Club, or other organization that has invited you to speak. In the debate be invariably courteous to the other teams in your handling of their arguments. Don't *defy* or *challenge* them and use the other terms that connote antagonism. Don't address them directly and accusingly. Let your attitude be friendly, gentlemanly at every turn. While others are speaking, don't show disdain, don't confer loudly, or otherwise distract attention.

B. Teamwork on the Platform and Work of Each Speaker. The first speaker for the affirmative has the advantage of an opportunity to present his speech exactly as he has prepared it. His manner should be easy, conciliatory, and judicial. His business is to explain in simple, interesting terms the meaning of the proposition and the real issues upon which the decision hinges. This analysis should be brief and understandable; it should lead logically to the argument proper. The first negative opponent must rise to the requirements of the moment. His ability in extemporaneous discussion must immediately make itself felt. He must agree or disagree with the affirmative analysis; he must point out sharply the real difference between the two sides and take the edge from the impression made by the opening speech. The alternating speakers thereafter must continually adapt themselves to the occasion. Cut and dried speeches must be discarded. The performance must be extemporaneous. Fair play and sound reasoning alone must win. Whatever happens, the speaker must keep his head; he must keep the audience with him; he must make them see his case; he must avoid the temptation to ramble among inconsequential details; he must stick to the main points and must insist upon debating only essential issues.

Teamwork demands strict conformity to the case as mutually worked out. The two speakers will type carefully this unified case and in the debate will each summarize it, especially at the end of the second affirmative main speech and again at the end of the second rebuttal period. Each speaker, too, will continually revert to his case as he defends each proposition and as he refutes the counteraffirmative argument.

C. Time Limits. Time limits are strictly observed. A two-minute warning from the timekeeper is usually given. Time cards are usually used. After the final tap of the bell or flash of the last time card, the speaker is allowed only to finish his sentence; he must speedily retire. Student debaters clamor for much time on the platform; the audience, however, becomes bored after one hour. Hence the sharp warnings and the compromise between the zealous debaters and a less enthusiastic audience.

D. Sportsmanship. After the debate be a "good sport." Avoid condescension, ill-concealed bitterness, obvious pride; you are a representative college man or woman. The judge or the rival speakers may have tried your soul. Quote Emerson to yourself or to some other person; at any rate, understand before you enter this competitive exercise that your emotional and intellectual stability are to be maintained.

VI. CRITICISMS OF DEBATING

A. Sincerity and Debating. Debaters have often been criticized for their alleged insincerity. "Debaters," we are told, "talk glibly on either side and represent doubtful intellectual honesty." The charge has little foundation. Certainly you will at every point respect your own beliefs—if they are firmly grounded in preliminary analysis and discussion.

As far as possible, set forth only that side of the case that reflects your real convictions. Some truth is found in the indictment that glibness is often encouraged at the sacrifice of conviction. If, for example, the debater has a long-established belief that any preparation against war is wrong, he should not be expected to talk in a public intercollegiate contest in support of such preparedness.

Usually this problem of student sincerity may be solved by each institution's having two teams which present opposite sides of a given question. Then, too, in regard to many issues undergraduate opinion is so little developed that the question of well-grounded conviction is absent. Concerning many social, political, and economic questions, students, like other human beings, have comparatively little knowledge and are ready to investigate and discuss either side. Full care should be taken, I agree, to encourage the genuine expression of the student's independent opinion.

B. *Competition and Debating.* "Isn't the impetus of true conviction," you may ask, "sufficient to call out the best student minds and to guarantee at least as complete preparation as that which now takes place without competitive debate?" It is to be doubted whether discussion for the mere sake of setting forth undergraduate opinion will attract numbers of students or lead them to undergo that vigorous preparation made by the debater who is out to win. "But," you may object, "that is just the trouble: teams are out to win. And that object degrades the whole principle of competition!" We recognize and encourage it in the economic world and in the scholastic world. University systems of awarding honors both in America and in England are based upon the theory of competition. In England the stimulus to scholarship rests upon an elaborate system of competition for prizes and honors. The fact that competition may be carried to excess does not prove that it is not valuable as a stimulus.

EXERCISES AND PROBLEMS

1. Give a five-minute speech or present a written report (500 words) upon some phase of one of the following topics: (*a*) Debating in Roman education. (*b*) Debating in medieval universities. (*c*) The debating training of certain American orators of the Revolutionary period. (*d*) The training in debate of Webster (or some other representative speaker). (*e*) The first intercollegiate debate of my college. (*f*) The advantages and disadvantages of membership in a debate league. (*g*) The aims and programs of Pi Kappa Delta (or some other honorary college forensic organization). (*h*) The advantages and disadvantages of debate tournaments. (*i*) Financing college debating. (*j*) The student-activity fee and debating. (*k*) A program for team preparation of an intercollegiate debate. (*l*) Sincerity and bilateral argument. (*m*) Platform behavior in debate. (*n*) Time cards in debate. (*o*) Procedure during a debate. (*p*) The arguments for and against debating. (*q*) Competition in debating.

2. Attend an intercollegiate debate and hand to the instructor a written criticism of the speakers.

3. Criticize a printed debate in the most recent volume of the *Uni-*

versity Debater's Annual or other book containing full-length college debates. Let your criticism include comment on (*a*) analysis, (*b*) argument and evidence, (*c*) rebuttal, (*d*) organization and style, (*e*) persuasiveness, (*f*) teamwork, (*g*) general effectiveness.

4. Summarize and criticize the case for the affirmative and of the negative in a debate on a proposition of policy in the latest volume of the *University Debater's Annual.*

5. Summarize and criticize the case for the affirmative and of the negative in a debate on a proposition of fact in the latest volume of the *University Debater's Annual.*

6. Report to the class the case prepared by your teammate and you for a later classroom debate. Explain in detail how you will treat each proposition.

7. Report to the class five or six types of negative cases that might be developed on a given proposition of policy announced for classroom debate.

8. Prepare a written report (300 words) in which you criticize the style of the four speakers in a debate in the *University Debater's Annual* (or you may make a comparison of the style of the four speakers).

9. Prepare a written report (300 words) in which you criticize the style of the four speakers in a debate in a recent *Bulletin of America's Town Meeting of the Air.*

10. Submit to the instructor a ten-minute written debate in which you are later to participate.

11. Report to the class your criticism of a radio debate to which you recently listened.

CHAPTER 25

Debate: Refutation
and Rebuttal

I. CHARACTER OF REFUTATION AND REBUTTAL

Refutation is the process of removing objections, of under-
mining inhibitions, and thus of gaining complete attention. It
consists of arguments and evidence presented to destroy the
proof resulting from counterarguments and evidence.

By the very nature of the process of debate he who advocates
a point of view finds that his proposals are in direct conflict with
other resolutions. When a hearer or reader does not accept the
proof presented to him, it is because obstacles in his mind, or
inhibitions, compete with, or resist the influence of, the proposals. These opposing ideas may come from a definite opponent,
as in debate, or merely from an audience. At the outset the hearers may be on the whole either indifferent, neutral, or favorable
to the proposition. The problem of the speaker, who in effect
declares, "I advocate," or "I affirm," is to counteract the effect of
some real or imaginary opponent who may immediately after-
ward suggest to the mind of the audience, "I question," or "I
deny." The removal of an inhibition, which consists of anything
which blocks the acceptance by another of an idea, is the process
of refutation.

How does rebuttal differ from refutation? The two terms

have equivalent meanings. Refutation is the term borrowed from rhetoric; rebuttal is derived from law. We shall use the terms interchangeably.

II. Importance of Refutation and Rebuttal

For the speaker to prepare and present the so-called constructive case is sometimes to give only one-half the proof in debate. For debate does two things: first, it creates positive belief; secondly, it destroys unbelief. Most amateur debaters err in evolving impressive constructive cases and in ignoring too largely the refutatory elements. Genuine debate can be completed only by giving to the audience a clear-cut contrast between the constructive proof on the one hand and the destructive proof on the other. Effective debating, therefore, requires a thorough understanding of refutation and skill in its use.

Skill in rebuttal distinguishes the genuine debater from a merely clever public speaker. The ability to single out, to restate clearly, and immediately to dispose of outstanding objections to one's position is an art requiring long practice. It is, however, of great practical value. The businessman or salesman, after he has unfolded his proposition, finds it necessary to deal directly with vigorous or half-expressed objections that strike at the basis of his argument. The legislator, after his prepared remarks upon the bill have been stated, must rally to vigorous defense as amendments, substitutions, counterbills, and endless criticisms are heaped upon the resolution. The candidate for office must likewise run the gantlet of censure from political enemies and must early and late rebut each major indictment. Whenever in practical affairs arguments are advanced, there comes a veritable battle in which alternate attack and defense succeed each other. Rebuttal, skillfully veiled though it may be in persuasive terms, is the indispensable basis for the successful conclusion of the issue. In spite of our hopes for the development of a type of discussion that may be free from bilateral virulence the fact remains that once the contentions are sharply arrayed against each other, there arises an intellectual clash, and in that clash effectiveness in give-and-take rebuttal is the deciding factor. Many a well-knit constructive debate has failed because it has neglected to consider the power of a rival argument.

III. Position of Refutation and Rebuttal

One of the major problems of refutation is to decide at what point in the speech to insert refutatory material. Should it precede the constructive material or succeed it? Or should refutation and construction be interwoven? The answer will depend largely on the subject, the attitude of the audience toward the subject, and on whether the occasion is one of debate. Refutation should in general be inserted wherever and whenever it will be most effective.

If the argument to be advanced is unpopular or if another writer or speaker has presented a strong case, then the first duty of a writer or speaker is to clear the atmosphere by disposing of the objections.

If, however, the audience attitude is on the whole favorable or neutral and if no outstanding objections have been raised, then the material to be refuted may be left until the constructive case is largely developed.

Refutation should, nevertheless, always be followed by a summary of positive statements which will give as a final impression a constructive suggestion to the audience. Undue stressing of material to be refuted may impress on the minds of the audience ideas which otherwise would command little attention. In general, opposing ideas should be taken up at the point where they logically arise. If an opponent has not already stated these objections, this type of reply is known as anticipatory refutation.

In formal debate it has been customary to have a main speech, composed almost entirely of constructive arguments, usually ten or twelve minutes long; and a second speech, five or six minutes long, filled with a discussion of the opposing arguments, called a *rebuttal*. When this conventional division is followed, a small amount of rebuttal material is sometimes inserted at the beginning of the first presentation of the negative side. It aims to refute some specific and especially impressive statement of the first affirmative speaker.

The tendency in recent years to adopt the more informal style in debate has led to the practice of limiting each speaker to one speech, freely filled with refutatory material, and a final rejoinder, largely composed of summary, which is presented by the opening speaker, the mover of the motion.

IV. Techniques of Rebuttal

Your preparation may have centered on your constructive speech. Or you may have debated with your squad so that you are familiar only with their ideas. In public debate you deal with a case or cases new to you. The point of view may seem strange to you and may baffle you. To avoid such unnecessary disaster, your preparation must be so systematic and complete as to arm you for whatever logic or twists of logic may be presented to you.

A. *Study Both Sides.* Your goal is to know the other side as thoroughly as does its defender. It is good training to argue on both sides. You should know exactly what the arguments are to be, the available materials, and both the strength and weakness of those arguments.

B. *Collect and Classify Rebuttal Cards in Advance.* Rebuttal statements are not the casual thoughts or bits of information that come to mind as a speaker hears his case dissected by an opponent. On the contrary, the worth-while speech of reply grows out of a systematic preparation which carefully anticipates the situation. All the arguments of the opposition are listed by a skillful rebutter as he evolves his own argument. Numerous objections to his points of view are set down on cards or slips of paper, to be answered later. In practice debates and in his review of printed debates on the subject, as found in magazines, Congressional records, and elsewhere, he jots down fairly and concisely each of the main pillars and subpillars of the arguments and the evidence which goes to support them.

Under each argument to be refuted the debater briefs concisely his reply, including the specific evidence which he intends to use in connection with each point. Cards of standard library size should be used, with the general topic placed at the top, and immediately beneath or on the same line, the more specific topic discussed. For example, if the question is, *Resolved, That a Federal Department of Education should be established with a secretary in the President's cabinet,* the general topic would include "need for research," "teachers' salaries," "illiteracy," "unequal educational opportunities," "physical education," "increased efficiency," "consolidation of departments," "Federal bureaucracy," "political effects," "dangers of centralization," "inadequacy of state control," and "cost." Thus the debater may list under a dozen heads as many as fifty major arguments, which cover practically every idea that may be brought up by the opposition. These arguments, thus classified, are ready for instant use in the crisis.

Specimen Rebuttal Card

Illiteracy   *New York State*

1. Although it is argued that ....
...................................., yet this argument is false, for
   A.
   B.
   C.
   D.

Source of information

C. Practice Rebuttal with the Aid of Your Accumulating Evidence. On many occasions before a given debate, you will go over your "evidence" cards and add to them. In an empty room meet an imaginary debater and refute him by reference to your material. State the opposing argument clearly. Then reply. Do not try to memorize the cards. Absorb mentally only the gist of each. Familiarize yourself with your quotations so that you can refer to them without labored reading. Practice these rebuttals until you have assimilated the content.

D. Adapt This Material to Opposing Arguments. Beginning debaters, including high-school speakers, often memorize rebuttal cards and echo them freely. The results are invariably mechanical—"canned rebuttals."

What you need is an understanding of the facts and ability to adopt these facts to what is offered by the other team. Your practice speaking and that in the public debate, therefore, must be *extemporaneous.* Think out previously the various arguments that you are to deal with, refute extemporaneously, and so avoid the later malpractice of stereotyping memorized items and ideas.

E. State Clearly the Arguments to Be Refuted. Much of the art of refutation lies in the clearness with which the inhibitory ideas to be removed are stated. Often refutation is not understood by the audience and is confused with constructive material because the refutatory ideas are hazily expressed. The novice who is defending government ownership of coal mines will declare, "Something was said about a bureaucracy," whereas the genuine debater will more definitely put it, "The argument has been advanced that government ownership of coal mines would lead to a huge bureaucracy in Washington," and then will proceed to a definite analysis and destruction of the charge. The rule for briefing refutation should be referred to at this point. Note that, in the following example of briefing, the argument to be refuted is stated as a conclusion, and the reply is developed as a piece of deductive reasoning:

I. The argument that government ownership of coal mines would lead to extravagance in administration and to a higher cost of coal is fallacious, for
  A. Efficient managers would continue to direct the coal industry, for
    1. The same managers who now operate the mining industry would continue to function under government ownership.

F. Refute the Central Ideas. During the practice debates and during your solo practice, you will refute everything and (I hope) brilliantly. Any idea big or little you will orally examine and deal with. You will either deny, admit, agree with, or rebut each opposing argument and bit of evidence.

During the formal debate, however, you will refute only the chief propositions. Your private rebuttals of thirty minutes will now have to be completed in four or five minutes. Obviously, you are to select. Since the affirmative and negative cases are built around issues, your task is to destroy the major contention. If you undermine this chief proposition, all the scaffolding will also topple. This suggestion, like all others, must be applied flexibly. If, for example, a concrete bit of opposing evidence has scored heavily with judge and audience, your obligation is to refute it immediately and sufficiently.

G. Refute a Point Sufficiently to Satisfy the Audience. What constitutes sufficient refutation of a point? Only the audience can decide. As best you can, you will guess what is sufficient for the group. What would easily satisfy one set of listeners would be hardly enough for another.

In a debate on the economic control of wages and prices, a negative speaker spent his entire speech showing that prices were declining, that conditions would right themselves, and that government controls were unnecessary. The affirmative reply was brief:

The speaker has argued at length that things are all right and that you consumers have no need of controlling prices. He seems to think that by saying so, he has reduced prices. But you need only to remind him that the price of his butter has gone up ten cents during the past week, that his beef has gone up twelve cents per pound, that wheat has advanced to the highest point in recent years.

The answer was apparently enough for this consumer audience, reminded of their recent grocery bills.

On the other hand, you need to be sure that you have offered sufficient refutation to overthrow the issue under discussion. Your obligation is not only to weaken the other position but to fill the vacuum with your own proposition. It is usually not enough in refutation to give a quotation and a single comment. If an argument is illogical, make clear the fallacy. If the facts are distorted or the assumptions unproved, take time to give substantial reply. The criterion for sufficiency of refutational treatment, as I suggested above, is the audience reaction or attitude.

H. In Refutation and Rebuttal Insert Additional Evidence. Refutation and rebuttal are not simply a reiteration of what you have said. Fresh and interesting evidence are called for. New argument, however, is not in order. Following legal practice, rebuttal is purely for purposes of dealing with the arguments and evidence already introduced. For you to launch on a fresh argument in support of the *practicability* of your proposition when you have ignored such issue in your first speech is bad procedure—unless the other team has demanded that you face that issue.

I. Avoid Refuting Points Not Made. Sometimes the beginner is so eager to give refutation already prepared or is so interested in filling five minutes that he refutes "straw men" or arguments not advanced by the other side. The technique suggests either ignorance or manipulation. In either case your hearers will no doubt adversely score you.

J. Avoid Crediting the Other Side with Argument and Evidence Stated but Not Developed. Often you will refute at length an idea merely mentioned by your opponents. Your assumption here is that the speaker has unfolded a wealth of argument and evidence to support an issue. Your very elaboration of this argument in your reply may give the hearer an impression of the weight of the opposing point and its treatment. Usually you should content yourself with, "The speaker asserted that the proposition is workable. He offered no reasons or evidence to support his statement. We should therefore like to inquire. . . ." The purpose of your question is to invite the next speaker to deal more fully with the argument—or admit its weakness.

K. Listen Attentively and Take Down the Substance of the Opposing Argument.

L. Use General Methods of Refutation. Refutation, in its attack on unsupported assertion and unreliable evidence or fallacious argument, will use the general methods suggested in the preceding chapters for testing evidence and argument. You will, therefore, challenge personal observations, expert authority, statistics, unsupported assertions, false assumptions, hasty generalizations, false causal reasoning, ignoring the question by attacking personalities, appealing to prejudice, appealing to tradition, begging the question, arguing in a circle, and using question-begging words.

M. Use Special Methods of Refutation. Special methods of exposing the weakness of opposing arguments include asking questions, *reductio ad absurdum*, method of residues, method of dilemma, exposing inconsistencies, adopting opposing arguments, exposing irrelevant arguments.

1. Asking questions. The purpose of asking questions is to bring forth again the issues, to see that the other side faces such fundamental questions, and, if possible, to elicit a reply to the issues or questions. Your aim is not to confuse but to clarify. Your sole interest is in keeping to the subject and to see that the other arguer makes clear his position and his arguments with respect to the issues.

2. Reductio ad absurdum. A common method of refutation is that of reducing an argument to an absurdity. The debater seemingly accepts for the moment the argument to be refuted and then shows that the logical conclusion is absurd. For example, the proposition used to be advanced that this country should not relinquish control of the Philippines until the Filipinos were fit to use their freedom.   In reducing such argument to an absurdity we should discover and state the general principle and then show that the practical application would not be acceptable even to those who have unwittingly advanced it.   The broad principle in this case is "Freedom should be given only to those who have demonstrated their ability to use it wisely." Applications would be (a) "Boys should never go into the water until able to swim." (b) "No one should attempt to operate an automobile until he is able to drive it properly."   By referring the general principle to a case that is more familiar to our experience than the one cited in the rival argument and by making clear that the two cases are analogous, we may compel the author of the argument, or, at any rate, those who listen, to admit the weakness of the principle.   In such case whether the refutation is effective depends upon (a) whether the principle assumed is clearly stated, (b) whether the analogous case is sufficiently close to the experience of the audience, and (c) whether the example meets the tests of valid analogy.

To acquire facility in the use of *reductio ad absurdum* the debater should be constantly on the alert to discover arguments of his opponent that are based on any of the following false, but commonly used, general assumptions:

That a mere sequence between two things is sufficient to establish a causal relationship between them;

That what is true of a part is also necessarily true of a whole, and vice versa;

That what is true in a peculiar instance is also true in an ordinary instance and vice versa;

That what is true of a term employed in one sense is also true of the same term employed in an entirely different sense;

That no true proposition is in any way associated with a man having faults; and no false proposition is in any way associated with a man who appears to be faultless;

That no proposition is false if the people are for it; and no proposition is true if the people are against it;

That when any person lacks information to prove a proposition, the proposition is false; and whenever any person lacks information to disprove a proposition, the proposition is true; and

That whenever a proposition is supported by authority that inspires reverence or respect, then the proposition must be true.[1]

[1] W. C. Shaw, *The Art of Debate*, pp. 128–129, Allyn and Bacon, 1922.

3. *Residues.* The method of residues can be put into use when the debater reduces the case to a definite number of possible conclusions and shows that all but one are impracticable. This method consists of reducing the argument to a disjunction and drawing a logical conclusion. For the disjunction to be satisfactory the possibilities must be exhaustive and mutually exclusive. For example, a student who advocated government ownership of coal mines showed that three courses of action were possible: a continuation of uncontrolled private monopoly, the establishment of rigid Federal regulation, or government ownership. The speaker then proved that the first two policies were indefensible. The presumption was that government ownership was the only feasible solution. The argument reduced to a disjunction would be as given below:

I. Private monopoly or Federal regulation or government ownership is the only solution of the coal problem.
II. Private monopoly is unsatisfactory.
III. Federal regulation or government ownership is the only solution of the coal problem.

I. Either Federal regulation or government ownership is the only solution of the coal problem.
II. Federal regulation is unsatisfactory.
III. Government ownership is the only solution of the coal problem.

Although a strong presumption occurs when the alternatives are ruled out, nevertheless the wise debater will proceed with a positive justification of the choice remaining. For it is extremely difficult to enumerate and to dispose of all the possibilities. In the case above the speaker overlooked state regulation of the coal industry, as applied in Pennsylvania.

Characteristic arguments, in which a new policy is advocated, are required to prove that the proposed policy is the best policy. In developing this issue the speaker invariably resorts to the method of residues. Once we grant that some action must be taken, it becomes a problem of exploring each possible avenue of escape. The speaker advocating a blanket amendment to the Federal Constitution, giving women equal rights with men, showed that the legal, economic, and social inequalities called for a remedy. The possibilities were (*a*) special state legislation or (*b*) Federal legislation. The inadequacy of special legislation

naturally led to the conclusion that Federal legislation was necessary. (And it was taken for granted that the only way to have
Federal legislation was to pass a blanket amendment—an assumption violently challenged by the other side.)

4. The dilemma. Another one of the effective methods of un-
dermining an argument is that of using the dilemma. This type
of refutation consists of making clear that an argument leads
logically to two possible solutions, both of which are untenable.
These alternatives are the *horns* of the dilemma. The opponent,
forced to choose one of these horns, becomes hopelessly impaled.
The dilemma, like the method of residues, shows that a given
possibility cannot be logically accepted. The remaining alternative, which the author of the method of residues would accept,
the rival speaker would show is also to be rejected, leaving dangling in mid-air, or on the two horns, the one who advanced the
premise. Since the dilemma is literally limited to two horns,
an expansion of the number of possibilities presented against the
other side would lead to a trilemma if three horns are employed;
to a tetralemma if four; and if many, to a polylemma.

The dilemma in its syllogistic form has for its major premise
a compound sentence made up of hypothetical propositions or
of a combination of hypothetical and disjunctive propositions.
The minor premise under the first of these conditions would
either affirm the two consequents or deny the two consequents.
Under the second condition the minor premise would deny the
two alternatives given in the major premise. An example will
make this explanation clear:

I. If the United States enters the federal world government, this
country must either abandon its sovereignty or refuse to abide by
the decisions of such government. (Compound hypothetical, disjunctive proposition.)

II. But this country can neither abandon the sovereignty nor refuse
to abide by the decisions of the federal world government.
(Categorical denial of both alternatives.)

III. This country cannot enter the federal world government. (Denial
of the common antecedent.)

The example above, reduced to a brief, would be stated as
follows:

I. The United States could not enter the federal world government,
for
  A. To enter the government would mean either loss of sovereignty
     or refusal of this country to abide by the decisions of that body.
  B. To accept either of these alternatives would be impossible, for
     1. To lose our sovereignty would be impossible.
     2. To refuse to abide by the decisions of such government
        would be impossible.

The valid dilemma is one of the most powerful of all forms
of refutation. So difficult is it, however, to develop clearly and
logically this device that few debaters succeed in handling it effectively. First of all, you need to make the dilemma clear—to
strip it of verbiage and attendant arguments that may conceal
the real disjunction. To assure yourself that your statement is
definite and exact, you will find advantage in framing the dilem-
matic argument as a syllogism. Secondly, you need to be sure
that the alternatives exhaust all the possibilities. The disjunction must be complete. Most dilemmas are faulty in this respect. Thirdly, you need to be assured that neither of the horns
may be accepted without serious injury to the case. Often the
acceptance of one of the alternatives is shown to have no disastrous consequences. Fourthly, you should prove, and not merely
assume, the proposition containing the horns.
  An example is the following:

  a. If a man is honest, he will land in the poorhouse; and if he is
dishonest, he will land in jail.
  b. But a man is either honest or dishonest.
  c. He will land in the poorhouse or land in jail.

The dilemma is obviously false in that many honest men and
some dishonest ones land in palaces.
  To refute a dilemma look for the middle ground and evade
the "either-or" aspect of the problem.
  5. *Exposing inconsistencies.* Still another method of winning
a case is that of bringing to light inconsistencies in the counterargument. Easy is it in the course of an extended discussion to
drop statements that are contradictory. Woe to you in discussion if your inconsistencies are exposed. If in one instance you
appear to argue against yourself, how much faith can the auditor

have in the remainder of your case? In a debate a speaker contended that compulsory arbitration of disputes in the coal industry was necessary because the unions have grown so powerful
that they would dictate to the government itself. A succeeding
argument attempted to convince the audience that compulsory
arbitration was practicable in this country because the unions,
although bitterly opposed to this method of settling disputes,
would bow to the will of the arbitration board. The listeners
naturally found it difficult to reconcile the two contentions. In
a number of debates on the subject of government ownership of
coal mines, railroads, or other utilities, supporters of the affirmative have fallen into apparent inconsistency, first, by stressing the
point that public ownership would result in reduced prices to
the public because of the doing away of private-monopoly rates;
secondly, by emphasizing the contention that government ownership would greatly improve the lot of the employees by reason
of the higher wages and shorter hours.

6. *Adopting opposing arguments.* (*Turning the tables.*)
Most effective is that debater who can appropriate the arguments or evidence offered by the other side and can interpret this
material of proof offered in such a way as to win his own case.
One debater in contending that we need a blanket amendment
to give equal rights to women in the United States argued that
four states failed to give equal contractual rights to men and
women. The opposition used this same evidence to prove that
the legislation was unnecessary because only four states still had
this discrimination—clear evidence of the fact that there had
been a steady and rapid change in state laws to meet the situation pointed out by the affirmative. A debate on the proposition
Resolved, That the American university is a failure argued that
the higher institutions were failing because college athletics
were so highly magnified, as many as 100,000 spectators attending an intercollegiate football game. The rejoinder was that the
stressing of athletics was the very reason why the university was
and is a success; that physical fitness and interest in these events
were a healthy sign and that it should be fondly hoped that the
audiences of 100,000 would more often swell to 150,000.

7. *Exposing irrelevant arguments.* Favorable results often
follow a clear-cut explanation of the irrelevant arguments advanced in a discussion. The refutation, however, must make it

evident that the arguments are irrelevant. The impression of a speaker is distinctly bad if those who listen feel that he has either deliberately or ignorantly engaged in insignificant or idle talk.

In general, strong refutation depends upon a wide knowledge of the question and upon mental alertness. Continually, the keen debater will ask: (a) Does the opponent use hasty generalization with too few examples, with untypical instances, with inaccuracy of fact, and with faulty causal connection? (b) If statistics are used, are the instances numerous, is the sampling systematically done, are exceptions to be noted, and do the figures cover a sufficient amount of time? (c) Are there false analogies in that the points of difference outweigh the points of likeness, in that negative instances may be cited, in that there is lack of causal connection, or inaccuracy in the use of facts? (d) Are there fallacies of mistaken causal relation in which the assumed cause is merely another effect of the real cause, in which it has operated after the effect has been noted, is inadequate to produce the effect, or is interfered with in its action by other counteracting causes? (e) Does the opponent beg the question by arguing in a circle, by assuming a more general truth which involves the point at issue, or by using question-begging words? (f) Does he ignore the question by appealing to passion, prejudice, humor? By discussion of personalities? By shifting ground, refuting an argument not advanced, appealing to tradition, custom, authority, ignorance, or by using exceptional instances? (g) Are the authorities open to attack? (h) Can the argument be reduced to an absurd conclusion? (i) Can the case be reduced to a dilemma from which there is no escape? (j) Can the case be reduced to three or four principles, only one of which can be shown to be feasible? (k) Can the tables be turned so that an opponent's arguments and evidence are used to prove the case?

V. The Rebuttal Speech

Some critics of debate, especially those who advocate the open forum, have advised the abandonment of the rebuttal speech because of its artificiality. As long as contest debating maintains its supremacy, however, the demand for this speech will doubtless continue. It was evolved as a device to give each speaker opportunity to defend his own issue and to reply to any part of the case of the other side. Substitutes for it have been worked out, as, for example, a system of cross-examination of one team by the other or by the audience; but its fairness in giving to the audience and the judge a more complete impression of a team is generally recognized.

It has all the elements of any other speech—organization, thought, language, and delivery.

A. Organization of the Rebuttal Speech. The second speech should contain no added arguments but should, of course, include fresh evidence. It should be well organized. The tendency of debaters when they rebut is to take up a promiscuous assortment of detached points. The result is a mixture of materials, an obscurity of thinking, and a lack of logical sequence of ideas. The material of rebuttal should be selected intelligently, arranged logically, and stated clearly and convincingly. The high-water mark of debating should be attained in the rebuttal. It is impossible to draw up a formula for the structure of every rebuttal speech. The exigencies of an individual debate will alone decide the character and content of the appropriate rebuttal. Nevertheless, a general plan, to be applied with flexibility, is here recommended.

1. Statement of issue. Because most rebuttals are scattered and incidental, it is highly desirable to organize the material under a general head or about a general issue. Note how scattered as rebuttal is the following first sentence: "The affirmative speaker argued that, whereas it cost $4 to mine a ton of coal, the retail price for the same was as high as $17." A much clearer approach from the point of view of good debate and of the audience would be to proceed as follows:

An outstanding issue is, Is government ownership and operation of the coal mines necessary? The speaker for the affirmative argued that such program is necessary because of the high price of anthracite coal under the present plan of private monopoly. He told us, for example, that whereas the cost of mining a ton of coal was $4, it has been retailed for as much as $17. In reply, . . .

The second of these methods makes clear the relation of the opposing speaker's argument to the main issue and, moreover, the relation of the specific evidence to that argument.

2. *A clear statement of an argument advanced by the opponent under that issue.* Sometimes the relation of opposing arguments to each other and to the rebuttal may not be clear. It is, therefore, a great help to all concerned if the speaker will state the whole matter in terms of fundamental issues, as suggested in the preceding paragraph. The principle here to be observed is that of stating the opposing argument rather than restating one's own case. When the rebuttal opens, it is high time to attack rather than defend. It should also be added that the attack should be made upon a main argument rather than upon minor ones. It is sometimes a temptation to pick out a weak but vulnerable spot in the opposition and attack it with such vigor as forcefully to impress the audience. In the long run, however, audiences, or at least skilled judges, decide in favor of those debaters who in rebuttal systematically take up all the major arguments constituting the opposing case. Hence we suggest stating the opposing arguments in relation to the three or four issues involved in the debate.

3. *A statement of the specific evidence presented by the other side.* After the stating of the issue and of the opposing argument, the use of evidence is next noted. Under one general argument will usually be found several bits of evidence. These should be taken up and disposed of in turn. The problem, again, is to begin with issues and arguments rather than with the evidence itself. The rebuttal will be more effective if this evidence, like the argument to which it is related, is clearly and fairly stated. It is a great achievement to quote accurately and fully the argument and evidence to be refuted.

4. *Refutation by specific means.* Thus argument and evidence are to be refuted by all the devices mentioned in the preceding sections. The typical and easiest methods of refutation are those of attacking the accuracy of the facts, showing the misuse of authorities, exposing hasty generalizations, false analogy, and false causal relation. In addition, fresh evidence, not touched upon in the main speech, should here be introduced.

5. *Summary of one's argument.* After the arguments and evidence have been analyzed and refuted in turn, it is then logical for the speaker to revert to his own constructive case and to that of his collaborators and to summarize the points as concisely and vigorously as possible. A few words of appeal may be added.

This summary will enable the skillful debater to show a sharp contrast between the rival positions and to strike a balance which will be favorable to his cause.

6. *A statement of what remains for the opposition to prove.* Although the rebuttal is logically complete at this point, added clearness and force will no doubt result if the speaker adds the final step of enumerating the specific line of argument which the other side must develop to maintain its case successfully. This statement of what remains to be proved may be partly set forth in the form of questions. Of course, if we are considering the final affirmative rebuttal, it is obvious that the speaker will not ask questions other than rhetorical ones of his opponents when the rules of debating compel the negative to remain silent.

On many occasions the formula outlined above will be almost entirely discarded and changed. Many debaters, for example, prefer to end their rebuttal with a so-called appeal rather than with a statement of what remains to be done. The framework, however, can be profitably applied.

Examine the following first affirmative rebuttal on the subject *Resolved, That the several states should enact legislation providing for a system of complete medical service available to all citizens at public expense.*

Statement of issue.	The first major issue in this discussion is the question, Does the present medical service in the United States call for the adoption of public medicine in the various states? The defender of private medical care and service, in grappling with this problem, gave the stock reply.
Statement of argument advanced by the negative.	"We need," he said, "no state medicine, because public health has steadily improved, and voluntary insurance, less dangerous, will probably patch up the system."
Statement of evidence advanced by the negative under that argument.	Let us briefly examine this position of our critic. It is true, as the speaker argued, that perhaps you may live, on an average, fifteen years longer than did your Revolutionary ancestors. We

Affirmative concedes a fact.	are gratified that our death rate is lower than that of Great Britain, France, or any other European country and that we have more doctors per capita than have these other nations.
Restatement of the issue for clarity and emphasis.	But the real question is, Are we making sufficient progress in the control of health? The more mature members of this audience doubtless recall the results of the examination of three million drafted men for the World War. The Surgeon-General's report
Citation of fresh evidence to refute the negative evidence.	showed at least one third with physical defects, and one man out of every five rejected because of serious disabilities.
Citation of evidence with which the negative is familiar.	Let the visiting speakers recall again that, according to the report of the Committee on Costs of Medical Care, with its six surveys of school children, from 65 per cent to 95 per cent of these boys and girls had serious health defects. Let the gentlemen reflect again on the report of this same committee, which indicated that, of thousands of industrial workers examined, 40 per cent had defective sight and 60 per cent defective teeth. Such evi-
Citation of authoritative evidence to justify a broad generalization.	dence the Life Extension Institute confirms in its conclusion that one hundred thousand young men examined had "an appalling number of defects."
Clinching affirmative argument by persuasive question.	Does not American preventive and curative medicine need vast improvement? Even though our creaking automobile represents a real advance over the one Dad urged over the dusty roads, should we not swap our 1925 model for today's best?
Summary of the previous affirmative argument, supplemented by restatement of subissues.	Our own argument, may I remind you, analyzed the high and unpredictable costs of medical care. You and I have asked, How can the 15 per cent of American families with incomes under

twelve hundred dollars meet these average costs of more than one hundred dollars per year for each family? How can these same families, who, according to figures from the Department of Agriculture, are unable to provide a diet essential for a reasonable standard of living, raise the cash for hospitals, nurses, dentists, and doctors?

Statement of a second issue.

Exact quotation of negative speaker's words.

Consider further the speaker's answer to our question, Do conditions not demand our socialization program? He said, "Let's have voluntary insurance." Do you not note some inconsistency between the vehement conclusion that all is well and the equally positive declaration that what we need is voluntary insurance? You who carry insurance understand the principles of a sound protective service.

Exposure of the negative's lack of evidence to support his point.

Did the speaker tell you how he would build up his reserves? How he would fix premiums? How he would benefit those who could not pass the exams? How he would persuade the unwilling to sign up? In hardly more than one sentence, he eulogized the French and British systems. Did he not ignore the fact that most of these countries, faced with failure of their voluntary systems, have adopted the compulsory plan? Let the speaker read again the conclusion of the majority of the Committee on the Cost of Medical Care. I quote:

Specific quotation from authority.

"Families with low or irregular incomes cannot be covered by any form of voluntary insurance." How futile is such a remedy!

Summary of the affirmative case and of specific data related to the argument.	Ladies and gentlemen, if our tuberculosis, infantile paralysis, or black and yellow fevers of tomorrow are to have proper control and extermination, you and I are to look to socialized medicine. If the submerged 15 per cent are to have reasonable medical protection, we must provide for them state medicine rather than voluntary insurance. The logic is clear: conditions require our proposal.
Statement of what the negative must prove —"putting it up to you" technique.	Let the visiting speakers who succeed me explain whether present medical costs are not beyond the reach of the twelve-hundred-dollar income class. Let them further analyze their solution of private insurance. Let them, for example, make clear how the twenty million families on the minimum-subsistence level can be sold these old-line or new-line policies. Rather will the American people look to public medicine as one of the feasible methods of obtaining social security.

The first affirmative rebuttal speech, although mechanical, exemplifies pretty well the organizational plan suggested above. The marginal notes indicate the phases of the structure.

B. Content. This speech, in addition to framework, contains ideas. The thought or content includes a restatement of issues, new evidence, and much persuasive material to enforce the thought. Enough transitions, summarizing, and topical statements are inserted to make the argument entirely clear.

EXERCISES AND PROBLEMS

1. Compare the relative merits of the two rebuttal speeches on opposite sides of a debate in a recent volume of *The University Debater's Annual.* Consider the effectiveness in (*a*) statement of is-

344 ARGUMENTATION, DISCUSSION, AND DEBATE

sues, (*b*) statement of the opposing arguments, (*c*) use of transitions and summaries, (*d*) freedom from hackneyed terms, (*e*) use of the rhetorical question, (*f*) refutation by the method of residues, (*g*) refutation by the method of dilemma, (*h*) refutation by the method of *reductio ad absurdum*, (*i*) refutation by exposing inconsistencies, (*j*) refutation by exposing irrelevancies.

2. (*For the instructor.*) Secure a wire or tape recording of the four rebuttals following the constructive speeches of a classroom or other practice debate. Have the squad or class criticize at length the rebuttal skills.

3. (*For the instructor.*) Have an affirmative speaker present an argument for six minutes. Then, after a negative speaker has refuted it for four minutes, have these two debaters alternate for thirty minutes, replying to each other in three-minute rebuttals.

4. Refute (in writing) an argumentative speech published in a recent issue of *Vital Speeches of the Day* or one reported in a recent newspaper.

5. Before the debate class present a four-minute refutation of a recent editorial.

6. Write a short analysis and criticism of the rebuttal techniques of Lincoln in the final Lincoln-Douglas debate.

CHAPTER 26

Debate: Special Types

I. THE CROSS–EXAMINATION

One proposal, typical of many, for making the debate more interesting to an audience, for spurring on the speaker to more complete preparation, for ensuring more satisfactory rebuttals, is the so-called cross-examination, or Oregon, plan of debating.[1] According to this procedure, two (sometimes three) speakers are on a team. The first affirmative speaker presents the entire affirmative case in, say, twelve minutes; then the first negative has an equal amount of time for presenting the entire negative case. The second negative cross-examines the first affirmative for eight minutes, and the second affirmative cross-examines the first negative (also for eight minutes). The second negative then presents a summary of the negative case, and finally the second affirmative summarizes his side, each of these final speeches being limited to eight minutes. The cross-examination is limited to specific questions; the chairman rules concerning the relevancy of the questions and of the answers. Critic judges vote at the end.

If a third speaker for each team is desired, he may present the rebuttal summary for his side, or he may cross-examine the entire opposing team.

[1] J. S. Gray, "The Oregon Plan of Debating," *Quarterly Journal of Speech Education,* Vol. XII, pp. 175–179, April, 1926.

The following is a specimen schedule of an intercollegiate cross-examination debate (modified Oregon plan) as held between the University of Michigan and Iowa State University at Ann Arbor, on Feb. 19, 1948:

First affirmative speech—six minutes
First negative cross-examines first affirmative—five minutes
First negative speech—six minutes
Second affirmative cross-examines first negative—five minutes
Second affirmative speech—five minutes
Second negative cross-examines second affirmative—five minutes
Second negative speech—five minutes
First affirmative cross-examines second negative—five minutes
Negative summary by first negative—four minutes
Affirmative summary by first affirmative—four minutes

A shift-of-opinion ballot was used, and an oral critique was given by a Michigan faculty member.

The cross-examination type may be used without decisions. The sponsors of the cross-examination plan intended the type to supply interest to audience and speakers without the presence of a judge. If a speaker is to maintain his case, his preparation must be thorough; the performance is usually free from academic dryness. Sometimes the examiner and examinee lose their composure and thus defeat the goal of platform amity and persuasiveness. The chairman is highly important in limiting the questions and replies and in preserving the general decorum. The rebuttals are especially valuable in instructing the audience concerning the issues and in making clear the significance of the previous questions and replies.

For successful conduct of the cross-examination debate these suggestions concerning preparation and presentation should help:

1. Prepare beforehand the questions covering the entire subject. Try these questions on a debate colleague.
2. Let your series of questions framed beforehand be grouped about the central issues and about the most important evidence.
3. In the debate itself don't hesitate to shape your questions in view of the arguments presented and the cross-examination statements made.
4. The two speakers should stand on opposite sides of the rostrum, partly facing each other, but also including the audience in the

conversation. The chairman may remain seated behind these two speakers.

5. The dialogue should be loud enough for all to hear easily.

6. Questions should be brief. They should invite yes or no replies.

7. Questions should aim to bring out issues and essential facts. Trick questions and those asking for detailed facts not ordinarily at hand are objectionable.

8. Replies should not consume more than a sentence or two. Long speeches are out of place. The examiner who permits the examinee to filibuster by continued speechmaking is making a strategical mistake. The chairman should check such eloquence.

9. The chairman will decide matters of relevancy and other details of procedure.

10. Avoid belligerency in questions and replies.

11. Avoid interrupting other members of the dialogue.

12. Retain your sense of humor.

13. Have a pattern in your questioning. Begin with facts, analogous cases, definitions, or preliminary assumptions.

14. Show the significance of the statements, concessions, or silences in response to your questions. Ask additional questions. Since the audience does not always get the connection between your line of inquiry and the arguments you would support, your chief job is to make clear the relevancy of your questions. So frame your questions and bring out the implications of the replies that your final speech is easier to make convincing to the audience.

15. In the final summary relate the general issues and contentions to the specific facts and arguments. Especially important is it to indicate (*a*) admissions, (*b*) inconsistencies, (*c*) errors in statements of fact or lack of knowledge concerning the available evidence, (*d*) errors in inferences from facts, (*e*) dilemmas facing the other side, (*f*) your appropriation of their arguments and facts to prove your own case.

On the whole, the cross-examination technique, if it can be kept free from the methods of the shyster lawyer, is a highly effective means of developing student speakers and of enlisting the interest of the audience.[2]

[2] Harold P. Zelko, "Can a Pre-debate Agreement Improve Cross-Examination?" *The Gavel*, Vol. XXIV, No. 3, 1942; John R. Fitzpatrick, "Congressional Debating," *Quarterly Journal of Speech*, Vol. XXVII, pp. 251–255, April, 1941; Kenneth G. Hance, "The Dialectic Method in Debate," *Quarterly Journal of Speech*, Vol. XXV, pp. 243–248, April, 1939.

II. Heckling

The heckling procedure, borrowed from the British custom of open-air speechmaking, especially the cross-examination of candidates for Parliament, allows the opposing speakers, and in some cases the audience, the privilege of interrupting the speaker with questions. Usually, each speaker has ten minutes. The order is first affirmative, first negative, second negative, second affirmative. Each member is assigned to one and one only for the cross-examination.

Each is allowed to proceed without interruption for the opening two minutes and the final two minutes. The chairman should prevent the heckler from abusing his privileges. Time is taken out for heckling. No time limits are set for such cross-examination, but procedure for this part of the program needs to be agreed upon in advance. The cross-examination must be limited to direct, pertinent questions. The chairman must be skilled and continually control the direction of the debate.

The arguers must here exercise the same courtesy and fair play required in the more conventional debating. Interruptions must be worth while in clarifying the issues and statements. Time limits must be carefully agreed to in advance; the entire program should be limited to about an hour. In general the method smacks of the Congressional style and has the obvious virtues and perhaps the vices of the tense occasions when a Senator rises to ask, "Will the gentleman yield?" The purpose is to get at the facts and issues and not to confuse or provide an interesting diversion.

III. Direct Clash

The direct-clash debate was introduced under the direction of Edwin H. Paget in North Carolina colleges in 1931–1932. The plan is somewhat as follows:

A. *Number of Speakers.* Two speakers or more make up each team.

B. *Period of Definition and Analysis.* Five or eight minutes may be given to a leader of each side to define and analyze the question. The negative will indicate clearly his point of agreement and disagreement with the affirmative analysis. The subsequent debate must be limited to the issues on which there is clear disagreement.

C. The First Clash. A member of the affirmative presents his argument in support of the first main issue (or perhaps a phase of it) in a three-minute speech.   The first negative speaker then replies to this specific issue in a two-minute rebuttal. He is followed in order by the second negative, the second affirmative, the third negative, and finally by another affirmative who summarizes. This entire process covers fifteen minutes; it includes seven speeches, one of three minutes and six of two minutes.

D. Second Clash. The successive clashes duplicate the method of the first one, except the negative generally advances the first contention (although the affirmative may lead in presenting each clash).

E. Function of the Judges. Three judges or one may be used. The chairman allows a momentary pause after any speech for the judges to confer. If at any time after the first two speeches the judging committee decides that one side has obtained a clear advantage on the point, that clash may be abruptly ended. The single judge, or chairman of the judging board, will announce, with reasons, the one side that has been awarded the point and score.   If the argument proceeds for the full seven speeches, the judge or judges shall then give their decision as is done in any other debate.

The final decision is the sum of the decisions on each issue. To prevent a tie, it is desirable to have an odd number of clashes.

If the debate is decisionless, the chairman may serve also as critic; he may intersperse the speeches with questions and at the end offer comment. Sometimes a vote by the audience after each clash or at the end of the program will enliven the occasion.

IV. British Parliamentary Type

This open-forum system, practiced for years in this country, has also been characteristic of the well-known British debating clubs of the Oxford Union Society and of the Cambridge Union Society at Oxford.   In 1921 a Bates College debate team argued at Oxford.   From 1921 until 1939 numerous British and other international teams visited this country.

International debating was revived after World War II, with the coming of a Cambridge team to some twenty American colleges, and an Oxford three-speaker team (September, 1947, to February, 1948) to more than fifty colleges and universities in all sections of the United States. Oxford debated the following subjects: (1) The social and economic arguments for the nationalization of basic industries are overwhelming. (2) The danger of war can best be averted by an all-purpose Anglo-American alliance. (3) The working of modern democracy demands a liberal rather than a vocational education. (4) If full employment is to become an international reality, America must radically alter her traditional economic policy.

At Iowa State University, for example, the teams were split. Two Iowans and one Oxford speaker advocated alliance with Great Britain; two Oxonians and one Iowan opposed. Each speaker had twelve minutes for his single argument. The audience at the end voted by depositing a ballot, "Affirmative" or "Negative," on the merits of the question. The negative won. Because of the length of the program no open forum followed the debate.

This philosophy of debate is based upon the British parliamentary tradition with the cabinet and government holding leadership in the House of Commons only as long as it reflects public opinion. When the cabinet or ministry loses that support, it resigns, and, in theory, an election is called, and the new constituency again speaks the majority will. By contrast, our American system has fixed tenure of office, Constitutional and Federalistic restraints that, to some extent, remove the officeholder from close contact with the electorate. Ours is Congressional government, and our debaters operate under such tradition. The younger Englishman adapts his ideas, arguments, language, and delivery exclusively to the audience. The participating hearers are, after all, the court of last appeal and determinants of his success or failure.

The essence of the British procedure is to emphasize the question rather than the merits of the debate; to concentrate on the audience rather than the judges; to vote at the end on the resolution; to adapt ideas, language, delivery, and the other elements of speaking, to the *audience itself*. The audience vote is all important.

The Oxford Union Society, for example, is a literary social club, founded in 1823, and includes several hundred students from the twenty-odd colleges. The Union, with the presiding officer's dais and the benches for the government and the opposition, duplicates the House of Commons.

Each of the three or four speakers of the evening is assigned to the side that represents his convictions. With little or no reference to his colleagues he gives his individual argument, usually some fifteen minutes long. If he persists, no bell shuts him off. A polite note from the secretary may remind him of the time. He follows no brief, reproduces no carefully worked-out manuscript. The constant heckling may inspire him to unexpected power in argument. He tries to be natural, informal, conversational; he scores with his wit, invective, and persuasiveness more than with statistics. No judges are there to pass on the merits of the debate. The aim is to establish conviction rather than to obtain a technical decision; to arrive at a dependable judgment rather than to play a game.

An open forum follows, with perhaps fifteen or twenty speeches from the floor. Finally, not long before midnight, the three or four hundred members divide and vote on the merits of the question, usually a problem of national or international policy, but occasionally philosophy, such as *Resolved, That this House pities its grandchildren.* Thus the British system exemplifies the judgeless, open-forum, parliamentary discussion. What are the advantages and disadvantages of this system as compared with the competitive debate?

In general the plan presumably fosters genuine conviction because each speaker talks only on that side which represents his real mental attitude. Moreover, the open-forum, audience-decision plan establishes an intimacy between the speaker and the audience which makes for better speaking and approaches the public-speaking conditions of life after college. The style is thus more personal, persuasive, humorous, and interesting.

The chief disadvantage is that it may make for superficial preparation and thus destroy the thoroughness of training, one of the accomplishments of the American debate. Furthermore, with the substitution of a vote on the merits of the question for that on the merits of the debate the competitive element completely disappears. The result is likely to be a loss of interest on the part of the audience. On the whole the influence on American college debating has been salutary.[3]

V. Problem Solving

The problem-solving debate was developed at the University of Washington.[4] The philosophy back of the method is that of stressing genuine conviction rather than competitive debating skill. The aim approaches that of discussion with its cooperative thinking.

The topic is stated as a question. Three speakers compose each of the two teams. The first speaker on each team analyzes the problem; the second, in each case, presents a typical solution in line with his colleague's analysis; the third speaker for each team compares the two solutions. The time should be more or less evenly distributed among speakers with a total of not more than one hour. Ample time should be left for the audience. If a decision is in order, a ballot may be used which weights each team as first or second in regard to analysis, solutions, and evaluation. The judges consider (1) scientific research, (2) elimination of prejudice, and (3) effective use of cooperation in finding a solution.

This Washington type of debate has been highly effective before extension audiences. The method outlined above is flexible enough for it to be adapted to meet audience needs and wishes.

VI. Legislative Session

As a direct means of training college students for active and practical participation in the political life of the times, the convention or legislative type has grown in popularity. A state

[3] For analysis of international debating see A. Craig Baird, "Shall American Universities Adopt the British System of Debating?" *Quarterly Journal of Speech Education,* Vol. IX, pp. 215–222, June, 1923; E. L. Hunt, "English Debating Reconsidered," *Quarterly Journal of Speech,* Vol. XXI, pp. 98–102, February, 1935; I. S. Lloyd and H. L. Richmond, "Seen from an American Platform: the 1947 Cambridge Union Tour," *Quarterly Journal of Speech,* Vol. XXXIV, pp. 50–53, February, 1948; A. Craig Baird, "How Can We Improve International Debating?" *Quarterly Journal of Speech,* Vol. XXXIV, pp. 228–230, April, 1948.

[4] See F. W. Orr and Albert L. Franzke, "The University of Washington Plan of Problem-solving Debate," University of Washington Extension Service, No. 8, 1938, and No. 610, 1940.

legislature, the United States Congress, or even the United Nations (or, earlier, the League of Nations) served as the pattern. Sometimes effort is made to duplicate closely the personalities of legislative body, as, e.g., when a student speaker becomes "the Senator from Ohio," or "the Security Council representative from China."

Probably the first of these student assemblies was the Model League of Nations Assembly, sponsored by the School of Citizenship and Public Affairs of Syracuse University in 1927.[5] A two-day student convention of New York State problems was held at Syracuse in April, 1933.[6] These congresses multiplied, both in colleges and high schools. The National Student Congress, of Pi Kappa Delta, was held at Topeka, Kansas, in 1938, with 40 student senators and 125 representatives. In 1939 the first National Student Congress of Delta Sigma Rho, the honorary intercollegiate forensic fraternity, was held at Washington, D.C. "One hundred and thirty students from 38 colleges participated."[7]

With the ending of World War II these student congresses revived. The fourth Delta Sigma Rho Congress was held in Chicago for two days in April, 1949. The program was as follows:

Thursday, March 31

5:00–10:00 P.M. Registration period
8:00–10:00 P.M. Preliminary caucuses
        Each delegate was registered as "Left Center," "Right Center," or "Independent." Caucuses were held to nominate Speakers and Clerks of the Assembly.

Friday, April 1

9:00–10:00 A.M. Opening assembly
        Officers were elected and delegates were assigned to the committees
10:00–12:00 A.M. Committee meetings
        Each committee attempted to frame a bill em-

---

[5] Joseph F. O'Brien, "The Historical Development of Student Assemblies," in Lyman S. Judson (ed.), *The Student Congress Movement,* pp. 9–23, The H. W. Wilson Company, 1940.

[6] Milton Dickens, "Intercollegiate Convention Debating," *Quarterly Journal of Speech,* Vol. XX, pp. 30–37, February, 1934.

[7] See Lyman S. Judson, *op. cit.*

bodying the legislation proposed for the special
problem assigned to that committee.

2:00–5:00 P.M.   Committee meetings
The Committees framed their bills and completed their committee work.

8:00–10:00 P.M.   Joint Conference Committee meeting
Three representatives from each committee
made up a Joint Committee dealing with the
given topic. The duty of the Joint Committee
was to fuse the several dissenting views and
produce a majority bill and a majority leader.
A minority bill and minority leader could also
be designated.

Saturday, April 2

9:00–11:30 A.M.   General assembly
12:30–3:00 P.M.   General assembly
Bills were passed upon.[8]

What is the value of these congresses? An Evaluation Committee of this Third Student Congress concluded as follows:

> The committee is firmly convinced that the Congress is a very
> worthwhile forensic experience; that the value to the student both in
> speaking, association with other students, and increase of knowledge
> on important current problems is great; and that the Congress def-
> initely should be retained as the principal feature of the Biennial
> meeting of Delta Sigma Rho.[9]

The Iowa University Student Senate, inaugurated on Mar. 16
and 17, 1945, and held annually since then, usually discussed
foreign policy. The objects, as defined for the 1945 session, were
first, to answer specifically the question, What should be the foreign policy of the United States as formulated in 1945? second,
to provide college and university students with opportunity for
further research in the problem of America's international relations and policies and to provide experience in the task of formulating those policies; third, to provide these students with

[8] For complete program of this Fourth Student Congress of Delta Sigma
Rho, see *The Gavel*, Vol. XXXI, pp. 43–46, March, 1949.

[9] Report of the Evaluations Committee of the Third National Student
Congress, *ibid.*, Vol. XXX, pp. 7–8, November, 1947. See also Louis
Ehninger and Mary Graham, "The Student Congress Movement Comes of
Age," *ibid.*, pp. 5–6.

additional opportunities in group discussion, parliamentary debate, and public speaking.[10] The two-day session included an opening session for organization, a series of committee meetings to analyze the problem, sessions to frame committee conclusions, and a final session to pass on these resolutions submitted by each of the ten committees. An attitude scale on the representative aspects of foreign policy was submitted at the outset of the conference and the results reported at the closing session.

According to Ray, these definite goals were accomplished:

1. It attempted to secure more concentrated and prolonged preparation on a limited discussion topic than is often done for such intercollegiate conferences.

2. It stressed realistic goals of formulating and expressing carefully reasoned opinions on the issues.

3. It encouraged also the general participation of the delegates as a whole in all phases of the problem (in addition to the experience of a more authoritative specialization or an assigned area).

4. It retained the features of criticism and rating of each individual and so permitted the competitive factor to be retained. (At the end of the conference the "superior" and "excellent" performers were announced.)

5. It retained the element of individual public speaking to supplement round table techniques.

6. It incorporated extended application of parliamentary law.

7. It required careful formulations of resolutions.

8. It gave somewhat full reflection, in the general sessions, of concrete resolutions.

9. It added to the usual record of such resolutions a comprehensive attitude compilation on the problems.[11]

If the Congressional plan is to succeed, (1) the rules of procedure must be carefully and specifically worked out beforehand; (2) students must have special training for committee work; (3) abbreviated rules of parliamentary law must be drawn up and distributed by mimeograph or other means to the participants; (4) practice in parliamentary law must be given before the gathering, but these legal practices should be reduced to a minimum; (5) one subject only should be used for the session; (6) a committee of more than a dozen members should be avoided; (7) the atti-

[10] Robert Ray, "The Iowa University Student Senate," *The Quarterly Journal of Speech* Vol. XXXII, pp. 454–457, December, 1946.

[11] *Ibid.,* p. 457.

tudes and techniques of discussion should prevail in the committee meeting; (8) speeches from the floor should be limited to
three minutes; (9) the presiding officer should know his business
and should be aided by a parliamentarian whose rulings should
be final; (10) the meeting should be so organized and directed
that the major emphasis is on discussion of the problem rather
than on parliamentary juggling; (11) any tendency to mock-
heroic imitation of the United States Senate must be prohibited
since the aim of the gathering is to discuss seriously an important
matter and not to imitate bad political speaking.

The procedure makes a successful variation of a classroom
program. It may well be added to an intercollegiate debate
tournament. If sufficient student interest in a topic of the day
(state or national) can be developed, if those participating are
somewhat mature in their knowledge of debate, parliamentary
law, and committee discussion, and if a skilled chairman directs
the session, the Congressional type of debating has great possibilities in correlating college debating with practice in political
thinking and leadership.

VII. Intercollegiate Forensic Conference and Tournament

In wide practice are the intercollegiate forensic gatherings, in
which for two or three days the students compete in debate, discussion, extempore speaking, dinner speaking, and general public speaking or original oratory. The following is a sample program (in which sixteen colleges and universities participated in
March, 1949):

Friday, March 4

8:00–9:00 A.M.	Registration
9:15 A.M.	Meeting of the directors (who also were the judges)
9:15 A.M.	Meeting of the participants, directors, judges, and chairmen
10:20 A.M.	Discussion period I
	The problem was: "What policy should the United States follow to control inflation and deflation?"
11:20 A.M.	Discussion period II
	Solutions
12:20 P.M.	Drawings for extempore speaking

1:30 P.M.   Extempore speaking (two sections)
2:30 P.M.   Discussion period III
                 Solutions (continued)
3:30 P.M.   After-dinner speaking preliminaries
4:20 P.M.   Debate, round I
7:00 P.M.   Debate, round II
8:30 P.M.   Debate, round III

Saturday, March 5

8:20 A.M.   Discussion, period IV
9:20 A.M.   Debate, round IV
10:30 A.M.   Public speaking
12:00 Noon   Forensic luncheon and finals of the dinner speaking
                 program
1:45–3:00 P.M. Parliamentary session (discussion, period V)
                 Resolutions discussed and voted up or down
3:05 P.M.   Announcement of results of the conference in all
                 events

The speakers in all events, including the discussion sessions, were judged as *superior, excellent, good, fair,* or *below standard.*

Such program encourages versatility and invites participation by the student in the type of speaking in which he is most proficient.

VIII. Radio Debating

A. Prevalence of Debating and Discussion over the Radio. One of the most significant social changes in the recent history of public speaking and debating has been the growing application of argument to radio audiences.

Whereas the political speaker of former generations made history if he was able to command an audience of thirty thousand, a national leader of today, especially if he happens to be a President defending his policies or appealing for reelection, may number his listeners by the millions. Likewise, if the school or college debater of other days talked to more than a thousand, he was lucky; now he often addresses thousands upon thousands over some major radio station or even over a national chain.

Intercollegiate debaters take for granted that their season's schedule will include at least one radio debate. Many state universities own their own stations and broadcast weekly debates; other colleges and universities have time regularly alloted to them on commercial stations. Even high-school speakers go on the air, especially in presenting final debates in the state debate leagues. Even transatlantic debating broadcasts have been scheduled. Oxford University, for example, broadcasting from London, has debated with Columbia University, speaking from New York. More and more will college debaters have opportunities over the air as the FM stations develop. Consideration, then, should be given to the technique of debating and discussion as that procedure may be affected by the use of radio.

B. *Similarities of Radio and Other Speaking Situations.* Radio debating is in general the same as debating before the visible audience. The same methods which produce effective arguments before the pedestrian, organized, or specialized "eye-to-eye" audiences usually succeed over the air. Good debaters on the college platforms usually make good debaters in the broadcasting studio. No new principles are applicable in the latter situation.

C. *Differences between Radio and Nonradio Debating Conditions.* The imposition of the microphone and the receiving set between the debater and his auditor does modify somewhat the problem of adaptability of material and style of presentation. The speaker is alone with the announcer and perhaps a few other colleagues or opponents. Over the air he hopes that many people are listening. But in his heart he suspects that their dials are either off or are tuned elsewhere. Certainly, the speaker has little opportunity for the circular response, no opportunity to convey by gestures, posture, or bodily movement his ideas, and little opportunity to create interstimulation among his hearers (note how television modifies these delivery restrictions); for although they may number thousands, they are widely scattered. Further, the speaker is probably aware that the mechanism of the machine favors certain vibration frequencies; it distorts certain sounds; it is unable to transmit fully the change in pitch and intensity. Its sensitiveness may result in the broadcasting of scratching papers, the turning leaves of books, jingling coins, or clearing of the throat. These conditions make for difficulty.

D. *Suggestions for the Radio Debater.*
1. Decide in advance what type of audience you intend to address.
2. Be sure your subject has contemporary appeal.
3. Make your entire program short and your speech brief. A

thirty-minute speaking program over the radio is long enough. Your individual speech also should be short, probably not exceeding six minutes. Four six-minute speeches, with perhaps two rebuttals of two minutes each, make a debate of normal length. Debates as short as fifteen minutes have been broadcast.[12]

4. Intersperse formal debates with symposia and informed discussions.

5. Analyze your subject with special reference to your audience.

6. Simplify the structure of your speech.

7. Introduce refutation that both meets the case of the opposition and removes the inhibitions of the audience.

8. Decide upon the specific appeals and frame your logic to make them effective.

9. Exploit your own personality in addressing your unseen audience.

10. Write and rewrite your speech.

11. Speak extemporaneously.

12. Let the radio language be both easily understood and interesting.

13. Cultivate a pleasing radio voice.

EXERCISES AND PROBLEMS

1. (*For the instructor.*) Let each member of the class report on one of the references listed for this chapter.

2. (*For the instructor.*) Assign a special type of debating for investigation and report by each member.

3. Criticize a cross-examination debate printed in one of the recent debate annuals.

4. Criticize in a written report (500 words) a debate between British and American universities as stenographically reported in one of the recent debate annuals.

5. Attend an international debate between universities and criticize it (in a four-minute oral statement) accompanied by a written statement of 500 words. Note especially the differences in methods of pointing arguments, the oral style, and the delivery.

6. Cooperate in the conduct of an undergraduate Congressional session; or attend one as an observer. Give a 200-word criticism of the procedure.

7. Conduct a cross-examination debate on the national college debate question for the present season.

[12] See *University Debater's Annual: 1943–1944*, pp. 11–30, The H. W. Wilson Company, 1944.

8. Conduct a "heckling" type of debate on the same question.

9. Conduct a problem-solution debate on the same question.

10. Conduct a fifteen-minute radio debate on the same question.

11. Listen to a recording of a practice debate—which debate you hope to give later in the classroom. Present to the class a brief report of this trial debate, including a statement of how you propose to improve in your later appearance.

12. Attend a student congress or assembly as a visitor. Later report (500 words) your criticism of the final assembly and your suggestions for improvement.

13. Listen to a radio debate and report to the class your answers to the following questions concerning each speaker: (*a*) Could you understand clearly? (*b*) If not, why not? (*c*) Was the speaker interesting? Why, or why not? (*d*) What words, if any, were mispronounced? (*e*) Was the speaker's voice too high? Too low? Was the rate too fast? Too slow? Was the quality satisfactory? (*f*) Was he conversational? (*g*) Was the enunciation or pronunciation over-exact? (*h*) Was the vocabulary limited? Pedantic? Literary rather than idiomatic? (*i*) Was the language concrete? (*j*) Were the sentences unduly involved? (*k*) Were too many ideas developed? (*l*) Was the organization satisfactory? (*m*) Was the speech persuasive? (*n*) For which side did you vote? Why?

14. Prepare and deliver a six-minute speech for a radio audience. If it is not possible to deliver the speech over the air, do so by a class-room public-address system; or present your speech to the class from behind a screen.

CHAPTER 27

Judging Debaters and Debates

I. Debating, the Critic Judge, and the Audience

Debating is a practical art. Its purpose is primarily to argue a case and to motivate an audience to arrive at a decision and take action. Its typical scene is the courtroom, the legislature, the political rally, the executive or conference room of some organization—industrial, religious, educational, business, military, political, or otherwise.

In addition to its mission of settling practical problems of criminal and civil trials, lawmaking, settlement of labor controversies, and the like, or as a preliminary to such efforts, debate also is conducted for learning purposes. It hopes to give knowledge to an audience. On other occasions it also hopes to teach the performers themselves better ways of debating. Audience instruction and stimulation, for example, occurs when the radio chains present debates as sustaining programs, or when two college teams take to the air. It is expected that the listeners will later act (or vote), partly as a result of their response to this immediate debate.

In its role as a learning medium for the audience, debating also gives excellent training to the speakers themselves. School and college debates are chiefly for such end. Although they are often staged for sport's sake and are promoted as intercollegiate competition, their place in higher learning is justified only because of their value as education. They are good training for prospective teachers, preachers, lawyers, statesmen, businessmen, social and government workers, housewives, and other citizens. To gain maximum benefit from such collegiate speaking, the debater should have criticism. Hence we provide a judge or judges at the end of a performance. This learned authority not only criticizes the team and the individuals, but he often awards a decision to the team "doing the better debating." This award is a sop to the many who wish their institution to excel on the platform as it allegedly excels in other academic and extracurricular activities. The award is one of several motivating devices to ensure good performance.

To further this debate training the speaker not only gets advice from a judge but attempts to convince and persuade the audience. This audience response, whether by show of hands or ballot, is "on the merits of the question." A life situation, quite apart from academic debating as a sport, is duplicated. The debater, his skills evaluated by a judge and his proposition voted up or down by his hearers, thus serves a dual role as a wielder of good technique and as a practical molder of public opinion.

II. The Decision on the Merits of the Debate: the Critic Judge

A. Criteria of Judgment. The critic judge applies certain standards of excellence. What are they? Despite the continued indictment of these judges as incompetent and uncertain as to their bases of evaluation, we do have a pretty well-defined group of criteria for them to follow although we shall probably never agree to every detail of a "nationwide uniform ballot," nor is it necessary that we do so.

Instructions traditionally stipulate that "material is more important" than form. Judges are expected to give credit for (1) skill in definition and analysis, (2) skill in argument, (3) quality and quantity of evidence, (4) excellence in organization, (5) skill in audience adaptation in the use of persuasive materials (ethical and pathetic proofs), (6) effective oral language, (7) skill in refutation and rebuttal, (8) effective delivery, and (9) general effectiveness. These items overlap; they probably do not have equal weight; and other categories may be considered, such as directness of clash, teamwork, the case, and strategy.

Those mentioned above, however, are representative and, properly interpreted, cover the field of criticism. Since much of the confusion attending judging stems from confusion over these criteria, may we briefly review each.

1. *Definition and analysis.* The debater must define terms accurately, clearly, and reasonably. If, for example, in a proposition of policy, he insists that "should" implies merely theoretical desirability but carries no requirement of practicability, the judge should put down that debater as deficient in his understanding of proposition framing. The judge, too, must look carefully at the analysis—the division of the material into partitions under issues and the clear statement and repetition of these main questions. If the analysis is peculiar and seemingly devised merely to throw the other team off guard, this critic should penalize accordingly. His own well-formulated understanding of the definitions and issues should enable him to note quickly immaturities as well as logical grasp.

2. *Argument and evidence.* The judge notes the effective use of specific instances, analogy, authority, causal reasoning, proper testing of assumptions, and absence of fallacies in the chief propositions.

3. *Evidence.* The judge asks, Is the evidence relevant, accurate, reliable, abundant, consistent, and persuasive?

4. *Structure.* The critic, again, notes the clearness, order, and proportion of each speech and its contribution (or lack) to the team's "case."

5. *Audience adaptation.* Again the judge will be sensitive not only to the dry argument but to the persuasive elements. He will give credit for pathetic and ethical proofs (emotional proofs) that motivate the hearers through appeals to duty, economy, and loyalty.

6. *Language.* The critic will view language as a means and not an end. He will observe condensation, concreteness, connotative usages, originality, and similar features of acceptable oral style.

7. *Refutation and rebuttal.* Debate success hinges on effective rebuttal. This critic will follow the give and take, especially as it develops in the second series of speeches. He considers selection of points to be refuted, general and special methods, position and amount, and the inclusion of new evidence.

8. Delivery. The judge evaluates directness of communication, extempore skill, conversational mode, sincerity, and effectiveness in voice and bodily activity.

9. General effectiveness. Since the judge is not bound by details and since his scrutiny of minutiae may blind him to the general movement of the debate, he may well size up the performance in the light of its over-all effectiveness. "General effectiveness" he may dispense with if his judgment of each category is continually related to the synthesis of skills.

B. Method of Rating Individual Performance. The ballot (page 365) has been used for rating individual debaters in a classroom situation. It is for purposes of training and not for competition. The "superior" and other ratings of debaters can thus be grouped. If it is desired, the totals for each team can be made and the "winning" team announced as that one having the highest numerical score.

C. Rating of Individuals and Teams in Intercollegiate Competition. The rise of the intercollegiate tournament, in which as many as fifty teams may debate in four or five rounds within a two-day period, calls for a more accurate and simplified ballot than the one below. The judge will continue to keep before him all the criteria here suggested. He will, however, for purposes of reporting, merely describe the debaters as "superior," "excellent," "good," or "fair" and may submit on paper a few criticisms of help to that debater, to be given in carbon to him either immediately after the debate or at the end of the tournament.

Below is a typical judge's ballot for such purposes. It includes (1) the rating of each performer, (2) rating of each team, (3) criticism of each speaker (on reverse side of the sheet—one-half of the carbon copy to be given to the team concerned), and (4) if the sponsors so desire, a judge's vote for the affirmative or negative "on the merits of the debate." The ballot puts the emphasis where it belongs—on the skills of the debater rather than on the "winning" or "losing." A speaker may win against an inferior team and yet have little to boast about as to his ability as an arguer.

Criticism blanks of this type, or those somewhat similar, have been used repeatedly and successfully in both secondary-school and intercollegiate debate activities.

Round_____ Time_____ Place (Room)_____ Subject_____

_____

| (Affirmative) | (Negative) |

Instructions to judges: You are requested to rate each speaker on each of the items included on the sheet, assigning the number between "1" and "5" which best describes your evaluation of the speaker's achievement in that function. Superior is 5; Excellent, 4; Good, 3; Standard or Fair, 2; Below Standard, 1.

Individual Ratings

1st Aff._____ 1st Neg._____

1 2 3 4 5		1 2 3 4 5
	Analysis..................	
	Evidence.................	
	Argument................	
	Audience adaptation........	
	Adaptation to opponents and refutation...............	
	Organization..............	
	Language.................	
	Voice and bodily action......	
	General effectiveness........	
	..........Totals..........	

2nd Aff._____ 2nd Neg._____

1 2 3 4 5		1 2 3 4 5
	Analysis..................	
	Evidence.................	
	Argument................	
	Audience adaptation........	
	Adaptation to opponents and refutation...............	
	Organization..............	
	Language.................	
	Voice and bodily action.....	
	General effectiveness........	
	..........Totals..........	

Norms for each performance: Below Standard, 0–12; Fair, 13–20; Good, 21–27; Excellent, 28–35; Superior, 36–45.

_____

(Judge)

JUDGE'S BALLOT

Aff. _____ Neg. _____

    (Name of institution)   (Name of institution)

    (First affirmative)   (First negative)

    (Second negative)   (Second affirmative)

In my opinion the debating done by the affirmative was

Superior
Excellent
Good   } Encircle correct designation
Fair
Below Average

In my opinion the debating done by the negative was

Superior
Excellent
Good   } Encircle correct designation
Fair
Below Average

In my opinion the performances of the individual speakers were as follows:

        (Superior, Excellent, Good, Fair, or Below Average)

The performance of the first affirmative was _____

The performance of the second affirmative was_____

The performance of the first negative was _____

The performance of the second negative was _____

In my opinion the _____ was more effective in

            (affirmative or negative)

debating.   (By prior agreement this part of the ballot may be ignored.)

_____   _____
Place   Number of round in tournament

_____   _____
Date and hour   Judge

Note to judge: (1) Pass Judge's Ballot, sealed, to the chairman. (2) On the reverse side of this ballot, fill out the criticism of each individual. Carbons and a duplicate sheet will be provided so that a copy of the written criticism can be given to each. Note that on this sheet (and the corresponding carbon copy) a separate section is reserved for the criticism of each debater. Each of these four sections can thus easily be detached and handed to the individual concerned.

D. Number of Judges. How many judges should be used? Formerly, three judges, representative men from the community or the state, who conferred at the end of the discussion and sometimes engaged in a second debate of their own, were universally used. Those selected were former debaters; they were lawyers, teachers, or, occasionally, businessmen or preachers, sometimes a college president or United States Senator. They gave great dignity to the occasion but were often limited in their expert knowledge of debate technique.

E. The Rise of the Expert Judge. The practice of having a single expert judge has been widespread since 1920. Three or five judges who possess the necessary qualifications and who are willing to submit to the duty have been hard to find. (An even number of judges has been taboo as offering an opportunity for a tie.) With the coming of the tournament it has been convenient to have the debate director of each school judge teams other than his own.

F. Qualifications of the Critic Judge. If the purpose of the program is to train debaters, then the best critic will be a teacher of debating. In theory at least, he lays aside his prejudices and votes for the team which demonstrates on the platform greater ability as debaters. It has been counted a bargain to pay him for his services. After the contest his explanation of his vote and his criticism of the teams are regarded as highly helpful to the cause of good debating. He should (1) know the technicalities of debate, (2) know the subject and be familiar with it as it has been argued in the classroom, (3) put aside his bias on the subject, (4) have no close ties with the speakers or institutions involved.

G. The Critic Judge in the Progress of the Debate. In the contest itself he should give his undivided attention to his job. He should take rather full notes. He should not look (or be) bored. Each page of his notebook may be given over to a single speaker. One-half of the page may contain a summary of the argument; the other half, a criticism of argument, evidence, and delivery. A reserve page may be used for assembling and organizing the general comments related to the items outlined on a previous page. At any point in the debate the critic should be able to rise and report which side is at present more effective.

H. The Oral Report of the Critic Judge. His oral explanation to the debaters and audience should be well organized. It should be brief (most critiques are long and rambling). It may be pleasant but should not be sprinkled with funny stories. The judge should be definite. "The affirmative is better in delivery," is vague. "The first affirmative speaker was delightfully conversational and pleasant in his approach to the audience and other debaters," is better. If possible, the judge should meet the speakers for individual criticism.

III. Decision on the Merits of the Question

A. The Audience Vote on the Question. In a democracy the people's vote is important. The vote registers support of, or opposition to, the legislation implied in the proposition. If legislatures and jurymen and all others in "life situations" vote concerning the question and not concerning the skills of the arguers, why should college debaters not experience similar speaking conditions?

The British student debaters, as I suggested above, have no judges to decide "who does the better debating." At the end of the debate the Oxford Union members vote the resolution up or down. Their debating and voting duplicate the House of Commons practice. In this country, too, the members of a legislature, after their debating is done, do not chiefly ask, "Did so and so make a good speech?" but, "How am I to vote on this proposition?"

In debate training, this experience of securing audience approval is important. In addition to audience attention, applause, and similar responses, the vote is concrete evidence of approval or disapproval. When the Oxford speakers, for example, debated at Iowa University, two Iowans and one Britisher supported the resolution, *This House approves an all-purpose Anglo-American alliance.* The audience vote was two-to-one for the negative. What did these ballots prove concerning the teams? Little. The vote did suggest that this Middle Western audience of November, 1947, was decidedly of the opinion that an Anglo-American alliance would be objectionable.

In your debating, adjust your ideas, arguments, language, rebuttal tactics, and delivery to enlist the support of your voting listeners. Furthermore, you should see to it that an audience vote is taken.

B. The Shift-of-opinion Ballot. We are concerned, however, with the extent to which the debater influences the vote. Even though he cannot secure a majority, his efforts have been successful if he diminishes the strong majority against him. Charles James Fox, one of the British Parliament's greatest debaters, was during his long public career in the majority for only eighteen months. Winston Churchill, before 1938, was repeatedly in the minority in the British Commons as he warned against the growing German aggression. Gradually the Commons came to his point of view. His speeches were without question "successful" even though the votes were heavily against his position.

If debating effectiveness is to be measured and if the appeal is to be made to the audience, then some plan is necessary for measuring the audience change of opinion as a result of the debate. A vote before the debate, followed by one after the debate, the same audience participating as judges in both cases, has been used as more enlightening than a vote at the end only. The ballot, often called the "Western Reserve" ballot because used and experimented with extensively there by Professors Howard Woodward and William A. D. Millson, would be arranged somewhat as follows:

Before the debate	After the debate
_____ Favorable to the proposal	_____ Favorable to the proposal
_____ Neutral or undecided	_____ Neutral or undecided
_____ Opposed to the proposal	_____ Opposed to the proposal

The vote would be based upon conviction about the question and not upon the "merits of the debate." A comparison of the votes before and after the discussion will enable you to measure the shift of opinion.

The ballots may be collected and counted while the open forum is in progress. Group the ballots, according to the votes cast before the debate, into three sections: *affirmative, neutral, negative.* Then, on the basis of the votes after the debate, classify each of the piles into three subpiles labeled *unchanged, neutral, negative* (if, for example, the affirmative pile is used as a basis). Next tabulate the figures and calculate the final score. This method, if a fairly accurate means of measuring changes of opinion can be worked out, will eliminate the critic judges, substitute a more direct type of arguing, and at the same time pre-

serve the contest element. The following is a sample audience
ballot, with a method of scoring:

AUDIENCE BALLOT

Each member of the audience is requested to record his opinion on
the question _____ both before and after the debate.
(State the resolution)
This vote is to represent the individual conviction on the question and
is in no sense to be construed as a vote on the relative merits of the
two teams.

Before the debate I am
(Mark X in the proper space before the debate)
_____ Favorable to the affirmative of the proposition.
_____ Neutral on the proposition.
_____ Opposed to the affirmative of the proposition.

After the debate I am now
(Mark X in the proper space immediately after the ending of the
final speech)
_____ Favorable to the affirmative of the proposition.
_____ Neutral on the proposition.
_____ Opposed to the affirmative of the proposition.
Signed _____

A change of vote from favorable to neutral would represent
a loss of one point; from favorable to unfavorable, two points;
a change from unfavorable to favorable, a gain of two points;
from neutral to favorable, one point. The winning team may be
determined by ascertaining the ratio of the total points accumulated for a given side to the total opportunities for scoring.
The total opportunities for a given side would be a sum equal
to twice the number of votes recorded for the opposing side
previous to the debate, plus the number of neutral votes recorded before the debate.

How valid is such audience measurement? Much depends
upon the number of voters and the conditioning of the audience
to focus on the arguments rather than on ways and means of
manipulating the ballot. Alan Monroe, investigating the Western
Reserve ballot, concluded:

1. The shift-of-opinion ballot, scored in the manner suggested by
Millson, seems to be a reasonably valid measure of the shift of opinion produced in an audience by a speaker.

2. Results obtained in this manner should be adequately reliable if obtained from a voting audience of thirty or more, but wherever possible, the specific reliabilities of the data should be checked by the formulae presented above.

3. The results obtained with the ballot should not be accepted as significant or meaningful unless the statistical reliability of these results is computed; otherwise, results due in large part to chance variables may be erroneously accepted as significant.

4. With proper regard for statistical reliability, the shift-of-opinion ballot deserves a wider use in experimental studies because of its simplicity, and the ease of scoring and computing results.[1]

For purposes of determining audience reaction to a debate, the shift-of-opinion ballot can be usefully applied.

EXERCISES AND PROBLEMS

1. Give a four-minute oral report to the class concerning the qualifications of a critic judge.

2. Read a debate in the *University Debater's Annual* (*e.g.*, edition of 1939–40) together with the critic judge's report. Decide (within the evidence of the printed debate) whether the critic voted properly.

3. Apply to each debater of a printed debate the rating scale as suggested in this chapter (omit "delivery"). Compare your ratings with those of your coursemates.

4. Serve as one of the judges for a classroom debate. Write (maximum 300 words) your criticism of each debater and of the debate as a whole. Compare your judgment with that of another student judge.

5. Serve as a judge of a classroom debate. Follow the criteria suggested in this chapter. Give a brief extempore criticism of the debate. (Three minutes.)

6. Report concerning the problem: Does listening to a debate on

[1] Alan H. Monroe, "The Statistical Reliability and Validity of the Shift-of-opinion Ballot," *Quarterly Journal of Speech,* Vol. XXIII, pp. 577–585, December, 1937.

Cf. W. A. D. Millson, "Review of Research in Audience Reaction," *Quarterly Journal of Speech,* Vol. XXIV, pp. 464–483, October, 1938; pp. 655–672, December, 1938.

See also Ernest Henrikson, "The Audience Reaction Ballot: An Evaluation," *Quarterly Journal of Speech,* Vol. XXIV, pp. 48–61, February, 1938.

the whole strengthen existing opinions of listeners? (Consult the references.)

7. Report concerning the problem: Does the side of the argument first presented have an advantage? (Consult the references.)

8. Serve as one of a committee of three to administer and interpret a shift-of-opinion vote on a debate. Report to the class your results and any criticism of your procedure.

APPENDIX A

Specimen Brief

Preliminary Brief[1]

Resolved, That the United Nations should now be revised into a World Federal Government.

Affirmative Brief

Introduction

I. The cause for discussion is as follows:

    A. Present conditions indicate the United Nations is not succeeding.

The American Mercury, 94:32, July, 1947, "U.N. Must Control Aggression."

        1. Russia, France, Britain, and the United States are engaged in a "cold war."

            a. Russia has blockaded the western sectors of Berlin.

Ibid., 94:97, July, 1947, "Russian Imperialism," Stanford, Neal.

            b. Military forces are alerted in Berlin.

        2. Actual warfare in Palestine has not been prevented by the United Nations.

        3. Fighting continues in China and Korea.

---

[1] Prepared by students at the State University of Iowa, with special contribution by Eleanor Kistle and Merrill Baker, summer, 1948.

The Nation, 166:413–415, Apr. 17, 1948, "Palestine—Operations Chaos," Shultz, L.

4. Governments of Rumania, Bulgaria, Yugoslavia, Albania, Hungary, and Poland have allegedly been taken over by Russian controlled Communists.

5. Boundaries for Greece and Turkey are not settled.

6. International control of atomic energy has allegedly failed in the United Nations.

Newsweek, 31:23–24, Apr. 26, 1948, "Peace Without Vetoes."

B. Security Council veto power has prevented action aimed at solving world problems.

1. The veto forced a disarmament program in the General Assembly.

2. The veto has prevented organization of a police power.

II. In any solution common goals are suggested as follows:

A. Peace should be a primary aim.

Littlefield, Henry W., *New Outline History of Europe*, 1815–1947, 13th ed., Barnes & Noble, Inc., 1947.

1. World War II killed nine million men.

2. World War II cost eight hundred billion dollars.

3. World War II cost untold millions in property damage.

4. World War II resulted in privation and suffering for millions.

B. World economic stability should be a primary aim.

1. The depression, 1929–1940, affected all peoples.

Chase, Stuart, *For This We Fought*, pp. 77–98, The Twentieth Century Fund, Inc., 1946.

2. Europe and Asia are suffering severely from unstable economic conditions caused by war.

3. The world is an economic unit.

C. Freedom of religion, speech, press, and assembly should be a primary aim.

1. Tyranny begets oppression by fostering fear and violence.

2. Tyranny suppresses the minority by the developing of channeled thought.

D. Scientific development should be a primary aim.

Chase, Stuart, *Tomorrow's Trade*, pp. 146–156, The Twentieth Century Fund, Inc., 1945.

1. We stand at the threshold of an atomic age.

2. Science strives to give man his basic needs.

3. Much remains to be done in medical, agricultural, and industrial development.

III. Terms of the proposition should be defined as follows:

A. *The United Nations* refers to the present organization of 58 nations with headquarters at Lake Success, New York.

B. *Should be revised* indicates amendment of the U.N. charter to include the structure and functions of government.

Encyclopedia of Social Sciences, Vol. VI, p. 173, "Federation," Macmahon, Arthur W.

C. *By World Federal Government* we mean:

1. The government would function in three main areas.

   a. It would make laws governing international relations as to war, armaments, immigration, trade, natural resources, atomic energy, and monetary standards.

   b. It would interpret these laws and determine violations.

   c. It would punish offenders individually, with no respect for race or former nationality.

2. The government would be constructed in four main divisions.

   a. It would have a lawmaking body containing representatives of all nations.

b. It would have a judicial branch for interpreting laws and punishing offenders.

c. It would have an executive branch for administration of the laws.

d. It would have a military branch to control insurrection and enforce law and order.

3. The government, similar to the United Nations, would be fundamentally different in three respects.

a. It would have power to enforce laws made by the legislative body.

New York Times, IV, 8:6 Apr. 4, 1948, "The U.N. Structure," Meyer, Cord, Jr.

b. It would have central authority over individuals living in member-states.

c. It would include all the nations of the world among its member-states.

Black, Henry C., *Black's Law Dictionary* (3d. ed.), pp. 758–759, West Publishing Company, 1933.

4. The government would be federal in nature, an organization superimposed upon a group of states to form a union under one central authority, but not destroying the power of the states to control local affairs.

IV. The history of the case is as follows:

A. Men have been looking for peace through world organization for hundreds of years.

Harper's Magazine, 193:396, November, 1946, "World Government Now," Pelcovits, N.

1. Dante, in 1313, proposed a universal empire to struggle against the papacy.

2. Rousseau had a plan for perpetual peace.

3. William Penn wrote of a world government plan.

Schapiro, J. Salwyn, *Modern and Contemporary European History,*

4. Congress of Vienna, 1814–1815, attempted to unite Europe.

a. Russia, Britain, Austria, Prus-

pp. 55–58, Houghton
Mifflin Company, 1946.

Schevill, Ferdinand, *A
History of Europe from
the Reformation to the
Present*, pp. 735–55,
Harcourt Brace and
Company, Inc., 1947.

The Atlantic Monthly,
178:56–60, August,
1946, "From the League
to the U.N.," Salvemi-
ni, G.

Charter of the United

sia, and France dominated the
conference.

b. Some minor matters were settled.

c. The Concert failed.
   (1) England grew suspicious
       of the others.
   (2) France disagreed with
       the others.
   (3) Revolutions in 1830 and
       1848 destroyed it com-
       pletely.

5. The League of Nations was designed to promote world peace.
   a. Economic and political sanc-
      tions were to be used against
      violators of its policy.
   b. Its creed was collective action
      for collective security.
   c. Member nations retained com-
      plete sovereignty.
   d. The United States did not en-
      ter the League.
   e. Many failures mark the
      League's history.
      (1) Great Britain and France
          finally resolved an Ital-
          ian-Greek dispute in
          1923.
      (2) Indecision characterized
          the reply to China's
          appeal when Japan at-
          tacked.
      (3) Economic sanctions were
          ineffective when Italy at-
          tacked Ethiopia.
      (4) Nonaction marked Po-
          land's seizure of Vilna, a
          part of Lithuania.
      (5) Germany moved into the
          Rhineland and no effec-
          tive action was taken.

6. The United Nations is the new-

Nations, Art. 9, 10, 11, 12, 13, 23, 24, 25, 26, 46, and 108, Chaps. XII, XIII, and XIV.

est attempt at securing world peace.

a. Nine members are in the Security Council.

b. All members are in the General Assembly.

c. Security Council members may veto its acts.

(1) Settlement proceedings may be vetoed.

International Concilia-tion, 413:441–535, September, 1945, "Test of U.N. Charter."

(2) Military and economic sanctions may be vetoed.

(3) Charter amendments may be vetoed.

d. The Security Council may investigate problems and recommend solutions.

United States Department of State Bulletin, v. 14, no. 351, pp. 467–475, Mar. 24, 1946, "Composition of Organs, Commissions, and Committees of the United Nations," Myers, D. P.

e. The General Assembly may recommend that the Security Council consider problems.

f. Police power is provided but is not existent.

g. Other agencies of the United Nations are included:

(1) An International Court of Justice exists along with the Secretariat, Economic and Social Council, Trusteeship Council, Economic Commission for Europe, and the Military Staff Committee.

Forum, 107:204–211, March, 1947, "Soviet American Cooperation," Plischke, E.

(2) Specialized agencies include the Food and Agriculture Organization and the Educational, Scientific, and Cultural Organization.

B. Today there is much agitation for World Government.

V. The conflicting arguments are:

A. The affirmative argue:

1. Present conditions make a change necessary.
   a. The world is in a terrible state.
   b. Causes of the present difficulties are inherent in the existing system.
   c. Only World Federal Government will correct the existing situation.
2. World Federal Government will eliminate present difficulties.
3. World Federal Government will be practicable.
   a. It can be established.
   b. It will work when established.
   c. It will bring many benefits.

B. The negative argue:
1. Present conditions do not warrant a change to World Federal Government.
   a. We have problems, but world relations are improving.
   b. Existing agencies can solve our problems.
   c. If existing machinery is inadequate, means other than World Federal Government will be sufficient.
2. World Federal Government will not solve present difficulties.
   a. It will not meet existing problems.
   b. It will create new and greater problems.
3. World Federal Government is not practicable.
   a. It cannot be established today.
   b. If established, it would not function.
   c. It has many disadvantages.

VI. The main issues thus suggested are:
   A. Does the present system call for a

change to World Federal Government?

1. Does the world situation indicate the necessity for a change?
   a. Are there existent political evils?
   b. Are there economic deficiencies?
   c. Are social and cultural levels out of balance with scientific and technological?
   d. Are there military evils?
2. Are alleged defects and evils inherent?
   a. Are there inherent functional defects?
   b. Are there inherent structural defects?
   c. Is there insufficient power of enforcement?
3. Are proposals other than World Federal Government sufficient for correction of the alleged defects and evils?
   a. Can elimination of the U.N. veto correct alleged difficulties?
   b. Can isolationism correct alleged difficulties?
   c. Would an immediate atomic war solve alleged problems?
   d. Is Wallace's "two-world" proposal adequate?
   e. Are other proposals adequate to meet the alleged difficulties?

B. Will World Federal Government meet and correct the alleged defects and evils?
1. Will it correct the alleged political evils?
2. Will it remedy the alleged economic deficiencies?

3. Will it correct the alleged social and cultural lag?

4. Will it remove alleged military evils?

C. Will World Federal Government prove practicable?

1. Can it be created?

2. If created will it function effectively?

3. Can the decisions of its organs be enforced?

VII. The affirmative will prove:

A. Amendment of the United Nations Charter to form a World Federal Government is necessary.

B. World Federal Government will prove practicable.

C. World Federal Government will have desirable economic, political, social, and military results.

Discussion

First Affirmative

I. Amendment of the United Nations Charter to establish a World Federal Government is necessary, for

A. Present conditions threaten world peace, for

1. Economic conditions endanger stability, for

Survey Graphic, 37:158–162, March, 1948, "Food and European Recovery," Thorp, Willard.

a. France's economy is critical, for

(1) France needs food badly, for

(*a*) Much of last year's crop was destroyed by unfavorable weather.

(*b*) The present Marshall Plan provides only survival rations.

United States News, 24:51, Feb. 20, 1948, "Continued Increase of Prices in France."

Ibid., 24:60, Mar. 12, 1948, "France's Failure to Boost Exports."

The Nation, 166:371, Apr. 3, 1948, "Beachhead We Forgot," Downes, Donald.

New Republic, 118:8, Mar. 1, 1948, "Britain Fights Bankruptcy."

World Report, 3:12–13, Oct. 7, 1947, "Britain's Economic Peril Speeds Arms Reduction."

Ibid., 3:3, Oct. 21, 1947, "Worldgram."

Ibid., 3:9–11, Oct. 21, 1947, "Britain's Plan to Survive the Winter."

(2) France needs money badly, for
  (a) Without monetary aid she cannot stem the inflationary tide.
(3) France needs raw materials, for
  (a) Supplies are low.
  (b) She cannot rely on coal and ore from eastern Europe.
b. Italy has many similar economic problems, for
  (1) She is suffering from inflation.
  (2) Wages have not met price increases.
c. The British Government is taking drastic measures to solve economic problems, for
  (1) England is almost bankrupt, for
    (a) Her trade deficit is 1.5 billions.
    (b) Her operating deficit is 2.7 billions per year.
  (2) British military forces are being reduced, for
    (a) The services (1947) had 1,290,000 men.
    (b) By 1949 the services had only 850,000 men.
  (3) Planned economy is being instituted in Britain, for
    (a) Government agencies are planning employment through laws governing vocational placement.

Ibid., 3:23, Oct. 7, 1947, "Will Britain Be Forced to Draft Labor?"

         (*b*) Government agencies are planning production and supply for coal and steel.

         (*c*) Britain is planning savings, for
            i. 1947 was to see 1.25 billions saved.
            ii. Government expense is to be cut 80 millions per year.

     (4) Britain is curtailing imports, for
         (*a*) Cuts are to be 832 million per year.
         (*b*) Tobacco and other products are off the import list entirely.

Vital Speeches, 14:345– 346, Apr. 1, 1948, "Survival of Freedom," Truman, President Harry S.

  d. Russia and the United States have competing economic plans for European rehabilitation, for
     (1) Russia ignores the Marshall Plan and offers controlled economy.
     (2) The U.S. goes ahead with the Marshall Plan.

 2. World political turmoil endangers world peace, for

The Nation, 165:200– 202, Aug. 30, 1947, "What's Our Game in Greece?"

  a. Greece is the scene of actual struggle between Russia and the U.S., for
     (1) Russia is aiding the guerrilla forces.
     (2) The United States sends arms and supplies to the nationalist forces.

Newsweek, 31:19, May 31, 1948, "Stage of Put Up or Shut Up."

  b. Russia and the United States cannot agree on the control of Germany, for

(1) They cannot occupy Berlin in peace.

(2) A western German state is in the making.

c. Bulgaria and Greece have recently failed to resume diplomatic relations, directly affecting Russo-American relations, for

(1) Russia supports Bulgaria and the U.S. backs Greece.

New Republic, 118:12–16, Mar. 29, 1948, "Italy's Dark April."

d. Italy's Communists are waging war on the U.S. and the Marshall Plan, affecting Russo-American relations, for

(1) Russia and the United States are battling for political support from Italy.

Harper's Magazine, 196:317, April, 1948, "Battle for Post-war France," Bourdet, Claude.

e. In France political factions cause friction between Russia and the United States, for

(1) Communist forces oppose U.S. aid.

(2) The U.S. backs more conservative French leaders than does Russia.

Vital Speeches, 13:527–539, June 15, 1947, "Waging World Peace," Lippmann, Walter.

3. Military problems among the nations offer a threat to world peace, for

World Report, 3:33–35, Oct. 21, 1947, "Communist Attack on the Marshall Plan."

a. The United States, replacing British control where Britain can no longer maintain troops, affronts Russia, for

(1) Russia calls it imperialistic action, for

(a) The *Communist Manifesto* so states.

Vital Speeches, 13:527–529, June 15, 1947, "Waging World Peace," Lippmann, Walter.

b. Both the U.S. and Russia are guilty of violating their military agreements, for

(1) Russia has crossed the Byrnes-Bevin-Molotov military line in Europe.

Ibid., 14:359–362, Apr. 1, 1948, "Actions Speak Louder Than Words," Byrnes, James.

The Atlantic Monthly, 176:43–45, November, 1945, "Einstein on the Atomic Bomb," Swing, R. G.

United States News, 24:23, June 4, 1948, "Pattern for Arms Spending."

Time, 50:30–31, Oct. 13, 1947, "Russia's War Plans."

Chase, Stuart, *Tomorrow's Trade*, pp. 8–21, 45–71, The Twentieth Century Fund, Inc., 1945.

    (2) Russia supplies the Chinese Communists.

    (3) Russia is infiltrating into the Near East.

    (4) The U.S. has fought for political freedom in Poland, Hungary, Rumania, Italy, and Korea.

  c. Control of atomic energy is still causing friction, for

    (1) Control still rests with the United States.

    (2) Both the Baruch and Gromyko plans for international control have been rejected.

  d. An arms race has begun among the nations, for

    (1) The U.S. is allegedly arming, for

      (a) Atom bombs are being stockpiled.

      (b) Congress approved a 56 group Air Force.

      (c) 2.5 billions worth of materials is stored.

    (2) Russia is expanding her military, for

      (a) In 1948 there were 30 new divisions.

      (b) Stalin said that he intends to have the world's largest air force and navy.

B. Present conditions and their causes are deeply rooted in our existing economic, political, military, and social relations, for

  1. Economic incentive leads nations to nationalism and conflict, for

    a. States attempt to become self-sufficient.

    b. States dump surplus goods on

the world market, but buy none in return.

c. Emphasis upon stockpiling natural resources leads to acquisition of new lands.

d. Competition over resources and markets leads to war, for

(1) Political control over the world depends upon economic control.

Survey Graphic, 37:158–162, March, 1948, "Food and European Recovery," Thorp, Willard

e. The nation which controls the money controls the world's politics, for

(1) International monetary standards are governed by some stable currency or exchange medium, for

(a) It was once the gold standard or the English pound, but today it is the dollar.

Jackson, Robert H., *The Case Against the Nazi War Criminals,* pp. 20–21, Alfred A. Knopf, Inc., 1946.

f. World War II resulted, in part, from crushing Germany economically, for

(1) The Germans were starving and any German government which fed them was acceptable.

2. Political barriers create conflicts which lead to global war, for

Eagleton, Clyde, *International Government,* p. 480, The Ronald Press Company, 1948.

a. Many nations become involved in boundary disputes, for

(1) Russia and America have been drawn into the Greek boundary problems.

(2) Iran's border disputes have nearly provoked war.

(3) China's borders are a point of tension between Russia and America.

Ibid., p. 476.

b. Present attempts to extend boundaries both political and

physical have resulted in the "cold war" in Europe, for

(1) Aid to Greece and Turkey puts them in the United States sphere.

(2) Political pressure on Italy brings her within the United States orbit.

Vital Speeches, 14:359–362, Apr. 1, 1948, "Actions Speak Louder than Words," Byrnes, James F.

(3) Russia is attempting to extend her area of influence to all Europe, for

(a) She has made satellites of many eastern European countries.

(b) The Communist party attempts domination in western Europe.

United States News, 24:23, June 4, 1948, "Pattern for Arms Spending."

3. Present military structures make war possible by almost any nation, for

a. The atom bomb makes large manpower reserves unnecessary.

Time, 50:30–31, Oct. 13, 1947, "Russia's War Plans."

b. Nations are re-arming.

c. Germany proved how formidable may be a lone nation's power against the world, for

Jackson, Robert H., *The Case Against the Nazi War Criminals,* p. 111ff., *Alfred A. Knopf, Inc.,* 1946.

(1) It took less than 20 years to build her military might of World War II.

C. Existing proposals, except World Federal Government, for dealing with the above problems are objectionable and inadequate, for

1. The United Nations, as now constituted is inadequate, for

United Nations Charter, Chap. V, Art. 10–16; Chap. VII, Art. 27; Chap. XIV; X, Art. 62; Chap. XII, Art. 77; Chap. XIX, Art. 18.

a. It is not based upon law backed with power to enforce that law, for

(1) The general assembly does not make laws, but only recommendations.

International Concilia-
tion, 413:441–553, Sep-
tember, 1945, "Text of
U.N. Charter."

United States Depart-
ment of State Bulletin,
v. 14, no. 351, pp. 467–
475, Mar. 24, 1946,
"Composition of Organs,
Commissions, and Com-
mittees of the United
Nations," Myers, D. P.

New York Times, IV,
8:6, Apr. 4, 1948, "The
U.N. Structure," Meyer,
Cord, Jr.

Black, Henry C., *Black's*
Law Dictionary (3d
ed.), pp. 392–393,
West Publishing Com-
pany, 1933.

    (2) The International Court
of Justice is limited to
fact finding and treaty
interpretation.
    (3) The Security Council can-
not take action against
the "Big Five" nations, for
        (*a*) Any of them can veto
any action.
        (*b*) The U.N. has no po-
lice power.
    (4) The Economic and Social
Council can only study
and recommend.
    (5) The Trusteeship Council
can supervise only terri-
tories voluntarily released.
  b. No large nation will surrender
the veto, for
    (1) If there were majority
rule in the Security Council, the six little nations
with 133 million people
could control the five
large nations with nearly
one billion people.
    (2) At San Francisco and
since, both Russia and the
United States have in-
sisted upon the veto
power.
2. An International Confederacy of
Nations would not be adequate,
for
  a. The inherent nature of confederacy is that of weakness, for
    (1) Central authority is not
intended to be so strong
as to control the member-
states.
    (2) Member-states may with-
draw at will.

World Affairs, 106:54, March, 1943, "It Must be Done Again," Behrendt, R. F.

Reves, Emery, *The Anatomy of Peace* (8th ed.), p. 81, Harper & Brothers, 1946.

The Atlantic Monthly, 179:39–42, March, 1947, "Disarmament— Where Do We Go From Here?" Finletter, Thomas K.

New York Times, 3:1, pp. 2, 7, Sept. 2, 1945, "Victory Statement," MacArthur, Douglas.

Chase, Stuart, *For This We Fought,* p. 111–124, The Twentieth Century Fund, Inc., 1946.

    b. Such a plan would rely upon power politics, for
        (1) Such a system permits secret alliances.
        (2) Large nations would retain control.
    c. Nations could wage war, for
        (1) There would be no force to prevent them.
    d. Confederacy has failed at other times, for
        (1) The ancient Greek Delian Confederacy failed.
        (2) Confederacy has failed twice in the U.S.

3. Isolationism is not an adequate choice, for
    a. The world is a unit in which nations cannot exist in seclusion.
    b. Airborne atom bombs may be dropped anywhere.
    c. Isolation has failed miserably in the past.

4. Immediate war with Russia is impracticable, for
    a. We want to prevent war.
    b. Weapons more destructive than the atom bomb might be used, for
        (1) It would be total war in every sense.
    c. There is strategic evidence that Russia might defeat the United States.

5. Preparedness in itself is not an adequate solution, for
    a. Military experts indicate there is no defense against the atom bomb.
    b. Vast arms programs drain the wealth of a nation.

c. Arms races spread fear and suspicion.

d. Armed nations eventually go to war, for

(1) Insignificant incidents can provoke war.

Life, 24: 52–54, June 21, 1948, "World Constitution," Jessup, John K.

6. The "Hutchins" plan is not practicable, for

a. It proposes regional division which would accentuate the present east-west split.

b. Construction of the central authority is too vague.

c. There is little reason to believe that the nations will accept the regional division.

Second Affirmative

II. World Federal Government would prove practicable, for

A. Many nations indicate they favor a federalized United Nations, for

Christian Science Monitor Magazine, p. 3, June 28, 1947, "U.N. in Fact or Form?" Lindstrom, R. D.

1. The new constitution of France grants to its executive branch the authority and power to transfer such aspects of national sovereignty to a world organization as may reciprocally be agreed upon among the nations.

2. China's constitution grants similar authority to her executive branch.

3. Great Britain's leaders have spoken for World Federal Government, for

New York Times, 16:1, May 15, 1947, "Text of London Address on May 14, 1947," Churchill, Winston.

a. Churchill has said, "Unless some effective world super government for the purposes of preventing war can be set up . . . the prospects for peace and human progress are dark."

b. Bevin has said, "I am willing to sit with anybody, of any party, of any nation, to try to devise a franchise or a constitution for a world assembly, with limited objective . . . the objective of peace."

4. United States policy is toward
   Vital Speeches, 12:426– World Federal Government, for
   428, May 1, 1946, "Real *a.* The Humber resolution favor-
   Parliament to Keep ing a change of the U.N. to
   Peace," Roberts, Owen J. world government has been
   approved by 19 states.

   b. Truman has said that we must move toward a world government.

   c. MacArthur has said that world government is the next logical step.

5. Cuban and Philippine delegates to the U.N. have asked for a world government.

Christian Century, 64: 6. It is indicated that eight Euro-
1196, Oct. 8, 1947, pean nations and 40 of those pres-
"World Government ent at the San Francisco meeting
Sought by 1955." on the U.N. are ready for World
Federal Government.

The Reader's Digest, B. The machinery for World Federal
48:109–117, February, Government can be organized and
1946, "World Govern- operated, for
ment Is the First Step," 1. The executive branch can be
Reves, Emery. formed from the present Security
Council, for
a. The leadership and basic pattern already exist.

2. The legislative branch can be formed from the present General Assembly, for
   a. Representation of nations already exists.
   b. Present representation could be altered to fit the needs of the new government.

Meyer, Cord, Jr., *Peace* 3. An international military force
or Anarchy, pp. 170– can be organized effectually, for

175, Little, Brown &
Company, 1947.

Schapiro, J. Salwyn,
*Modern and Contempo-
rary European History,*
pp. 911–916. Houghton
Mifflin Company, 1946.

*Political Science Quar-
terly,* 62:11–26, March,
1947, "Issues of the Nu-
remberg Trial," Wechs-
ler, Herbert.

*New York Times Maga-
zine,* p. 12, June 16,
1946, "The Nuremberg
Trials," Jackson, Robert
H.

    a. Provision for such a force is
made in the present U.N.
Charter.
    b. Each nation can contribute a
proportional share of the military force.
    c. Military forces from several
nations can operate under central control, for
        (1) Such control was effected
in World War II, for
            (*a*) Eisenhower was Al-
lied commander in
the European thea-
ter, and MacArthur
in the Pacific thea-
ter.
    d. Such a force would be so de-
ployed that revolt by any nation could be suppressed, for
        (1) There would be bases the
world over.
        (2) No one nation would be
as strong as the collective
force of the other nations.
4. International laws can be interpreted by the International Court
of Justice, for
    a. Such a court is in existence.
    b. There is a body of interna-
tional law.
    c. All law has developed from a
nucleus through judicial interpretation.
    d. International courts will work,
for
        (1) The International Mili-
tary Tribunal functioned
smoothly with four na-
tions represented on the
bench.
5. Language barriers can be overcome, for

        a. They have been overcome in the United Nations meetings.

        b. They were overcome at the Nuremberg Trials.

III. Federal World Government will bring desirable economic, political, social, and military benefits, for

  A. World affairs would be governed by a strong central authority, for

    1. International problems would be met by international legislation.

    2. International legislation would be administered by an executive of international choice.

    3. International legislation would be interpreted by an international court.

    4. International legislation would be enforced by an international police force.

The Atlantic Monthly, 177:53–60, March, 1946, "Timetable for World Government," Finletter, Thomas K.

  B. The supreme authority of member nations would be checked, for

    1. Power to declare war would rest with the central authority.

    2. Power of law enforcement would rest with the central authority.

    3. International military power would check any rebel states.

    4. By nature "federal" implies delegation of sovereignty to a central power.

  C. Central control would minimize war, for

Ferguson, Wallace K., and Geoffrey Brun, *A Survey of European Civilization,* pp. 552–553, 882–911, Houghton Mifflin Company, 1942.

    1. Federations, in the past, have brought peace to member-states, for

        a. The federation of Italy brought peace.

        b. The federation of Germany brought peace.

        c. The federation of Scotland and England brought peace.

One World or None, pp. 61–65, (Masters, Dexter, and Katherine Way, eds.), McGraw-Hill Book Company, Inc., 1946, "Can We Avert an Arms Race by an Inspection System?" Szilard, Leo.

The Atlantic Monthly, 180:27–33, October, 1947, "Peace Is Still Possible," Meyer, Cord, Jr.

Chase, Stuart, *Tomorrow's Trade*, pp. 1–8, The Twentieth Century Fund, Inc., 1945.

Kemmerer, Edwin W., *The ABC of Inflation*, p. 11, McGraw-Hill Book Company, Inc., 1942.

Chase, Stuart, *Tomorrow's Trade*, pp. 8–24, The Twentieth Century Fund, Inc., 1945.

2. The atom bomb and other arms would be controlled, for
   a. Inspection would be possible, for
      (1) Aerial surveys, effective during World War II, could be used.
      (2) Operations cannot be camouflaged against infrared photography.
      (3) Large industry is easily spotted.
3. Many of the incentives for war would be removed, for
   a. The nations would be working toward a common goal.

D. Central control will promote economic stability and prosperity, for
1. Energy now spent on war could be used to improve the world living standard.
2. World inflation could be controlled through joint effort to stabilize currency, for
   a. The World Bank would be utilized.
   b. Production could be synchronized.
3. Efficient use of world resources will result in more of everything for all, for
   a. At present many areas do not produce that for which they are best suited.
   b. Much of the world's manpower is squandered in nonproductive effort.

E. Central control will promote health and educational standards, for
1. Through central agencies scientific advances may be utilized by all.

2. Educational problems will be
solved by joint action.

3. The present United Nations commissions have made many advances in this area.

Conclusion

I. Since present conditions threaten world peace;

II. Since existing agencies and proposed solutions other than World
Federal Government are inadequate;

III. Since Federal World Government would prove practicable;

IV. Since Federal World Government would bring desirable economic, political, social, and military benefits;

Therefore, a Federal World Government should be established.[2]

[2] This student brief, partly because its length was restricted, has left
many questions concerning practicability unanswered. The reader and
critic will wish to know specifically how the proposed government is to be
established, who is to join, and exactly how it will operate politically, economically, militarily, and ideologically.

Suggested Library Sources for Readings on Current Problems

The following types of sources for readings on problems for argumentation, discussion, and debate are intended to be suggestive only. Obviously, we cannot list here exhaustive lists of sources in each category. For detailed explanation of a given source consult your librarian or the *Guides to Reference Books* listed below. Most debaters will dip into most of the categories of materials here listed.

I. Guides to Reference Books

Mudge, Isadore G., *Guide to Reference Books* (6th ed.), American Library Association, 1936; Shores, Louis, *Basic Reference Books* (2d ed.), American Library Association, 1939. These give publishers, dates, and other data concerning most of the references listed below.

II. Encyclopedias

Encyclopedia Americana; New International Encyclopedia; Encyclopædia Britannica; Nelson's Complete Encyclopedia; Catholic Encyclopedia; Encyclopedia of Social Science; Cyclopedia of Education.

III. Dictionaries and Word Books

Webster's New International Dictionary of the English Language; Funk and Wagnalls' New Standard Dictionary of the English Language; J. A. H. Murray's Oxford English Dictionary; New Century

Dictionary of the English Language; Clarence Barnhart's *American College Dictionary;* Peter M. Roget's *International Thesaurus of English Words and Phrases;* James C. Fernald's *English Synonyms and Antonyms;* F. A. March's *Thesaurus Dictionary of the English Language.*

IV. Yearbooks and Handbooks

The Americana Annual (1923–); *New International Year Book* (1907–); *Britannica Book of the Year* (1937–); *The World Almanac and Book of Facts* (1868–); *Statesman's Yearbook* (1864–); U. S. Census Bureau, *Sixteenth Census of the United States* (1940 and later); *Economic Almanac* (1946–47); *Pan American Year Book; American Year Book* (1910–1921, 1925–); *Reference Shelf.*

V. Catalogues and Indexes

United States Catalog; Cumulative Book Index; Publisher's Weekly; English Catalogue of Books; Essay and General Literature Index (1900–1933); *Speech Index* (1935–); *Readers' Guide to Periodical Literature* (1900–); *International Index to Periodicals* (1907–); *Industrial Arts Index; Art Index; Agricultural Index; Education Index; Index to Legal Periodicals; Engineering Index; Index Medicus; Catholic Periodical Index; Public Affairs Information Service; Vertical File Service Catalog; Book Review Digest* (1905–); *New York Times Index; Union List of Serials.*

VI. Directories

Stephen, Leslie, and Sidney Lee, *Dictionary of National Biography* (1921–22 with later supplements); Johnson, Allen, and Dumas Malone, *Dictionary of American Biography* (1928–37); *National Cyclopaedia of American Biography; Who's Who* (1848–);*Who's Who in America* (1900–); *International Who's Who* (1940–); *Leaders in American Education;* and similar "Who's Who" books.

VII. Bibliographies

Bibliographical Index (1938–); *United States Library of Congress,* special bibliographical lists; see also bibliographies listed in Mudge's *Guide to Reference Books* under the special subjects, such as religion, social science; see also the bibliographies listed in *Reference Shelf* and in the *Debater's Handbook* series (annual).

VIII. Pamphlets

Vertical File Service Catalog (1932–) for pamphlets; *Public Affairs Information Service; World Almanac* (lists addresses of organizations "with a purpose" that provide much special material).

IX. Government Documents

United States Census Report; Commerce Yearbook; Commerce Reports; Monthly Labor Review; U.S. Office of Education Reports; Congressional Documents, including (*a*) *Senate Documents,* (*b*) *Senate Reports,* (*c*) *House Documents,* (*d*) *House Reports; Congressional Record; Congressional Committee Hearings; Catalogue of Publications of the United States; U.S. Bureau of Foreign and Domestic Commerce; Executive Publications,* including (*a*) State Department, (*b*) Treasury Department, (*c*) Department of National Defense—Army, Navy, Air, (*d*) Justice Department, (*e*) Post Office Department, (*f*) Interior Department, (*g*) Agriculture Department, (*h*) Commerce Department, (*i*) Labor Department, (*j*) Independent agencies, such as Library of Congress, U. S. Civil Service Commission, Atomic Energy Commission, Tennessee Valley Authority; consult Superintendent of Documents, U.S. Government Printing Office; *Catalogue of Public Documents;* the government of each state also supplies a large amount of material.

X. Periodicals

The following classifications are illustrative only:

A. GENERAL NEWS: *Time, Newsweek, Fortune, United States News.*

B. GENERAL LITERATURE: *The Atlantic Monthly, Catholic World, Harper's Magazine, Jewish World Review, Yale Review, The New Yorker.*

C. OPINION: *The Nation, New Republic, The American Mercury.*

D. "MASS APPEAL": *The American Magazine, Collier's, The Saturday Evening Post, Life.*

E. REVIEWS: *New York Herald Tribune Books, New York Times Book Review, Saturday Review of Literature.*

F. DIGESTS: *The Reader's Digest* and many other "digests."

G. ECONOMICS AND INDUSTRY: *American Economic Review, American Federationalist, American Institute of Banking Bulletin, American Journal of Economics and Sociology, Barron's Weekly, Business Week, Brookings Institution Pamphlets, CIO News, Commercial and Financial Chronicle, Consumer's Research, Economist, Financial World, Fortune, Monthly Labor Review, Nation's Business.*

H. EDUCATION: *American Oxonian, American Scholar, Educational Review, English Journal, Journal of Proceedings of the Association of American Universities, School and Society.*

I. GOVERNMENT, LAW, AND CURRENT HISTORY: *American Historical Review, Americas, American Political Science Review, Asia, British Weekly, China Monthly, Congressional Digest, Current History, Far*

Eastern Quarterly, Foreign Affairs, Foreign Policy Association Reports (also *Headline Books*); *International Conciliation, Journal of Negro History, Pan American Union Bulletin, Pan American, Political Science Quarterly, Public Opinion Quarterly, United States News, World Affairs.*

J. NATIONAL DEFENSE: *American Legion Monthly, AVC Bulletin, Army and Navy Journal.*

K. SOCIOLOGY: *American Journal of Sociology, American Sociological Review, Journal of Applied Psychology, Social Action, Survey Graphic.*

L. ATOMIC ENERGY: *Bulletin of the Atomic Scientists* and similar sources.

M. SPEECH: *Broadcasting, The Debater's Magazine, The Forensic* (Pi Kappa Delta), *The Gavel* (Delta Sigma Rho), *Quarterly Journal of Speech, The Speaker* (Tau Kappa Alpha), *Talks, Vital Speeches of the Day, Bulletin of America's Town Meeting of the Air, American Forum of the Air, Northwestern Reviewing Stand, The University of Chicago Round Table, Speech Activities.*

XI. NEWSPAPERS

Debaters will read at least one representative daily. For material in the newspaper files, refer to the *New York Times Index*, to be used as a date index. With the date as a guide, this index can be applied to any paper.

XII. RADIO BROADCASTS

Radio stations will supply sources of their broadcasts of debates, speeches, and discussions. Examples of programs of great value to debaters are University of Chicago Round Table; America's Town Meeting of the Air; American Forum of the Air; People's Platform; Northwestern Reviewing Stand.

SCHOOL AND COLLEGE DEBATE AND DISCUSSION MATERIALS

University Debater's Annual; Debater's Magazine; Reference Shelf; Debate Index; Intercollegiate Debates; Debate Handbook. Extension Divisions of State Universities and Directors of State or Regional High-school Speech or Forensic Leagues will recommend materials on subjects for debate and discussion.

Outline of Parliamentary Law

Debate and discussion should be conducted in accordance with the principles of parliamentary law. Every debatable motion includes (1) the making of the motion; (2) the seconding; (3) the stating of the motion by the chair; (4) the discussion; (5) the vote by acclamation, division, silent assent, roll call, or balloting; and (6) the announcing of the vote. We present first the main motion, next the amendment, and thirdly the amendment to the amendment. We vote first on the amendment to the amendment, next on the amendment, and thirdly on the main motion. Motions are principal and secondary. Only one main motion may be before the house at a time. Secondary motions are privileged, incidental, or subsidiary. It is necessary to keep in mind the order of precedence of motions. The main motion is lowest in rank because all other motions are intended to facilitate its disposition. Privileged motions have precedence over subsidiary motions, and these two groups both have priority over the main motion. Incidental motions have among themselves no order of precedence and may be proposed at any time. Moreover, they must be disposed of before other motions, except those of the privileged group, are considered.

The table on page 401 is intended to give the student help in handling representative motions. This outline should be supplemented by the study of a complete guide to parliamentary law. It is not intended to be exhaustive, but it will be sufficient for the purposes of most small group deliberations, and for the conduct of larger assemblies.

TABLE OF PARLIAMENTARY MOTION

Motions	Need of second	Amendable	Debatable	Vote required	May be postponed	May be reconsidered	May be laid on table	May interrupt speaker
I. Privileged Motions								
1. To adjourn.........	Yes	No	No	Majority	No	No	No	No
2. To fix time for next meeting	Yes	Yes	No	Majority	No	No	No	No
3. Question of privilege........	No	No	No (usually)	Chairman	No	No	No	Yes
4. Special orders..........	No	No	No	Two thirds	No	No	No	Yes
II. Incidental Motions								
5. Point of order..........	No	No	No	Chairman	No	No	No	Yes
6. To withdraw a motion.....	No	No	No	Majority	No	Yes	Yes	No
7. To suspend a rule..........	Yes	No	No	Two thirds	No	No	No	No
8. To reconsider...........	Yes	No	Yes	Majority	No	No	Yes	No
9. To appeal from chair........	Yes	No	Debate limited	Majority	No	Yes	No	Yes
III. Subsidiary Motions								
10. To lay on table.........	Yes	No	No	Majority	No	No	No	No
11. Previous question........	Yes	No	No	Two thirds	No	If lost, no	Yes	No
12. To postpone to a definite time	Yes	Yes	Yes	Majority	No	Yes	Yes	No
13. To commit, refer, recommit	Yes	Yes	Yes	Majority	No	Yes	Yes	No
14. To amend.........	Yes	Yes	Yes	Majority	Yes	Yes	Yes	No
15. To postpone indefinitely.....	Yes	No	Yes	Majority	Yes	Yes	No	No
IV. Principal Motion								
16. Any main question.........	Yes	Yes	Yes	Majority	Yes	Yes	Yes	No

Source: A. Craig Baird, *Public Discussion and Debate* (rev. ed.) Ginn & Company, 1937.

The business of most meetings may be accomplished by the process of presenting and seconding a motion, discussing and amending it, and voting on it. Special parliamentary procedure to postpone or block action, to speed up business, to recall motions already passed, or to act on rules of order may be easily abused. Since the object of the session should be to facilitate discussion and business, the undue exercise of parliamentary gymnastics is to be discouraged. The chairman, even though he may not be familiar with every bypath, should apply common sense to the situation. He should exercise his best judgment in his interpretation and simplification of any legal complexities. Rules are merely a means. His aim is to protect free debate rather than to encourage legal sparring.

APPENDIX D

Supplementary Reading

CHAPTER 1. AIMS, RELATIONSHIPS, APPLICATIONS

BLACK, MAX: *Critical Thinking*, Chap. 13, "The Grounds of Belief," pp. 227–243, Prentice-Hall, Inc., 1946.

BRYCE, JAMES: "The Influence of Democracy on Thought," in his *The American Commonwealth*, 2 vols., Vol. 2, pp. 822–831, The Macmillan Company, 1921.

CHAFEE, ZECHARIAH, JR.: *The Inquiring Mind*, pp. 3–9, Harcourt, Brace and Company, Inc., 1928.

CONANT, JAMES BRYANT: "Free Inquiry or Dogma?" *The Atlantic Monthly*, Vol. 155, pp. 436–442, April, 1935.

CROCKER, LIONEL, *Argumentation and Debate*, pp. 1–17, American Book Company, 1944.

EWBANK, HENRY L., and J. J. AUER: *Discussion and Debate*, pp. 3–23, F. S. Crofts & Co., 1941.

LIPPMANN, WALTER: "The Indispensable Opposition," *The Atlantic Monthly*, Vol. 164, pp. 186–190, August, 1939.

MURPHY, RICHARD: "The Forensic Mind," in Herbert A. Wichelns and other editors, *Studies in Speech and Drama in Honor of Alexander M. Drummond*, pp. 451–472, Cornell University Press, 1944.

NICHOLS, ALAN: *Discussion and Debate*, pp. 22–30, Harcourt, Brace and Company, Inc., 1941.

WALLAS, GRAHAM: *Social Judgment*, Chap. III, "The Art of Judgment," pp. 43–61, George Allen & Unwin, Ltd. (London), 1934.

WILSON, WOODROW: "The Parliament of the People," in his *New Freedom*, pp. 90–110, Doubleday & Company, Inc., 1913.

CHAPTER 2. SUBJECTS, PROPOSITIONS, AND QUESTIONS

EWBANK, HENRY L., and J. J. AUER: *Discussion and Debate,* Chap. V, "Locating and Defining the Problem," pp. 77–91, F. S. Crofts & Co., 1941.

FOSTER, WILLIAM TRUFANT: *Argumentation and Debate* (2d rev. ed.), Chap. I, "Phrasing the Proposition," Houghton Mifflin Company, 1932.

OLIVER, ROBERT T.: "What's Wrong with Debate Questions," *The Debater's Magazine,* Vol. II, pp. 12–13, March, 1946.

O'NEILL, J. M., CRAVEN LAYCOCK, and ROBERT L. SCALES: *Argumentation and Debate,* Chap. II, "The Proposition," pp. 13–32; Chap. III, "The Burden of Proof," pp. 33–54.

RAHSKOPF, HORACE G.: "Questions of Fact vs. Question of Policy," *Quarterly Journal of Speech,* Vol. XVIII, pp. 60–70, February, 1932.

CHAPTER 3. RESEARCH TECHNIQUES

ADLER, MORTIMER J.: *How to Read a Book,* Part II, Simon and Schuster, Inc., 1940.

EWBANK, HENRY L., and J. J. AUER: *Discussion and Debate,* pp. 93–105, F. S. Crofts & Co., 1941.

LEWIS, NORMAN: *How to Read Better and Faster,* The Thomas Y. Crowell Company, 1944.

NICHOLS, EGBERT R., and JOSEPH H. BACCUS: *Modern Debating,* pp. 105–134, W. W. Norton & Company, 1934.

SHORES, LOUIS: *Basic Reference Books* (2d ed.), American Library Association, 1939.

CHAPTER 4. REFLECTIVE THINKING AND ARGUMENTATIVE TYPES: PRELIMINARY SURVEY

BURTT, EDWIN ARTHUR: *Right Thinking,* pp. 3–16, 17–30, 289–315, Harper & Brothers, 1946.

CLARKE, EDWIN LEAVITT: *The Art of Straight Thinking,* pp. 7–72, Appleton-Century-Crofts, Inc., 1929.

DEWEY, JOHN: *How We Think* (new ed.), Chap. I, "What is Thinking?" pp. 3–16; Chap. V, "Actual Thinking," pp. 71–78; Chap. VI, "Examples of Influence or Testing," pp. 91–101, D. C. Heath and Company, 1933.

MANDER, A. E.: *Logic For the Millions,* Sec. III, "What May We Believe?" pp. 49–76, Philosophical Library, Inc., 1947.

ROBINSON, JAMES HARVEY: *The Mind in the Making,* Harper & Brothers, 1921.

THOULESS, ROBERT H.: *How to Think Straight,* Chap. XII, "The Need for Straight Thinking," pp. 164–170, Simon and Schuster, Inc., 1941.

WERTHEIMER, M.: *Productive Thinking,* Harper & Brothers, 1945.

WOOLBERT, CHARLES HENRY: "The Place of Logic in a System of Persuasion," *Quarterly Journal of Speech Education,* Vol. IV, pp. 19–39, January, 1918.

CHAPTER 5. DEFINITION

BLACK, MAX: *Critical Thinking,* Chap. 2, "Definition," pp. 185–208, Prentice-Hall, Inc., 1946.

DEWEY, JOHN: *How We Think* (new ed.), pp. 136–148; 159–164, D. C. Heath and Company, 1933.

EWBANK, HENRY L., and J. J. AUER: *Discussion and Debate,* Chap. V, pp. 77–92, F. S. Crofts & Co., 1941.

MANDER, A. E.: *Logic for the Millions,* Sec. VI, "Explanation," pp. 115–136, Philosophical Library, Inc., 1947.

NORTHROP, F. S. C.: *The Logic of the Sciences and the Humanities,* Chap. II, "The Analysis of the Problem," pp. 19–34, The Macmillan Company, 1947.

ROBINSON, DANIEL S.: *The Principles of Reasoning* (2d rev. ed.), Chap. V, "Definition and Division," pp. 52–72, Appleton-Century-Crofts, Inc., 1936.

THOULESS, ROBERT H.: *How to Think Straight,* Chap. I, "Emotional Meanings," pp. 3–20; Chap. X, "Vagueness and Related Evils," pp. 132–146, Simon and Schuster, Inc., 1941.

See also references for Chap. 16, "Argumentative Composition: Divisions of Discourse."

CHAPTER 6. ANALYSIS AND ISSUES

BAIRD, A. CRAIG, and FRANKLIN H. KNOWER: *General Speech,* Chap. 6, "Ideas and Organization: Dividing the Subject," pp. 65–79, McGraw-Hill Book Company, Inc., 1949.

BRIGANCE, WILLIAM NORWOOD: *Speech Composition,* Chap. IV, "The Divisions of the Speech," pp. 66–119, F. S. Crofts & Co. 1937.

CROCKER, LIONEL: *Argumentation and Debate,* Chap. III, "Analysis of the Proposition," pp. 29–58, American Book Company, 1944.

DEWEY, JOHN: *How We Think* (new edition), pp. 71–78, 91–101, D. C. Heath and Company, 1933.

NICHOLS, EGBERT R., and JOSEPH H. BACCUS: *Modern Debating,* Chap. IX, "The Development of the Debate Case," pp. 135–150, W. W. Norton & Company, 1934.

O'NEILL, J. M., CRAVEN LAYCOCK, and ROBERT L. SCALES: *Argumen-*

tation and Debate, "The Issues," pp. 42–67, The Macmillan Company, 1917.

ROBINSON, DANIEL S.: *The Principles of Reasoning* (2d rev. ed.), Chap. V, pp. 52–72, Appleton-Century-Crofts, Inc., 1936.

ROWELL, EDWARD Z.: "Argumentative Analysis," in W. Arthur Cable (compiler and ed.), *Cultural and Scientific Speech Education Today,* pp. 88–95, Expression Company, 1930.

SELLARS, R. W.: *The Essentials of Logic* (rev. ed.), Chap. IV, "Classification and Division," pp. 46–58, Houghton Mifflin Company, 1925.

WICHELNS, HERBERT A.: "Analysis and Synthesis in Argumentation," *Quarterly Journal of Speech Education,* Vol. XI, pp. 266–272, June, 1925.

CHAPTER 7. ORGANIZATION: THE OUTLINE AND THE BRIEF

COOLEY, ROGER WILLIAM (ed.): *Brief-making and the Use of Law Books* (4th ed.), West Publishing Company, 1924.

CROCKER, LIONEL: *Argumentation and Debate,* Chap. XV, "The Brief," pp. 233–244; App. VI, "Example of a Debate Brief," pp. 302–318, American Book Company, 1944.

FOSTER, W. T.: *Argumentation and Debate* (2d rev. ed.), Chap. III, "Constructing the Brief," Houghton Mifflin Company, 1932.

KNOWER, FRANKLIN H.: "Studies in the Organization of Speech Material–I," *Journal of Educational Research,* Vol. XXXIX, pp. 220–230, November, 1945.

MILLER, EDD, "Speech Introductions and Conclusions," *Quarterly Journal of Speech,* Vol. XXXII, pp. 181–183, April, 1946.

CHAPTER 8. EVIDENCE: PRINCIPLES AND TYPES

BAKER, GEORGE PIERCE, and HENRY B. HUNTINGTON: *The Principles of Argumentation* (new edition), pp. 67–177, Ginn & Company, 1925.

BURTT, EDWIN R.: *Right Thinking,* Chap. XIX, "Criteria of Evidence," pp. 400–425, Harper & Brothers, 1946.

CLARKE, EDWIN LEAVITT: *The Art of Straight Thinking,* pp. 104–123, 221–302, Appleton-Century-Crofts, Inc., 1929.

CROCKER, LIONEL: *Argumentation and Debate,* pp. 60–100, American Book Company, 1944.

EWBANK, HENRY L., and J. J. AUER: *Discussion and Debate,* Chap. VIII, "Exploring the Problem: Evidence," pp. 117–150, F. S. Crofts & Co., 1941.

LEE, IRVING: *Language Habits in Human Affairs,* Chap. VII, "Facts First–Then Works," pp. 115–152, Harper & Brothers, 1941.

O'NEILL, J. M., CRAVEN LAYCOCK, and ROBERT L. SCALES: *Argumentation and Debate*, Chap. VI, "Evidence," pp. 80–113, The Macmillan Company, 1917.

SMITH, HAROLD E.: "The Use of Statistical Data in Debate," *Quarterly Journal of Speech*, Vol. XXVI, pp. 426–431, October, 1940.

WIGMORE, JOHN HENRY: *The Science of Judicial Proof* (3d ed.), Little, Brown, & Company, 1937.

CHAPTER 9. EVIDENCE: TECHNIQUES AND TESTS

See references for Chap. 8.

CHAPTER 10. ARGUMENT: GENERALIZATION

BOSANQUET, BERNARD: *Implication and Linear Inference*, The Macmillan Company, 1920.

BURTT, EDWIN ARTHUR: *Right Thinking*, pp. 455–486, Harper & Brothers, 1946.

CLARKE, EDWIN LEAVITT: *The Art of Straight Thinking*, pp. 124–161, Appleton-Century-Crofts, Inc., 1929.

CROCKER, LIONEL: *Argumentation and Debate*, Chap. VII, "Proving the Proposition by Induction," pp. 102–112, American Book Company, 1946.

DEWEY, JOHN, *How We Think* (new edition), Chap. V, pp. 71–78, D. C. Heath and Company, 1933.

EWBANK, HENRY L., and J. J. AUER: *Discussion and Debate*, pp. 46–73, 219–284, F. S. Crofts & Co., 1941.

ROBINSON, DANIEL S.: *The Principles of Reasoning* (2d rev. ed.), Chap. XV, "The General Nature of Induction," pp. 203–211; Chap. XVII, "Probability," pp. 229–236; Chap. XVIII, "Statistical Methods," pp. 237–250, Appleton-Century-Crofts, Inc., 1936.

SELLARS, R. W.: *The Essentials of Logic* (rev. ed.), Chap. XIV, "The Logic of Systematic Investigation," pp. 164–177; Chap. XIX, "Statistics and Averages," pp. 239–255, Houghton Mifflin Company, 1925.

CHAPTER 11. ARGUMENT: ANALOGY

BURTT, EDWIN ARTHUR: *Right Thinking*, Chap. XVI, "Causal Laws and the Principles Guiding Their Verification," pp. 316–341, Harper & Brothers, 1946.

CLARKE, EDWIN LEAVITT: *The Art of Straight Thinking*, pp. 194–206, Appleton-Century-Crofts, Inc., 1929.

ROBINSON, DANIEL S.: *The Principles of Reasoning* (2d rev. ed.), Chap. XXIII, "The Method of Analogy," pp. 298–306, Appleton-Century-Crofts, Inc., 1936.

THOULESS, ROBERT H.: *How to Think Straight,* Chap. VIII, "Pitfalls in Analogy," pp. 103–118, Simon and Schuster, Inc., 1941.

WALLACE, KARL: "On Analogy: Redefinition and Some Implications," in Herbert A. Wichelns and other editors, *Studies in Speech and Drama in Honor of Alexander M. Drummond,* pp. 412–426, Cornell University Press, 1944.

See also the references for Chapters 12, 13, and 14.

CHAPTER 12. ARGUMENT: CAUSAL REASONING OF AUTHORITY

BALDWIN, J. M. (ed.): *Dictionary of Philosophy and Psychology,* "Cause," Vol. I, pp. 163–168, The Macmillan Company, 1925.

Columbia Associates in Philosophy: *An Introduction to Reflective Thinking,* pp. 63–96, Houghton Mifflin Company, 1923.

DEWEY, JOHN: *Logic,* Chap. XXII, "Scientific Laws—Causation and Sequences," pp. 442–462, Henry Holt and Company, Inc., 1938.

McBURNEY, J. H., and KENNETH HANCE: *The Principles and Methods of Discussion,* Chap. XI, "The Modes of Reasoning in Discussion," pp. 182–203, Harper & Brothers, 1939.

ROBINSON, DANIEL S.: *The Principles of Reasoning* (2d rev. ed.), Sec. VII, "Causality and Will in Experimental Methods," pp. 253–286, Appleton-Century-Crofts, Inc., 1936.

THONSSEN, LESTER, and A. CRAIG BAIRD: *Speech Criticism,* Chap. 13, "The Character of the Speaker," pp. 383–391, The Ronald Press Company, 1948.

CHAPTER 13. ARGUMENT: DEDUCTION

BLACK, MAX: *Critical Thinking,* Chap. 2, "Deduction and Informal Argument," pp. 12–30, Prentice-Hall, Inc., 1946.

CLARKE, EDWIN LEAVITT: *The Art of Straight Thinking,* pp. 207–220, Appleton-Century-Crofts, Inc., 1929.

DEWEY, JOHN: *Logic,* Chap. XXI, "Scientific Method: Induction and Deduction," pp. 419–441, Henry Holt and Company, Inc., 1938.

MANDER, A. E.: *Logic For the Millions,* Sec. VIII, "Deductive Reasoning," pp. 155–174, Philosophical Library, Inc., 1947.

McBURNEY, J. H., and KENNETH HANCE: *The Principles and Methods of Discussion,* Chap. XI, "The Modes of Reasoning in Discussion," pp. 182–203, Harper & Brothers, 1939.

SCHILLER, F. C. S.: *Logic for Use,* Chap. XIV, "Syllogistic Reasoning," pp. 269–286; Chap. XV, "The Theory of Proof," pp. 286–319, George Bell & Sons, Ltd. (London), 1929.

CHAPTER 14. OBSTACLES TO STRAIGHT THINKING

BIRD, CHARLES: *Social Psychology,* pp. 305–344, Appleton-Century-Crofts, Inc., 1940.

BOGASLOVSKY, BORIS B.: *The Technique of Controversy*, Chap. I, "The Puzzle of Modern Reasoning," pp. 1–19; Chap. II, "Sophisms, Paradoxes and Common Sense," pp. 20–35, Harcourt, Brace and Company, Inc., 1928.

BURTT, EDWIN ARTHUR: *Right Thinking*, pp. 45–78, Harper & Brothers, 1946.

CLARKE, EDWIN LEAVITT: *The Art of Straight Thinking*, pp. 303–362, Appleton-Century-Crofts, Inc., 1929.

MANDER, A. E.: *Logic for the Millions*, Sec. IX, "Testing our 'Grounds' for Belief," pp. 175–192, Philosophical Library, Inc., 1947.

MCBURNEY, JAMES H., and KENNETH G. HANCE: *The Principles or Methods of Discussion*, "Obstacles to Reflective Thinking," pp. 204–242, Harper & Brothers, 1939.

ROBINSON, DANIEL S.: *The Principles of Reasoning* (2d rev. ed.), Chap. XIV, "Fallacies," pp. 187–200, Appleton-Century-Crofts, Inc., 1936.

THOULESS, ROBERT H.: *How to Think Straight*, Chap. II, "All and Some," pp. 20–30; Chap. IV, "Some Logical Fallacies," pp. 47–56; Chap. XI, "Prejudice," pp. 147–163, Simon and Schuster, Inc., 1941.

CHAPTER 15. OBSTACLES TO STRAIGHT THINKING (CONCLUDED)

See the references for Chaps. 8, 10, 11, 12, 13, and 14.

CHAPTER 16. ARGUMENTATIVE COMPOSITION: DIVISIONS OF DISCOURSE

BLACK, MAX: *Critical Thinking*, Chap. 10, "Ambiguity," pp. 167–184, Prentice-Hall, Inc., 1946.

BORCHERS, GLADYS: "An Approach to the Problem of Oral Style," *Quarterly Journal of Speech*, Vol. XXII, pp. 114–117, 1936.

BRIGANCE, WILLIAM NORWOOD: *Speech Composition*, Chap. V, "The Psychology of Gaining Acceptance," pp. 120–196; Chap. VI, "The Use of Words," pp. 197–275, F. S. Crofts & Co., 1945.

CROCKER, LIONEL: *Argumentation and Debate*, pp. 265–289, American Book Company, 1944.

GILMAN, WILBUR E., BOWER ALY, and LOREN D. REID: *Speech Preparation*, Chap. V, "Composing the Speech," pp. 94–135, Artcraft Press, 1946.

SPENCER, HERBERT: *The Philosophy of Style*, Appleton-Century-Crofts, Inc., 1871. Also in W. T. Brewster, *Representative Essays on the Theory of Style*, pp. 167–208, The Macmillan Company, 1911.

THONSSEN, LESTER, and A. CRAIG BAIRD: *Speech Criticism*, Chap. XV, "The Style of Public Address," pp. 405–433, The Ronald Press Company, 1948.

410   ARGUMENTATION, DISCUSSION, AND DEBATE

UTTERBACK, WILLIAM E.: "Psychological Approach to the Rhetoric of Speech Composition," *Quarterly Journal of Speech Education,* Vol. X, pp. 17–22, February, 1924.

WOOLBERT, CHARLES H.: "Speaking and Writing—A Study of Differences," *Quarterly Journal of Speech Education,* Vol. VIII, pp. 271–285, June, 1922.

CHAPTER 17. ARGUMENTATIVE COMPOSITION: LANGUAGE

ALY, BOWER: "The Rhetoric of Semantics," *Quarterly Journal of Speech,* Vol. XXX, pp. 23–30, February, 1944.

BAIRD, A. CRAIG, and FRANKLIN H. KNOWER: *General Speech,* Chap. 10, "Language," pp. 132–158, McGraw-Hill Book Company, Inc., 1949.

BLACK, MAX: *Critical Thinking,* Chap. 9, "The Uses of Language," pp. 147–166, Prentice-Hall, Inc., 1946.

CHASE, STUART: *The Tyranny of Words,* Chap. XIII, "Turn With the Logicians," pp. 226–243, Harcourt, Brace and Company, Inc., 1938.

FLESCH, RUDOLPH: *The Art of Plain Talk,* Harper & Brothers, 1946.

HARRIMAN, PHILIP LAWRENCE (ed.): *Encyclopedia of Psychology,* "Language and Psychology," pp. 319–332; "Language, the Psychology of," pp. 332–341; "Semantics, Language," pp. 838–870, Philosophical Library, Inc., 1946.

HAYAKAWA, S. I.: *Language in Action,* pp. 15–39, Harcourt, Brace and Company, Inc., 1941.

JOHNSON, WENDELL: *People in Quandaries,* Chap. I, "Verbal Cocoons," pp. 3–20; Chap. V, "The World of Not-words," pp. 91–111; Chap. VI, "The World of Words," pp. 112–142; Chap. VII, "The Process of Abstracting," pp. 143–168; Chap. VIII, "Three Basic Notions," pp. 160–184, Harper & Brothers, 1946.

LEE, IRVING: *Language Habits in Human Affairs,* Chaps. VIII, "A Shell of Words," pp. 153–176, Harper & Brothers, 1941. (Read the entire book.)

OVERSTREET, HARRY A.: *Influencing Human Behavior,* pp. 50–70, 87–109, 125–139, W. W. Norton & Company, 1925.

See also the references for Chap. 16.

CHAPTER 18. PERSUASION: TECHNIQUES OF MOTIVATION

BAIRD, A. CRAIG, and FRANKLIN H. KNOWER: *General Speech,* Chap. 17, "Adapting the Speech to the Listeners," pp. 298–314, McGraw-Hill Book Company, Inc., 1949.

BIRD, CHARLES: *Social Psychology,* pp. 29–60, 127–141, 258–304, 345–368, Appleton-Century-Crofts, Inc., 1940.

BORING, EDWIN G., HERBERT S. LANGFELD, and HARRY P. WELD, and collaborators: *Introduction to Psychology* (5th printing), Chaps. II, V, VI, XII, John Wiley & Sons, Inc., 1944.

DOOB, LEONARD W.: *Propaganda*, Henry Holt and Company, Inc., 1935.

HOLLINGWORTH, H. L.: *The Psychology of the Audience*, Chaps. III, VI, VII, VIII, IX, pp. 19–33, 41–160, American Book Company, 1935.

LUMLEY, FREDERICK ELMORE: *Means of Social Control*, Chap. VIII. Appleton-Century-Crofts, Inc., 1925.

OGBURN, WILLIAM F., and MEYER F. NIMKOFF: *Sociology*, Chap. X, "Suggestibility: Crowds and Publics," pp. 272–305, Houghton Mifflin Company, 1946.

OLIVER, ROBERT T.: *The Psychology of Persuasive Speech*, Chaps. IV, VII, VIII, IX, X, XI, pp. 9–120, 199–333. Longmans, Green & Co., Inc., 1942. (See also the bibliographies at the ends of chapters.)

OVERSTREET, HARRY A.: *Influencing Human Behavior*, pp. 9–49, 71–86, 143–169, W. W. Norton & Company, 1925.

ROBINSON, JAMES HARVEY: *The Mind in the Making*, "On Various Kinds of Thinking," pp. 33–40; "Rationalizing," pp. 40–48, Harper & Brothers, 1921.

SMITH, B. L., H. D. LASWELL, and R. D. CASEY: *Propaganda, Communication and Public Opinion*, Princeton University Press, 1946.

WOOLBERT, CHARLES H.: "Conviction and Persuasion: Some Considerations of Theory," *Quarterly Journal of Public Speaking*, Vol. III, pp. 249–264, July, 1917.

WOOLBERT, CHARLES H.: "Persuasion: Principles and Method," *Quarterly Journal of Speech Education*, Vol. V, pp. 12–25, 101–119, 211–238, January, March, May, 1919.

See also the references for Chaps. 4, 8, 10, 11, 12, 13, 14, and 16.

CHAPTER 19. DELIVERY

ANDERSON, VIRGIL A.: *Training the Speaking Voice*, Chap. VII, "Voice and Personality," pp. 203–222, Oxford University Press, 1942.

BAIRD, A. CRAIG, and FRANKLIN H. KNOWER: *General Speech*, Chap. 13, "The Speaking Voice," pp. 208–237, McGraw-Hill Book Company, Inc., 1949.

BARNES, HARRY: *Speech Handbook*, "The Fundamental Processes of Speech," pp. 5–25, Prentice-Hall, Inc., 1943.

BRYANT, DONALD C., and WALLACE, KARL R.: *Fundamentals of Public Speaking*, Appleton-Century-Crofts, Inc., 1947.

FAIRBANKS, GRANT: *Voice and Articulation Drill Book,* Harper & Brothers, 1940.

GRAY, GILES W., and CLAUDE M. WISE: *The Bases of Speech* (rev. ed.), Harper & Brothers, 1946.

JERSILD, A. T.: "Modes of Emphasis in Public Speaking," *Journal of Applied Psychology,* Vol. XII, pp. 611–620, 1928.

MURRAY, ELWOOD: *The Speech Personality,* J. B. Lippincott Company, 1944.

PARRISH, WAYLAND MAXFIELD: *Speaking in Public,* Charles Scribner's Sons, 1947.

SARETT, LEW, and WILLIAM TRUFANT FOSTER: *Basic Principles of Speech,* Houghton Mifflin Company, 1946.

THONSSEN, LESTER, and HOWARD GILKINSON: *Basic Training in Speech,* D. C. Heath and Company, 1947.

WINANS, JAMES A.: *Speech-making,* Chap. II, "Conversing with an Audience," pp. 11–45, Appleton-Century-Crofts, Inc., 1938.

WOOLBERT, CHARLES H., and J. F. SMITH: *The Fundamentals of Speech* (2d rev. ed.), Harper & Brothers, 1934.

CHAPTER 20. DISCUSSION: AIMS, RELATIONSHIPS, TECHNIQUES

AUER, J. JEFFERY: "The Citizen's Roundtable," *Adult Education Bulletin,* Vol. XIII, pp. 68–73, February, 1949.

AUER, J. JEFFERY, and HENRY L. EWBANK: *Handbook for Discussion Leaders,* Harper & Brothers, 1947.

BEARD, CHARLES A.: *The Discussion of Human Affairs,* The Macmillan Company, 1936.

BURTT, EDWIN ARTHUR: *Right Thinking,* pp. 708–741. Harper & Brothers, 1946.

BUSCH, HENRY MILLER: "Discussion in the Administrative Process," *Adult Education Bulletin,* Vol. XIII, pp. 85–88, February, 1949.

CHAMBERLAIN, NEIL W.: "Group Discussion and Collective Bargaining," *Adult Education Bulletin,* Vol. XIII, pp. 77–84, February, 1949.

EICHELBERGER, CLARK M.: "Discussion in the United Nations," *Adult Education Bulletin,* Vol. XIII, pp. 88–90, February, 1949.

DEWEY, JOHN: *How We Think* (new edition), pp. 107–118, D. C. Heath and Company, 1933.

EWBANK, HENRY L., and J. J. AUER: *Discussion and Debate,* F. S. Crofts & Co., 1941.

KELTNER, JOHN W.: "Goals, Obstacles, and Problem Formulation in Group Discussion," *Quarterly Journal of Speech,* Vol. XXXIII, pp. 468–473, December, 1947.

LEE, IRVING J.: "Why Discussions Go Astray," *Etc.: A Review of General Semantics,* Vol. IV, pp. 81–88, Winter, 1947.

McBurney, James H., and Kenneth G. Hance: *The Principles and Methods of Discussion,* pp. 1–25, Harper & Brothers, 1939.

Phillips, C. F., and J. V. Garland: *Discussion Methods,* The H. W. Wilson Company, 1939.

Schreiber, Julius: "Discussion in the Armed Forces," *Adult Education Bulletin,* Vol. XIII, pp. 73–77, February, 1949.

Studebaker, John W.: *The American Way,* McGraw-Hill Book Company, Inc., 1935.

Thompson, Wayne N.: "Discussion and Debate: A Re-examination," *Quarterly Journal of Speech,* Vol. XXX, pp. 288–299, October, 1944.

Thonssen, Lester: "The Social Values of Discussion and Debate," *Quarterly Journal of Speech,* Vol. XXV, p. 117, February, 1939.

Utterback, William E.: "Group Discussion," *Adult Education Bulletin,* Vol. XIII, pp. 67–68, February, 1949.

Walser, Frank: *The Art of Conference,* Harper & Brothers, 1933.

Chapter 21. Discussion: Patterns and Outlines

Baird, A. Craig: *Discussion: Principles and Types,* Chaps. 6 and 7, pp. 54–87, McGraw-Hill Book Company, Inc., 1943.

Dewey, John: *How We Think* (new edition), pp. 71–78, 91–101, 136–148, D. C. Heath and Company, 1933.

McBurney, James H., and Kenneth G. Hance: *The Principles and Methods of Discussion,* pp. 162–181, Harper & Brothers, 1939. See the references for Chaps. 5, 6, 20.

Chapter 22. Discussion: Special Types

Auer, J. Jeffery: "Discussion Programs and Techniques in the Armed Forces," *Quarterly Journal of Speech,* Vol. XXXII, pp. 303–310, October, 1946.

Dickens, Milton, and Marguerite Heffernan: "Experimental Research in Group Discussion," *Quarterly Journal of Speech,* 35:23–29, February, 1949.

Fansler, Thomas: *Discussion Methods for Adult Groups,* American Association for Adult Education, 1934.

Hopkins, H. D.: "The Public Forum," *The Debater's Magazine,* Vol. II, pp. 209–212, December, 1946.

Keltner, John W.: "Trends in Discussion Research," *Adult Education Bulletin,* Vol. XIII, pp. 91–95, February, 1949.

Pellegrini, Angelo M., and Brent Stirling: *Argumentation and Public Discussion,* "New Forms and New Objectives in Public Discussion," D. C. Heath and Company, 1936.

Studebaker, John W.: *The American Way,* McGraw-Hill Book Company, Inc., 1935.

Studebaker, John W., and Chester S. Williams: *Forum Planning Handbook*, U. S. Office of Education, 1939.

Utterback, William E.: "Decision through Discussion," *New York Times*, 1946.

Chapter 23. Discussion: Leadership, Participation, Evaluation

Albig, William: *Public Opinion*, Chap. VI, "Leadership," pp. 92–117; Chap. X, "Attitude and Opinion," pp. 170–180; Chap. XI, "Measurement of Opinion," pp. 181–198; Chap. XII, "Attitude Scales," pp. 198–214, McGraw-Hill Book Company, Inc., 1939.

Bird, Charles: *Social Psychology*, pp. 142–228, 369–395, Appleton-Century-Crofts, Inc., 1940.

Leigh, Robert D.: *Group Leadership*, W. W. Norton & Company, 1936.

Simpson, R. H.: *Study of Those Who Influence and of Those Who Are Influenced in Discussion*, Teachers College, Columbia University, 1938.

Tead, Ordway: *The Art of Leadership*, Chap. X, McGraw-Hill Book Company, Inc., 1935.

Timmons, W. J.: "Discussion, Debating and Research," *Quarterly Journal of Speech*, Vol. XXVII, pp. 415–421, October, 1941.

Young, Kimball: *Social Psychology*, Chap. XV, "Leadership, Authority, and Prestige," pp. 361–395; Alfred A. Knopf, Inc., 1930.

Chapter 24. Debate: Principles and Techniques

Baird, A. Craig: "How Can We Improve International Debating?" *Quarterly Journal of Speech*, Vol. XXXIV, pp. 228–230, April, 1948.

Crocker, Lionel: *Argumentation and Debate*, pp. 209–232, American Book Company, 1944.

Ewbank, Henry L., and J. J. Auer: *Discussion and Debate*, pp. 410–424, F. S. Crofts & Co., 1941.

Judson, Lyman S. (ed.): *The Student Congress Movement*, The H. W. Wilson Company, 1940.

Leigh, Robert D.: *Modern Rules of Parliamentary Procedure*, W. W. Norton & Company, 1937.

Nichols, Alan: *Discussion and Debate*, Part II, Chap. 7, "The Intercollegiate Debating World," pp. 205–240, Harcourt, Brace and Company, Inc., 1941. (See especially bibliography, Appendix Eleven.)

Nichols, Egbert R., and Joseph H. Baccus: *Modern Debating*, pp. 65–93, W. W. Norton & Company, 1936.

RAY, ROBERT F.: "The Iowa University Student Debate," *Quarterly Journal of Speech*, Vol. XXXII, pp. 454–456, December, 1946.

SUMMERS, HARRISON B., and FOREST L. WHAN: *How to Debate*, Part I, The H. W. Wilson Company, 1940.

CHAPTER 25. DEBATE: REFUTATION AND REBUTTAL

CROCKER, LIONEL: *Argumentation and Debate*, pp. 138–175, American Book Company, 1944.

EWBANK, HENRY L., and J. J. AUER: *Discussion and Debate*, pp. 468–491, F. S. Crofts & Co., 1941.

NICHOLS, ALAN: *Discussion and Debate*, Part II, Chap. 6, Harcourt, Brace and Company, Inc., 1941.

NICHOLS, EGBERT R., and JOSEPH H. BACCUS: *Modern Debating*, pp. 135–170, W. W. Norton & Company, 1936.

O'NEILL, J. M., CRAVEN LAYCOCK, and R. L. SCALES: *Argumentation and Debate*, pp. 344–365, 420–429, The Macmillan Company, 1917.

ROBINSON, D. S.: *The Principles of Reasoning* (rev. ed.), pp. 178–210, Appleton-Century-Crofts, Inc., 1930.

CHAPTER 26. DEBATE: SPECIAL TYPES

CROCKER, LIONEL: *Argumentation and Debate*, pp. 46–58, American Book Company, 1944.

DENSMORE, G. E.: *Contest Debating*, Chaps. VI and VII, George Wahr, 1939.

EWBANK, HENRY L., and J. J. AUER: *Discussion and Debate*, pp. 343–409 and 425–467, F. S. Crofts & Co., 1941.

GULLEY, HALBERT: "Debate versus Discussion," *Quarterly Journal of Speech*, Vol. XXVIII, pp. 305–307, October, 1942.

HOLM, JAMES NOBLE: *How to Judge Speech Contests*, Chap. VI, Platform News Publishing Company, 1938.

MILLER, EDD: "Special Types of Debate," *The Debater's Magazine*, Vol. II, pp. 145–146, September, 1946.

NICHOLS, ALAN: *Discussion and Debate*, Part II, Chaps. 4 and 6, Harcourt, Brace and Company, Inc., 1941.

NICHOLS, EGBERT R., and JOSEPH H. BACCUS: *Modern Debating*, "Historical Sketch of Intercollegiate Debating," pp. 383–391, W. W. Norton & Company, 1936.

POTTER, D. M.: *Debating in the Colonial Chartered Colleges*, Teachers College, Columbia University, 1944.

SUMMERS, HARRISON B., and FOREST L. WHAN: *How to Debate*, Part IV, The H. W. Wilson Company, 1940.

University Debater's Annual, 1948–1949, The H. W. Wilson Company, 1949.

Chapter 27. Judging Debaters and Debates

Crocker, Lionel: *Argumentation and Debate,* pp. 177–185, American Book Company, 1944.

Ewbank, Henry L., and J. J. Auer: *Discussion and Debate,* pp. 371–389, 492–509, F. S. Crofts & Co., 1941.

Hay, D.: "Debate and Measurement of Attitudes," *Quarterly Journal of Speech,* Vol. XXII, pp. 62–66, February, 1936.

Knower, Franklin H.: "Experimental Studies of Changes of Attitude," *Journal of Abnormal and Social Psychology,* Vol. XXX, pp. 522–532, 1936.

Lund, F. H.: "The Psychology of Belief," *Journal of Abnormal Psychology,* Vol. XX, pp. 63–81, 174–196, April, July, 1925.

Monroe, Alan: "The Statistical Reliability and Validity of the Shift-of-opinion Ballot," *Quarterly Journal of Speech,* Vol. XXIII, pp. 577–585, 1937.

Nichols, Egbert R., and Joseph H. Baccus: *Modern Debating,* pp. 328–379, W. W. Norton & Company, 1936.

Robinson, Karl F.: "An Experimental Study of the Effects of Group Discussion upon the Social Attitudes of College Students," *Speech Monographs,* Vol. VIII, pp. 34–57, 1941.

Thompson, Wayne: "Is There A Yardstick for Measuring Speaking Skill?" *Quarterly Journal of Speech,* Vol. XXIX, pp. 87–91, February, 1943.

Thonssen, Lester, and A. Craig Baird: *Speech Criticism,* Chap. 17, "The Measures of Effectiveness," pp. 448–461, The Ronald Press Company, 1948.

Timmons, William M.: "Discussion, Debating, and Research," *Quarterly Journal of Speech,* Vol. XXVII, pp. 415–421, October, 1941.

Index

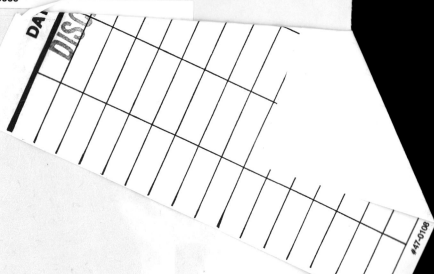